WEDGWOOD
JASPER

Robin Reilly

WEDGWOOD JASPER

with over 600 illustrations, 71 in colour

Thames and Hudson

BOOKS BY THE SAME AUTHOR

History and Biography

The Rest to Fortune: The Life of Major-General James Wolfe
The Sixth Floor
The British at the Gates: The New Orleans Campaign in the 1812 War
William Pitt the Younger
Josiah Wedgwood

Art and Ceramics

British Watercolours
The Collector's Wedgwood
Wedgwood (2 volumes)
Wedgwood Portrait Medallions: An Introduction
Wedgwood: The New Illustrated Dictionary

With George Savage

Wedgwood: The Portrait Medallions
The Dictionary of Wedgwood

Parts 2 and 3 and the Appendices of this edition have been reprinted, with minor corrections and revisions, from *Wedgwood* by Robin Reilly (Stockton Press, 2 vols, 1989). The Introduction, Part 1 and Bibliography have been specially prepared for this edition.

British Library Cataloguing-in-Publication Data
A catalogue record for this book is available from the British Library

ISBN 0-500-01624-0

Printed and bound in Singapore by CS Graphics

Contents

Note to the Illustrations

In more than two centuries of production, the Wedgwood firm has been responsible for manufacturing tens of thousands of different shapes, ornaments and designs, and it is inconceivable that all of them could ever be published. The costs of photography and printing, photographic plate-making and publishing are high, and most museums now charge substantial reproduction fees for the use of existing photographs. Generous illustration is essential to books on pottery and porcelain, and too many authors have been obliged by rising costs to rely upon reproducing photographs which have become stale through over-use. An unusually high proportion of the illustrations in this book, including almost all of the colour plates, was photographed especially for it. With few exceptions, the colour plates and the black and white photographs from the Buten, Born, Kadison, Laver and Zeitlin collections were taken by Brent Burgess, formerly Wedgwood's chief photographer, and I am grateful to him for achieving excellent results with hired equipment under conditions that were never comparable with those of his studio.

Some explanation is required to clarify the method and conventions followed in the captions:

1. Wedgwood trademarks. No attempt has been made to differentiate between the various sizes of marks used. All marks are impressed unless otherwise stated (e.g. 'enamelled', 'incised'). Typefaces are shown as upper case ('WEDGWOOD'), upper and lower case ('Wedgwood') or lower case ('wedgwood'). Workmen's marks (generally incised) have been included where they are known. A full discussion of trademarks appears in Appendix B.

2. Dating of pieces illustrated. The word '*circa*' (abbreviated to '*c.*') is used to indicate an approximate date extending five years on either side of the date given (e.g. '*c.*1785' means that the piece was made between 1780 and 1790). Where two dates are given ('*c.*1780–90') the earlier is the first date at which the piece could have been made. Where the qualifying '*c.*' does not appear, there is reason to believe that the date or dates given are precise.

3. When eighteenth-century examples have not been readily accessible, nineteenth- or even twentieth-century pieces have been used to illustrate particular ornaments or designs.

Introduction

By far the most widely collected of all Wedgwood wares from the 18th century until the present day is jasper, the invention of the first Josiah Wedgwood and the style for which the firm has been most famous ever since. Apart from a brief illustrated monograph, which I wrote for a collectors' series in 1972, no book devoted exclusively to Wedgwood's jasper has ever been published.

In 1989 my two-volume study of Wedgwood wares from the earliest production until 1968 was published. It is now regarded as the standard work on the subject and the necessary reference for collectors, museums, libraries, dealers and auction houses. The enormous costs of a text of more than half-a-million words with 3,800 illustrations, and the consequently high price of the book, however, restricted its distribution to a fraction of the number of those who required it. *Wedgwood Jasper* contains the whole of the text, illustrations, appendices and notes which refer to jasper from both volumes of the larger work, providing the only comprehensive history and description of Wedgwood's jasper ever published in a single volume.

The book is arranged in three parts. The first, which has been written especially for it, is little more than a narrative chronology of the firm and its principal products. It is intended only to put events, inventions, developments and styles in sequence and to help to distinguish between the various members of the family who worked the firm, among whom the names of Josiah, Thomas, Francis and John have been endemic. It is necessarily cursory and superficial. Those who require more detailed information about the first Josiah Wedgwood or the uniquely varied products of the Wedgwood firm during more than two and a quarter centuries of manufacture will find it in my recent biography, *Josiah Wedgwood* (1991), the original two-volume study, *Wedgwood* (1989), or *Wedgwood. The New Illustrated Dictionary* (1994).

The second and third parts are reprinted without alteration except for essential minor adjustments to footnotes and other references. The organisation of the original work, designed as far as possible to preserve a coherent narrative, reserving the most detailed information about the ware to the extended captions to the illustrations, has been preserved.

The basic requirement of any study of Wedgwood is an exhaustive examination of Josiah Wedgwood's letters and memoranda. They contain an extraordinarily personal and complete account of his invention and development of what was surely the most significant innovation in ceramic history for nearly a thousand years. Some of this material, including much of the Wedgwood–Bentley correspondence, has already been published, but the printed versions, notably Lady Farrer's edition of Wedgwood's letters, have been generally erratic and incomplete, leading to misinterpretations and misconceptions which have been repeated until they have taken root. This study of Wedgwood's jasper is the result of more than thirty years of original research. By far the most important discoveries relating to jasper made during this period were those of the '1777 Memorandum' (see pp. 87–9), which makes certain the distinction between jasper of the 18th-century and that of later periods, and the evidence showing the withdrawal of jasper from production during much of the first half of the 19th century. Without this crucial information, it is not surprising that so much jasper has been wrongly dated.

In the preparation of this book my debt to previous published work has been slight. My debt to primary source material, on the other hand, is evident, and my long journey through the archives has been made both easier and more enjoyable by the unstinting help given to me by Dr Ian Fraser, formerly the archivist at Keele University, and his successors, Christine Fyfe and Martin Phillips. Gaye Blake-Roberts FMA, the Curator of the Wedgwood Museum at Barlaston, and her assistants Lynn Miller and Sharon Gater, have selflessly shared their research with me. Evidence of their generosity, for which I am sincerely grateful, is to be found in the text and notes. The illustrations were obtained through the co-operation of many collectors and dealers, the authorities of museums and the directors and staff of auction houses in three continents. These sources are acknowledged in the text, but it is necessary to repeat my thanks to them all. Finally, I must record my continuing gratitude to the Trustees of the Wedgwood Museum for allowing me unrestricted access to the Wedgwood archives and providing illustrations and photography from the great collection in their care.

RR. Somerset, 1994

PART ONE

THE WEDGWOODS,
MASTER POTTERS

JOSIAH WEDGWOOD AND HIS WORK

For at least 13,000 years man has made pottery by forming damp clay into shapes suitable for use or ornament and exposing them to heat. The formula for porcelain, on the other hand, was not discovered by Chinese potters until about 1,200 years ago and remained a closely guarded secret until the eighteenth century. Porcelain has always been valued for its beauty and strength.* Its manufacture has engaged the energies and the fortunes of princes; its modellers and designers have commanded respect and rewards; and the finest objects of porcelain have long been regarded as works of art. 'Art' is a word seldom applied to pottery before 1876,[1] although the principal difference between pottery and porcelain lies in the ingredients and the heat of the fire, and most people cannot tell them apart.

Historians have persisted in describing English pottery before 1760 as a peasant craft: 'rough and crude, carelessly and inefficiently manufactured'; 'very primitive' and made by potters who were 'poor and ignorant'.[2] Even the most casual acquaintance with the work of John Dwight of Fulham or the Elers brothers at Bradwell Wood before the end of the seventeenth century, the tin-glazed earthenwares of Bristol, Lambeth and Liverpool, or Staffordshire saltglazed stoneware, much of it boldly decorated in polychrome enamels, is sufficient to dispel the illusion that English pottery before 1759, when Wedgwood opened his first factory, was primitive, or the work of the poor and ignorant.

Nevertheless, it is true that Josiah Wedgwood transformed both the product and the methods of its production and distribution, and in consequence also the way in which it was regarded and the market it could command. Before 1765, when Wedgwood's refined creamware received the approval of the Queen, Staffordshire pottery seldom reached the tables of the rich and it was little appreciated outside Britain. By the end of the century, English creamware was used by royalty and the aristocracy, as

---

*The idea that porcelain is fragile is a comparatively modern one, arising partly from the concept that anything of beauty is by definition also fragile and partly from the vulnerability of European 'soft-paste' porcelains.

well as the increasingly prosperous middle class, and was imitated throughout Europe, where its popularity had all but destroyed the traditional manufacture of tin-glazed earthenware. No less remarkable was the elevation of English ornamental pottery to a position of prestige and influence previously reserved for the porcelain of Meissen and Sèvres. So sudden, so complete and so influential a transformation requires some explanation and it is readily to be found in the work of Josiah Wedgwood.

Although much has been deduced from insufficient evidence, scarcely anything is known of Josiah Wedgwood's childhood. The date of his birth is not recorded and appears not have been known even to his sons.[3] The most likely date is also that of his baptism, which took place at St John's, Burslem on 12 July 1730. Josiah was the youngest child of Thomas and Mary Wedgwood of the Churchyard Pottery, Burslem, a small concern owned by the Wedgwoods since the middle of the seventeenth century, when Thomas's grandfather established a potworks there. Thomas died in June 1739, at the age of fifty-two, leaving the pottery to his eldest son, also Thomas, with instructions to support the younger children. Although the Churchyard Wedgwoods were far from prosperous, Thomas's purchase of a family pew in the parish church for the considerable sum of £7 indicates that neither were they uncomfortably poor, but other members of the family were both more successful and more affluent.

The young Josiah walked the 7-mile round journey to school in Newcastle-under-Lyme, probably until, at the age of fourteen, he was apprenticed to his eldest brother to learn the 'Art of Throwing and Handleing'.[4] In return he undertook, during the next five years, not to 'imbezil or waste' his master's goods, play cards, dice or any other unlawful games, 'haunt or frequent' taverns or ale houses, nor commit fornication or contract marriage. The inclusion in the contract of the difficult 'Art of Throwing' on the wheel, the most highly rated of all the potter's skills, is significant: only those who were expected to become master potters served such an apprenticeship. During the period of this apprenticeship, probably around 1745–6, Josiah suffered a severe attack of smallpox,[5] which weakened his right knee to such an extent that he was unable to use the 'kick-wheel' which provided the motive power to the throwing wheel. On a later occasion, when he chose to throw some important commemorative vases himself, the wheel was turned by his partner.

Josiah remained with his brother for about three years after the end of his apprenticeship before entering into partnership with John Harrison and Thomas Allders in 1754. Two years later he was taken into partnership by Thomas Whieldon, one of the most respected potters in England. During the following five years, the young Wedgwood conducted his first experiments to improve the lead-glazed creamware earthenware body, which was already providing some competition for more conventional

1

2

3

1. *Small Whieldon or*
Whieldon-Wedgwood
creamware teapot with
crabstock handle and spout,
floral knop and turned foot,
coloured predominantly with
grey and touches of green
and yellow. The sides are
ornamented with applied
Tudor roses, buds and leaves
on trailed stems running
from handle to spout, a form
of ornament associated
particularly with
Whieldon, as is the
combination of colours.
Height 3⅝" (9.3 cm).
Unmarked. c.1750–60.
Temple Newsam
House, Leeds

2. *Creamware teapot in the*
form of a cauliflower, with
scroll handle, cauliflower
spout and floret knop,
decorated in green and
ivory-yellow glazes. Height
4⅛" (10.4 cm).
Unmarked. Wedgwood,
c.1763. Temple
Newsam House, Leeds

3. *Creamware plate, with*
feather-edge and rose-
moulded centre, transfer-
printed in Liverpool by
Sadler & Green with
prints of 'exotic' birds.
Diameter 9½" (24.2 cm).
Unmarked. Wedgwood,
c.1770.
Author's collection

tin-glazed and saltglazed wares, its shapes and the coloured glazes used for its decoration. As Josiah was later to write in his Experiment Book: 'I saw the field was spacious, and the soil so good, as to promise an ample recompence to anyone who should labour diligently in its cultivation'.[6] In 1759 he entered that field on his own account, renting a small pottery, the Ivy House Works, from his kinsmen, John and Thomas Wedgwood, of the Big House, Burslem, for £10 a year.

During the next ten years – at the Ivy House and, from the end of 1762, at the Brick House – Wedgwood perfected his creamware, renamed 'Queen's ware' after he had supplied a 'complete sett of tea things'[7] to Queen Charlotte, introduced well-modelled tableware shapes with enamelled and transfer-printed decoration, and began to explore the

4

5

4. Thomas Bentley (1730–80). Portrait medallion, black jasper dip, 5″ × 3½″ (12.6 × 8.8 cm). Mark: WEDGWOOD. *This portrait was modelled by Joachim Smith in 1773–4 as a companion to that of Josiah Wedgwood (Plate 5). Although both portraits must surely have been produced soon after they were modelled, most of the surviving eighteenth-century examples are in black and white, perhaps indicating that a special memorial edition was issued in 1781. (See Appendix H:II).*
Manchester City Art Gallery

5. Josiah Wedgwood (1730–95). Portrait medallion, black jasper dip, 5″ × 3½″ (12.6 × 8.8 cm). Mark: WEDGWOOD. *Modelled by Joachim Smith in 1773–4 as a companion to that of Bentley (Plate 4). (See Appendix H.II).*
Manchester City Art Gallery

market for ornamental wares. He had acquired two partners: his cousin Thomas, employed as a journeyman from May 1759 and promoted to partner in the manufacture of 'useful' wares in 1766; and his kinswoman, Sarah Wedgwood, a considerable heiress, who became his wife on 25 January 1764. In the spring of 1762, following an accident to his vulnerable knee while on a visit to Liverpool, Josiah was introduced to Thomas Bentley, a cultured and experienced merchant, who became his most intimate friend and, from 1768, his partner in the manufacture of ornamental wares. Josiah's letters to Bentley, which have survived almost intact,[8] provide the nucleus of evidence for one of the best documented partnerships in industrial history and are the basis of all studies of eighteenth-century Wedgwood.

The Wedgwood & Bentley partnership, formed specifically for the manufacture of 'ornamental Earthenware or Porcelain Viz Vases, Figures, Flowerpots, Toylet Furniture* & such other Articles as they shall from Time to Time agree upon',[9] lasted until Bentley's death in 1780. It had been planned by Josiah for several years and, in preparation, he had already bought the Ridgehouse Estate, a property of some 350 acres close to Burslem, where he built a new factory, which he named 'Etruria'. Conscious of the need for better communications with London and the port of Liverpool, Josiah had taken a leading part in the promotion of turnpike roads and canals. The Trent & Mersey canal, begun in July

---

*Articles, such as patch boxes, powder bowls, jars for cosmetics, pin trays and small candlesticks, for a lady's dressing-table.

6

*6. Sarah Wedgwood
(1734–1815) at the age of
forty-six. Enamel on
Wedgwood earthenware by
George Stubbs RA, 20″
× 16″ (51 × 40.5 cm),
signed and dated 1780. The
portrait was painted as a
companion to that of Josiah
Wedgwood (see Plate 15)*

1766 and finished in 1777, linked the Potteries with Liverpool on the west coast and Hull on the east as well as providing access at greatly reduced costs to materials from the West Country. As Treasurer to the company formed to administer it, Josiah was aware that the special value of the Ridgehouse Estate was its position directly in the path of the proposed canal.

The entire plan was threatened in April 1768 by further injury to Josiah's weakened right knee, which he described as 'over walk'd & over work'd'[10]. Four weeks later his leg was amputated in his own house by a local surgeon, without anaesthetic. Bentley stayed in Burslem until the immediate danger was past. Within three weeks of the operation Josiah was dressing his own wound and by the first week in July he was sufficiently recovered to visit his factories and go 'rambleing into Cheshire'.[11] Soon afterwards he was fitted with a wooden leg, one of several models which he wore for the rest of his life.

The production of ornamental vases was an innovation in English pottery. By the end of 1768, when the Wedgwood & Bentley partnership books were opened, Wedgwood had three different types in production: Queen's ware, variegated (in imitation of natural stones, such as agate) and black basaltes (Wedgwood's refined black stoneware). Less than a year later the first so-called 'encaustic' vases, in the style of antique red-figure vases, were painted at the Wedgwood & Bentley decorating studio in Chelsea. New London showrooms, opened in Great Newport Street, became a fashionable meeting place. From 1772, when all of Wedgwood's production for both partnerships was manufactured at

7. *Two Queen's ware vases of simple form with vertical engine-turned stripes and turned feet, the elaborate artichoke finials constructed by hand from separately moulded leaves. Height 14" (35.6 cm) and 13" (33.0 cm). Unmarked. Wedgwood, c.1765. The use of the artichoke for the finials was especially appropriate for Wedgwood's first showrooms, opened in 1765 at the 'Sign of the Artichoke', Cateaton Street, London.*

8. *Pear-shaped vase with gilded handles and band of laurel, the white terracotta body decorated with coloured slip to imitate agate, on a square white biscuit terracotta plinth. Height 11" (27.8 cm). Mark:* Wedgwood & Bentley. *c.1773.* City Museum & Art Gallery, Stoke-on-Trent

9. *Black basaltes vase, Shape No. I in Wedgwood's Ornamental Shapes Book, ornamented with* Venus and Cupid *(see Appendix J:I, 77 and 79). Square plinth. Height 13" (32.8 cm). Mark:* WEDGWOOD & BENTLEY ETRURIA *impressed around screw.* c.1775. Dwight & Lucille Beeson Collection, Birmingham Museum, Alabama

7

8

9

10

11

(Facing page)
10. Black basaltes and encaustic-painted 'First Day's Vase', Shape No. 49 in the Ornamental Shapes Book, one of six made to mark the official opening of the Etruria factory on 13 June 1769. The vases were thrown personally by Josiah Wedgwood with his partner Thomas Bentley turning the wheel for him. The form of the vases was copied from one in the Hamilton collection and the painting, also copied from Hamilton's Antiquities, represents Hercules in the Garden of the Hesperides. The inscription on the reverse reads: June XIII.M.DCC.LXIX/ One of the first Days Productions/at/Etruria in Staffordshire/by/ Wedgwood & Bentley. Height 10" (25.4 cm) Unmarked. Wedgwood & Bentley, 1769. On loan to City Museum & Art Gallery, Stoke-on-Trent

11. Four pieces from the 'Frog' service, enamelled in monochrome: custard or ice cup painted with a view taken 'Near Richmond, Surry'; oval compotier from the dessert service with a view of Windsor Castle; cover dish showing Sir William Mann's lake in Surrey; and tureen and cover with a view of Earl Gower's mansion at Trentham. Wedgwood, 1774. Hermitage Museum, St. Petersburg. Photograph, Wedgwood.

Etruria, virtually everything made there was marked with the name 'Wedgwood', or 'Wedgwood & Bentley', impressed in the clay, instead of a painted device such as was used by the comparatively few potters and porcelain manufacturers who marked their goods.

Two orders for Queen's ware, both from the Empress Catherine II of Russia, helped to establish Wedgwood's reputation in Europe. The first, for a dinner and dessert service in the painted *Husk* pattern, confirmed his ability to produce tableware of the highest quality; the second, for the great 'Frog' service of 952 pieces painted with landscapes for the Chesmenski Palace, was for the largest and most prestigious pottery service ever made and its successful production raised Wedgwood's reputation far beyond that of any contemporary rival. Its completion was marked by the removal of the London showrooms to more spacious premises in Greek Street, where they opened on 1 June 1774.

By this time the Wedgwood & Bentley name had become as famous for ornamental wares as that of Wedgwood was for tableware. A new, hard white terracotta body had superseded Queen's ware for the production of 'variegated' vases and the range of colours and shapes had been extended; and black basaltes vases were made in great variety, some ornamented with swags, festoons and cameos, some given a greenish patina in imitation of antique bronze, others painted in the encaustic colours which Wedgwood had patented in 1769. The shapes of Wedgwood's vases were seldom original, but he altered their appearance with ornament or decoration to disguise their sources, which were books of engravings or existing models in porcelain or metal. His principal sources were the engravings illustrating the work of the Comte de Caylus and the collection of Sir

12. Sir William Chambers (1723–96). Portrait medallion, solid blue and white jasper, 3¾" × 2⅛" (9.5 × 7.3 cm). Mark: WEDGWOOD. *Modelled by Charles Peart in 1787. (See Appendix H:I.)* Scottish National Portrait Gallery, Edinburgh

12

William Hamilton, from which he took shapes and red-figure decoration for vases as well as classical border patterns for tableware decoration. He copied and adapted examples of Sèvres porcelain and made full use of shapes designed and published by European artists, such as Bernard de Montfaucon, Jacques de Stella, Joseph Marie Vien, Fischer von Erlach and Edmé Bouchardon, as well as those of the British architects Sir William Chambers, James 'Athenian' Stuart, and the brothers Adam. In August 1772 he boasted to Bentley that he had 'upwards of 100 Good Forms of Vases'[12] available.

Wedgwood announced his ambition to become 'Vase maker general to the Universe' and as early as May 1769 he noted the great gathering of coaches to his London showrooms.[13] The 'Vase madness' generated by his vases was not confined to fashionable society; it had spread to that part of society which sought to be fashionable. 'We must', he told Bentley in 1769, 'endeavour to gratify this *universal passion*'.[14] But it was not only vases that Wedgwood & Bentley had succeeded in introducing to an increasingly large market. Black basaltes figures, plaques, cameos, seals, tablets for chimneypieces, portrait medallions, ornamental candlesticks and library busts, closely resembling bronze in their appearance, poured from Etruria into the houses of the rich and fashionable, and of those who imitated them. Under the guidance of Bentley and of such knowledgeable and influential patrons as Sir William Hamilton, Wedgwood had become a convinced neoclassicist at a time when the porcelain manufacturers were trapped in the rococo style. By the end of 1772, when he began the long series of experiments which led to the invention of jasper, Wedgwood had become the high priest of the 'true style' in pottery and the leading manufacturer of ornamental wares in the industry.

13. White terracotta biscuit portrait medallion of Sir William Hamilton, modelled by Joachim Smith and first produced in 1772 (see Appendix H:I). Oval height 7" (17.7 cm). Unmarked. Wedgwood, c.1772.
British Museum

The invention of jasper occupied much of Wedgwood's time for two years, and its development to the perfection he required of it before he would stake his reputation by taking it to market took three more. It was not until the beginning of 1782, some ten years after he began his painstaking sequence of recorded trials, that he was ready to offer jasper vases to the public.

Thomas Bentley did not live to see them. He died suddenly in November 1780, at the age of fifty. Both as an intimate friend and as a business partner he was irreplaceable. Josiah had consulted him upon every subject, whether business or personal, for fifteen years. It was often Bentley who decided the timing of introducing new products to the market and it was Bentley who regularly called upon the King and Queen, who sought the patronage of ambassadors abroad and foreign diplomats in England, and who cultivated the custom of London society in the Wedgwood showrooms, which he had managed since 1769. It was Bentley, too, who advised Wedgwood on matters of taste, style and fashion. Wedgwood described Bentley's letters to him (now sadly lost) as 'my Magazines, Reviews, Chronicles, & I had allmost said my Bible'.[15] His abilities had been perfectly complementary to Josiah's: Wedgwood's inventive genius and technical expertise with Bentley's commercial experience and entrepreneurial skill; Wedgwood's urgent ambition and driving, tireless energy with Bentley's education, taste and restraining good sense; Wedgwood's vision and Bentley's perceptiveness. And always in the background, reliably producing Queen's ware, the essential foundation without which the Wedgwood & Bentley partnership could never have been contemplated, was Josiah's partner in the production of 'useful' wares, his cousin Thomas.

*14. Thomas Bentley
(1730–80). Josiah
Wedgwood's partner in the
manufacture of Ornamental
wares, 1768–80. Portrait,
oil on canvas, 35¼" ×
27¾" (89.8 × 70.5 cm),
attributed to Joseph Wright
of Derby. 'He possessed A
warm and brilliant
imagination' (from the
inscription on his tomb in
Chiswick Church).*
Wedgwood Museum

14

By the end of 1780 Josiah had achieved his principal goals. His
Queen's ware, acknowledged to be the finest earthenware manufactured
for domestic use anywhere in the world, was imitated from Russia to the
United States of America, and, although he had never considered price
to be the first consideration, he had produced his tableware in such a
range of prices that it had become generally affordable. His ornamental
wares, which by then included the cane and rosso antico bodies (both
refined versions of wares previously available in Staffordshire) as well as
the earlier black basaltes and jasper, had captured a large and profitable
market which had not previously been known to exist. His vases, a sensa-
tional innovation when they were first marketed, had created a fashion
which had already lasted for more than a decade. With the introduction
of jasper vases, on which he had been working for three years, Josiah's creative work seemed to be done. He was prematurely aged by continuous
overwork, stress, amputation and minor illnesses over the years, but his
ambition was not yet satisfied.

After 1780 he gave more of his time to other interests, but he still
found the energy for experiment. His invention of the pyrometer, an
instrument to measure temperature in pottery ovens during firing, was his
last major technical contribution to the industry. Without it, he would
probably have been unable to produce his jasper copies of the Portland
vase,* the crowning achievement of his life as a potter.

Josiah had always preferred the use of original models, when they
could be obtained, to those readily available to other potters, and in 1768

*See pp. 215–35.

15

*15. Josiah Wedgwood
(1730–95). Portrait in
ceramic colours on
Wedgwood earthenware,
oval 20″ × 16″ (50.8 ×
40.7 cm), by George
Stubbs R.A. Signed and
dated 1780. (See Plate 6).*

he had confided to Bentley his dream of creating in London 'a Colony of Artists, Modelers, Carvers &c'.[16] This had been partly realised in the Chelsea Decorating Studio, where the *Husk* and 'Frog' services and the encaustic-decorated vases had been painted. Wedgwood's financial success made it possible for him to commission original work from artists of his own choice. Twenty years later he set up a modelling studio in Rome,[†] under the direction of John Flaxman junior and Henry Webber, to model bas-reliefs from the antique.

Patronage was extended beyond his business. His portrait, and a companion portrait of Sarah, were commissioned from Sir Joshua Reynolds; George Stubbs, for whom Wedgwood made ceramic supports for paintings, completed portraits of Josiah (Plate 15), Sarah (Plate 6), and her father, and a large family group set in the grounds of Etruria Hall; work was bought and commissioned from Joseph Wright of Derby; and part of the decoration of Etruria Hall was by John Flaxman.[17]

During his twenty-five years as a manufacturer Josiah had found little time for politics. In his early struggles to improve communications by road and canal to the Potteries he had made powerful friends, notably Lord Gower and the Duke of Bridgewater, and he had seldom missed the opportunity to commemorate senior political figures whenever he believed that their portraits, on teapots or medallions, had commercial value. Generally he was careful to refrain from the production of pieces whose political comment could make him powerful enemies. Only the

[†]See pp. 147–55.

16. *French Revolution portrait medallions, deep-blue jasper dip. (Clockwise, from top left) comte de Mirabeau, Jacques Necker, duc d'Orléans, marquis de Lafayette, Louis XVI, Jean Sylvain Bailly. All diameter 2⅜″ except Orléans 2¹⁄₁₆″ and Louis XVI 2⅝″; all marked* WEDGWOOD. *c.1789–90. The applied borders are respectively* fleur-de-lis *for the King and his Director-General of Finance, anthemion for prominent revolutionaries, and laurel for the duc d'Orléans.* Dr and Mrs Alvin M. Kanter Collection

American Revolution, of which he had been an ardent admirer, had stirred him to strong political comment, and even then he had confined it to his letters to Bentley. The French Revolution also gained his approval, and he commemorated it with portraits of the leading figures (Plate 16), prudently chosen from both sides. As first chairman of the General Chamber of Manufacturers, which he had founded, Josiah had been closely concerned with negotiations for the abortive Irish Trade Treaty, which he had strenuously opposed, and the French Trade Treaty of 1786, which he had supported. Neither had gained him popularity with manufacturers and the trade advantages promised by the second had been eliminated by the Revolution. His active support for the Society for the Abolition of the Slave Trade was made public by his production of a medallion in jasper (see Plates 49 and C1), modelled from the seal of the Society. Generally, his political views were shared by his closest friends – Bentley, Erasmus Darwin (his 'favourite Aesculapius', who attended all the family), Joseph Priestley, to whom he supplied free chemical wares for his scientific experiments, R.L. Edgeworth, Matthew Boulton, his most worthy rival in the manufacture of ornamental wares, and James Watt — most of whom were members of the Lunar Society, whose meetings he sometimes attended.

After the death of his 'useful' ware partner, Thomas Wedgwood, in 1788, Josiah assumed the whole burden of the business. In 1790, shortly

after his successful production of the Portland vase, he decided to retire and to hand over the control of his firm to his three sons. He died on 3 January 1795.

THE UNWANTED INHERITANCE

Although all three had been trained in factory techniques and management, none of Josiah Wedgwood's sons wished to take an active part in the business. For several years the entire responsibility rested with his nephew, Tom Byerley, a partner from 1790 until his death in 1810. Josiah's eldest son, John, and his youngest brother Tom, both resigned their partnerships during Josiah's lifetime. The younger brother, Josiah II, to whom the factory was bequeathed, thought it not worth continuing and was persuaded only by necessity to manage it. His ability was rather greater than his enthusiasm and his period of control, which lasted for nearly fifty years was not without merit. He presided over the introduction of some fine underglaze-blue printed wares, a new 'White ware' earthenware body, early lustre decoration of excellent quality and the first, although unsuccessful, production of bone china; and the basaltes, cane and rosso antico bodies were kept in production with the addition of new ornaments. But the inexplicable loss of the ability to make large jasper pieces, and its consequent withdrawal from production, was a sad blow to the business from which it took many years to recover.

17. *Dr Erasmus Darwin (1731–1802). Portrait in ceramic colours on Wedgwood earthenware, painted by George Stubbs RA, 1783. Oval 26" × 20½" (66 × 52 cm). Unmarked, but signed and dated by the artist.* Wedgwood Museum

18. *Thomas Byerley (1742–1810), Josiah Wedgwood's nephew and, from 1790, partner. Portrait medallion in blue jasper dip modelled by William Theed, 1810. Oval 4" × 3" (10.2 × 8.35 cm). Mark:* WEDGWOOD. *c.1810. (See Appendix H:III.)* Wedgwood Museum

19

Josiah II's eldest son, Josiah III, was made a partner in the firm in 1823 but he was little interested in it and resigned in 1841 leaving its management to his younger brother Francis, yet another reluctant potter, who shortly afterwards attempted to sell the Etruria factory and the entire estate by auction. The factory failed to find a buyer and Francis continued to manage it until his retirement in 1876. The period of his management saw the introduction of Carrara (Wedgwood's Parian), and Majolica, and the employment of Emile Lessore, who created a new style of earthenware decoration which gained prestige for the firm at international exhibitions. Most important for Wedgwood's future was the reintroduction in 1860 of solid colour jasper, a goal towards which Francis had been working for more than twenty years.

YEARS OF RESOLUTION

Francis was succeeded at Etruria by his eldest son, Godfrey, who shared control with his younger brothers Clement and Laurence. Under their guidance bone china was successfully reintroduced. Godfrey was particularly interested in design and was largely responsible for the employment of Lessore and of Thomas Allen, Wedgwood's first qualified art director. Fashion, and thus styles of decoration and ornament had changed. The international exhibitions in London in 1862 and in Paris in 1867, 1878 and 1889 had stimulated demand for Japanese designs, which were

20
21

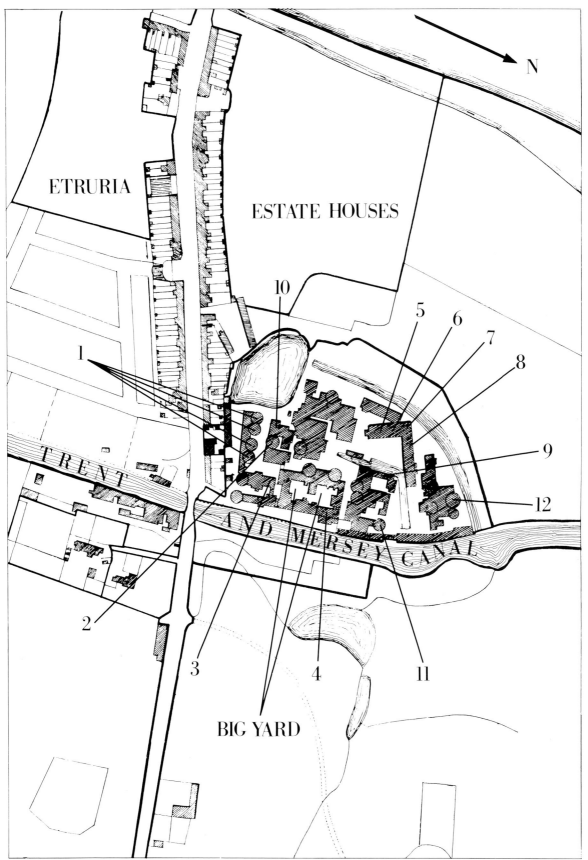

N

ETRURIA

ESTATE HOUSES

10

5
6
7
8

1

9

12

2

3

4

11

BIG YARD

TRENT AND MERSEY CANAL

23. Godfrey Wedgwood (1833–1905), eldest son of Francis Wedgwood. From a drawing by Edward Clifford, c.1882. Godfrey was a partner in the firm from 1859 to 1891, at first with his father and later with his brothers, Clement and Laurence.
Photograph: Wedgwood

24. Francis Hamilton Wedgwood (1867–1930), eldest son of Clement Wedgwood. 'Major Frank' was a partner at Etruria from 1889, and chairman and managing director of the company, incorporated in 1895, until his death thirty-five years later.
Photograph: Wedgwood

adapted for Majolica and translated, with variable success, to tableware designs. Attempts to apply them, even in the most modified form, to jasper, however, failed, as earlier attempts to ornament jasper with any but neoclassical or romantic bas-reliefs had failed. Godfrey's most lasting personal contribution to the firm, was his purchase at auction in 1887 of the Mayer manuscripts, which include Wedgwood's letters to Bentley and now form the core of the enormous Wedgwood archive deposited at Keele university.

When Godfrey Wedgwood retired in 1891, management of the firm passed to his brother Laurence with Cecil Wedgwood (Godfrey's son) and Francis Hamilton Wedgwood (Clement's son, 'Frank') as equal partners. This partnership was dissolved four years later on the incorporation of the firm as Josiah Wedgwood & Sons Ltd, when it was controlled by Cecil, Francis Hamilton and Laurence's son, Kennard. The newly formed company suffered severe reverses but by 1913 the demand for revived neoclassical design had restored its fortunes and the outlook was bright. Kennard had moved to New York, where he founded a subsidiary company to service North America, leaving Cecil and Frank in effective control of the parent company. The outbreak of World War I, in which Cecil was killed, slowed recovery but did not extinguish it. Thomas Allen had been succeeded as art director by John Goodwin and the invention by Daisy Makeig-Jones of *Fairyland Lustre* decoration raised Wedgwood, for the first time, to the first rank of ornamental bone china manufacturers. During the first thirty years of the century the work of Alfred and Louise Powell helped to restore Wedgwood's reputation for fine craftsmanship in earthenware tablewares.

The 1930s was a period of remarkable change for Wedgwood. The Wall Street crash and the world depression which followed threatened the survival of even the greatest international businesses. Smaller companies, such as Wedgwood, whose sales to North America formed a substantial part of their turnover, were especially vulnerable. Frank Wedgwood had died in 1930 to be succeeded as Chairman by Kennard. In England, four young cousins of the fifth generation had joined the company: Josiah V (son of Frank's brother, Josiah Clement, later Lord Wedgwood), John Hamilton (son of Frank's brother Ralph), Hensleigh Cecil and Frank's son Tom. Josiah became managing director, a position he held for thirty-one years. The cousins were supported by two executives of exceptional ability: Norman Wilson, then perhaps the most energetic and inventive pottery manager in Britain, later to be Production Director and Managing Director; and, from 1934, Victor Skellern, who succeeded Goodwin as art director. Together they formed what was one of the strongest management teams ever seen in the Potteries and they lost no time in laying the foundations of a permanent revival in the company's fortunes. During this period, the work of John Skeaping, Keith Murray and Eric Ravilious was of particular importance in keeping the company in the forefront of earthenware design. No less important were the techni-

25

25. Three-colour jasper spherical vase or 'Moon Flask' of pale-blue jasper dip ornamented with white fans and branches of prunus blossom, framed lilac jasper portrait medallions and octagonal cameos, supported on four solid white jasper spherical feet. Mark: WEDGWOOD. *c.*1875. *A bizarre piece, evidently intended to satisfy the fashionable taste for Japanese styles but bearing little resemblance to anything Japanese.*
Christie's, New York

26. Solid pale-blue and white jasper plaque, 'Adam', modelled by Anna Zinkeisen in 1924. Diameter 6⅜″ (16.2 cm). Mark: ADAM BY ANNA ZINKEISEN WEDGWOOD MADE IN ENGLAND 1959 *(replica made in 1959). 'Adam' and 'Eve' plaques were originally made in solid blue and white, green and white and black and white jasper between 1925 and 1929.*
Wedgwood Museum

27. Solid pale-blue and white jasper 'Apollo' vase designed by John Goodwin in 1930 to celebrate the bicentenary of Josiah Wedgwood's birth. The body of the vase is engine-turned and ornamented with the Latin inscription: CC POSTNATUM CONDITOREM ANNO VIGET ARS ETRURIAE REDINTEGRATA *(freely translated as: Two hundred years after the birth of the founder, the thriving art of Etruria is revived). The vase was issued in a limited and numbered edition of fifty of which No. 1 was presented to HM Queen Mary. Height 9½″ (24.1 cm).*
Sotheby's, London

26

27

cal improvements made at Etruria, including the installation of the first gas-fired and oil-fired tunnel ovens.

THE LAST OF ETRURIA

By 1935 continuing subsidence of the Etruria site had made long-term planning impossible, and the directors agreed to buy the 380-acre Barlaston estate and there to build the most modern pottery and porcelain manufactory in Europe, using electricity for all firing. Keith Murray and his partner Charles White designed the factory while the internal layout and equipping of buildings was assigned to Tom Wedgwood and Norman Wilson. The foundation stone was laid on 10 September 1938 and building was allowed to proceed, in spite of the outbreak of war a year later, until the completion of the earthenware factory in April 1940. The bone china factory remained at Etruria until 1949. Wedgwood's production was severely rationalised during the war, and almost all ornamental ware, including jasper, was discontinued. When Norman Wilson returned from war service in 1946, one of his first tasks was the development of a new jasper body which was suitable for modern firing methods.

Kennard Wedgwood was persuaded to retire in 1946, when he was succeeded by Hensleigh. Josiah V became Chairman of the parent company, retaining the position of Managing Director. On 13 June 1950 six 'Last Day's Vases' were thrown on the wheel at Etruria and the old factory was closed.

A NEW AGE

The Wedgwoods seized the opportunities of the 1950s, when the home market was opened for decorated wares for the first time since 1940. The first Wedgwood Rooms (specialist retail shops – mostly in respected department stores – staffed and stocked by Wedgwood) were opened in 1953, providing the company with a direct connection, then unique in the industry, with the public who bought its goods. The home market became stronger than ever before and the American company, which had failed to make the same progress, was given new impetus by the appointment of Arthur Bryan as president. New overseas companies were established in Canada and Australia.

Josiah V was succeeded as managing director in 1961 jointly by Maitland Wright and Norman Wilson, but he remained chairman, with his cousin, Sir John Wedgwood, as his deputy. Sir John's son Martin joined the company in 1962, the first member of the seventh generation to do so. Wedgwood's success during this period, which was due to vigorous and intelligent management, high quality of design and production and a sales staff of exceptional ability, was achieved against strong competition, not only from British manufacturers but also from imported wares, notably from Scandinavia, Germany and Japan. Wedgwood's bone china, which had established an unrivalled reputation in North America during the war, was especially important to the company's prosperity and

28. Josiah Wedgwood V (1899–1968), second son of Josiah Clement Wedgwood DSO, (Josiah IV), first Baron Wedgwood of Barlaston. Josiah V was managing director from 1930 to 1961 and chairman from 1946 to 1967.
Photograph: Wedgwood

29. Norman Wilson (1902–85), potter, designer and inventor. As Works manager at Etruria, Wilson played a crucial part in the modernisation of the Etruria Works and in the subsequent planning of the Barlaston factory. He was production director at Barlaston from 1946 to 1961 and joint managing director with Maitland Wright from 1961 until his retirement.
Photograph: Wedgwood

continuing prestige, and there was a strong revival in demand for jasper, the production of which was deliberately controlled to maintain its reputation for excellence and desirability.

Arthur Bryan was appointed managing director in 1963. Sir John Wedgwood and his son Martin resigned from the company in 1965. Two years later Wedgwood became a public company and Josiah V retired. He died on 5 May 1968. He was succeeded as chairman by Arthur Bryan, who had already embarked on an ambitious policy of acquisition which was to make the Wedgwood Group the world's largest pottery and porcelain manufacturer.

During much of the period of twenty years before it was itself taken over by Waterford, Wedgwood was the only one of the 'Fine China Group' of manufacturers – Wedgwood, Royal Worcester, Spode, Minton, Crown Derby, Doulton – to retain its independence. It was a period of unprecedented expansion, both in turnover and profits, substantially fuelled by acquisitions and soaring inflation but nevertheless impressive. It was put into reverse in 1981–2, when adverse trading conditions and high interest rates on borrowings halted a £9.5 million programme of expansion and required nearly twenty per cent of the workforce to be laid off, but the underlying strength of the company was not damaged. By 1986, the number of companies in the Group had grown to eleven, and a fourth overseas company had been established in Tokyo. The long-established policy of commissioning 'outside' designers was maintained, notably in the work of Richard Guyatt, Sir Eduardo Paolozzi, Glenys Barton, David Gentleman and Wendy Ramshaw, the last of whom was responsible for some innovative jasper jewellery. Other

30. Sir Arthur Bryan (b.1923), the first chief executive of Wedgwood to be appointed from outside the family and the last chairman and managing director of the independent company. He was knighted in 1976 for services to exports.
Photograph: Wedgwood

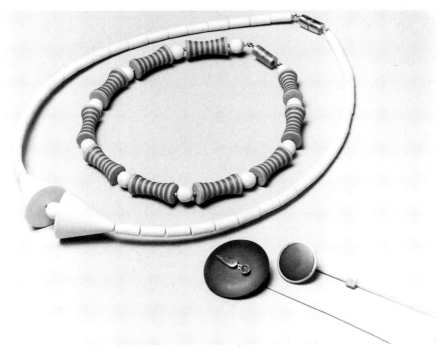

31. Jasper jewellery designed for Wedgwood by Wendy Ramshaw in 1982. The collaboration between the artist and Wedgwood resulted in three categories of jewellery: individual pieces made up by her from jasper or basalt supplied to her specifications; limited editions also made by the artist; and pieces produced in larger quantities from her prototypes. Wedgwood's cooperation, described by Wendy Ramshaw as 'a generous form of patronage', enabled her to take advantage of materials and the extraordinary skills of turners that would not otherwise have been available to her.
Wedgwood Museum

Wedgwood

jasper introductions, such as the 'fashion' colours (taupe, teal and pink) and the translation of Beatrix Potter's 'Peter Rabbit' from lithographed nurseryware to jasper were less well judged.

In 1985–6 Wedgwood became the target of take-over bids, the most pressing being from London International Group, already the owners of Royal Worcester and Spode. Sir Arthur Bryan (knighted in 1976 for services to export) described the offer as 'unwelcome, hostile and unattractive in every sense' and had it referred to the Monopolies Commission while he considered other proposals. Finally, in October 1986, an offer of £253 million was agreed with Waterford Glass and the two companies were consolidated as Waterford Wedgwood.

Jasper continues to be produced, and some attempt has been made to change its appearance by the revived use of engine-turning, jasper dip and different ornaments. It remains, however, obstinately neoclassical. It is an error to suppose that it can remain perennially fashionable. The classical foundations of its original style of ornament have given it a longer life than that of any other ornamental pottery or porcelain, but it has been a life occasionally interrupted by the rejection of classical models. Such intervals have not, historically, been of long duration. Josiah Wedgwood wrote of his black basaltes: 'the black is sterling and will last for ever'.[18] Jasper, if it is not permanently degraded into giftware, may last as long.

32. Wedgwood's first jasper 'Christmas Plate' ornamented with a relief of Windsor Castle. Produced in 1969, the limited edition quickly sold out and the plate became a collector's piece, leading a section of the public to believe that all future editions of this type would also rise as dramatically in value. Greatly increased demand, however, led to the production of greatly increased quantities.
Wedgwood Museum

32

The Colour Plates

C1. *Oval frame of twenty-five jasper cameos illustrating many different coloured grounds including the comparatively rare yellow and brown, and a remarkable trial piece of a vivid green and black dip. Among the subjects are three 'Slave' medallions (cf. Plate 49), a portrait of George, Prince of Wales, two figures of Aesculapius, two of Apollo and the* Dipping of Achilles. *c.1776–90.* Wedgwood Museum

C2. *Two pale-blue and white jasper cameos mounted in cut steel as shoe buckles, probably by Boulton & Fothergill. (Above) solid grey-blue and white jasper with slightly darker-blue dip cameo of the* Bourbonnais Shepherd *after the design by Lady Templetown (see Appendix J:I.251). Oval height 2½" (6.1 cm) including mount. Mark:* WEDGWOOD. *c.1785. (Below) Pale-blue and white jasper dip cameo of* Poor Maria *after the design by Lady Templetown (see Appendix J:I.251), mounted in cut steel with beads of steel, glass and jasper. Oval height 3½" (8.9 cm) including mount. Mark:* WEDGWOOD. *c.1785. The subject was inspired by Joseph Wright of Derby's painting,* Maria and her dog Sylvio, *1777, depicting the character from Laurence Sterne's popular* Sentimental Journey, *published in 1768. Wedgwood Museum*

C3. *Cut-steel comb set with two small blue jasper dip rosettes and a centre cameo of doves on an altar, length 4" (10.2 cm). Mark:* WEDGWOOD *(on cameo). c.1785–90. Cut-steel bracelet set with nine circular cameos (a tenth missing) in tricolour jasper dip of blue, lilac and white with Cupid ornaments. Length 6" (15.2 cm). Mark:* WEDGWOOD. *c.1790. Small necklace of seventy-two matched blue and white jasper beads, each ¼" (0.63 cm) long. Length (including metal link beads) 19½" (50.0 cm). Unmarked. Wedgwood, c.1785–90. Wedgwood Museum*

C4. *Two silver-mounted jasper buttons (Plates 41 and 42) and a circular blue and white jasper cameo set in a cut-steel beaded mount as a clock pendulum. The cameo is ornamented with signs of the zodiac, first supplied to Wedgwood by Mrs Landré in 1776 (cf. Plates 46 and 56). Marks: None visible. Buttons, c.1785; pendulum c.1790–1800. Wedgwood Museum*

C5. *Four scent bottles. (Top left) a cut-glass bottle with a gold screw-top, the body inset with a black and white jasper cameo of a girl with doves attributed to Emma Crewe. Height 2⅝" (6.6 cm). (Top right) long octagonal bottle with metal screw-top. Solid pale-blue and white jasper ornamented with the figure of 'Winter' from the set of the Horae (cf. Plate 48). 4" × 1¾" (11.2 × 4.4 cm). (Bottom left) oval blue and white jasper dip bottle with metal screw-top, ornamented with the figure of a warrior with his armour. Height 3½" (8.9 cm). (Bottom right) round bottle with unmounted screw-top. Pale-blue and white jasper dip, ornamented with portraits of George III and Queen Charlotte within a laurel border. Diameter (without screw-top) 1¾" (4.4 cm). Marks: None visible. Wedgwood, c.1785–90. Wedgwood Museum*

C6. *Solid white jasper plaque with applied white reliefs and four octagonal jasper grounds for cameos showing the four stages in the making of a tricolour jasper dip cameo ornamented with* Cupid in his Car drawn by Lions. *5½" × 8¼" (14.0 × 20.8 cm). Mark:* WEDGWOOD O. *Made by 'Bert' Bentley, 1922. The method of production illustrated by the plaque has remained unchanged for more than two hundred years. Wedgwood Museum.*

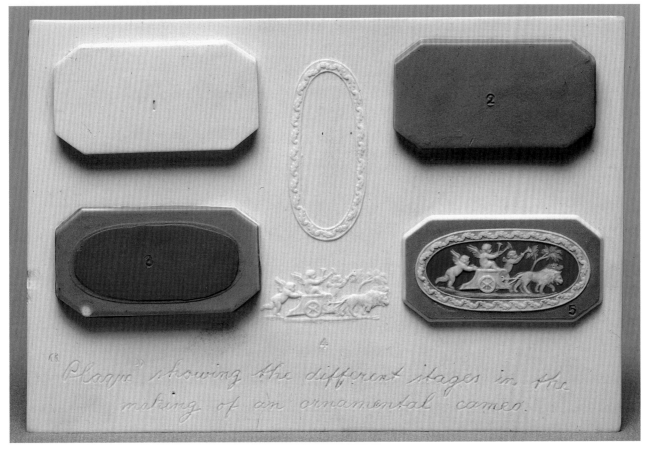

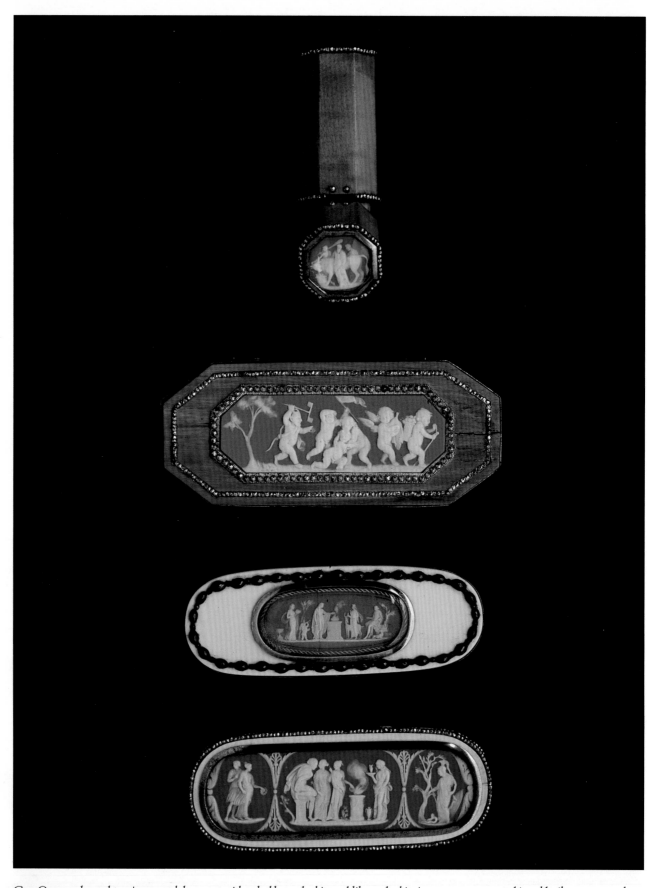

C7. One wooden and two ivory patch boxes set with pale-blue and white and lilac and white jasper cameos mounted in gold, silver or cut steel, and an octagonal pin box with hinged lid inset with a cameo under glass. Lengths 3½″–4½″ (8.9–10.8 cm). No marks visible. c.1785–90.
Wedgwood Museum

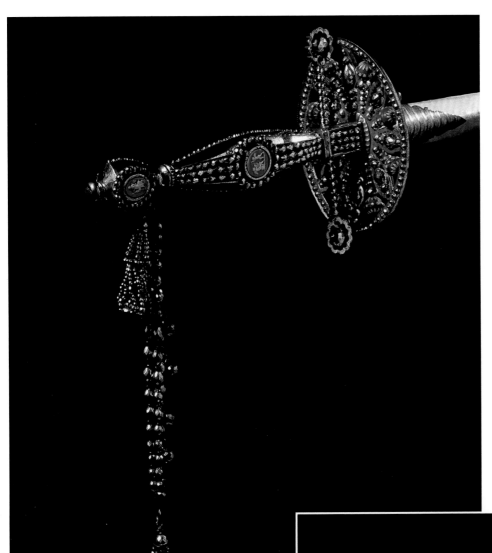

C8. Cut-steel hilt and guard of a court sword, the hilt ornamented with four pale-blue and white jasper cameos, and the guard with eight pale-blue and white jasper beads. Length (hilt and guard) 6" (15.2 cm); (sword in vellum and steel scabbard) 28½" (97.8 cm). c.1790. The case for the hilt bears the name of 'I.Dawson, small steel worker, Goldsmith and Jeweller, 21, Hyde Street, Bloomsbury, London'. Josiah made some trial sword or dagger handles in 1777, writing to Bentley on 22 October (E25–18787): 'The Griffins head makes an excellent handle for an Hanger but I wish you had given me some dimensions for the length & thickness. The Tritons head will make another for a Sea Captain, & a Tygers head we have wo^d make a third.' He writes that he will send the griffin first for Bentley's inspection. None of these pieces appears to have survived, so it is not known whether they were to be made in jasper or black basaltes. It seems most likely that they were never put into production.
Nottingham Castle Museum

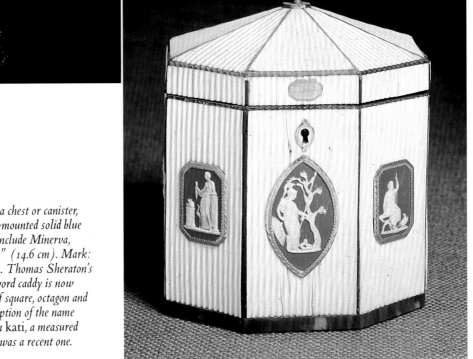

C9. Ribbed ivory and tortoiseshell tea chest or canister, each of its eight sides inset with a gold-mounted solid blue and white jasper cameo. The subjects include Minerva, Hope, Juno and Neptune. Height 5¾" (14.6 cm). Mark: (Juno) WEDGWOOD. c.1790–1800. Thomas Sheraton's catalogue of 1803 mentions that 'the word caddy is now applied to various kinds of tea chests of square, octagon and circular shape', suggesting that the adoption of the name (probably a corruption of the Malayan kati, a measured quantity of about twenty-one ounces) was a recent one.
Nottingham Castle Museum

C10. *Chocolate-brown jasper dip portrait medallion of Admiral Keppel, attributed to William Hackwood, 1779. 4" × 3¼" (10.2 × 8.2 cm). Mark: Wedgwood & Bentley. 1779–80. The chocolate brown is a rare colour for eighteenth-century jasper and particularly so for portrait medallions. (See Appendix H:I.) Private collection*

C11. *Green jasper dip portrait medallion of Josiah's brother-in-law, William Willet, modelled by William Hackwood in 1776. Oval 4" × 3¼" (10.2 × 8.2 cm). Unmarked. 1776. Josiah wrote of this portrait: 'A stronger likeness can scarcely be conceiv'd' (see p. 110 and Appendix H:II.) Wedgwood Museum*

C12. *Pale-blue jasper dip portrait medallion of Edward Bourne in laurel wreath and fluted black jasper frame, modelled by William Hackwood in 1779. Oval 6½" × 5½" (16.5 × 14.0 cm). Unmarked. c.1779. (See p. 111 and Appendix H:II.) Wedgwood Museum*

C13. *Two experimental portrait medallions:*
(right) Carl von Linné (Linnaeus), solid white and
yellow jasper; (left) Voltaire, solid yellow and white
jasper. Ovals height 3¼″ × 2¾″ (8.2 × 7.0 cm).
Mark: (both) Wedgwood and Bentley. c.1777.
(See Appendix H:I.) Wedgwood Museum

C14. *Pale-blue jasper dip portrait medallion of*
Josiah Wedgwood in a rosso antico and black basaltes
frame, modelled by William Hackwood in 1782.
Oval 5¼″ × 4½″ (13.3 × 11.4 cm). Unmarked.
c.1782. (See Appendix H:I.)
Wedgwood Museum

C15. *Solid yellow and white jasper portrait medallion of George Washington, copied from a medal by Voltaire struck in Paris in 1777. Oval 3¼″ × 2¾″ (8.2 × 7.0 cm). Mark:* Wedgwood & Bentley. *1777–80. (See Appendix H:I.)* Formerly Eugene D. Buchanan Collection

C17. *Deep-blue jasper dip portrait medallion of Sarah Siddons, modelled by John Flaxman junior, 1784. Oval 4½″ × 3½″ (11.4 × 8.9 cm). Mark:* WEDGWOOD. *(See Appendix H:I.)* Wedgwood Museum

C16. *Deep-blue jasper dip portrait medallion of William Pitt the younger, modelled by John Flaxman junior, c.1786. Oval 3⅝″ × 2⅞″. Mark:* WEDGWOOD. *c.1786. (See Appendix H:I.)* Wedgwood Museum

C18. *Solid grey and white jasper portrait medallion of Gustavus III, King of Sweden, in a polished frame of the same material, attributed to Flaxman, 1777. Oval 3¹⁵⁄₁₆″ × 3³⁄₁₆″ (10.0 × 8.0 cm). Mark:* WEDGWOOD & BENTLEY. *1777–80. (See Appendix H:I.)* Formerly Eugene D. Buchanan Collection

C19. Solid grey–blue and white jasper plaque, Panther and Bacchanalian Boys *(see Appendix J:I.195)*. *Oval 7½″ × 10″ (19.0 × 25.4 cm). Unmarked. Wedgwood & Bentley, c.1778.* Mr & Mrs Byron A. Born Collection

C20. *Blue jasper dip plaque,* Marriage of Cupid and Psyche, *the second version first modelled in 1774. Oval 8″ × 11¾″ (20.3 × 29.7 cm). Mark:* WEDGWOOD. *c.1785. (Cf. Plates 134–6.)* Nottingham Castle Museum

C21 and C22. Pair of blue jasper dip tablets, The Muses with Apollo *(see Appendix J:I.204), attributed to Flaxman. Each 6⅛" × 15¾" (15.5 × 40.0 cm). Mark:* WEDGWOOD & BENTLEY. *(See Plates 138–40.) c.1778–80.*
Kadison Collection

C23. Oval plaque, pale blue–grey jasper with blue jasper dip, ornamented with the figures of Ganymede and the Eagle *(see Appendix J:I.225). Oval height 7" (17.7 cm). Mark:* WEDGWOOD & BENTLEY. *c.1778. Josiah wrote to Bentley on 3 November 1777 to tell him that he had sent a jasper example of this subject to London, and again on 4 April next year: 'We shall send you three pieces of Jasper today from Sʳ Roger Newdigates models, which with the Eagle & Ganimede should be sent with our compliments to that good gentleman' (E25–18790; E25–18822).*
Wedgwood Museum

C24. *Solid blue and white jasper tablet,* An Offering to Peace, *after a design by Lady Templetown. 6″ × 11¾″ (15.2 × 29.7 cm). Mark:* WEDGWOOD. *c.1790. (See Appendix J:I.238.) This subject is usually catalogued as 'Sacrifice to Ceres' (Mr Wedgwood,* Exhibition Catalogue, *Nottingham Castle Museum, 1975, where it is attributed to Webber) or 'Offering to Ceres' (Eliza Meteyard,* Wedgwood and His Works, *1873, Plate VII, where it is erroneously identified with Flaxman's* An Offering to Flora. *Cf. Plate 145). No subject with either of these titles appears in Wedgwood's catalogues up to 1788. The figures, which are unmatched in style and size, were used with others in compositions for tablets and vases (e.g. tablet, 'Sacrifice to Ceres' in* Wedgwood Basreliefs, *Josiah Wedgwood & Sons Ltd, n.d. (c.1952), p. 13, where it is described as 'Designed and modelled by John Flaxman, 1779', and Meteyard,* Wedgwood and His Works, *Plate XXVI).*
Nottingham Castle Museum

C25. *Green jasper dip tablet,* Birth of Bacchus, *modelled by William Hackwood in 1776. 5″ × 10⅝″ (12.7 × 27.0 cm). Unmarked. c.1776. (See Appendix J:I.118.) The principal group of three figures, Hermes delivering the infant Dionysus to one of the nymphs of Nysa, is adapted from an earlier, and smaller tablet (see Appendix J:I.1); the figure on the left comes from the Arbury list (No. 5, see Plate 125); and the others appear as single figures or as part of different compositions, generally used to lengthen existing subjects. The surface of the figures on this tablet have a noticeable sheen, showing the 'vitrified surface' mentioned by Josiah in March 1776, and perhaps also the surface 'glaze' to which he referred on 10 March (see p. 81).*
Wedgwood Museum

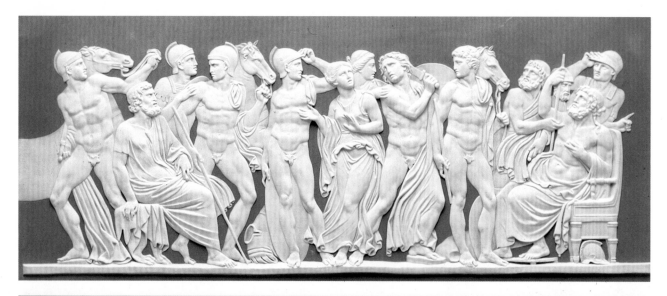

C26. *Green jasper dip tablet,* Achilles in Scyros among the Daughters of Lycomedes, *attributed to Pacetti, and adapted from the so-called sarcophagus of Alexander Severus and Julia Mammaea in the Capitoline Museum. 6¼″ × 15⅜″ (15.8 × 39.0 cm). Mark:* WEDGWOOD. *c.1788–95. This subject is almost invariably catalogued as 'The Sacrifice of Iphigenia' in spite of Dr Carol Macht's definitive evidence of the subject's source* (Classical Wedgwood Designs, *1957, p. 26).* Kadison Collection

C27. *Large grey–blue jasper tablet with pale-blue jasper wash on the upper surface only, ornamented with single figures and groups of boys after designs by Lady Diana Beauclerk (see Appendix J:I.241–3 and cf. Plates 179–81). 6″ × 22½″ (15.2 × 57.0 cm). Mark:* WEDGWOOD. *c.1787–90.* Nottingham Castle Museum

C28. *Solid grey–blue and white jasper teapot with engine-turned foot and lid, acanthus leaf-moulded spout and ribbed loop handle with leaf terminals, ornamented with* Sportive Love *and* Charlotte at the Tomb of Werther *modelled by William Hackwood from designs by Lady Templetown (see Appendix J:I.271–2 and cf. Plates 207 and C31). Height 6″ (15.2 cm). Mark:* WEDGWOOD. *c.1785–90.* Wedgwood Museum

C29. *Solid pale-blue and white jasper saucer dish, engine-turned and ornamented with a leafage border and a centre group of* Infant Academy *after Reynolds (cf. Plates 155 and 156); and a solid pale-blue and white jasper butter dish with engine-turned lid and foot, acanthus border, and ornaments of* Poor Maria *after the design by Lady Templetown and groups of boys at play. Diameter (saucer) 9¾" (24.7 cm); (butter dish) 5½" (14.0 cm). Marks: (saucer)* WEDGWOOD O 3; *(butter dish)* WEDGWOOD 3.
Wedgwood Museum

C30. *Solid pale-blue and white jasper two-handled cup, with white jasper handles and ornaments of* The Young Seamstress *after a design by Emma Crewe (see Appendix J:1.270) and* The Reading Lesson *attributed to Emma Crewe (probably the companion piece to* The Young Seamstress*), the interior lapidary-polished. Height 4" (10.2 cm). Mark:* WEDGWOOD S. *c.1790.*
Nottingham Castle Museum

C31. *Solid lilac and white jasper teapot and cup and saucer, ornamented with figures of* Domestic Employment *after Lady Templetown (see Appendix J:I.248) and* Bacchanalian Boys *after Fiammingo. Both pieces engine-turned. Height (teapot) 5″ (12.6 cm). Mark: (teapot)* WEDGWOOD 3; *(cup and saucer)* WEDGWOOD. *c.1785–95. (Cf. Plates 207 and C28.) All solid lilac jasper of this period is rare, and teawares seem to have been made only in trial quantities.* Nottingham Castle Museum

C32. *Blue jasper dip coffeepot with engine-turned lid and foot, white jasper handle and spout and ornament of* Domestic Employment *after Lady Templetown (see Appendix J:I.248). Height 8″ (20.3 cm). Mark:* WEDGWOOD A. *c.1785–90.* Wedgwood Museum

C33. *Pale-green jasper dip tea bowl and saucer, ornamented with figures of boys at play, the rim and interior of the bowl lapidary-polished. Both the bowl and saucer are as translucent as porcelain. Height 2½" (6.3 cm). Mark: (bowl)* WEDGWOOD O; *(saucer)* WEDGWOOD 3. c.1785. Nottingham Castle Museum

C34. *Pale-green jasper dip 'Brewster' shape teapot and slop bowl, both with engine-turning and ornaments of* Domestic Employment *after Lady Templetown. The teapot has a fluted handle with acanthus and shell terminals; the bowl has a lapidary-polished rim and interior. Height (teapot) 4½" (11.4 cm); diameter (bowl) 7¼" (18.4 cm). Mark: (both)* WEDGWOOD 3. c.1785–90. Nottingham Castle Museum

C35. *Two lilac jasper dip coffee cups and saucers: (left) can shape, tricolour with engine-turned dicing and applied green jasper quatrefoils; (right) translucent, with engine-turned fluting to the saucer and lower part of the cup, the upper part with applied bas-reliefs of children from the* Domestic Employment *designs, the interior lapidary-polished. Height (both) 2½" (6.3 cm). Marks: (left)* WEDGWOOD 3; *(right)* WEDGWOOD 3 O. c.1785–95. Nottingham Castle Museum

C36. Three can shape tricolour jasper coffee cups and saucers: (left to right) black dip, with engine-turned dicing and applied laurel stripes and green jasper quatrefoils; solid white jasper with applied green vine, quatrefoils and stars, lilac pendants and grapes, and blue cameos; green dip with four decorative bands of applied blue squares and green quatrefoils, and three bas-relief groups in compartments. Mark: (all) WEDGWOOD. *Height 2¾" (7.0 cm). c.1790.*
Nottingham Castle Museum

C37. Solid pale-blue and white jasper paint chest or box with lotus knop, 'dimpled' ground and ornament of boys playing musical instruments, fitted with a tray of twelve white jasper paint cups and a white jasper palette. Height 6¾" × 4¾" × 3¾" (17.1 × 12.0 × 9.5 cm). Mark: WEDGWOOD. c.1785–90. *Paint chests were produced in white terracotta stoneware and black basaltes and there are references to paint cups as early as 1771. A paint chest is illustrated in the London Pattern book for 1787 (Ms. 61–30635).*
Mr and Mrs Byron A. Born Collection

C38. Solid pale-blue and white jasper 'Vase teapot', the 'dimpled' ground ornamented with figures from Domestic Employment *designed by Lady Templetown, with solid white jasper double handle, laurel moulded spout and Cupid knop. Shape no. 303. Height 8" (20.4 cm). Mark:* WEDGWOOD C. *c.1787–95. In a letter to Thomas Byerley, dated 6 April 1787, Josiah wrote of '303 Teapots on high feet, & highly finished in every respect, 3 sizes – the largest I think is a guinea half – They are called Vase Tea pots' (Ms. 96–17711).*
Wedgwood Museum

C39. Tricolour jasper lidded cup and saucer of lilac dip with engine-turned dicing, ornamented with horizontal and vertical white jasper bands of laurel and green jasper quatrefoils, with solid white jasper handle and lotus knop. Height 4½" (11.4 cm). Mark: WEDGWOOD. c.1785–95. Kadison Collection

C40. Solid pale-blue jasper centrepiece bowl with applied white and yellow jasper strapwork in a basketweave pattern and applied flowers inside the bowl. Height 9" (22.8 cm); oval width 9¼" (23.5 cm). Mark: WEDGWOOD. c.1785–95. A particularly large and fine example of tricolour jasper on a solid jasper ground colour, a combination much rarer than three-colour jasper dip. Wedgwood Museum

C41. Solid pale-blue and white jasper figure of 'Venus rising from the sea, upon a pedestal richly ornamented with figures representing the seasons' (see Appendix L.28). Height 6½" (16.5 cm). Mark: Wedgwood & Bentley. 1779–80. This figure is listed separately from the 'Small statues on pedestals' which appear in the 1787 Catalogue (see Appendix L.38) and was evidently not included in that group of figures, none of which has been identified as having been made during the Wedgwood & Bentley period. It seems, therefore, that the pedestals illustrated in Plate 241 can have been made only for the figure of Venus. On the figure illustrated the rock upon which Venus crouches has been lightly tinted with a thin, pale-blue wash.
Private collection (Photograph: Courtesy of David Buten)

C42. *Lilac and white jasper dip and blue and white jasper dip chess set designed by John Flaxman junior in 1783–4. Height of queen 3½″ (8.9 cm). Mark: (all)* WEDGWOOD. *c.1785–95. (Cf. Plates 246–9.) The set is laid out on a late-eighteenth-century mahogany and satinwood chess and backgammon box.* City Museum & Art Gallery, Stoke-on-Trent (chess set); Author's collection (chess board)

C43. *Pair of solid blue and white jasper candlesticks in the form of tritons grasping whorled shells (sometimes erroneously described as cornucopias). Height 11″ (28.0 cm). Mark:* WEDGWOOD. *c.1785–95. Wedgwood's figures of tritons appear to have been modelled from a single figure, carved in wood, sent to Etruria towards the end of 1769 and described by Bentley as after a model by Michelangelo (E25–18278 28 December 1769). In January 1770 Josiah estimated that 'a single Triton . . . will always take a man near two days to begin & finish it' (E25–18281 3 January 1770); and six months later could make only three pairs a week in black basaltes (E25–18306 2 June 1770). Tritons were produced also in the 'straw' colour and bronzed basaltes (E25–18308 8 June 1770). Cf Plate 250.*
Mr & Mrs David Zeitlin Collection

C44. Pair of solid blue and white jasper candlesticks in the form of tree trunks entwined with vine and ivy, with figures of Cupids, one with a basket of grapes, the other with a fire of wood and leaves, representing Autumn *and* Winter. *Height* 10¾″ *(27.2 cm). Mark:* WEDGWOOD. *c.1785–90. The figures are often attributed to Hackwood, and less frequently to Flaxman, but no evidence has been found to substantiate either claim.*

Nottingham Castle Museum

C45. *Pair of solid blue and white jasper tripod vase–candlesticks with reversible lids, the bodies with spiral fluting and ornament of acanthus leaves. Height (as vase with lotus finial) 9⅝"* (24.5 cm); *(as candlestick) 10¾" (27.3 cm). Mark:* WEDGWOOD ⩔ . *c.1785–90. (Cf. Adams vase–candlestick, Plate 299.)* Kadison Collection

C46. *Pair of candelabra of cut glass with black and white jasper (dip?) drums mounted in ormolu bases. The cut-glass drops are of yellow and white glass. Height 11" (38.0 cm). No marks visible. Wedgwood, c.1790.* Wedgwood Museum

C47. *Pair of solid lilac and green jasper flower-holders in the form of figures of Cupid with a bird's nest and Psyche with a butterfly, perhaps representing* Spring *and* Summer. *Height 8¾″ (22.2 cm). Mark:* WEDGWOOD. *c.1785–95. It is possible that these figures are the work of the same modeller as the* Autumn *and* Winter *candlesticks, and were intended to form a garniture of the Seasons but documentary evidence of this is lacking. (Cf. Plate 257.)*
Buten Museum

C48. *Two solid green and white jasper and solid lilac and white jasper square bough-pots or pedestals ornamented with bas-relief figures of Cupids representing the Seasons. Height 6½″ (16.5 cm). Mark:* WEDGWOOD. *c.1785–95. These bas-reliefs have been erroneously identified with those invoiced to Wedgwood by John Flaxman senior in 1775 (see Appendix J:I.114–17 and 231–4). The shape was designed for more than one purpose: it could be used as a pedestal for a vase; with a flat perforated grid as a bough-pot or flower-holder; or with a shaped holder as a bulb-pot. (Cf. Plate 273.)*
Buten Museum

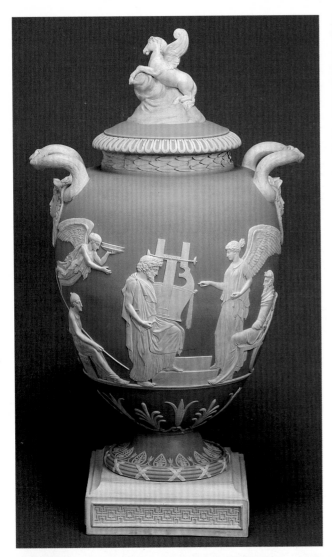

C49. Greenish-buff jasper dip 'Pegasus' vase, with solid pale-blue jasper clouds beneath the feet of the Pegasus figure and eggs at the centre of the snake handles, on a solid white jasper plinth. Height 18″ (45.7 cm). Mark: WEDGWOOD. c.1786. Only two examples of the vase in this rare colour have so far been found (the second is in a private collection in America). (See captions to Plates 262 and 263.) Nottingham Castle Museum

C50. Solid pale-blue and white jasper snake-handled vase, ornamented with Venus in her Chariot drawn by Swans, with attendant Cupids, and Cupids watering the Swans after designs by Charles Le Brun. Height 16½″ (42.0 cm). Mark: WEDGWOOD. 1786–90. (Cf. Plate 276.) Wedgwood Museum

C51. Pair of solid pale-blue and white jasper wine and water ewers ('Sacred to Bacchus and Neptune') after models supplied by John Flaxman senior in 1775 (Cf. Plates 278A and B). Height 15″ (38.0 cm). Marks: (wine) WEDGWOOD K; (water) K (no Wedgwood impressed mark). c.1786–90. Nottingham Castle Museum

C52. *Solid blue and white jasper 'ruined column' vase. Height 7¾″ (19.6 cm); base 8¼″ × 4¼″ (21.0 × 10.6 cm). Mark:* WEDGWOOD. *c.1786–95. (See caption to Plates 287–9.)* Kadison Collection

C53. *Solid pale-blue and white jasper vase or bough-pot, the shape adapted from the 'Michelangelo lamp', first made in basaltes, the supporting 'Persians' in solid white jasper, the bowl ornamented with a floral scroll, and the upper part with rose festoons and a pierced grid. Height 11⅝″ (29.5 cm). Mark:* WEDGWOOD. *c.1790–1800. The bowl of the vase is attached to the foot by a bolt which runs through the length of the stem. There is a noticeable difference in shade between the base and stem, and the bowl and grid, the former being of a greyish-blue and the latter a clear pale blue, but, although the two parts were probably not fired together, there seems to be no reason to suspect that they vary substantially in date of manufacture or that they were 'married' from two other pieces.* Kadison Collection

C54. Green and white jasper dip cylindrical pedestal bough-pot with white jasper grid on solid white jasper hexagonal plinth on raised feet. The body of the bough-pot is ornamented with Blind-man's-buff, designed and modelled by John Flaxman junior in 1782 'to decorate the sides of teapots' (see Plate 133). Height 7½" (19.0 cm). Mark: WEDGWOOD. *c.1786. Cylindrical pedestal shapes of this type were used also as bases for lamps and vases. The solid white jasper foot suggests a date before or shortly after 1786 (see caption to Plate 265).*
Nottingham Castle Museum

C55. *Tricolour jasper flower-pot or cachepot and stand, the lilac dip body with vertical engine-turned stripes ornamented with moulded strips of green jasper in a basketwork pattern. Height (pot) 3¼" (8.2 cm); diameter (stand) 4½" (11.5 cm). Mark:* WEDGWOOD Z. c.1790. Buten Museum

C56. *Tricolour jasper bough-pot and stand of green jasper dip with vertical engine-turned stripes ornamented with moulded strips of yellow jasper in a basketwork pattern, the solid white jasper pierced grid ornamented with green jasper leaves and yellow jasper quatrefoils. Diameter (without handles) 9" (22.8 cm); height (without stand) 4¼" (10.8 cm). Mark:* WEDGWOOD. c.1795. Kadison Collection

C57. *The 'Hope' copy of Wedgwood's jasper Portland Vase, supplied to Thomas Hope, one of the original subscribers, in June 1793 (see Plates 318 and 316A). The figures are identified as Thetis, reclining in her sanctuary, watched by Hermes and Aphrodite. Height 10⅛" (25.8 cm). Unmarked. Wedgwood, 1793.* Wedgwood Museum

C58. *A fine example of the solid blue jasper Portland Vase of which a number were made in 1791 (see p. 230). This particular vase was*
presented to the British Museum by Josiah II in 1802. There is no obvious reason to suppose that the vase was produced specially for the purpose
of this presentation, and no record has been found of the production of solid blue copies during the previous ten years, so this vase was most probably
among those made during the temporary shortage of 'Barberini black' clay in April 1791. Josiah II's choice of this colour to present to the British
Museum suggests that no black copy of sufficiently fine quality remained in stock in 1802. Although imperfect, the vase is well undercut and
attractively shaded. The blue body appears to have shrunk rather more in firing than the black clay. Height 9¾" (24.7 cm). Unmarked.
Wedgwood, 1791.
British Museum

C59. Solid pale-blue and white jasper group, 'Britannia Triumphant', on tall cylindrical pedestal. Height 32″ (81.3 cm). c.1802. (See Plates 335–8.) Beeson Collection, Birmingham Museum, Alabama (group); Wedgwood Museum (pedestal)

C60. Jasper, cane and drabware caddy spoons and caddy shells with a contemporary jasper salt spoon. Length (caddy spoons) 3½″ and 2⅛″ (8.9 and 5.4 cm); (salt spoon) 2½″ (6.3 cm). Mark: WEDGWOOD. *c.1815–28.*
Mr and Mrs Byron A. Born Collection

C61. Pair of yellow-dip jasper spill vases ornamented with 'light blue wreathed laurel' ornaments. Height 3½″ (8.9 cm). Mark: WEDGWOOD. *c.1814. These pieces appear in Bateman's orders from March 1814.* Wedgwood Museum

C62. Ormolu clock by Thomas Reynoldson, Hull, fitted with a jasper face, pillar supports and decorative panels, and a French movement by H. Marc, Paris. Height 13¾″ (34.9 cm). Mark: None visible. c.1878. Possibly made for the 1878 Exhibition in Paris.
Buten Museum

C63. *Three canopic vases, two in jasper dip and the third in cane ware with grey ornaments. Height (jasper) 10" (25.5 cm); (cane) 9⅞" (25.1 cm). Mark:* (left and centre) WEDGWOOD; *(right) unmarked. c.1865–75. Mr and Mrs David Zeitlin Collection*

C64. *Pair of jasper-dip wine coolers ornamented with water-lilies in modelled slip. Height 11½" (29.2 cm). Mark:* WEDGWOOD. *c.1880. (Cf. Plates 386 and 387.)* Buten Museum

C65. Two solid blue jasper vases with carved and modelled slip ornaments of garlands of flowers. Height 9¼″ and 9⅜″ (23.5 and 23.8 cm). Mark: (left) WEDGWOOD DW[?]O; *(right)* WEDGWOOD X × 941. *c.1886. (Cf. Plates 386 and 387.)* Buten Museum

C66. Tobacco jar of diced black jasper dip with ornaments of yellow quatrefoils and white olive foliage. Height 8". Mark: WEDGWOOD. *c.1880–1900.*
Wedgwood Museum

C67. (Left to right) yellow-buff jasper-dip vase, a wide band on the body being dipped in black and ornamented with Dancing Hours *figures. Height 7⅞" (20.0 cm). Mark:* WEDGWOOD 4XA. *1924. An example of a comparatively rare form of three-colour jasper. Turquoise-dip bas-relief ware bowl. Diameter 7¼" (18.5 cm). Mark:* WEDGWOOD. *c.1880–90. All teaware made in this colour appears to be of the jasper-dipped stoneware body. Crimson jasper dip bas-relief ware mug. Height 5⅛" (13.2 cm). Mark:* WEDGWOOD ENGLAND. *c.1910. (Cf. Plate 408.) Yellow-buff-dip pillar candlestick with black ornaments. Height 7" (17.8 cm). Mark:* WEDGWOOD ENGLAND 3. *c.1930.*
Buten Museum

C68. Crimson-dip jasper spill vase and bas-relief ware teapot, the teapot with glazed interior, the spill vase ornamented by Bert Bentley. Height (spill) 7½" (19.0 cm); (teapot) 3½" (8.9 cm). Marks: (spill) WEDGWOOD MADE IN ENGLAND o: (teapot) WEDGWOOD ENGLAND. c.1930.
Wedgwood Museum

C69. Solid blue and white jasper chess set designed by Arnold Machin in 1938 and produced before 1940 in black basalt, jasper, Queen's ware and bone china. Height (king) 5½" (14.0 cm). Mark: WEDGWOOD MADE IN ENGLAND. Replicas made in 1969.
Wedgwood Museum

C70. *Coloured stoneware ('porcelain') chess pieces after the models by John Flaxman junior (Plates 246 and C42). Height 2⅜″ to 4¼″ (6.2 cm to 10.7 cm). Marks: (blue pawn and Celadon queen)* WEDGWOOD ~ ~ ; *(drab queen)* WEDGWOOD 12 ~ ~ ; *(knight)* WEDGWOOD. *c.1810–20.* British Museum

C71. *(Rear left) solid pale-blue and white jasper Portland vase. Height 9⅞″ (25.0 cm). Mark:* WEDGWOOD *(on foot rim). c.1880. (Rear right) crimson jasper-dip Portland vase. Height 10¾″ (27.3 cm). Mark:* WEDGWOOD *(on foot rim). c.1930. (Front left) olive-green-dip bas-relief ware Portland vase without base disc. Height 5″ (12.7 cm). Mark:* WEDGWOOD ENGLAND *(on base). c.1910. (Front right) bright-blue-dip bas-relief ware Portland vase. Height 4″ (10.2 cm). Mark:* WEDGWOOD *(on base). c.1863.* Buten Museum

PART TWO

JASPER, 1774–95

Josiah Wedgwood's jasper, the triumphant outcome of more than 5,000 recorded experiments, was his most important contribution to ceramic art, and the most significant innovation in ceramic history since the Chinese invention of porcelain nearly a thousand years earlier. Jasper is a dense white stoneware which, when thinly potted and fired at a slightly higher temperature than usual (above 1,250° centigrade), may be translucent like porcelain. The body may be stained to provide a wide variety of colours, ornamented, engine-turned, laminated and lapidary polished; and, although the result is seldom pleasing, it may be glazed, painted in enamel colours and gilded. At its finest, it combines intrinsic beauty with unusual versatility and it has remained continuously in production (except for a short interval in the nineteenth century and periods of wartime government restrictions) for more than two hundred years.

The qualities which made it especially suited to neoclassical ornament and appealed to cultivated taste in the eighteenth century, achieved for jasper a widespread mass popularity which has sometimes been diminished but never eliminated. No ornamental style in ceramics has attracted a comparable popular market over so long a period, and the commercial benefits accruing to the firm have far outweighed the constricting influence it has sometimes exercised upon design development.

Josiah's almost unbroken series of experiments to produce white earthenware and stoneware bodies has made it difficult to disentangle the development of the white 'terracotta'* from the invention of jasper. The reference most often quoted as the first relevant to jasper is dated 13 January 1771, when Josiah wrote to Bentley of his intention 'To make a white body, succeptible of being colour'd & which shall polish itself in burning Bisket'; but he went on to speculate how this new body would enable him 'to make wonderfull pebbles & other fine things',[1] and his description fits the terracotta body better than the jasper. The white terracotta was already in production in its earliest form of 'polished biscuit', and was later to be advertised in the Catalogues as 'Fine white Terracotta' (1774), 'white waxen Biscuit' (1779) and 'white Porcelain *bisqué*' (1787). Even Bentley's demand in 1772 for 'a finer body for Gems' was satisfied

*See p.17

by 1774 when the white body was described as 'proper for cameos, por-traits and bas-reliefs'. Josiah's response to the demand is, however, rele-vant: 'I think a China [porcelain] body wo^d not do. I have several times mixed bodies for this purpose, but some have miscarried, & others have been lost or spoild for want of my being able to attend to, and go thro' with experiments.'[2] At the time, his health was poor, and he was indulging himself in one of his valetudinarian fits when he feared for the future of the ornamental business without the benefit of his own inventive brain to direct it.

As late as December 1772, therefore, Josiah had made no conscious progress towards the invention of jasper, and the development of the white terracotta was still in an early stage. Nor is there evidence that Wedgwood had, at that time, any clear conception of the direction in which his experiments might lead him. Within eighteen months, however, he had isolated, though not fully understood, the materials he needed, and six months later he was able to send samples to Bentley which the latter approved. Although the partners pronounced themselves satisfied with the new body, it was to be a further three years before it could be made with certainty in the colours required, and at least three more before it could be used for the production of vases. Nevertheless, it is notable that the bulk of Josiah's great number of experiments was completed within the space of the two years from December 1772 to December 1774.[3]

Wedgwood's progress in the development of any ceramic body, or glaze or technique, was empirical. He was using materials which were full of unidentified impurities and which consequently produced infuriat-ingly unpredictable variations in behaviour. Josiah was, as has been demonstrated,[4] a competent chemist, and had available to him the advice of such distinguished scientists as Joseph Priestley, Samuel Galton and John Whitehurst, but chemical analysis was still in its infancy. Josiah's frustrations and his successes were the results of trial and error.

The composition of jasper was Josiah's most closely guarded secret, and William Burton and Sir Arthur Church are among the writers who have taken the trouble to have the body subjected to modern methods of chemical analysis. Burton, himself chemist for five years at the Etruria Works, concluded that it contained 'finely divided barium sulphate with the addition of the smallest possible amount of clay'. Church published a more detailed formula: 'Sulphate of baryta 59 parts; clay 29; flint 10; car-bonate of baryta 2'.[5] Josiah's own formula was unveiled in response to a request from Bentley in February 1776: 'You desire to know a mixture,' Josiah replied, 'Will you be content to have part of it now, & the remaineder another time – It is too precious to reveal all at once.'[6] The fig-ures that follow are Josiah's code numbers, and the identifications in French are in Bentley's hand:

17 Cailloux [calcined flint]
22 Argile des Potiers [Purbeck clay]
20 Albatre [alabaster]

24 Saphire [zaffre & cobalt]

74 [cawk (barium sulphate)]

Three days later, Josiah revealed the quantities for white jasper: 'Our Jasper is one of 17 six of 74 three of 22 & ¼ of 20,'[7] giving the proportions as:

Calcined flint 1

Purbeck clay 3

Alabaster (fired and washed) ¼

Sulphate of barium 6

A knowledge of this formula is of some assistance in the understanding of Josiah's many difficulties with the body, and may perhaps yield some clues to his original intention.

Josiah's invention of jasper was no more accidental than his refining of creamware: it was a deliberate development, making use of accessible materials, to produce a finer white body than the terracotta biscuit. The general principles of its manufacture – a high proportion of a fusible substance (barium sulphate) held in shape during firing at high temperature (about 1,200°–1,250° centigrade) by refractory clay while fusion took place – were those of porcelain manufacture. Some thinly potted and high-fired jasper conforms to both the Chinese and the European definitions of porcelain: it emits a bell-like tone when struck, and it is translucent. Josiah himself described jasper as 'my porcelain'.[8] It is tempting to construe these facts as evidence that jasper was the accidental by-product of experiments directed towards the manufacture of porcelain, and this is a deduction that cannot be disregarded.

The manufacture of 'true' (Chinese) porcelain was an almost universal ambition throughout Europe in the eighteenth century. Its secret, which remained closely guarded, was discovered at Meissen, where it was first produced in 1709.[*] Artificial ('soft paste') porcelain, made from white-burning clay and what was, in principle, ground glass, had been made in Europe since the end of the sixteenth century, first in Florence and later at St Cloud, and reached its peak of perfection at Vincennes. In England, it was made first at Chelsea and Bow, where bone ash was added to the body. At the Worcester porcelain factory, from 1752, the body contained soaprock.[†]

In 1768, William Cookworthy, a Quaker apothecary and chemist of Plymouth, who had been experimenting with Cornish materials similar to those of China,[‡] took out a patent for their use. Both the factory, removed to Bristol in 1772, and the patent were bought by Richard Champion and, in 1774, he applied for an extension of the patent for fifteen years. Josiah Wedgwood led the Staffordshire potters, who were

[*]The invention was the result of experiments by J.F. Böttger. The Royal Saxon Porcelain Company was established at Meissen in 1710.

[†]Hydrated silicate of magnesium, noted for resistance to thermal shock.

[‡]Local kaolin of much the same properties as the Chinese, and Cornish or growan stone, a feldspathic rock similar to petuntse.

excluded from the use of Cornish materials, in their petition to the House of Lords to deny the extension. In the face of such powerful opposition, and the likely costs of a prolonged dispute, Champion compromised and amended his application to refer to the use of Cornish clay and stone only for the manufacture of porcelain. By 1781 he was bankrupt, and turned to Wedgwood for assistance. Josiah, no longer interested in porcelain manufacture, helped Champion to sell his patent to a company of eight Staffordshire potters.[*]

The development of artificial porcelain is of little relevance in this work. Josiah Wedgwood certainly knew how to make it – the Bow recipe was noted in his Experiment Book on 13 February 1759 – but never showed much interest in doing so. It was commercially an extremely hazardous undertaking, as the many failures in the industry, including Chelsea and Bow, showed, and there were already too many competitors in the field. Further, production of porcelain would certainly damage the sales of Queen's ware and there would be little advantage in taking such a risk for an artificial porcelain.

It would, however, be mistaken to suppose that Josiah was not interested in the manufacture of 'true' porcelain. He conducted experiments for it at least as early as 1773, when he obtained samples, probably of both kaolin and petuntse, from Samuel More,[9] to whom they had been sent from China by the naturalist John Bradby Blake.[†] Even earlier references to 'porcelane' and 'Experiments which I expect must be perfected by the *Spath Fusible*' indicate previous attempts in 1767, and, by October of that year, Josiah was well informed about the work of the comte de Lauraguais,[‡] who had recently produced the first recorded French hardpaste porcelain.[10] Josiah's Commonplace Book shows also that he had studied the work of du Halde[§] and Faujas de St Fond, corresponded with Bradby Blake, and taken advice from Richard or Josiah Holdship, the partners in the Worcester porcelain factory from 1751 to 1759.

David Rhodes's expenses in May 1775 include payments for pieces of Chelsea, Plymouth, Liverpool, Worcester, Derby, Lowestoft and Bristol porcelains, some of them 'broken ware',[11] and it is hard to escape the conclusion that these were required for some form of analysis or experiment.

---

[*]Charles Bagnall, William Clowes, John Daniel, Joshua Heath, Samuel Hollins, Anthony Keeling, John Turner of Lane End, and Jacob Warburton. Later, after Turner and Keeling had withdrawn, the company became the New Hall Company of Shelton. The company made 'true' porcelain from 1781 to 1835.

[†]John Blake, who became a supercargo to the East India Company, went to Canton in 1766, where he obtained plants and seeds for propagation. His death in 1773 at the age of twenty-eight seems to have put an end to Wedgwood's trials with Chinese materials.

[‡]Louis-Léon-Felicité, duc de Brancas (1733–1824), produced an imperfect grey true porcelain in his laboratory at the Château de Lassay about 1765, using kaolin from Alençon.

[§]Jean Baptiste du Halde (1674–1743), a Jesuit who published in 1725 *Description géographique, historique, & c de la Chine*, based on letters and reports of missionaries. It was translated into English and was the fount of much early information about Chinese ceramics.

At the end of 1775, however, Josiah responded to an offer from Matthew Horne:* 'our experimental work is over, & for my own particular, it does not suit with my business to begin upon Porcelain at present';[12] and in February 1776 he wrote: 'I do not wish to purchase any English process, & much less the Bow, which I think one of the worst processes for China making.'[13] By then he no longer needed it.

In a detailed and unusually technical letter written about a month earlier, he comments to Bentley on the processes of porcelain manufacture, outlines his preferences in materials, and continues: 'I have given you my idea of the best plan for making *perfect Porcelain* with uniform success, and it is the plan I intend to proceed upon as time will permit, but I may probably make a *white ware* for Painting before the other plan is perfected into Manufacture. . . . I will send you some Pitchers of 74 Porcelain and you will let Mr Rhodes try his skill in glazing them.'[14] By '74 Porcelain' he was referring to the white jasper of which barium sulphate (code number 74) formed so large a proportion, but it is plain that, the perfection of jasper notwithstanding, he had not yet abandoned his intention to manufacture 'true', hardpaste porcelain at some later date. It may have been the remarkable success of jasper, and the fact that its manufacture was, for a time, confined to Wedgwood & Bentley, that persuaded him not to pursue that aim. It is probable too that, even after he was confident of the jasper body in 1777, his trials with different colours and techniques of ornamenting kept him sufficiently busy, and that there was little space or spare capacity in the factory for so demanding a product as porcelain. Last, he was fully aware of the commercial hazard involved in porcelain production and the complication it would add to his already wide variety of manufacture.

The question remains whether the series of trials which led to the invention of jasper was a diversion, originally temporary, on the way to the manufacture of porcelain; or designed, through the use of similar principles and materials to those of porcelain, to create an original ceramic body that might be an end in itself. Josiah's obvious and intimate interest in the details of porcelain manufacture, and the evidence, not only of his knowledge of the techniques and materials involved but also of experiments in their application, lends weight to the supposition that he knew, with some precision, what the outcome of his experiments was likely to be. Though his initial intention may have been to produce hardpaste porcelain, the direction of his work from the end of 1772 was towards a new ceramic body which, though undoubtedly a porcellaneous stoneware, was not defined by its composition as porcelain.

The search for this new body, and its development, absorbed much of Josiah's time and energy for more than two years. If one considers that he was, simultaneously, engaged in managing his business and,

*Matthew Horne wrote to Wedgwood in 1775 claiming to be able to make porcelain figures 'four or five feet high without supports or props' and offering himself for employment (Wedgwood Ms. 2–18628 n.d. 1775).

throughout part of 1773 and 1774, personally directing the production of the 'Frog' service for the Russian Empress, it is no surprise to find him complaining of stress and overwork.

In response to Bentley's demand at the end of 1772, Josiah wrote to him in February 1773 of having made 'some very promising experim[ts] lately upon fine bodies for Gems & other things'.[15] Nothing much more is heard of these until March 1774, and it is clear that he had had little time to spend upon them during the past fourteen months: 'I have', he writes, 'for some time past been reviewing my experiments, & I find such *Roots*, such *Seeds* as would open & branch out wonderfully if I could nail myself down to the cultivation of them for a year or two. And the Foxhunter does not enjoy more pleasure from the chace, than I do from the prosecu-tion of my experiments when I am fairly enter'd into the field, & the far-ther I go, the wider the field extends before me.' After reviewing some of those 'Roots which have been selected & put into cultivation', he recalls Bentley's warnings and adds: 'but the too common fate of schemes is ever before my Eyes, & you have given me many excellent lectures upon the bad policy of hurrying things too fast one upon another.'[16]

By July he is deep in Experiments: 'M[oor]stone & Spaith fusible are the two articles* I want, & the several samples I have of the latter are so different in their properties that no dependence is to be had upon them. They have plagued me sadly of late. At one time the body is white & fine as it should be, the next we make perhaps, having used a different lump of the Spaith, is a Cinamon color. One time it is melted to a Glass, another time dry as a Tob: Pipe. . . . I have now begun a series of experi-ments upon materials which are easy to be had in sufficient quantities, & of qualities allways the same.'[17]

By the end of August his experiments have borne fruit, but he is in difficulties:

> I shall send by tomorrows Coach a number of heads of Lady C F's Daughters.† They are all made, not only of the same materials, nominally, but out of the same Dish in which we grind these mat-erials & all ground together, & all fired in the same sagar, & yet you will see what a difference there is amongst them. Two, & Two only are pretty good, when the ground is cover'd [enamelled]. I am at work upon more solid materials, & have no doubt of succeeding in making these heads &c one time like another, but of what size I

---

*Moorstone: a feldspathic rock or 'china stone', similar in properties to the Chinese petuntse and Cornish growan stone. Josiah wrote of it: 'As Moor stone varies so much, being a compound, mixed at random perhaps by the waves & Tides of the Ocean, I despair of making it a Principal ingredient in a Porcelain Manufactory' (E25–18645 21 January 1776). 'Spaith Fusible' or Spar: Josiah's name for the fusible part of his composition (in this case carbonate of barium – 'No. 19') as distinct from the refractory clay.
†Lady Charlotte Finch (1725–1813), governess to the daughters of George III. Horace Walpole called her 'the cleverest girl in the world'. Portraits of her daughters, Henrietta and Matilda, were modelled, with that of Lady Charlotte, in 1774. See Appendix H:I.

33   34

33. *Trial white jasper portrait medallion of Mrs Matilda Fielding, the ground enamelled in purple. Oval height 1 ¾" (4.3 cm). Unmarked. c.1774. Matilda Fielding was one of the daughters of Lady Charlotte Finch, and this example of her portrait, modelled by Joachim Smith, is possibly one of the trials to which Josiah refers in his letter of 30 August 1774 quoted on p. 74. (See Appendix H:II.)* Manchester City Art Gallery

34. *Solid pale-blue and white jasper portrait medallion of Lady Charlotte Finch, modelled by Joachim Smith. Oval height 3" (7.6 cm). Mark:* WEDGWOOD & BENTLEY. *c.1775. The rough texture of the blue ground indicates the early date of this portrait. 'Lady Cha', second daughter of the Earl of Pomfret, and governess to the royal children, was described by Horace Walpole as 'a woman of remarkable sense and philosophy' (The Last Journals of Horace Walpole, 1910, Vol. I, p. 125). (See Appendix H:I.)* Private collection

cannot at present ascertain. I am really sorry we cannot gratify the Ladies, & Mr Smith[*] in the time they deserve. . . . I cannot work miracles in altering the properties of these subtle & complicated (though native) materials I had built my fabrique upon.[18]

There is a note of distraction in the last paragraph of his letter: 'If I had more *time*, more *hands*, & more *heads* I could do something – but as it is I must be content to do as well as I can. A Man who is in the midst of a course of experim[ts] sho[d] *not be at home* to anything or anybody else but that cannot be my case. Farewell – I am almost crazy but am allways Y[rs] most affec[tionate][ly].[19]

Only four days later his confidence is restored and he writes: 'I believe I shall make an excellent white body, & with *absolute certainty* without the fusible sparr.' On 5 September he promises by the next day's coach samples of gems 'of the new white composition of *less delicate materials*' and is sure of being able to make heads of this with perfect consistency and at little expense. The body is 'so delicate a color & so fine in every other respect', and he is preparing a quantity of it for use.[20]

Early in November he is able to report that he has made the first 'small oval Statue Bass reliefs', and asks Bentley to 'try how they will ground [take a ground colour]'. He intends to 'proceed, by degrees to larger & larger Bass reliefs of the same composition'. He is experiencing trouble with blistering, however, and suspects the 'Spath Fusible', but sends Bentley an example of a different white composition, 'a seed of consequence', containing 'neither Zaffer, smalt nor anything but white materials'. It is 'a beautiful Onyx color', and he begs his partner not to lose it since it is the first specimen of its kind and unique. Later in the

[*]Joachim Smith (*fl.*1758–1803), modeller in wax, and among the earliest (if not the first) to provide Wedgwood with relief portraits in wax to copy in basaltes, terracotta and jasper. See Plates 4, 5, 13, 33 and 34, and Appendix H:I.

month he has the results of Bentley's experiments, made in London, to colour the grounds. This was done in various enamel colours, and Josiah is fairly satisfied with them but notes that – as with cameo heads on por⁄phyry grounds – there is some difficulty in 'preserving the outlines clean & sharp, & this in the small figures is not practicable'. Bentley has evidently tried also some stained slip grounds, probably in the various shades of browns and dark reds easily available to him, and Josiah expresses some doubts about the propriety of clay grounds.[21]

By 12 December an important development has taken place, Josiah is somewhat coy about telling Bentley what it is, only hinting at it by telling him not to enamel any more 'onyxes' in black or blue as he believes he can in future do much better at Etruria. Six days later the secret is revealed with his sending '4 black & Blue onyx Intaglios', of which he modestly asks Bentley's opinion. 'They have', he writes, 'this advantage over the enam[elle]ᵈ ones that the blue, as well as the black may be pol⁄ish'd, & I wish you woᵈ have these 4 polish'd all over to try how they will look in that way.' From this it is plain that these samples are the first of the blue and black stained clay body and, although much remained to be done before it was perfected, this may truly be considered the first refer⁄ence to coloured jasper.[22]

Josiah had already told Bentley of the increased importance that lap⁄idary polishing was likely to assume in their work: 'Polishing will from henceforth be a capital branch of our Manufacture, & I think you should if possible have it perform'd in your own Building. If you can hire a proper person, I will ingage he shall not want employment. – This operation may probably be applied to *Vases* – snuff box lids it will certainly come in for soon.' He had no doubt of being able 'to give a fine white composition any tint of a fine blue, from the Lapis Lazuli, to the lightest Onyx' and proposed 'making the heads of this composition, & sometimes the Grounds, but each separate – by this means we shall be able to under cut the heads a little. The Grounds must be even & polish'd, & the under side of the heads ground even so as to lie perfectly flat upon the polish'd ground & then Mr Rhodes must fix them with a little Borax &c in his Enamel kiln. I am now making a few blanks & heads, of which I have not the least doubt but you will make the finest things in Europe.' By Boxing Day 1774 he had made laminated seals in blue and white.[23]

Now that he was certain of his new composition, Josiah greatly regretted having made portrait medallions in it for Joachim Smith. The latter was reported to have had dealings with William Duesbury at the Derby porcelain works. Josiah wrote to Bentley:

If Mr Smith has been dabling with the person you aprehend, he may have done us a very essential injury, & I wish both he, & his [wax] heads had been at Jericho before we had anything to do with either, as he may infuse many notions into D[uesbury]'s brain which he has learnt from seeing our things, & the free conversations we have

had with him upon these subjects. – Your Burd[et]ᵗˣ* & Sm[ith]s &
all such flighty unsolid Genius's are very dangerous people to have
any sort of connection with – They are absolutely mad themselves,
& yet, in their own conceit, are too wise to be guided by anybody
else.²⁴

It was, of course, the Derby factory's white biscuit porcelain that he feared
as competition to his new body, and in January 1775 he was approached
by 'a Man from the Derby China works' who sought employment at
Etruria. Josiah suspected him of being 'sent to learn something from us'
and did not hire him, but 'learnt from him that they have been making
h[ea]ds for Smith, & have many more to make'.²⁵

Whatever the accuracy of his suspicions, Josiah believed that he
would lose the services of Joachim Smith and decided that it would be
best to 'drop all connections' with him; but he wanted, as he informed
Bentley, to have 'if possible a Modeler of our own for Portraits'. 'We
can now certainly make the finest things in the world for Portraits,' he
wrote, 'Pray try to obtain another modeller.' It is no coincidence that,
less than two weeks later, Bentley reported that he had 'met with a
Modeler' and wrote favourably of the young John Flaxman. The connection with Smith nevertheless continued, for at the end of the year Josiah
was still repeating his apprehension of Smith's dealings with Derby 'or
some other China Folks' and told Bentley: 'if you can prevent that
connection it will be very well, but if not, he [Smith] must not, in my
opinion be connected with them & with us too.' Smith's name is not
mentioned again.²⁶

Wedgwood's arrangement with Joachim Smith is not clear. He refers
to portrait medallions in the white terracotta and jasper as being made
'for' Smith, and the same preposition is used in describing the Derby biscuit porcelain 'heads'. In September 1774 Josiah sent samples of white
jasper medallions to London for Smith's approval and asked Bentley to
'tell him I am preparing a quᵗʸ of this body for his use, & whatever he
sends shall *now* be done immediately'.²⁷ This seems to indicate that it was
Wedgwood who was commissioned by Smith, rather than the reverse,
and that Smith was distributing the Wedgwood reproductions of his wax
portraits. If this was the true situation, Josiah's complaint of Smith's 'per-
fidy'²⁸ in going to Derby for reproductions which he was having difficulty
in obtaining from Wedgwood was not well justified. However, Smith's
letter of 8 February 1775 making excuses for not being able to send
Wedgwood any moulds or models 'for some months past'²⁹ supports the
belief that he was, as Josiah suspected, dealing simultaneously with
Wedgwood and Derby.

By the end of 1774 Josiah was making intaglios in two colours, by
laminating blue and white ('onyx') jasper, and had his first experience of
jasper 'staining'.† The intaglios, he told Bentley, were 'not quite right . . .

*P.P. Burdett, the engraver.
†Also known, less elegantly, as 'bleeding', this problem has persisted with certain colours.

for the blue stains thro' the white in the intaglio part, but the white (when the colours are revers'd) will not stain thro' the blue'. He had also laminated white with black and red, but it appears from his reference to 'the compositions not uniting cordially together' that he may have been attempting to fuse the white jasper body with black basaltes rather than black jasper.[30] He was soon to discover that, whereas the similarity in composition of the other 'dry bodies' – black basaltes, cane and rosso antico – allowed them to be united in any combination, jasper would accept lamination or ornament only from jasper. Nor could it be used to ornament the other dry bodies.[*]

On New Year's Day 1775 Josiah confided to his partner that he was 'at some loss how to have the principal material [for jasper manufacture] without making a noise', and suggested that Bentley might 'get a Friend to order it up to Town – disguise it there & send it to me hither in boxes or Casks'.[31] This was not the shortest route for material obtained from Derbyshire, but Josiah was well aware that his invention could be protected only by the utmost secrecy, and that even the most stringent security could not guarantee his monopoly for more than a year or two at best. Four days later he returned to the problem:

> The only difficulty I have is the mode of procuring & conveying *in Cog the raw material*. . . . It is something round about by way of London, but if it was sent by the West Indies the expence would not be worth naming in comparison with other considerations. . . . I dare not have it the *nearest way*, nor *undisguis'd*, though I should only wish to have it pounded & put thro' a coarse hair sieve, but even this I would not have done with your People, nor have them see it at all. Could not Mr More[†] set some poor Man to work upon it in some of the uninhabited buildings at the Adelphi.[32]

On 15 January 1775, because his letter was to go 'by the Coach & not by the Post', he gave Bentley 'a full description of the substance', admitting that he had 'not a single piece [left] unpounded'. 'It is', he wrote, 'a white Chalky looking substance, in form generally flatt, about an inch, or from one to two inches thick, & often enclosing small lumps of lead Ore'. It was known as Cauk (or Cawk), and he had found it in great quantity at mines between Matlock and Middleton, Derbyshire, when he and his father-in-law, Richard Wedgwood, had been searching for '*spath fusible* or No. 19 which he afterwards found for us upon Middleton Moor, & call'd it *Wheat Stone*'. Josiah sent Bentley a small sample of the pounded cauk but cautioned him that supplies of it must not be pounded "till it is under our management or that of our friend, for the Lead Ore must be carefully picked out of it at the time . . . & before it is made small'.[33]

---

[*]Later it was found possible to use jasper dip with a stoneware of a closely related composition. See p. 249.

[†]Samuel More, secretary to the Society of Arts.

'I am not yet certain', he continued, 'but some of the 19s may do as well as the 74 (for that is my N° for this Cauk & so I shall hereafter call it), but the different specimens of 19 I have had, have possess'd very different qualities one from another, as they regard my experiments, & the 74 has been all alike, no one piece differing from another, which is of great consequence to us, & would induce me to give the preference to 74, if 19 should be equal to it in every other respect.'[34] The confusing similarity, and yet the crucial differences, between 'Spath fusible' or 'Wheat Stone' (No. 19) and 'Cauk' (No. 74) were the principal cause of Josiah's early difficulties with the manufacture of jasper. Both are forms of barium, but the first is barium carbonate, or witherite, and the second barium sulphate, barytes or heavy spar.

It was in this situation, when his invention was not perfected, that Josiah was most concerned with secrecy: 'If our Antagonists should overtake us at this stage, we cannot again take another step before them, to leave them behind again.' But he was confident: 'we shall leave them at so great a distance & they have so many obstacles to surmount before they can come up to us, that I think we have little to apprehend on that account.' In due course, when he had established a satisfactory lead, he would meet any competition, 'taking it for granted that they will in time come at our compositions &c, we shall still have *variety of subjects – Execution – Character, & connections* in our favour sufficient to continue us at the head of this business, & lastly we must not forget a good resolution we have long since made of not permitting any apprehension of being robbed of our inventions, prevent our putting them into execution.'[35]

At the beginning of 1775 Josiah had declared himself 'absolute' in the white jasper, blue, 'likewise a beautiful Sea Green, & several other colors *for grounds* to Cameo's, Intaglio's &c', and was confident of being able to make bas-reliefs 'from the Herculaneum size [15 inches × 12 inches ovals] to the least Marriage of Cupid &c, & in heads from Peter the Great [17 inches × 14 inches oval] to the smallest gem for rings'.[36] This claim proved to be over-optimistic. He had not yet solved the problem of staining, when coloured grounds 'bled' into the white reliefs, but he was experimenting with two possible methods: first 'that those heads & figures which can be made separately, undercut a little at the edges, then fixed to the ground & fired biscuit will be less liable to staining; and second, that 'the Heads & Figures which can be *made & fired* separate, & fixed on afterwards, will be totally free from this inconvenience, & may have the great advantage of a perfectly even, & polish'd ground. This will be the ultimate perfection of our Cameo's.'[37]

Far more serious, Josiah had underestimated the difficulties still to be overcome. For nearly two years more he struggled with intractable materials which seemed to have a will of their own. In July 1775 he was irritated that, although his 'mixture' had not been varied at all, the results were 'by no means alike'. Next month he complained: 'I have so many of these raw materials, & different compositions under my

36

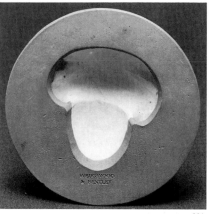

36A

35. *Three early solid pale-blue and white jasper trial medallions with moulded frames:* (left to right) A Vestal, Orestes at Delphi *and* Hercules and the Nemean Lion. *Oval 4½" × 3½" (11.4 × 8.9 cm). Unmarked. c.1775. These examples illustrate the problems encountered with blistering and cracking of the jasper composition in firing.* Wedgwood Museum

36. *Solid pale-blue and white jasper head of Medusa. Diameter 5" (12.7 cm). Mark:* WEDGWOOD & BENTLEY. *c.1776. A fine example of the superb head attributed to John Flaxman, 1777 (see Appendix J:1.94). The jasper is of beautiful quality and, in spite of a depth of relief which exceeds 1½" (3.8 cm), shows some translucency with transmitted light.* Kadison Collection

36A. *The reverse of the Medusa medallion illustrated in Plate 36, showing the deeply scooped back.*

immediate care, & in which nobody can assist me that I am almost crazed with them.' He had ordered fifty tons of white clay from Bruges,[38] and was experimenting with clays from Cornwall, still unsure of his materials and, with mounting costs, still unable to produce and market the new body with certainty. 'I have had', he wrote, 'too much experience of the delicacy, & unaccountable uncertainty of these fine white bodies to be very sanguine in my expectations – And Crisp* – Poor Crisp haunts my imagination continually – Ever pursuing – just upon the verge of overtaking – but never in possession of his favourite object! There are many good lessons in that poor Man's life, labours & catastrophe. . . . Fate I suppose has decreed that we must go on – we must have our Hobby Horse, & mount him, & mount him again if he throws us ten times a day.'[39]

The beginning of 1776 brought new hope. On 4 January Josiah reported that the blue and white bodies were still difficult to fire, but two days later he was ready to send two plaques: 'A Night & Day.

---

*A reference to Nicholas Crisp(e), a jeweller and potter at Lambeth, for whom the sculptor John Bacon worked as a modeller. Alan Cunningham (*Lives of the Most Eminent Painters*, III, p. 201) describes him as 'an eminent maker of porcelain', and he has been erroneously credited with founding the Bow porcelain factory. Wedgwood knew of him as a potter who had failed in the pursuit of 'true' porcelain, and mentions this in the account of his 'Journey into Cornwall, in company with Mr Turner in search of Growan Stone and Clay', ed. Geoffrey Wills, published in Wedgwood Society *Proceedings*, Vols. 1 and 2, 1956–7. See also A.G. Toppin, 'Nicholas Crisp, Jeweller and Potter', English Ceramic Circle *Transactions*, Vol. I, 1933.

The best we have made of the new white', and 'A Medusa large, & very fine – 2 heads blue grounds – too fine to sell', and added: 'I think we improve in the Science of firing, & that seems to be the only point we are deficient in respecting this very fine body.' Unusually, eight days passed before he wrote again; but on 14 January he was calmly triumphant: 'I believe I can now assure you of a conquest & a very important one to us. No less than the firing of our fine *Jasper* & *Onyx* with as much certainty as our *Basaltes*.' He had fired successfully nearly a hundred portrait medallions and 'the two bodies, blue & white agreed perfectly together.' On the 18th he was so confident that he was 'mixing two Tons w' of the fine Jasper composition!', and laying it up 'in a cellar to ferment'. One unexpected property of the composition was its coldness to the touch. Unlike other clays, it did not appear to take up heat from the atmosphere, and the man employed to take it 'out of the Tub complain'd of it being bitter cold'.[40]

It looked as if Josiah's troubles with jasper were at an end; but they were not. On 10 March 1776 he wrote to Bentley:

I have been a good deal perplex'd, & am still, with the two Tons of Jasper composition I told you I had mix'd & was grinding at the Flint Mill. – It was very good. The whole is now gro^d & proves very different from the specimen above mention'd for all the pieces made of it have a glaze upon the surface equal almost to Glazed China. I can attribute the change to nothing but the *different mode* of grinding. Perhaps when ground in our little Mill, the particles are uniformly small, but when ground in a large Flint Mill with Stones of near half a Ton weight, most of the particles in the composition are crush'd. . . . I have long known that the surface of our Jasper will be rough, & harsh, or smooth & polish'd in proportion to the fineness (small-ness) of the particles in the composition. This failure is a sad mis-fortune to us.[41]

37

37. *Solid pale-blue and white jasper medallion of a head of Medusa or Gorgon's head. Diameter 4"* *(10 cm). Mark:* Wedgwood & Bentley. *c.1778. (See Appendix J:I.95) The reverse of the medallion is pierced with six large firing holes.* Manchester City Art Gallery

Early in February he had reported a good kiln load, 'not a single piece discolor'd, blister'd, or shewing any tendency to either of those disorders, so that I may now surely be confident of our being absolute of firing this delicate substance.' He needed urgently to know whether Bentley could enamel on white jasper 'for you will no doubt want other color'd grounds besides blue which must be enamel'd, & I would much rather make them white in Jasper than our 1211 or Granite body.'* In view of his claim thirteen months earlier to have perfected 'a beautiful Sea Green, & several other colors', this clear indication that only the blue was 'absolute' is surprising. A week later he sent Bentley some more trials of different colours, but he was evidently unsure of his ability to make them for he sent a second letter on the same day, somewhat peremptorily 'desiring' his partner to 'let Mr Rhodes have no rest 'till he ascertains with certainty whether our jasper will or will not enamel'. The first answer was that it would not, and Josiah wrote: 'the foundations of your miscarriages are laid in our imperfect firing of the Biscuit.' He recommended choosing only the perfectly fired pieces with a 'vitrified surface' for enamelling.[42]

The problem was finally resolved by the successful production of colours made, in the same manner as blue jasper, by staining the clay with metal oxides. Nevertheless, Josiah still required some additional method of colouring the grounds of jasper medallions and tablets so that imperfections caused by 'short' firing could be disguised. 'It is', he wrote in July, 'a pity to throw these things away, which are sound & good in other respects. . . . I have sent you these to try what you can do with them either in selling them as they are at a lower price, or colouring the grounds afresh in any way you can. Water color, with Mountainies [*sic*] wax Varnish would make them into very good Pictures; & it is absolutely necessary we should take some course with such imperfections as these.'[43]

This is the earliest evidence of 'Tinkering' with jasper, but Wedgwood was to go in for this almost to the extent that he 'tinkered' with basaltes vases.† In July 1777, just a year later, he congratulated Bentley on his putting Hutchins 'to stopping the Jaspers', adding, 'I daresay he will do them neatly and we shall always have occasion for such a hand.'[44] In May next year he explained in a memorandum: 'We cannot make the stopping matter for the Jaspers of the same color. It is very hard & will be durable. Whether they would be mended by painting the figures all over & leaving the ground (if perfect) as it is, or painting the stopping of a color nearer to the rest of the figure might perhaps be worth trying.'[45] The bas-reliefs were cracking in firing or in cooling, or failing wholly to adhere to their grounds. Some, it seems, even cracked during the journey from Etruria to London.[46]

---

*A reference to the white terracotta body used for 'granite' vases, plinths, flowerpots, cameos &c.
†'Tinkering' was Josiah's own word for this practice.

This was not the only problem still to be solved. In June 1776 Josiah wrote in frustration: 'This Jasper is certainly the most delicately whimsical of any substance I ever engag'd with; & as such unavoidable losses attend it, we must endeavour to make the living pay for the dead, which we may the more easily do as we shall have no rivals yet awhile, & those pieces that are good are fine enough to ask any price for. If we can once conquer the difficulties we now labour under, these very difficulties will have been an advantage to us.'[47]

The losses were, indeed, frightening, and must sometimes have given Josiah cause to wonder if the manufacture of jasper could ever be commercially practicable. Towards the end of May he had reported a 75 per cent loss in firing jasper tablets, and even those which were fired and cooled successfully would sometimes, as Josiah told Bentley, 'crack upon the Road, & in your Drawers too I dare say'. He was trying to make the composition harder and firmer. 'These alterations', he wrote, 'cause me infinite trouble & vexation, & nothing less than the patience of Job could go through with them.' The use of old clay, he found, prevented the bas-reliefs from cracking in cooling, and he was laying up stores of it to mature. By August he believed that he had conquered the majority of his difficulties and he reported to Bentley, then in Paris, only one piece of jasper cracked in five or six 'burnings'; but he was still suffering severe losses in the production of the larger tablets. In November he decided to make no more tablets until specific orders were received for them. 'I apprehend', he wrote, 'we never shall make a *Perfect* one. Very few fine large things are perfect. Perhaps none.'[48]

At this time Wedgwood was making white jasper in two shades: 'a bluish white' and 'Ivory yellowish white'. Josiah described the latter as the 'natural colour'; the former was produced by 'a very little blue in the mixture'. As tables of quantities noted in his Commonplace Book show, the 'bluish white' became the standard for production. He was careful also to differentiate between the 'waxen body' and that of jasper. For later generations, discrimination between the bodies is complicated by the appearance at this stage of a 'glossy composition', which Josiah attributed to the mixture having been 'ground upon the Wind[mill]' whereas what he called 'the opaque' mixture was ground on a water mill. As he explained, the glossy composition was the more delicate in firing, and he attributed many of his problems to the difference in methods of grinding and the fineness of the composition.[49] The 'waxen' body, as he made plain in his letter of 24 September 1776, was not jasper at all, but a development of the terracotta, otherwise known as '1211' or 'granite body'.[50] Pieces catalogued as 'Waxen jasper' are generally examples of the finer composition, and more rarely the 'glossy' composition, of which few specimens have survived.

Josiah continued to experience problems with the jasper colours but, in March 1776, sent the first specimen of a yellow to London, and by the end of September he was experimenting with black: '*Black blue grounds* are what I have been attempting a long time.' He was able to make 'small Cameo Heads with blue–black grounds' from July 1776, without any other difficulty than 'their staining the white so abominably', but the aim, which was to produce a black vase with bas-relief figures in white or pale blue, could not be achieved until he understood that basaltes, which he was still trying to use as the ground, could not be ornamented with jasper. Even the blue gave him trouble, but principally because he did not properly comprehend Bentley's written suggestions about the particular shade of colour required. In one of his rare bursts of aggravation Josiah wrote: 'You ask if I could not make a middle tint of Blue. But you told me in a former letter that nobody bought a *pale* blue if a full-color'd one lay near it, which induc'd me to attempt a deeper color, & the white has suffer'd* by it.'[51]

Josiah's experiments to produce a deeper shade of blue led not only to the production of a fine colour but also, indirectly, to the development of a different technique. In April 1777 he mentioned a 'deep' or 'dark' blue, and on the 13th he sent Bentley 'two heads with exquisite blue grounds'. 'I wish', he wrote, 'we may be able to make you some Tablets in this way. They are color'd with the Cobalt @ 36/- Per lb which being too dear to mix with the clay of the whole grounds we have wash'd them over, & I think them by far the finest grounds we have ever made.'[52] This is the earliest reference to jasper 'dip', the technique of applying a thin wash of one colour over a ground of another, and is of special significance in explaining the reason for the introduction of the method. It has long been understood that Wedgwood introduced jasper dip because of the high, and rising, price of cobalt. What puzzled ceramic historians was why the cost of such small quantities of cobalt as would be used in pale blue jasper should make such an economy necessary. This is soon understood when the quantities required for the production of solid *dark-blue* jasper are considered.

The pigment, often known as 'smalt', used for cobalt blue – in its various forms for decoration by painting, transfer-printing, groundlaying or staining – was made by fusing zaffre (impure cobalt oxide), potassium carbonate and a form of silica to produce a deep blue–black glass. This was then ground to a fine powder. At this period the best-quality cobalt was obtained, in quantities kept small by the prohibition or rigorous control of exports, from deposits in Saxony. Demand always outstripped the permitted supply, and smuggling was punishable by death. Prices could thus be maintained at a high level, and by the end of 1777 they had risen to three guineas a pound. In spite of this, Josiah wrote: 'it is worth all the money. I do not know what to do about buying more.' Properly prepared and refined, in times of scarcity it was sold for as much as £4. Later, native deposits were found in Cornwall, but, in the meantime, Josiah was dependent upon imported supplies. In March 1777 he bought three pounds of it from 'a man who kept a warehouse in Altona [near

*From staining or 'bleeding'.

Hamburg]' who had 'found out the way of procuring it by means of some Jews, one of whom they say has been discover'd & hang'd for the practice'. 'It is probable', he added reasonably, 'there never may come any more such into the country.'[53]

The 'dip' technique greatly enhanced the versatility of the jasper body, generally superseding lamination, opening the way to engine-turned patterns cut through the dip to the base colour, and making poss-ible the creation of subtler shades of colouring than could be obtained in the solid body. At first the 'deep blue' dip medallions and plaques required extra finishing: 'it will be necessary', Josiah wrote, 'to paint the backs & edges with watercolours, they look so slovenly with the blue daubed upon the white.' This problem was soon overcome by bevelling the edges, which might then be polished. In October 1776, John Griffiths, a Birmingham lapidary, had been hired for a period of three years from New Year's Day 1777 at a wage of twenty shillings a week 'to do such work in the Lapidary branch of business, as the s[d] Wedgwood & Bentley shall employ him in, & to work such hours as is customary for Lapidarys to work, Viz. from six in the morning to six at night, or in proportion to that time'. By this agreement, too, Griffiths hired out his wife at ten shillings a week for the same hours and work, and undertook to instruct such others as Wedgwood & Bentley might hire. Lapidary polishing, which had become 'a capital branch of our Manufacture' in 1774 for laminated red and white seals, was now the technique used for finishing the finest cameos, medallions and tablets of both solid jasper and jasper dip.[54]

The technique of lamination was not altogether discarded. In August 1779, Wedgwood wrote to Bentley about the edges of bas-relief pieces 'losing their colour in polishing'. This could be remedied by lami-nating the grounds, 'which will at the same time take away the idea of the upper surface being a wash or enamel, as it will then appear, very natur-ally, to be one of the uppermost laminae under the white'.[55] Such a costly method of production was soon abandoned in favour of a strip of con-trasting colour inlaid along the edge, and was finally superseded by a band of thick jasper slip to produce the same effect. None of these decora-tive techniques appears to have lasted as a regular method of production beyond the turn of the century.[*]

On 25 January 1777 Josiah wrote that he could not control either the colour or the texture of his blue jasper seals: 'The deepest, & the palest are made from the same lump of Clay & fired not only in the same Kiln but in the same Sagar at the same time.' This was serious, for the failure applied equally to all jasper pieces. Three months later he proposed, 'if we think it safe', to send Bentley 'a sample of the finest blue ground you ever

[*]Nineteenth-century examples of jasper inlay exist, but they are rare and it is plain that the technique was seldom used. The line of slip is more often found, particularly on the feet of such pieces as tea canisters, but even this appears to have been reserved for particular shapes and occasional use.

saw'. In July he built a new kiln specially for jasper. Nothing, he believed, but the firing stood between him and the making of 'the finest things imaginable'. Bentley had heard this, or something much like it, many times before, but on 3 November Josiah wrote soberly: 'I have tried my new mixing of Jasper, & find it very good. Indeed I had not much fear of it, but it is a satisfaction to be certain, & I am now ABSOLUTE in this precious article & can make it with as much facility, & certainty as black [basaltes] ware. Sell what quantity you please. I would as readily engage to furnish you with this, as any pottery I make.' This was a bold claim after so many false hopes, but it was one that he was able to justify.[56]

The plain jasper body of this period is a beautiful milk-white, which shows no sign of the blue except by close comparison with the 'ivory yellowish-white' of the 'natural' composition. There were many variations in shades of blue, and of other colours, due to slight changes in composition, mixing and firing temperature. Most of these were accidental. A distinctive grey–blue is particularly associated with the last quarter of the eighteenth century. Josiah himself described two more shades: a 'middle' or 'deeper' blue; and a still 'deeper mazarine'. The last required 'a particular management in the fire' and pieces made of it 'should be paid for *as gems*'. By the middle of December 1777 he was able to offer Bentley a choice of 'green – yellow – lalock [lilac] – &c to the colour of the rooms'.[57]

Wedgwood's choice of colours, dictated largely by the metal oxides available for staining the clay mixture, bore a close relationship to the colours most favoured for interiors by Robert Adam.* These were not invariably to the taste of Josiah's customers, as he was to find when he entertained Lord Gower and Lancelot ('Capability') Brown at Etruria. 'Both', he told Bentley,

> objected to the blue ground, unless it could be made into Lapis Lazuli. I shew'd them a sea green, & some other colors, to which Mr Brown said they were pretty colors, & he should not object to them for the ground of a room, but they did not come up to his ideas for the ground of a tablet, nor would any other color unless it was a copy of some natural, & valuable stone. All other color'd grounds gave ideas of color'd paper – painting – compositions, casting, moulding &c &c & if we could not make our color'd grounds imitate marble, or natural stones, he advised us to make the whole white, as like to statuary marble as we could. This is certainly orthodox doctrine, & we must endeavour to profit by it.[58]

In effect, Josiah does not appear to have taken much notice of this advice and it is doubtful whether he would have profited by doing so.

*For example: the Library at Kenwood, 1767–9; the ceiling of the second Drawing Room at 20 St James's Square, 1772; the Top Hall at Nostell Priory, *c*.1773–5; and the ceiling of the Drawing Room at Mellerstain, *c*.1778. It is an error, however, to suppose that Adam's colours were invariably pastels: full, strong colours, including a rich crimson, were used for some of the rooms at Northumberland House, 1773–5, and the Sculpture Gallery at Newby Hall, 1767–72.

38

The shades of blue, green, yellow and lilac, with 'blue–black', pale grey and chocolate brown, were all made during the last years of the Wedgwood & Bentley partnership and beyond, in both the solid jasper and the jasper dip forms. Accidental variations of shade or tone have been given distinguishing names such as 'pink', 'peach', 'olive‑green', 'apple‑green' and 'mauve', all of which owe more to the invention of collectors and interior decorators than to Josiah Wedgwood. The common base for jasper dip was white, but pale blue was often dipped in one of the darker shades ('middle' or 'deeper mazarine'), and other colour combinations are known. Trials were made using solid green and yellow as bases for brown and blue dips, and a portrait medallion of the Earl of Chatham in the Wedgwood Museum (Plate 38) is an example of brown dip on grey–blue.

In connection with jasper dip, Josiah's memorandum on jasper compositions is of particular importance and appears to have been over‑looked by all earlier writers, either because they did not find it or because they failed to understand its significance.[59] It is dated 23 November 1777, some seven months after Josiah first mentioned the jasper dip technique to Bentley. Because it contains useful details of production techniques which have been imperfectly understood, and answers a number of questions which have puzzled historians and collectors in the past, it is quoted in full:

Memorandum Nov.ʳ 23 1777 Jasper Composition

To make it stand in the burning – The finer it is ground the more vitreous it is – The same composition, by being ground to different degrees of fineness, will, with the same treatment in other respects, and the same degree of heat in burning, produce either a coarse unvit‑rified body, or one that is nearly converted into glass, & especially upon the surface, and every stage between these two extremes may be produced by different degrees of grinding.

The coarser the body is, the less subject it will be to warp or bend in burning, & vice versa. In order therefore to give the body the stability in burning required, the materials must be coarsely ground, but then the surface will be coarse likewise, and as the articles to be made of this beautiful composition are not to be glazed, a kind of semipolish is required upon the surface, that the biscuit may look fine, & wash perfectly clean.

In order to produce this effect, take some of the composition, ground sufficiently to take the smoothness required, & make it into slip, in which dip your pieces, and when dry polish it. The slip may be thin to produce this effect, so thin perhaps as not to injure a figure.

To apply this to making Teacups of a fine polished white within and blue on the outside, & suppose them to be cast in moulds.

You must have three different kinds of Jasper slip ready, viz. Blue fine enough to take a semipolish in burning — White of the same quality — and coarser white.

Fill your mould with the blue slip, & empty again quickly. When it is a little dried, fill it with the coarse white, and let it stand till it is too dry to be disturbed by filling it again with the finer white, which is next to be done, and this must be emptied quickly like the blue.

When the cup leaves the mould, it must be put upon the lathe to be polished, & to have a foot put upon it, as it could not have one in the mould without it leaving a mark on the inside.

If Throwing & Turning is preferred to casting, the vessel must be thrown of the coarse body, slip'd within before it is turned with the fine white, and dipt after turning or whilst upon the chock in the fine blue.

What is said of a teacup will, by an ingenious Potter (and no other should have anything to do with these finer works & compositions) be easily applied to any other vessel.

The principal danger in this operation will probably arise from the dissimilarity in the *coarse* and the *fine* bodies, as they will not diminish alike in burning, they may tear one another to pieces in the first cooling, or in heating & cooling afterwards in use.

To counteract this disposition as much as possible, let the difference between the coarse & the fine be no greater than is absolutely necessary to produce the effect required — Let the middle or coarse part be thick, and the fine washes as thin as may be, that the middle part may be too strong to be broken by the others.

Let them cool very gently after firing.

A little more clay in the coarser part will make it stronger.

The memorandum is written in Alexander Chisholm's hand, evidently copied, after his employment in 1781, from Josiah's dated original. The descriptions provide information not recorded elsewhere. First, Josiah's use of two jasper bodies, one coarse and one fine, is revealed. The use of a coarse body to give jasper strength and help it to hold its shape under high firing temperatures is disguised by the thin covering of the fine body. This disguise has been so successful that it has remained undetected for two hundred years. It explains noticeable differences in quality, and delicate differences in colour, between the faces and backs of apparently solid blue or green tablets and medallions of this period; and the same differences have been noticed between the exteriors and interiors of vases made a little later. The method points the way to 'bas-relief' ware,* produced extensively in the nineteenth and twentieth centuries and previously thought to have been an early-nineteenth-century development. Last, the memorandum confirms the production of both solid jasper and jasper dip teacups by the end of 1777, and indicates that some of those believed to have been lapidary polished may have, instead, the natural 'semipolish in burning' of the most finely ground composition 'nearly converted into glass'.

It is notable that the memorandum is dated just twenty days after Josiah informed Bentley that he was now 'ABSOLUTE in this precious article', and could make it as easily as black basaltes. This success has always been attributed to the 'new mixing' he mentioned and the special kiln for firing jasper. No doubt these improvements played a part; but the essential change was, it is now clear, the introduction of the coarser, stronger body to provide the ground for the finer wash, even for those pieces which were to have the appearance of 'solid' jasper. True solid jasper pieces of the Wedgwood & Bentley period can therefore be assigned with some confidence to a date before November 1777.

On 15 December 1777 Josiah wrote a letter to Bentley which has been the subject of much controversy. 'I have often thought', he wrote,

> of mentioning to you that it may not be a bad idea to give out, that our jaspers are made of the Cherokee clay which I sent an agent into that country on purpose to procure for me, & when the present parcel is out we have no hopes of obtaining more, as it was with the utmost difficulty the natives were prevail'd upon to part with what we now have, though recommended to them by their *father Stuart,*† Intendant of Indian affairs. But then his Majesty should see some of these large fine tablets, & be told this story (which is a true one for I am not Joking) the first, as he has repeatedly enquir'd what I have done with the Cherokee clay. This idea will give limits, a boundary to the quantity which your customers will be ready to conceive may be made of these fine bass reliefs, which otherwise would be gems indeed. They want nothing but *age & scarcity* to make them worth any price you could ask for them. . . . A Portion of Cherokee clay is really used in all the jaspers so make what use you please of the fact.[60]

---

*See p. 250.
†James Stuart (1700–79), general agent and superintendent of Indian affairs in 1763.

As other writers have pointed out, it is scarely possible to believe this story unless the quantity of Cherokee clay used in each piece was infinitesimally small. The total quantity of this clay obtained in 1768 was only five tons and, if the evidence of the patent specification is to be believed,[*] it was an essential ingredient of encaustic colours for painting on black basaltes from 1769. Nor is it reasonable to ignore Josiah's own recipe for jasper, sent in two letters to Bentley.[†] The code number for Cherokee clay, '23', is notably absent from this.

It is not easy to guess what might have been Josiah's motive for wishing to publish such an unlikely story, or for his desire to set 'limits' or 'a boundary' to the number of tablets he could ever make of this quality. The most charitable explanation is that this claim was based on the use of quantities so small as to be scarcely worth mentioning, added since February 1776 when he revealed the recipe to his partner: such a quantity, for example, as might be required in a thin slip coating applied to the face of tablets – a technique introduced only about a month or so before Josiah made this extraordinary claim. Evidently he hoped to gain some benefit from the story in added prestige for his jasper, but it is likely that he intended also to mystify his competitors and to dissuade them, for as long as possible, from attempting to imitate it. Nothing further appears to have been said on the subject, and it is possible that Bentley's caution and good sense prevented more widespread dissemination of a story which, even if it were founded on truth, was unlikely to be believed.[‡]

Jasper never came to be the easiest of bodies to work or fire. There were occasional obstacles still to be overcome, and sophisticated techniques, such as 'diced' decoration and the ornamenting of vases, still to be mastered. Nevertheless, by the end of 1777 jasper was regularly in production in a fair variety of objects and colours. Josiah was ever conscious of the need for secrecy, proposing that supplies of cauk, the precious '74', should be delivered via London and Liverpool, and that Bentley should tell his supplier that he was 'in hopes of opening an exportation trade for it, & that he may be preparing at his leizure 50 or 60 barrels of 240 lb each'. 'I wish', he added, 'you would burn, or lock up safe this & all of my l^{rs} which mention this article. The secret is of some importance.'[61]

Trials were continued well into the next year with the intention of making a still harder body for seals, but most of the experiments after 1777 were in the different methods of decoration and ornament for a body which was in most respects as perfect as it was ever to be. From 1778 Josiah was able to concentrate upon extending the variety of objects he could make in it beyond the range of other dry bodies, and on making full use of his colours.

[*]Patent No. 939, 1769.
[†]Quoted pp. 70–1.
[‡]According to a note made by Francis Wedgwood, 'two arkfuls' of Cherokee clay still remained in the round house some forty-eight years later (Ms 60–32823 1824–5).

The date of the introduction of 'diced' patterns created on the engine-turning lathe is not known, but there appears to be no record of any such piece bearing an authentic mark of the Wedgwood & Bentley partnership and it is probable that this type of decoration dates from about 1785. The making of three-colour cameos required only a minor variation on the technique of ornamenting jasper dip (Plate C6), and it is surprising to find none recorded with the Wedgwood & Bentley mark. The existence in the British Museum of several bearing the impressed mark 'WEDG-WOOD &' may perhaps indicate the introduction of this style of decoration almost immediately after Bentley's death in December 1780 and before new punches had been made. This, however, is conjecture.

CAMEOS AND INTAGLIOS*

Cameos and intaglios formed a large part of Wedgwood's jasper production, and they were especially important in its early development because of the difficulty experienced in firing larger objects. Small bas-reliefs and intaglios were cheap as trial pieces, and the experience gained from them in the techniques of ornamenting, laminating, dipping, enamelling, undercutting, firing and lapidary polishing could be applied to the making of larger medallions and tablets. By 1779, when Wedgwood & Bentley published their last catalogue, their basaltes and white body cameos and intaglios were already well known. They had added few subjects since the publication of the second edition in 1774, but the introduction of blue and brown jasper (other colours were not advertised) had vastly increased the variety available.

The cameos and intaglios were, according to the preliminary remarks in the 1779 Catalogue, 'exactly taken from the finest antique Gems. The *Cameos* are fit for Rings, Buttons, Lockets, & Bracelets; and especially for inlaying in fine Cabinets, Writing-Tables, Bookcases &c. of which they form the most beautiful Enrichment, at a moderate Expence.' The price of cameos with '*several Figures*' was stated to be '*ten Times* less than any other durable Imitations that have ever been made in Europe', and the figures were 'much sharper than those that are made of Glass'. This last comment was a scarcely disguised thrust at the glass-paste cameos being produced at the time by James Tassie, though the rivalry between him and the partnership was always friendly, and they co-operated to the extent of exchanging models and purchasing them from one another.[62] 'The Ladies', Wedgwood (or perhaps Bentley) wrote in the Catalogue, 'may display their Taste a thousand Ways, in the Application of these Cameos; and thus lead Artists to the better Stile in ornamenting their Works.'

Cameos were to be had in 'Waxen biscuit'† or in 'the *artificial Jasper*, with blue or brown Grounds [jasper dip] . . . or in the blue Jasper [solid

*See Appendix E.
†The terracotta body.

39. *Nine jasper dip cameos: top row* (left) *a Lion, blue dip on grey–blue with bevelled edge, diameter 1⅛" (3.0 cm);* (centre) *double portrait of George III and Queen Charlotte (cf. Plate 98), blue dip on white, oval height 2¾" (7.0 cm), silver-mounted and suspended from a similarly mounted three-colour octagonal cameo;* (right) *rare oval portrait of Jesus Christ, blue dip on grey–blue, oval height 1⅛" (3.0 cm); middle row* (left) Time *(seated on clouds), blue dip on white, diameter 1½" (4.0 cm), lapidary-polished edge;* (centre) The Power of Love *(Cupid riding a lion), blue dip on white, diameter 1½" (4.0 cm);* (right) *a bull, blue dip on white, diameter 1½" (4.0 cm), lapidary-polished edge; bottom row* (left and right) *two navette-shaped cameos of* Hebe *and a* Marine Venus, *blue dip on white, height 2⅛" (5.5 cm), lapidary-polished edges;* (centre) Winter *(Cupid warming his hands before a brazier), blue dip on white, oval height 2" (5.0 cm). Marks: (portrait of Christ) Wedgwood; (others)* WEDGWOOD. *All c.1785–95.* Christie's, London

colour] at a very moderate price, for those who wish to form mythological Cabinets'. Subjects were divided, not always with due regard to accuracy, into ten categories and an appendix: Egyptian History; Gods and Godesses (*sic*); Sacrifices; Philosophers, Poets and Orators; Kings of Macedonia &c; Fabulous Age of the Greeks; The War of Troy; Roman History; Masks, Chymeras &c; and Illustrious Men. The appendix contained a fine assortment in which Pompey the Great and George III rubbed shoulders with 'An unknown Queen, in the King of France's cabinet', and the Earl of Clanbrasil appeared close by 'Leander in the Hellespont' and 'An Egyptian Figure, covered with Hieroglyphicks'.

Cameos vary in size from a quarter of an inch to 2½ inches in diameter or (oval) height, the edges usually at this period being bevelled and lapidary polished. They were sometimes made double-sided, having the appearance of two thin cameos fused back to back, with a deep groove running between them, for setting as jewellery.

The purposes for which cameos were mounted are almost too numerous to name. Letters and invoices contain references to the following, and this list is probably not comprehensive: bell-pulls, boxes, bracelets, brooches, buckles, buttons, cabinets, candlesticks, chairs, chatelaines, clock pendulums, combs, coach panels, commodes, door handles, *étuis*, hair pins, hat pins, hangers (swords), sword hilts, lockets, metal boxes, urns, vases and lamps, opera glasses (monocular and binocular), patch boxes, rings, smelling bottles, snuff boxes, tea caddies, toilet boxes, toothpick boxes, watches and watch keys, work boxes and writing boxes.

In addition to Matthew Boulton, to whom Wedgwood supplied quantities of cameos for mounting in ormolu, silver and cut steel, one of the earliest customers for black basaltes and white jasper cameos was the Birmingham japanner, Henry Clay, who used them for ornamenting writing boxes, dressing (table) boxes and tea caddies. In writing of these, Josiah's precarious spelling deserted him entirely: 'With regard to his

40. Blue jasper dip cameo of Hygeia pouring a libation. In the background the sovereign's crown represents the King (George III), whose temporary recovery from an attack of porphyria in 1789 the subject celebrates. Diameter 1⅞" (4.8 cm). Lapidary-polished edge. Mark: WEDGWOOD. *c.1789. This subject was designed also for an oval cameo, without the crown but with an added inscription.* Author's collection

41. Pale-blue jasper dip cameo of Bacchus, holding a wine cup and thyrsus, with an unidentified animal (perhaps intended for a panther), mounted in silver as a button. Diameter 1¼" (3.2 cm). Mark: None visible. Wedgwood, c.1785. This subject is sometimes erroneously identified as Hercules and Cerberus. Wedgwood Museum

42. Two pale blue jasper dip cameos of (left) Hercules, and (right) Apollo standing between an altar and a column supporting his lyre, both mounted in silver as buttons. Diameter 1¼" (3.2 cm). Mark: None visible. Wedgwood, c.1785. Wedgwood Museum

40

41

42A

42B

93

43. *Two blue jasper dip cameos: (left) A Centaur with bow (Sagittarius); (right) A running Horse; both modelled by Edward Burch RA (1730–1814). Diameter 1 ½" (3.8 cm). Mark:* WEDGWOOD. *Ledger entries for 1788–9 show that Burch modelled for Wedgwood '18 horses at 16s each' in addition to the same number of dogs, a large dog, a set of signs of the zodiac, and portraits of George III (see Plate 50) and Queen Charlotte. The Running Horse is after a drawing by George Stubbs.* Nottingham Castle Museum

44. *Pale-blue jasper dip cameo of a Leaping Horse, modelled by Edward Burch after Stubbs, mounted as a button. Diameter 1 ½" (3.8 cm). Mark: None visible. Wedgwood, c.1789. (See Plates 43 and 45.)* Wedgwood Museum

45. *Nineteen studies of horses modelled by Edward Burch and reproduced in solid blue and white jasper as a single oval plaque. Oval 15" × 11" (38.0 × 28.0 cm). Mark:* WEDGWOOD O. c.1920. *Although the ledger entries account for only eighteen such studies, there seems to be no reason to doubt the attribution of any of the figures. The elongated 'O' impressed (sometimes in conjunction with the initials 'BB') denotes work by A.H. ('Bert') Bentley, a modeller and ornamenter at Etruria, 1890–1937 (see p. 294).* Wedgwood Museum

43

44

45

Ecroitiers . . . there will be no impropriety in our shewing them, & selling them. . . . I wish you likewise to see some of his Cades.'[63] Clay's 'paper ware', so called to distinguish it from 'true' *papier-mâché* produced from pulped paper, was made from layers or panels of several thickness of paper dried in a hot stove, and it was used for the manufacture of japanned trays, chairs, tables, screens and cabinets, as well as the smaller objects which he ornamented with cameos. Other mounters supplied at this period included Thomas Copestake of Uttoxeter, William & Richard Smith, Birmingham, Green & Vale, Birmingham, and the Wolverhampton firm of William Hasselwood and John Vernon.

The popularity of antique cameos and intaglios among collectors made their reproduction a minor industry in which Tassie was supreme. The Wedgwood & Bentley 1779 Catalogue lists 440 cameo and 379 intaglio subjects. Tassie made a cabinet for Catherine the Great in 1782 which contained 12,000 intaglios and impressions of 6,076 different subjects, some of which were obtained from Wedgwood; and in 1785 Tassie bought a collection of 'above 17,000 sulphur impressions of Gems collected by Baron Philippe Stosch' to add to his stock of subjects.[64]

Wedgwood's intaglios were made primarily for seals, and the subjects were chiefly copies from antique gems, heraldic devices or intial letters or ciphers. In the 1779 Catalogue he drew attention to the improvements made possible by the introduction of jasper 'by polishing the bezels and giving a ground of pale blue to the flat surface of the stone, which makes them greatly resemble the black and blue onyxes, and equally ornamental for rings or seals. They are also made now in a fine blue jasper, that takes as good a polish as turquoise stone or lapis lazuli.' The Catalogue of intaglios was divided into two categories only: 'Antique Subjects', which embraced both the historical and the mythological; and 'Modern Subjects', mostly portraits ranging from Pope Clement XIV to 'The Washerwoman'.

46. *Three-colour jasper dip cameo in lilac, blue and white, ornamented with a central sacrifice subject and a border of signs of the zodiac. Diameter 1½" (3.8 cm). Mark:* WEDGWOOD. *c.1790. The signs of the zodiac are cruder than those assigned to Edward Burch, and may be those supplied to Wedgwood by Mrs Landré in 1776 (Ms. 1–56.)* Wedgwood Museum

47. *Pale-blue jasper dip cameo of the* Three Graces *(the goddesses Hera, Aphrodite and Athene), the edge lapidary-polished, mounted as a button. Diameter 1½" (3.8 cm). Mark: None visible. Wedgwood, c.1785.* Wedgwood Museum

46　　　　　　47

Both cameos and intaglios were used for profile portraits. 'If', Wedgwood & Bentley announced in their Catalogue, 'gentlemen and ladies choose to have models of themselves, families or friends, made in wax or cut in stones, of proper sizes for seals, rings, lockets, or bracelets, they may have as many durable copies of those models as they please, either in cameo or intaglio, for any of the above purposes, at a moderate expense.' A deft appeal was made to the middling class to join their betters in the exercise of patronage: 'If the nobility and gentry should please to encourage this design, they will not only procure to themselves *everlasting portraits*, but have the pleasure of giving life and vigour to the arts of modelling and engraving. The art of making *durable copies*, at a small expense, will thus promote the art of *making originals*, and future ages may view the productions of the age of George III with the same veneration that we now behold those of Alexander and Augustus.'

48. Set of four blue jasper dip on solid blue–grey jasper oval medallions ornamented with figures of the four Horae *(Seasons), identifiable as* (left to right) *'Summer', 'Winter', 'Autumn' and 'Spring'. Oval height 2½" (6.4 cm). Mark:* WEDGWOOD. *c.1785–90. These subjects have been variously catalogued as the Four Seasons and the Four Winds or Zephyrs, but their butterfly's wings identify them as the spirits who, in Greek and Roman mythology, personified the Seasons. The Four Winds are generally depicted as male.* Dr & Mrs Alvin M. Kanter Collection

49. White jasper cameo ornamented in black with the figure of a kneeling slave in chains, inscribed with the words: 'AM I NOT A MAN AND A BROTHER?', *mounted in gold to be worn as a pendant. Oval height 1⅜" (3.4 cm), including frame: Mark:* WEDGWOOD H. *c.1790. (See p.7 and cf. Plate C.1)* British Museum

50. Blue jasper dip cameo ornamented with a portrait of George III, modelled by Edward Burch, beneath the sovereign's crown and ribbons inscribed 'HEALTH RESTORED'. *Oval height 1½" (3.8 cm). Mark:* WEDGWOOD. *Issued to celebrate the King's temporary return to sanity in 1789. (Cf. Plate 40.)* Wedgwood Museum

48

49

50

51
52

51. *Cameos and small medallions in variants of jasper or stoneware bodies in imitation of Wedgwood's jasper:* top row (left) blue dip on pale blue ornamented with a copy of Flaxman's Sacrifice to Hymen (*Plate 135B*), *oval 2½" × 3¼" (6.5 × 8.8 cm), unmarked, possibly by William Adams of Greengates, c.1785–95;* (centre) *blue and white dip, ornamented with a relief of* 'The Death of Wolfe' *after Benjamin West, oval 1" × 1⅜" (2.5 × 3.5 cm), mounted in gold, unmarked, attributed to Adams, c.1785;* (right) *grey–blue and white dip, ornamented with the figure of Sterne's* Poor Maria (*cf. Plate C2*) *within a floral scroll border, oval 1⅞ × 2⅝" (4.8 × 6.7 cm), marked* TURNER *impressed, c.1785;* bottom row (left) *octagonal brown and white dip, ornamented with a sacrifice subject (cf. Plate 46), 2⅛" × 2¼" (5.4 × 5.7 cm), unmarked, attributed to Turner, c.1800;* (right) *bright-blue dip on pale blue ornamented with the figure of Galatea riding on a Hippocampus, oval 2" × 3¼" (5.1 × 8.3 cm), unmarked, possibly French, c.1800.*
Author's collection

52. *Chimneypiece in the Drawing Room at Berrington Hall, Herefordshire. The steel grate inset with Wedgwood cameos of blue and white jasper, the blue ground repeated in the grey–blue ground of the painted ceiling by Henry Holland, 1778–81.*
Photograph: Courtesy of *Country Life*

Any criticism of the business of commercial reproduction was bravely met and summarily confuted: 'Nothing can contribute more effectually to diffuse a good taste through the arts than the power of multiplying copies of fine things, in materials fit to be applied for ornaments; by which means the public eye is instructed; good and bad works are nicely distinguished, and all the arts receive improvement. . . . Everybody wishes to see the original of a beautiful copy.'

Prices were 'moderate' (a description much favoured by Wedgwood & Bentley): 'The model of a portrait in wax, when it is of a proper size for a seal, ring, or bracelet will cost about three guineas. . . . Any number of cameos for rings, in jasper, with coloured grounds, not fewer than ten, are made at 5s. each. Any number of cameos for bracelets in the jasper

53. *Late-eighteenth-century satinwood box ornamented with five jasper cameos set in gold mounts. Box 5" × 8½" × 2⅝" height (12.6 × 21.5 × 6.7 cm). Marks: None visible. The cameos are all of solid grey–blue jasper overpainted (perhaps at a later date) in dark reddish-brown. c.1795–1800.* Nottingham Castle Museum

54. *Marble and ormolu barometer with Derby biscuit porcelain figures on a marble base, the pedestal set with black and white jasper (probably dip) cameos of* Aurora *and* Bellerophon watering Pegasus, *standing on a tall satinwood plinth. Signed: 'Vulliamy London' and dated 1787. The female figure, often described as 'Andromache', was modelled by John Deare RA after an earlier design by John Bacon RA; the figure of the* putto, *though normally supplied by the Derby factory, was also occasionally produced for Benjamin Vulliamy by Wedgwood (see p. 237). Height 67" (170 cm), including satinwood plinth.* Victoria & Albert Museum, London

54A. *The Vulliamy barometer (Plate 54) shown on its plinth.*

with coloured grounds at 7s. 6d. each.' Three years earlier, Josiah had written to Bentley: 'Wax copies are sold at a Guinea, & shall we sell Jasper & Onyx at 7/6 – Forbid it the Genius of the Arts. Or to descend to the plain Stile of the Manufacturer we certainly cannot afford it, especially when we pay for the models.'[65]

53

54

54A

55. *Cylinder clock with French movement in an ebony case inset with five jasper cameos below the face and four small jasper roundels (one missing) on the sides. The cameo subjects include* Europa and the Bull, Ganymede and the Eagle *and* Marcus Curtius. *Height 16″ (40.6 cm). None of the cameos is marked except for the numbers '175' on the back of* Europa *and '75' (?) on the back of* Marcus Curtius. *Probably English, c.1790.*
Nottingham Castle Museum

56. *Cut-steel purse top inset with long oval blue and white jasper cameos of the signs of the zodiac in compartments. Length 5½″ (14.0 cm). No marks visible.*
Lady Lever Art Gallery, Port Sunlight

57. *Cut-steel chatelaine or fob chain set with two oval blue and white jasper cameos,* A Conquering Hero *and* Sacrifice to Peace, *with a pendant cut-steel watch case set with a circular cameo of* Apollo. *The reverse of the watch case is set with a miniature on ivory in the manner of Angelica Kauffmann. Length 8″ (20.4 cm). No marks visible. c.1790.*
Wedgwood Museum

58. *Cut-steel chatelaine or fob chain mounted with two double-sided blue and white jasper cameos:* Fortuna and Hope, *and* Fortuna and A Bacchante. *Length: 17″ (43.0 cm). No marks visible. c.1790.*
Wedgwood Museum

55

56

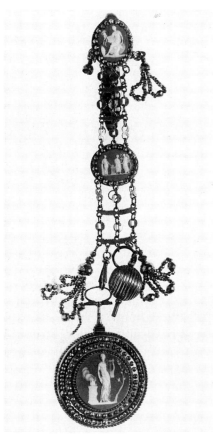

57

58

59. *A small collection of cut-steel mounted jewellery comprising six brooches of various shapes and a steel comb set with cameos, a necklace of blue and white jasper beads, and an octagonal scent bottle ornamented on both sides with figures of* Horae *(cf. Plate 48). Length (necklace) 19½" (50 cm); (comb) 4" (10.2 cm). Marks: (comb cameo)* WEDGWOOD; *none visible on the others.*
Wedgwood Museum

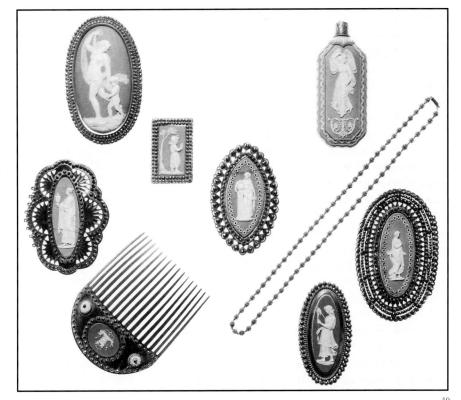

59

60. *Two oviform jasper dip bell pulls: (left) white jasper, dipped blue and dipped again in white, engine-turned to produce a blue intaglio pattern; (right) green jasper dip with acanthus and lotus-leaf ornament. Height 2¾" (7.0 cm). Unmarked. c.1785–95.*
Wedgwood Museum

60

61   62

61. *Pale-blue and white jasper scent bottle ornamented with portraits of Jean Sylvain Bailly and (reverse) Lafayette (see Appendix H:II) within borders of rose swags and paterae, the bottle having a white jasper screw-top with a scalloped sleeve. Diameter (without screw-top) 2″ (5.8 cm). Unmarked. (Cf. Plate 16.) Similar 'smelling bottles' were made with portraits of George III and Queen Charlotte, George III and the Prince of Wales, the Prince of Wales and the Duke of York, the Prince of Wales and Prince of Wales's feathers, and the Prince and Princess of Orange. c.1790.* British Museum

62. *Single-lens telescopic opera glass (Monocular) with ormolu and ivory mounts and a decorative sleeve of blue jasper dip ornamented with the* Marriage of Cupid and Psyche *(cf. Plates 134–6). Length 3″ (7.6 cm). No mark visible.* Wedgwood Museum

PORTRAIT MEDALLIONS*

Wedgwood's 'Cabinets of heads', series of flat circular and small oval medallions, moulded in one piece in black basaltes or white biscuit, had proved popular and, by 1774, fairly complete sets were available under the various headings of 'Heads of Illustrious Romans', 'Caesars and Empresses' and so on.† The 1779 Catalogue shows additions to several of the categories, including fifty-three more 'Kings and Illustrious Persons of Asia, Egypt & Greece', nineteen 'Illustrious Romans' and twenty-two Emperors previously ignored, besides a full set of sixty-nine Kings of France. None of these categories, which appear as Classes III, and V to IX, is specifically mentioned in 1779 as available in jasper, but many of the portraits included in them were made as small portrait medallions in blue and white jasper and, more rarely, in other colours.

The most important additions to the lists occurred in Classes X and XI, 'Heads of Illustrious Moderns from Chaucer to the Present Time' and 'Princes and Statesmen'. No less than fifty-four new heads are listed in the 1779 Catalogue, and all in these classes are made 'either in the *black Basaltes*, or *blue* and *white Jasper*; they are of various Sizes and different Prices, from One Shilling a piece to a Guinea, with and without frames of the same Composition; but most of them in one Colour [basaltes or white] and without frames are sold at One Shilling each.'

Unlike the earlier basaltes pieces, these jasper heads were made separately from their grounds, and with the introduction of two-colour relief portraits came the requirement for new techniques to sharpen detail and avoid staining. Josiah had written in December 1774 of making the heads and grounds separate and, by this means, being able 'to undercut the

*See Appendix H.
†'Cabinet Medals'.

63. Rare portrait medallion of Jesus Christ in solid grey–blue and white jasper. Height 3" (7.5 cm). Mark: WEDGWOOD & BENTLEY. *c.1776. (Cf. Plate 39 top right.) No source has been found for this portrait, but three versions of heads of Christ are listed in the 1773 Catalogue under Class VIII 'Heads of the Popes' (see Appendix F).* British Museum

64. Grey–blue jasper with dark-blue jasper dip portrait medallion of Marcus Aurelius Antoninus. Oval 6¼" × 4⅞" (15.9 × 12.6 cm). Mark: WEDGWOOD & BENTLEY. *c.1778. (See Appendix G, Class VII, 18.) This medallion illustrates the use of undercutting, particularly noticeable inside the ear and nostril, and in the folds of the toga, where the detailing is on the same plane as the ground and could not therefore be made in the mould. The portrait illustrates also the cracking (through the neck) sometimes experienced in firing.* Wedgwood Museum

heads a little'.[*] In the same letter he had suggested that the heads, ground flat on the under side, must be fixed 'with a little Borax &c' in the enamel kiln in London.[66] By the time jasper was perfected in January 1777, he had discovered that bas-reliefs of all sizes could be fixed like all sprigged ornament, by being lightly dampened with water while in the clay state and applied to the ground before firing. Undercutting then became a refinement by which the salient features might be made to stand out in crisp relief. This technique, which is simple but requires skill and precision, involves the 'sculpting' of the portrait, when it is in the 'leather-hard' (or 'cheese-hard') state before firing, to add detail that cannot be reproduced from a mould. Undercutting is especially noticeable on the finished article in such features as nostrils, eyes, ears, curls of the hair and folds of the dress, where the cutting is on the same plane with (horizontal to) the background.[†] Josiah drew Bentley's attention the effects of this technique in November 1778: 'you will easily perceive the difference in the hair, faces, fingers[‡] &c . . . which gives them the appearance, & nearly the reality of [original] models.'[67]

Staining of the white heads by the coloured grounds was a serious problem. Josiah had reported as early as July 1776 that he could make blue–black jasper grounds without difficulty apart from 'their staining the white so abominably', and in the same letter he asked Bentley to take note of a 'new edition' of portraits of the King and Queen. 'I wish they were better,' he wrote, 'You'l see how the blue has stain'd her Majesty. We must make those parts thicker; but that will take more time, new moulds &c., & we have clay, *everlasting*, moulds already.'[68]

Much of the difficulty was the result of unduly thin modelling of the original. 'I am aware', Josiah wrote in July 1776, 'of the necessity a

[*]See p. 76.
[†]Detail on a vertical or near-vertical plane only can be reproduced from a mould.
[‡]A reference to bas-relief figures on tablets and medallions.

Modeller will plead for making some of the parts so flat, in order to keep those parts back, & to give a proper relief to the whole. But you will soon see, by turning to our blue & white Jaspers, that we cannot admit of such delicate parts.' He agreed that 'In some things the blue shade which our ground is so apt to cast through the thin parts of the white, may be of advantage to the subject. As in . . . any parts of Drapery which require to be thrown back. . . . But when the naked part of the Figure is penetrated with the color of the ground, it is generally injurious. See the poor Queens Nose, & many other cameos.'[69] When the original model was made at Etruria the problem seldom arose, but the correction of work commis sioned from modellers in wax, or taken from plaster casts supplied from elsewhere, was sometimes more costly than the modelling of originals.

Josiah's reference to 'clay, *everlasting*, moulds' is not readily under stood without a knowledge of his method of moulding bas reliefs from models in metal, plaster, wax, ivory or wood. He described this in a letter written at the beginning of August 1777: 'we . . . can take a clay mould from a medal, that will last for ever, & continue its sharpness, but from a mould we must first make a medal, then burn it, & take a mould from this burnt medal. This clay mould must likewise be burnt, & lastly the medals requir'd must be made out of these clay moulds, so that the opera tions are multiplied, & the medal diminish'd very much by having our original in a mould, & not a medal.' Moulds were usually of plaster of Paris but, as Josiah explained, 'plaster [can]not bear a sufficient force in pressing to make such low reliefs perfect, & besides they soon lose their own sharpness.'[70] His 'everlasting' moulds were therefore of fired clay.

The method then was to take a relief model (or to make one in fired clay from a mould supplied), and to take from it an intaglio mould ('case mould'). From this first (intaglio) mould was made the master cast in relief ('block mould'), a replica of the original object. This block mould,

65. Dark blue dip on blue grey jasper portrait medallion of George Edwards (1694–1773), English naturalist and ornithologist, from a model (probably in wax) by Isaac Gosset. Oval height 3¼" (8.2 cm). Mark: WEDGWOOD & BENTLEY. *c.1779. (See Appendix H:I.) Another portrait showing evidence of undercutting in the nostril, ear and folds of the dress. The ground is impressed* 'EDWARDS' *below the truncation of the bust, and the reverse is incised with the formula '3 of No. 3 and 1 of New Mixd M' indicating that the medallion is a trial piece.* Wedgwood Museum

65

66   67

in fired clay, was used to make a working mould (intaglio) and it was from this that the repeated copies in relief of the original object were cast. When the working mould deteriorated through wear, a new one was made from the block mould. By this means the object itself and the original mould from it were protected from wear, and the sharpness of the relief could be maintained for long periods. Wedgwood's use of fired clay greatly prolonged the useful life of his moulds, a large number of which, subject to occasional repair, have remained intermittently in use for two hundred years.

Josiah's letter of August 1777 mentions also that the repeated operations of moulding and firing resulted in the original being 'diminish'd very much'.[71] This he explained in some detail so that Bentley should understand the need for original models of a suitable size, for, as Josiah put it, 'We can easily reduce, & must of necessity do it in making clay moulds – but cannot enlarge.' Shrinkage in firing reduced jasper and basaltes models by about one-eighth. 'In order to render our moulds everlasting & allways sharp,' Josiah told Bentley, 'they should be made of clay burnt. For this purpose when we have a mould given to us, we are under the necessity of taking a press in clay out of the mould, & burning it. This is one diminishing of size. – From this burnt impression we take a clay mould & burn that, which is a second lessening of the bassrelief, & from this mould we make the figures &c for sale which in our fine Jasper lessens the size very considerably.'[72]

The sources of Wedgwood's portrait medallions were many and varied. Many of the classical portraits were remodelled from casts of gems, a large number of which were supplied by James Tassie, either in a sulphur or the glass-paste composition which he had invented. Historical portraits were generally moulded from bronze or silver medals, but these too were often remodelled because they were too small for effective reproduction in jasper. The set of Kings and Queens of England, the Popes and the Roman History portraits were modelled after medals by the Dassier family.[*73] Heads of the French Kings were modelled by the Etruria modeller William Bedson from a set in Lord Bessborough's collection, but Josiah was not excited by them: 'they will serve to make a flourish in our next edition of the Catalogue but I fear will be of little farther use.'[74]

Josiah's enthusiasm was reserved for his 'Illustrious Moderns'. This should surprise no one for they remain uniquely interesting in ceramic history and provided him with a rare opportunity to create a modern gallery of portraits of his own choice and to commission original work. The first mention of this series of portraits is in his letter to Bentley dated 25 January 1777: 'I hope you have read Mr Eller's[†] fine letter & are preparing to send down the Heads of all the illustrious Men in all the Courts, & Countries of Europe to be immortalised in our artificial Jasper.'[75] From this it appears that the 'Illustrious Moderns' were embarked upon at Elers's suggestion and as a pendant to his request for a portrait to be modelled of his more celebrated father (Plate 110). There is ample evidence, however, that Wedgwood & Bentley were making portraits which were subsequently listed under this heading long before this date,[76] and it is clear that Josiah's comment was sarcastic. During the following three years Elers was a regular pest with his extravagant claims on behalf of his father and uncle, and an array of suggestions for Wedgwood production which ranged from the long-achieved to the ludicrous.[‡] Josiah often found it hard to restrain his irritation.[77]

[*]Dassier *et cie*, a Swiss family of medallists and engravers, of whom the foremost members were Jean Dassier (1676–1763) and Antoine Dassier (1718–80).
[†]Paul Elers (1700–after 1777) son of John Philip Elers.
[‡]His last, in October 1779, was that Wedgwood should rise above 'trifling trinkets' and manufacture water pipes 'for London first & then for all the world' (E26–18932 20 October 1779).

68   69

68. Dark-blue jasper dip portrait medallion of Lord Auckland, from a model in wax by Eley George Mountstephen, 1789–90. Oval height 4⅜" (11.1 cm). Mark: WEDGWOOD. *(See Appendix H:II.)* Brooklyn Museum, Emily Winthrop Miles Collection

69. Dark-blue jasper dip portrait medallion of Eleanor, Lady Auckland, from a model by Eley George Mountstephen, 1789–90. Oval height 4⅜" (11.1 cm). Mark: WEDGWOOD *(Cf. Plate 68 and see Appendix H:II.)* British Museum

70. *Green jasper dip portrait medallion of James 'Athenian' Stuart. Oval height 4⅛" (10.4 cm). Mark:* WEDGWOOD. *c.1785. A well undercut portrait on a ground dipped too thinly so that the white jasper of the medallion shows through the dip. (See Appendix H:I.)* Wedgwood Museum

71. *Green jasper dip portrait medallion of Granville Leveson-Gower, first Marquis of Stafford. Oval height 3½" (8.9 cm). Mark:* WEDGWOOD. *'Lord Gower' was one of Wedgwood's most influential patrons. The portrait is attributed to Hackwood, c.1782. (See Appendix H:I.)* Wedgwood Museum

72. *Blue jasper dip portrait medallion of Erasmus Darwin. Oval height 5" (12.6 cm). Mark:* WEDGWOOD. *The portrait is attributed to Hackwood, c.1779, after the portrait by Joseph Wright of Derby, 1770, now in the National Portrait Gallery, London. (Cf. Plate 17 and see Appendix H:II.)* Wedgwood Museum

73. *Black jasper dip portrait medallion of Honora Sneyd Edgeworth. Oval height 2¾" (7 cm). Mark:* Wedgwood. *c.1781. Incised on the reverse: 'Ground & head 2 of Last 1559 1 of 3614 Black wash'. Honora Edgeworth was the second wife of Wedgwood's friend Richard Lovell Edgeworth. (See Appendix H:II.)* Wedgwood Museum

70

71

72

73

74

75

74–5. *Blue jasper dip portrait medallions of Louis XVI and Marie Antoinette of France in contemporary carved and gilt wood frames. Oval heights 3" (7.6 cm). Marks:* WEDGWOOD. *c.1784. 74 modelled by Hackwood (and signed by him with his initials on the truncation) in 1778 after a medal by Renaud; 75 remodelled, probably by Hackwood, after a medallion by Jean Baptiste Nini. (See Appendix H:I.)* Wedgwood Museum

76

77

From about the end of 1777 the portrait medallions were made more often in jasper dip than solid jasper, and some which were previously believed to be solid blue or green are now, in the light of the evidence provided by Josiah's memorandum, seen to have been given a thin ground of fine slip. Solid grey, and yellow or brown dip are the rarest colours, but lilac is uncommon and blue–black seems to have been used very seldom before 1780.[78] Only blue and green, in various shades, both solid and dip, appear to have been in regular production for portraits.

The Wedgwood & Bentley portrait medallion of Admiral Keppel* provides an example of the extraordinary speed at which Josiah worked. On 25 February he was complaining that Bentley had failed to send him a head of Keppel 'when it is advertised every day in shade-etching & wax. . . . we should have had it a month since.' A week later he had an etching – 'an extreme bad impression', useless for modelling – and demanded a wax portrait to be sent as soon as possible. On 8 March he was still waiting for the model, but the Oven Books show that portraits of Keppel were fired only five days later, and this is confirmed by a letter written on the 14th, which shows that Josiah, despairing of receiving a suitable relief model in time to take best advantage of the market, had had the portrait modelled from the engraving (Plate C10). It has been traditionally ascribed to Flaxman, but, since it was modelled so hurriedly at Etruria, it is most likely to have been the work of William Hackwood. A second, more authentic portrait of Keppel was modelled later, perhaps in 1782, when he was raised to the peerage and became First Lord of the Admiralty.[79]

---

*News of Keppel's acquittal at the court martial following the indecisive engagement with the French fleet off Ushant in 1778, reached London on 11 February 1779. Keppel at once became a public hero.

The Modellers

Whereas Wedgwood's choice of portraits for reproduction in terracotta biscuit or black basaltes had been strongly influenced by the models available to be copied, he and Bentley evidently saw the jasper portraits of 'Illustrious Moderns' as meriting special attention and the costs of original modelling. The contrast of the white heads against coloured grounds emphasised any defects in moulding, and modellers at Etruria had already gained valuable experience in retouching moulds and remodelling from casts of bronze medals.

First in importance among Wedgwood's modellers was William Hackwood (Plate 78). He was not the most celebrated of the many whose work was reproduced in jasper, and the quality of his modelling lacked the sophistication of Flaxman's or Webber's; but his talent was prodigious, his output enormous, and he was one of the few whose work is sometimes identifiable and who was employed at Etruria rather than commissioned to work elsewhere.

78. Portrait of William Hackwood. Oils on canvas 13½" × 11½" (34.2 × 29.2 cm), probably by a local Staffordshire artist, c.1820. Hackwood was incomparably valuable as a modeller and 'mender'. He was responsible for finishing many of Wedgwood's finest black basaltes busts, for modelling a large number of portrait medallions, and for modelling or remodelling an even larger number of cameos, medallions and tablets. His work was seldom original, but the few pieces which appear to be entirely his own (e.g. the portraits of William Willet and Edward Bourne, Plates C11 and C12) show vigour and attention to fine detail.
City Museum & Art Gallery, Stoke-on-Trent

78

William Hackwood is first mentioned by Josiah in a letter dated 20 September 1769: 'I hired an ingenious Boy last night for Etruria as a Modeler. He had modeled at nights in his way for three years past, has never had the least instructions, which circumstance considered he does things amazingly & will be a valuable acquisition. I have hired him for five years, & with Denby & him I shall not want any other *constant* modeler at Etruria. Palmer,* & several others wo^d fain have hired the Boy but he chose to come to me.'[80] Hackwood chose, too, to stay – for sixty-three years.

At this time Charles Denby was Wedgwood's senior modeller at Etruria, with Boot working on figures. Denby was equally talented as a painter, and in May 1770 he was dispatched to London to work under Bentley and Rhodes in the Decorating Studio, where the 'Husk' service for the Empress Catherine was then being enamelled.[81]

In August 1770 Hackwood was noted as having spent three weeks on modelling a flower basket and was 'now ingaged in finishing basreliefs'. His first essay in portrait modelling was made a year later, just at the time when Bentley proposed to the King and Queen that their portraits might be reproduced in basaltes. Josiah approved: 'It was a good hint you gave them respecting their Portraits. I hope it will work & have its proper effect, & am fully perswaded a good deal may be done in that way with many of Their Majesty's subjects, but we sho^d if possible do this as we have done in other things – begin at the *Head* first & then proceed to the inferior members.' He added: 'Though we have made a sort of beginning in that way here for Hackwood has been three times at Crew by Mrs Crews† particular desire to model the head of her son and heir. I told her he was quite a novice in Portrait modeling but she wo^d have him try his hand & I could not refuse her. What he will make of it I do not know.' Unfortunately, this head, probably the first of Hackwood's portraits, has not been identified.[82]

During the next five years Hackwood proved his worth, restoring busts obtained from Hoskins & Grant, or Cheere or Parker,‡ remodelling such figures as the griffin candlestick, and repairing gems. Josiah reported that he was 'of the greatest value & consequence in finishing fine small work, & of this kind we shall have enough to employ him constantly'. By January 1776 Hackwood was working on important tablets,§ and six months later Josiah reckoned there was enough modelling and repairing in hand to last Hackwood and William Bedson two years. He could, he wrote, do with 'half a doz^n more Hackwoods'.[83]

---

*Humphrey Palmer, potter at the Church Works, Hanley.
†Frances Anne, wife of John Crewe (created Baron Crewe 1806); fashionable beauty and political (Whig) hostess and the friend of Fox and Sheridan. Her daughter Emma supplied Wedgwood with designs for jasper bas-reliefs (see p. 157). Her son, Sir John, second Baron Crewe, while a child, was painted in the character of Henry VIII by Sir Joshua Reynolds in 1776.
‡John Cheere (1709–87); Richard Parker (*fl.* 1769–74).
§See p. 145.

79

80

79. Solid pale-blue jasper with darker-blue jasper dip portrait medallion of David Garrick, modelled by William Hackwood in 1777. The ground below the truncation is impressed 'GARRICK'. Oval height 3½" (9.0 cm). Mark: Wedgwood & Bentley. c.1778. Examples of this medallion are signed 'Wm Hackwood' on the truncation. (See Appendix H:I.)
Christie's, London

80. Solid pale-blue jasper with darker-blue jasper dip portrait medallion of William Shakespeare, modelled by William Hackwood in 1777. The ground below the truncation is impressed 'SHAKESPEARE'. Oval height 4" (10.2 cm). Mark: WEDGWOOD & BENTLEY. c.1778. Signed 'Wm Hackwood' on the truncation. (See Appendix H:I.)
Christie's, London

On 5 July 1777 Josiah added a postscript to his letter to Bentley: 'I send you this head of Mr Willet* as a specimen of Hackwood's Portrait modeling. A stronger likeness can scarcely be conceiv'd. You may keep it as the shadow of a good Man who is marching with hasty strides towards the land of Forgetfulness.'[84] The portrait (Plate C11) is one of the finest known to be Hackwood's, and it is reasonable to assume that, unlike most of the portrait medallions, it was modelled from the life.

It was, perhaps, inevitable that Hackwood, still probably not yet twenty,† should have acquired a high opinion of himself. In March 1777 Josiah complained that he was 'growing very extravagant in his prices' and that he did not 'find it possible to keep him reasonable upon the sub-ject'.[85] Evidently this problem was resolved, for nothing more was written on the matter.

However, another problem arose, which may have been connected with the first: Hackwood was discovered to be signing his portraits. In December 1777 Josiah sent Bentley new portrait medallions of Shakespeare and David Garrick. 'You will see', he wrote, 'by looking under the shoulder of each that these heads are modeled by *Wm Hackwood*, but I shall prevent his exposing himself again now that I have found it out. I am not certain that he will not be offended if he is refus'd the liberty of puting his name to the models which he makes quite new, & I shall be glad to have your opinion upon the subject. Mine is against any name being upon our articles besides W & B, & if you concur with me I will manage the matter with him as well as I can.'[86] Hackwood had already signed portraits of the King and Queen, adapted from wax portraits by Isaac Gosset, and his portrait of Voltaire, probably modelled in 1777, and he went on to sign portraits of Edward Bourne in November 1778, of

*William Willet (c.1698–1778) was married to Josiah's sister Catherine.
†Hackwood's date of birth is not known, but it was probably about 1757.

Josiah Wedgwood in 1782 and of Lord Anglesey about 1821.[87] It has been generally supposed that Hackwood obeyed Josiah's prohibition against signatures and that these three exceptions were made either by special permission or without Josiah's knowledge. It is more likely that Josiah agreed to Hackwood's signing all original work after 1777 on condition that portraits remodelled from other artists' originals were unsigned.

The medallion of Edward Bourne (Plate C12), an old bricklayer at Etruria, is a masterpiece of portrait modelling. Josiah wrote of it: 'Old Bournes is the man himself with every wrinkle crink & cranny in the whole visage.'[88] It appears to have been modelled neither for family nor for commercial reasons, but purely as an exercise in modelling; but it was offered to the public and a small quantity, in various colours, was sold.

Hackwood's work was seldom original. He was employed primarily in 'mending' (amending and repairing) or remodelling the work of others and for this reason his style is not easily identified. His portrait models tend to be hunched at the shoulders and thick-necked, and the truncations are sharply cut. Early examples are always crisply undercut at the eyes, ears, nostrils and coat lapels.

It is likely that Hackwood was not the only modeller at Etruria to work on portraits obtained from commissioned artists, but no evidence of others has been found. Henry Webber is credited with the portrait of Sarah Wedgwood modelled in 1782,[89] but the attribution is based on tradition and probability rather than on any knowledge of Webber's style in portrait modelling. It is nevertheless hardly possible to believe that Hackwood was responsible for 'mending' every one of the 228 'Illustrious Moderns' listed in the 1787 Catalogue, in addition to all his work on busts, cameos, medallions and tablets. If, however, Bedson was responsible for part of the work of 'mending' and remodelling, no evidence has been found of it.

Of the commissioned artists, by far the most gifted and distinguished was John Flaxman. His work for Wedgwood is of the utmost importance in the development of jasper, bringing to it the technical excellence and originality of a professional sculptor and creative artist of the first rank. Without Flaxman, Wedgwood's eighteenth-century jasper would have lacked much of its most sensitive and stylish neoclassical ornament. Flaxman was not primarily a portrait modeller, but it was in this capacity that he was first commissioned by Wedgwood & Bentley.

John Flaxman junior was born in 1755 in York, the second son of a modeller and maker of plaster casts who, early next year, set up his studio at New Street, Covent Garden, London. The family was poor, and the young Flaxman suffered from ill-health and congenital curvature of the spine which deprived him of normal childhood diversions. 'So unhappily formed by nature',[90] he was nonetheless cheerful and intelligent, and showed, at an early age in his father's shop, great promise in drawing and modelling. In 1766 he won a premium from the Society of Arts, and

81. *Detail from the portrait of John Flaxman junior, RA, by George Romney, 1795. Oils on canvas (full portrait) 30″ × 25″ (76.2 × 63.5 cm).* National Portrait Gallery, London

81

82. *Green jasper dip circular portrait medallion of John Flaxman junior. Diameter 6″ (15.2 cm) excluding turned oak frame. Mark:* WEDGWOOD. *c.1790. This self-portrait was modelled c.1787. (See Appendix H:II.)* Wedgwood Museum

82

three years later enrolled as one of the first students of the newly founded Royal Academy Schools, where his fellow artists included John Bacon the elder and James Tassie. He exhibited at the Royal Academy for the first time in 1770, at the age of fifteen, and forty years later became the first professor of sculpture.

Flaxman was brought up in the tradition of baroque and rococo, though both were in decline. His father's original work was baroque in style, and Roubiliac and Scheemakers were among the customers for casts whose sculpture would have been familiar to the young Flaxman. At the Royal Academy he would have heard Reynolds advising students that 'a mere copier of nature can never produce any thing great', quoting Cicero's account of the sculptor Phidias, recommending 'a careful study of the ancient sculptors', and warning against the 'ridiculous style' of those who had 'given to Grecian Heroes the airs and graces practised in the court of Lewis the Fourteenth'.[91] Grace, elegance and, above all, simplicity were the ideals. The word 'neoclassicism' was unknown until late in the nineteenth century. Much of Flaxman's work might be described as modified baroque, in which the inspiration of nature was strengthened by the prevailing influence of classical forms and imagery, not excluded by them.

Flaxman's name first appears in Wedgwood's letters in September 1771, when Josiah wrote to Bentley describing the recent visit to Etruria of Sir George and Lady Strickland, and her father, a Mr Freeman of Schute Lodge. Josiah described Freeman as 'a man of Taste as you will be convinced when I tell you that *he admires our works exceedingly* but says our materials are so fine & we execute so well we should to be complete spare no expence in having the finest things abroad model'd for us. . . . He is a great admirer of young Flaxman & has advised his Father to send him to Rome which he has promised to do. Mr Freeman says he knows young Flaxman is a Coxcomb, but does not think him a bit the worse for it *or the less likely to be a great Artist.*'[92]

No further mention of Flaxman's name occurs until the beginning of 1775, when Wedgwood & Bentley were having trouble with Joachim Smith,* and Josiah proposed to 'drop all connections with Smith & if possible, have a Modeler of our own for Portraits'. On 14 January he wrote: 'I am glad you have met with a Modeler & that Flaxman is so valuable an Artist.' It is not clear that the two are the same, but the next day Josiah suggested that Flaxman might model 'a good Tablet for a chimneypiece', and by the middle of April the Flaxmans (father and son) had supplied a quantity of bas-reliefs and other pieces.†[93]

In July Josiah received an inquiry from Sir James Broughton for portraits of his two sons, preferably to be modelled three-quarter-face, for cameos to be set in a bracelet for his wife, and Josiah suggested that Flaxman might be 'more moderate' than Smith. Later experience was to

*See pp. 76–7, 123.
†See p. 114.

83   84   85

83. Wax portrait of Hermann Boerhaave, the Dutch physician, modelled by John Flaxman junior in 1782 and invoiced to Wedgwood on 8 July of that year (Ms. 2–30187). The portrait is modelled, using a sculptor's technique, direct on to glass, which is painted black on the reverse. Maximum height of relief 3⅛" (8.0 cm) (See Appendix H:I.) Formerly author's collection

84. Dark-blue jasper dip portrait medallion of Michel de Ruyter. Oval height 3⅜" (8.6 cm). Mark: WEDGWOOD. Modelled by John Flaxman junior in 1782 (see Appendix H:I). Brooklyn Museum

85. Solid blue and white jasper portrait medallion of Captain James Cook. Oval height 3¼" (8.3 cm). Mark: WEDGWOOD. Modern replica, c.1922. Attributed to John Flaxman junior c.1779, after the portrait by William Hodges. (See Appendix H:I.) Wedgwood Museum

show that Flaxman was one of the few modellers capable of producing convincing likenesses in the difficult three-quarter view, and some of his portrait medallions – notably those of Boerhaave, de Ruyter, Hein, Paul I of Russia and Captain James Cook – are almost full-face (Plates 83–5, 88 and C16). There is no record that the Broughton boys' portraits were made. Later in the month, Josiah made another suggestion: 'Suppose you were to employ Flaxman to model some Figures. They would do for Tablets, Vases, inlaying &c. We have nobody here that can do them.' He added: 'You have had a pair or two of Flaxman's figures, & shall have more.'[94]

This last remark raises the question whether the figures supplied were by the elder John Flaxman or by his younger son. The earliest record of work bought by Wedgwood from the Flaxmans' studio is a bill for goods supplied in March and April 1775.[95] This is receipted by John Flaxman junior on behalf of his father and, in view of Josiah's suggestion dated July that Flaxman should be employed to model 'figures' for tablets and vases, it may be deduced that the bas-reliefs already delivered were casts rather than original models, and that they were part of the elder Flaxman's stock in trade. The exceptions were charges for 'Moulding & making a cast from a Medall of Lennaeus',[*] and 'Mending a Wax medall & making a Mould from it'. The medal is unsigned, but the wax was probably the original by Inlander, modelled in 1773 (Plate C13).[96]

In a letter of 8 August 1775 there is positive evidence of original work by the younger Flaxman: 'I wish you', Josiah wrote to Bentley,

> to see Mr Flaxman before you leave London, & if you could prevail
> upon him to finish Mr Banks[†] & Dr Solander[‡] they would be an

[*]Carolus Linnaeus (Carl von Linné, 1707–78), Swedish botanist, physician and natural historian, chiefly distinguished for introducing a system for the classification of plants.
[†]Sir Joseph Banks Bt (1743–1802), naturalist, who accompanied Captain Cook on his voyage in 1768. President of the Royal Society, 1778–1802. Created baronet 1781.
[‡]Dr Daniel Charles Solander (1736–82), Swedish naturalist. Librarian to Sir Joseph Banks and accompanied him on Cook's 1768 voyage to the southern hemisphere.

acquisition to us, & as we shall now make with tolerable certainty any moderate sized Bassreliefs of the composition [jasper] sent you last. . . . I submit it to you whether we should not have some of the finest things that can be modeled, & Originals which have not been hackney'd in Wax & Plaister for a century past, & if you think we should would it not be saving time to set Mr Flaxman upon some business before you leave him.[97]

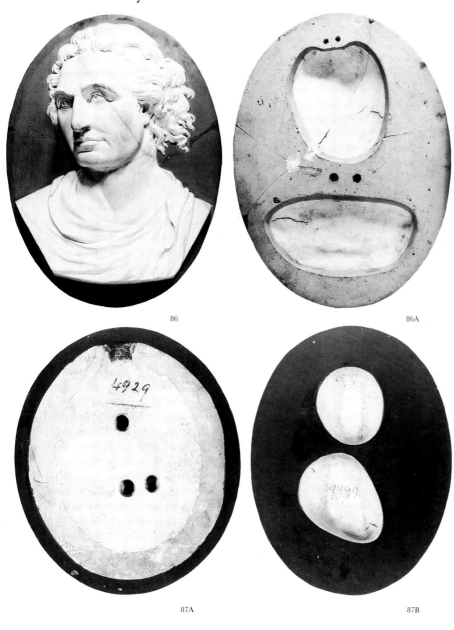

86

86A

87A

87B

86. *Solid blue and white jasper with darker-blue jasper dip portrait medallion of Captain James Cook. Oval height 9½" (24 cm). Mark:* WEDGWOOD & BENTLEY. *c.1779. A medallion of large size evidently adapted (probably by Hackwood) from the portrait illustrated in Plate 85. No other example of this medallion, which was unrecorded until 1982, has yet come to light (See* Wedgwood Society of Australia *Newsletter, No. 59, 1982, pp. 3–4.) (See Appendix H:I.)* Alexander Turnbull Library, Wellington, New Zealand

86A. *Reverse of the medallion illustrated in Plate 86 showing the two large thumb scoops and smaller pierced holes behind the relief to permit the escape of gases and to reduce stresses between the ground and the relief. In spite of these precautions, the medallion shows large firecracks in the white relief (visible in both thumb scoops) in addition to fractures due to impact.*

87A. *Pierced holes in the reverse of the framed portrait medallion of Edward Bourne (Plate C12), c.1778.* Wedgwood Museum

87B. *Reverse of a black jasper dip portrait medallion of Frederick I of Württemberg, illustrating two thumb scoops. Both show a network of stress cracks as well as small firecracks. Oval height 5¼" (13.2 cm). Mark:* WEDGWOOD. *c.1797.* Wedgwood Museum

87C. (Left) *reverse of a black basaltes portrait medallion of the French actor Pierre Louis Dubois de Préville, showing the single long thumb scoop and the inscription 'Preville'. Oval height 3⅞"* (9.8 cm). *Unmarked. c.1779. (See Appendix H:I.)* (Right) *reverse of blue and white jasper dip portrait medallion of Edward Bourne, showing two large pierced holes. Oval height 4¼"* (10.8 cm). *Unmarked. c.1795. This portrait is badly firecracked across the neck and down the cravat, and the body of the medallion is of a noticeably coarser jasper than the head and blue dip.* (Centre) *reverse of a solid blue and white jasper medallion of Euterpe, showing the smaller and more widely spaced holes typical of many mid-nineteenth-century plaques and medallions. Oval height 6½"* (16.6 cm). *Mark:* WEDGWOOD. *c1870.* Author's collection

88. *Black jasper dip portrait of Maria I of Portugal, modelled by John Flaxman junior in 1787 (see Appendix H:II). Oval height 4"* (10.0 cm). *Mark:* WEDGWOOD. British Museum

89. *Solid pale-blue and white jasper portrait medallion of Johann, Count Meerman (see Appendix H:II) modelled by John Flaxman junior in 1785. Oval height 4¼"* (10.8 cm). *Mark:* WEDGWOOD. *c.1785.* The late Eugene D. Buchanan Collection

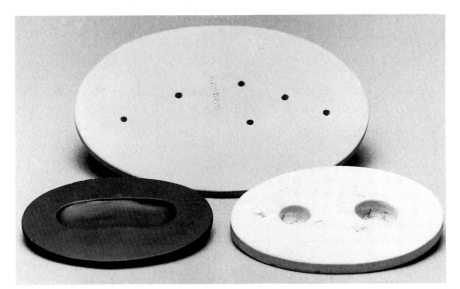

87C

88

89

90

91   92

90. *Solid pale-blue and white jasper portrait medallion of Anna Cornelia Mollerus, Countess Meerman (see Appendix H:II) modelled by John Flaxman junior in 1785. Oval height 4¼" (10.8 cm). Mark:* WEDGWOOD. The late Eugene D. Buchanan Collection

91. *Lilac jasper dip portrait medallion of Sir Joseph Banks (see Appendix H:I) modelled by John Flaxman junior in 1775. Oval height 3½" (8.9 cm). Mark:* WEDGWOOD. c.1785. Wedgwood Museum

92. *Solid pale-blue jasper dipped in darker-blue jasper portrait medallion of Dr Daniel Charles Solander, the Swedish botanist who accompanied Sir Joseph Banks on James Cook's voyage in 1768 and to Iceland in 1772 (see Appendix H:I) modelled by John Flaxman junior in 1775. Oval height 3¼". Mark: Wedgwood & Bentley. c.1778. This portrait of Solander, with that of Banks (Plate 91), was 'classicised' for the series of large portrait medallions produced in 1779. For these portraits, all the subjects had their wigs removed and classically draped robes or togas substituted for their eighteenth-century clothes.* Wedgwood Museum

The Banks and Solander portraits (Plates 91 and 92) appear to have been the first of Flaxman's original models for Wedgwood, and both profiles show characteristics of style which are to be seen in others of Flaxman's medallions: an upright figure, straight-backed, with well-defined eyes, mouth and nostrils; uncluttered dress, with the figure plainly truncated; and an especially noticeable thinness of jasper at the bridge of the nose, which often shows the ground colour through the white relief. Josiah complained of this last feature of Flaxman's modelling which was, he wrote, 'too flat in several parts to be made in color'd grounds, & we can sooner finish our own than raise his model'.[98]

As Flaxman's original wax models show (Plates 83, 111 and 112), his technique was a sculptor's, the portraits being modelled direct on to glass or slate grounds, using a hard greyish-white composition of his own, which contained a high proportion of white lead. The relief varied in thickness from a transparent coating of wax to about half an inch. It was a common practice for modellers to create their own compositions, and Flaxman probably developed his mixture specially for use in 'working' models from which plaster moulds would be taken.[99] This particular composition is not known in the work of any other modeller and is, indeed, quite unlike the softer mixtures used by such modellers as Isaac Gosset and John Charles Lochée for the reproduction of wax copies.

Nearly fifty portrait medallions of the 'Illustrious Moderns' series are documented as Flaxman's work or attributed to him on grounds of style or long tradition.* Research carried out in the past twenty years has removed from the list many portraits formerly attributed to him for less evident reasons. He continued to model portraits for Wedgwood at least until 1788, and probably as late as 1796, and he was responsible for a greater number of the 'Illustrious Moderns' than any other modeller.[100]

Among the eighteenth-century modellers of Wedgwood's portrait medallions, Flaxman was one of the few to be a professional sculptor. Of the rest, only John de Vaere and Henry Webber could claim that distinction: Edward Burch was a gem engraver and wax modeller; James Tassie was a wax modeller and the co-inventor and exploiter of glass paste for the imitation of gem stones; Isaac Gosset, John Charles Lochée,† Eley George Mountstephen, Charles Peart and Joachim Smith were all modellers in wax.

John de Vaere (*fl.*1785–1810) was born in France and attended the Royal Academy Schools in 1786. He was originally recommended to Wedgwood by Flaxman, and succeeded Webber as chief modeller in 1794. Documentary evidence of his having modelled five portrait medallions – Alexander Allardyce and the four admirals, Duncan, Howe, Nelson and St Vincent (Jervis)‡ – exists in receipts dated 1798,[101] but since much of his work for Wedgwood was completed during Josiah's lifetime, the existence of earlier portraits by his hand cannot be ruled out.

Henry Webber (1754–1826) was the son of a Swiss sculptor and a pupil of John Bacon the elder. He attended the Royal Academy Schools in 1774 and joined Wedgwood some eight years later on the recommendation of Sir Joshua Reynolds and Sir William Chambers.[102] He was head of the ornamental department at Etruria from 1785 to 1806. He was not a specialist portrait modeller and the only portrait medallion attributed to him is that of Sarah Wedgwood. This appears in the Oven Book for 13 and 20 April 1782, the same dates as the first firing of Hackwood's signed portrait of Josiah, and more than two months before Webber's recorded arrival at Etruria. Unless this model was sent to Etruria ahead of Webber's arrival (in which case Sarah must have sat to him at some even earlier date), this attribution must be reconsidered. If

*See Appendix H.
†Though better known as a modeller in wax, Lochée's sculpture, little of which has been identified, shows a technical mastery which it would be unjust to ignore. See note 106.
‡See p. 238.

Webber was responsible for others of the portrait medallions, the fact appears to be unrecorded.

None of the other portrait modellers whose work can be identified with certainty was formally employed by Wedgwood, and none is known to have modelled portraits, as Hackwood and Flaxman are known to have done, for Wedgwood's exclusive use. Edward Burch RA (1730–1814) provided a portrait of George III after his Academy Prize Medal entry of 1785, but is better remembered for his models of horses after Stubbs (Plates 43–5). James Tassie (1735–99), whose work has already been mentioned in connection with seals, produced more than 500 portraits, many of them modelled from life, in his glass paste, and he and Wedgwood occasionally supplied each other with models.[103] Most of

93

93. Portrait of the modeller James Tassie (1735–99) by David Allan. Oils on canvas 30" × 25" (76 × 64 cm). Scottish National Portrait Gallery, Edinburgh

119

94

95

94. *Solid blue and white jasper portrait medallion of James Byres, the Scottish architect and antiquary, modelled by James Tassie in 1779. Oval height 2⅝" (6.7 cm). Signed and dated on the truncation. Mark:* WEDGWOOD. *Nineteenth-century replica, c.1889. James Byres purchased the Barberini vase from Donna Cornelia Barberini-Colonna in 1780, and sold it to Sir William Hamilton (see p. 217 and Appendix H:I).* Scottish National Portrait Gallery, Edinburgh

95. *Dark blue jasper dip portrait medallion of Dr Joseph Black, modelled by James Tassie, 1788 (see Appendix H:II). Signed and dated on the truncation. A similarly signed and dated wax of this subject is in the Wedgwood Museum. Oval height 3½" (8.9 cm). Mark:* WEDGWOOD. c.1789. Wedgwood Museum

Wedgwood's reproductions of Tassie's originals are signed and dated on the truncation; others supplied by Tassie bear the single letter 'T' impressed (Plates 94 and 95). Evidently Wedgwood's aversion to artists' signatures could not be extended to models acquired from Tassie.

Wax portraits by Isaac Gosset (1713–99), and by Matthew Gosset (1683–1744) his uncle, were probably bought by Bentley from the younger Gosset's stock in London. It is unlikely that any was a commissioned work, and the most successful of them – those of George III and Queen Charlotte – were remodelled by Hackwood (Plates 96 and 97). Isaac Gosset's understated style of modelling in a smooth ivory wax of his own (or his uncle's) formulation, did not translate well into stoneware without considerable alteration to sharpen and deepen the relief.

96. *Blue jasper dip portrait medallion of George III, from a model by Isaac Gosset (see Appendix H:I). Oval height 3½" (8.9 cm). Mark:* WEDGWOOD. c.1785. Wedgwood Museum

97. *Blue jasper dip portrait medallion of Queen Charlotte, from a model by Isaac Gosset (see Appendix H:I). Oval height 3½" (8.9 cm). Mark:* WEDGWOOD. c.1785. Wedgwood Museum

96

97

98. *Solid blue and white jasper double portrait medallion of George III and Queen Charlotte, probably modelled by Hackwood after the wax portraits by Isaac Gosset. Oval height 1 ¼"* (3.2 cm). Unmarked. c.1776. Double portraits of the King and Queen were available in June 1776, and were mentioned in Josiah's letter to Bentley of 16 April 1777 (Wedgwood in London, 1984, 225th Anniversary Exhibition 1959–1984, No. M6; and E25–18747). *Wedgwood Museum*

99. *Deep-blue jasper dip portrait medallions of (left) Frederick Augustus, Duke of York and Albany and (right) George, Prince of Wales, modelled by John Charles Lochée in 1787 (see Appendix H:I). Oval height 3 ⅝"* (9.2 cm). Mark: WEDGWOOD. *These royal portraits well illustrate Lochée's ornate style.* Nottingham Castle Museum

    John Charles Lochée's style, on the other hand, was inclined to be over-flamboyant. Bentley gave him some work, which has not been identified, in 1774.[104] Lochée's portraits of the royal princes, modelled in 1787 when he was living in Rupert Street, London, are documented,[105] and others have been identified from manuscript references or attributed on grounds of his distinctive style.* Lochée's portrait medallions regularly display certain features recognisable also in his sculptured busts:[106] the truncation below the shoulder is concealed by an opulently folded cloak (sometimes fur-lined); ribbons and sashes are ornately creased or folded; the hair is naturalistically modelled; and lace is reproduced in fine detail (Plate 99).

    Unlike Flaxman, who sent his original models to Etruria, where moulds were taken from them, Lochée supplied moulds, keeping his original work for his own wax reproductions. Josiah II wrote critically to

*See Appendix H:II.

100. *Pale-blue jasper dip
portrait medallion of Lord
Hillsborough modelled by
Charles Peart in 1787 (see
Appendix H:I). Oval
height 4¾" (12.1 cm).
Mark:* WEDGWOOD.
'EARL OF
HILSBOROUGH' *(sic)
impressed below truncation.*
Private collection

101. *Solid blue and white
jasper dip portrait medallion
of General Sir Eyre Coote,
modelled by Eley George
Mountstephen in 1788 (see
Appendix H:II). Oval
height 5" (12.6 cm).
Mark:* WEDGWOOD.
c.1790.
British Museum

his father in 1788: 'Now you are in London it would be very kind if you would give Mr Lochée a lecture on modelling & making moulds – you know how he undercuts – & his moulds are in general very bad, some-times they appear to have had waxes taken out of them – & I believe always they are very full of pin holes.'[107] Three years later Lochée was declared bankrupt[108] and no more was heard of him. Now generally for-gotten,[109] Lochée was an accomplished portrait sculptor and wax model-ler, and the portraits reproduced by Wedgwood are attractively rococo and extravagant among the careful likenesses by Hackwood and the pur-ity of Flaxman's work.

Charles Peart (1759–98) was Lochée's pupil and assistant when the latter was working at Stowe in 1788, and his style, if the portrait of Lord Hillsborough (Plate 100) is to be taken as typical, shows signs of Lochée's influence.[110] His portrait of Sir William Chambers (see Plate 12), however, displays no hint of rococo leanings, and it seems likely that Peart's portrait modelling reflected more closely the style of the portrait used as a source than his own.

The work of Eley George Mountstephen (*fl.*1781–91) too is varied in style, perhaps for the same reason. His portrait of Sir Eyre Coote (Plate 101) is of special interest as a copy in high relief, in the difficult three-quarter-face view, of a marble bust by Nollekens.[111] This, and the profile portraits of Lord and Lady Auckland (Plates 68 and 69), the sources of which have not been identified, are distinctly rococo, as is his portrait of 'Philippe Egalité', duc d'Orléans; but that of Christopher Wyvill, mod-elled twelve years earlier than the rest, is of neoclassical severity. It does not appear likely that Mountstephen's style became, against the fashion, more rococo, and the conclusion must be that such of his work as was copied by Wedgwood is not illustrative of Mountstephen's own style.

Wedgwood's difficulties with Joachim Smith have been described above, and it seems that Smith was the first 'outside' modeller to supply Wedgwood with wax portraits for reproduction. Copies of his work made in biscuit terracotta predate even the jasper trials of Lady Charlotte Finch's portrait. His portraits of 'Lady Cha' and her daughters, and of John Bradby Blake (Plates 33, 34 and 104) are competent but undistinguished, giving little hint of the mastery displayed in that of Sir William Hamilton (see Plate 13) a portrait as dignified, elegant and finely modelled as any in the entire series. Some of the same admirable qualities may be seen in his portraits of Josiah and Bentley, both in Court dress, modelled in 1773 (Plates 4 and 5), and it is not hard to understand Josiah's reluctance to lose his services. No ceramic evidence of his connection with Duesbury's Derby factory has yet been found.

Two other sources of Wedgwood portraits are of particular interest: the ivory carvings of David Le Marchand (1674–1726) and Silvanus Bevan (1691–1765). Little is known about Le Marchand, but the quality

102. Blue jasper dip portrait medallion of the Prussian naturalist and philosopher, Johann Reinhold Forster, modelled by Joachim Smith, c.1776. Oval height 3½" (9.0 cm). Mark: WEDGWOOD. c.1785. Nottingham Castle Museum

103. Lilac jasper dip portrait medallion of Sir William Hamilton, modelled by Joachim Smith, c.1772. (Cf. Plate 13 and see Appendix H:I.) Oval height 4⅞" (12.4 cm). Mark: WEDGWOOD. c.1785. Brooklyn Museum, Emily Winthrop Miles Collection

104. Pale-blue jasper dip portrait medallion of John Bradby Blake, English naturalist working in China, who sent home samples of kaolin and petuntse used by Josiah in his early experiments for porcelain (see p. 72 and Appendix H:I). Modelled by Joachim Smith, c.1776. Oval height 1¾" (4.5 cm). Mark: WEDGWOOD. c.1785. City Museum & Art Gallery, Stoke-on-Trent

105. Carved ivory portrait medallion of Sir Christopher Wren by David Le Marchand, c.1723. Oval height 5" (12.7 cm). This portrait was copied by Wedgwood in black basaltes as early as 1773, and later reproduced in jasper (see Appendix H:I). National Portrait Gallery, London

102

103

104

105

of his identified portrait carvings is such as to leave no doubt of his artistry. George Vertue described him as 'an Ingenious Man for carving in Ivory' and added that he had 'done a vast number of heads from ye life in basso relief'.[112] At least seven of these, including those of Sir Christopher Wren and Sir Isaac Newton, were reproduced by Wedgwood. All but three appear in the 1773 Catalogue. The exceptions are the portraits of Charles Chester Eyre,* and the facing pair of Mathew Raper II and his wife Elizabeth (Billers). These last two were probably a private commission, perhaps from the owner of the originals.†

Silvanus Bevan was a practising apothecary and founder of the firm later to be known as Allen & Hanbury. His ivory carving was evidently no more to him than an agreeable diversion, and his style is crude in comparison with Le Marchand's. His portraits have, nevertheless, a certain vitality, and that of William Penn (Plate 108) has been described by Hugh Tait as 'the only reliable portrait of Penn known'.[113] Wedgwood acquired casts from an unspecified number of these carvings from his friend Samuel More, secretary of the Society of Arts, in 1778. He wrote to Bentley: 'Mr More has been so good as to send me some casts from a number of carvings in ivory of the heads of Drs. Mead, Sloane, Pemberton, Woodward and some others. Pray who is Doctr Pemberton'.‡[114] One unlisted portrait has been identified: that of the physician Sir Edward Hulse.

The portrait of William Penn is mentioned in a letter written nearly a year later, which reveals something of Josiah's attitude to his patrons and to the value of suitable gifts as advertisement. 'I have', he told Bentley on 9 October 1779,

> a letter from our good friend Mr More with a mould of a very poor head of the famous Penn which we shall do the needfull with & return the mould as desir'd. Mr More says – 'I have been reproach'd (& I dont love reproaches) that the person to whom I was oblig'd for the other heads has not yet got casts of them, I shall be glad therefore if you will order one or two sets of them to be made in *biscuit* for me to give to the person I had them from. Mr Bentley says they may be easily made in biscuit, if so, let me beg the whole number may be

*Identified by the author in 1984 from the signed, dated and inscribed ivory carving in the Victoria & Albert Museum. This portrait exists also in Tassie's glass paste.

†This would have been Mathew Raper III FRS of Twyford Hall, who gave Le Marchand's ivory bust of Newton to the British Museum. Both Terence Hodgkinson and John Kerslake have suggested that there was a close connection between Le Marchand and the Raper family, who are recorded as owning a number of his ivory carvings (Terence Hodgkinson, 'An Ingenious Man for Carving in Ivory', *Victoria & Albert Museum Bulletin*, Vol. I, No. 2, 1965, pp. 29–32; John Kerslake, 'Sculptor and Patron? Two Portraits by Highmore', *Apollo*, January 1972, pp. 25–9; see also Charles Avery, 'Missing, Presumed Lost: Some Ivory Portraits by David Le Marchand 1674–1726', *Country Life*, 6 June 1985, pp. 1562–4).

‡Dr Richard Mead FRS (1673–1754), physician to Queen Anne and George II, president of the Royal College of Physicians. He accumulated a valuable library collection of paintings and works of art. Sir Hans Sloane (1660–1753), eminent naturalist and physician, president of the Royal Society. Dr Henry Pemberton (1694–1771), physician and mathematician, Gresham Professor of Physic 1728. Dr John Woodward (1665–1728), physician and natural philosopher.

106

107

108

106. Double portrait of
Silvanus and Martha
Bevan from an ivory
carving by Silvanus Bevan
(see Appendix H:II) a
cast from which was sent to
Etruria in 1778. Oval
height 3 ¼" (8.3 cm).
Mark: WEDGWOOD
MADE IN ENGLAND.
Replica made in 1972. This
and a similar double portrait
of Timothy Bevan and his
wife Hannah were evidently
made for Silvanus Bevan
towards the end of 1779.
Apart from a few copies for
the family, it is unlikely that
any jasper copies of these
portraits were made in the
eighteenth century.
Wedgwood Museum

107. Solid pale-blue and
white jasper portrait
medallion of Dr Henry
Pemberton from the cast of
an ivory carving by
Silvanus Bevan sent to
Etruria in 1778 (see
Appendix H:I). Oval
height 3 ¾" (9.5 cm).
Mark: I Wedgwood &
Bentley. c.1778.
Brooklyn Museum,
Emily Winthrop Miles
Collection

108. Solid pale-blue and
white jasper portrait
medallion of William Penn
from the cast of an ivory
carving by Silvanus Bevan
sent to Etruria in 1779 (see
Appendix H:II). Oval
height 3 ⅛" (8.0 cm).
Mark: Wedgwood &
Bentley 1559. c.1779.
Brooklyn Museum,
Emily Winthrop Miles
Collection

sent me'. I do not now recollect why, but I was fully perswaded that
Mr More had had casts of the heads mention'd, however as that is
not the case, I will make some sets of biscuit ones if you chuse that he
should have those, rather than the jasper; but there is so little difference in the expense to us, between one & the other, & so evident &
so great difference in the value, & consequently in the complem[en]ᵗ
that I should prefer jasper to give away, & if you will give what you
have, we will make you more.[115]

The three portraits of Richard Mead (in ivory, wax and jasper) in the
British Museum (Plates 109A–C) provide an instructive illustration of
the changes that might be made in the transition from an original carving
to the jasper medallion. The wax in this example is described as being
signed 'J FLAXMAN',[116] but this signature must be open to doubt. Neither
the style of the modelling nor the wax composition bear any resemblance
to Flaxman's; nor is there any evidence that he undertook remodelling or
repairing work after the first receipted bill for April 1775.[117] By the
autumn of 1778 Flaxman was the most highly valued of Wedgwood's artists, and working on such important reliefs as the Muses and *The*

109A. Carved ivory portrait of Dr Richard Mead by Silvanus Bevan, a cast of which was sent to Etruria in 1778 (see Appendix H:I). Height of ivory carving 3½" (8.8 cm). Unmarked. British Museum

109B. Wax portrait of Dr Richard Mead after the ivory carving (A), showing alterations to the portrait, including the removal of the cloak over the truncation, resulting in a squarer appearance; but the cutting of pupils to the eyes has added vitality to a portrait that was originally more like a memorial bust. The truncation bears the inscription 'J. FLAXMAN' (see p. 125). Height of wax 2⅞" (7.3 cm). British Museum

109C. Solid grey–blue and white jasper portrait medallion of Dr Richard Mead from the wax portrait (B). Oval height 3⅜" (8.6 cm). Mark: Wedgwood & Bentley. c.1779. British Museum

110. Wax portrait of John Philip Elers modelled by William Hackwood in 1777 at the request of Elers's son (see p. 105 and Appendix H:II). On 19 July 1777 Josiah reported to Bentley: 'Mr Elers asks "if he could properly be indulged with about half a doz" more of the Portraits, for his friends are pretty numerous"? . . . He . . . seems disposed to write, & if I am not much mistaken to beg without ceasing' (E25–18772). Formerly author's collection

109A

109B

109C

110

Apotheosis of Homer, and it must be considered unlikely that a cast from an ivory carving, sent by More from London to Etruria, should have been sent back to London to Flaxman rather than 'repaired' by the most expert of repairers, William Hackwood, at Etruria. The wax in question does bear some resemblance in style to Hackwood's wax portrait of Elers (Plate 110), also nearly full-face and demonstrating the technical difficulties posed by such portraits. On the evidence available it seems probable that the British Museum wax was inscribed with Flaxman's name some time after it was modelled, perhaps in the hope that its value would be enhanced by the alteration.

Wax Models

The difference between original wax models for Wedgwood's portraits and reproductions from them is not always understood or recognised. A very large number of wax reproductions of Wedgwood portrait medallions exists. They are usually of poor quality, lacking undercutting, and cast from moulds taken from jasper or basaltes medallions. For this reason, they are approximately the same size as, or slightly smaller than, their Wedgwood counterparts. Genuine wax models, on the other hand, were required to be larger than the intended stoneware heads to allow for shrinkage in successive moulding and firing operations of about one-eighth. This rule applied to all bas-relief subjects.[118] Spurious waxes are often painted, presumably to disguise faults and inferior craftsmanship, and almost invariably they have been cast separately and fixed to their backgrounds (generally glass, painted on the reverse) with glue.

Flaxman's waxes were often modelled direct on to their grounds, which might be slate or glass, the wax being so thin in parts as to be transparent; Lochée, whose waxes were intended for commercial reproduction (in wax), supplied Wedgwood with moulds, but his first models, like Mountstephen's, were modelled direct on to their grounds of slate or glass, only the reproductions from casts being applied to grounds after the wax had hardened. The important distinction between original bas-relief work for reproduction in jasper – such as Flaxman's or Hackwood's – and work by modellers who intended to reproduce their own models in wax (Gosset, Lochée, Joachim Smith, Mountstephen) is that the wax models of the former are unique. In the latter case, there may be several surviving examples of each portrait. All models are larger than their stoneware reproductions by about one-seventh to one-eighth. No wax portrait that is the same size or smaller than Wedgwood's version of the same subject is likely to be an original model: it could only be so if it had

111. Greyish-white wax portrait of Captain James Cook, modelled by John Flaxman junior in 1784 (see Appendix H:1). Height of wax relief 4" (10.2 cm). Flaxman used a hard wax composition of his own, containing a high proportion of white lead, and modelled directly on to backgrounds of slate or glass painted a dark colour on the reverse. This portrait and other original models for Wedgwood by Flaxman, Hackwood, Lochée and Mountstephen (see Plates 83, 110, 112 and 113) were discovered, in very damaged condition, in London in 1972, and were carefully restored. At that time it was possible to examine Flaxman's wax composition in some detail.
Formerly author's collection

112. Greyish-white wax portrait of George, Prince of Wales, modelled by John Flaxman junior c.1783–4 (see Appendix H:1). Height of wax relief 4" (10.2 cm), modelled directly on to a glass ground painted black on the reverse. (Cf. Plates 83 and 111.)
Formerly author's collection

111

112

113. *Dark coral-pink wax portrait of Prince Charles von Ligne, modelled by John Charles Lochée (see Appendix H:I). This portrait was sent to Etruria in April 1787. Height of wax relief 3⅛" (8.0 cm). (See p. 127 and caption to Plate 111.)*
Formerly author's collection

114. *Pale-blue jasper dip small portrait medallion of Lord Thurlow (1731–1806) produced by Ralph Wedgwood, either at the Hill Top factory or at Ferrybridge, c.1796–1800. Oval height 1⅝" (4.1 cm). Mark:* Wedgwood & Co. *Lapidary-polished edge. This portrait is sometimes catalogued as 'William Penn', but is evidently from the same source as the Neale & Co. medallion of Lord Thurlow in black basaltes (see* Stonewares & Stone Chinas, *ed. T.A. Lockett and P.A. Halfpenny, City Museum & Art Gallery, Stoke-on-Trent, 1982, No. 89).*
Holburne of Menstrie Museum, Bath

115. *Sèvres blue and white biscuit porcelain portrait medallion of Henri IV in imitation of Wedgwood's jasper. Diameter 3½" (8.9 cm). Mark:* SEVRES *impressed on truncation; 'Mas' (? Jean or Louis Mascret) incised on reverse. c.1820.*
Victoria & Albert Museum, London

113

114

115

been remodelled in an enlarged version for production. Although the vast majority of waxes purporting to be original models are spurious, some original works have survived, and the recently published dogma that 'all wax models are merely wax casts (in some cases further remodelled)'[119] is demonstrably false.

TABLETS, PLAQUES AND MEDALLIONS*

The Wedgwood & Bentley Catalogue of 1774 lists ninety-three tablets, plaques and medallions ranging in size from 1¼ inches high, better described as cameos, to a pair of plaques, *Night* and *Day*, measuring 20 inches high by 14½ inches wide. Most of these were available either in black basaltes or the white biscuit body, some with encaustic-painted grounds or frames, and all at that date pressed in one piece and finished

*See Appendix J.

(undercut) while in the leather-hard state before firing. Jasper bas-reliefs in two colours posed a different problem, which Josiah solved by experiments on the smaller cameos and portrait medallions before embarking on trials with larger and costlier pieces.[*] As he wrote to Bentley on 6 August 1775: 'I am going upon a large scale with our Models &c which is one reason why you have so few new things just now, but I hope to bring the whole in compass for your next Winters shew & ASTONISH THE WORLD ALL AT ONCE, for I hate piddleing you know.'[120]

By 1777, when jasper pieces were included in the Catalogue for the first time, the number of medallions and plaques had been more than doubled, and by the end of the Wedgwood & Bentley period it had risen to at least 222.[†] The Ornamental Ware Catalogue of 1787 lists 275 in Class II ('Bas-reliefs, Medallions, Tablets &c'), including one rectangular tablet *Diana visiting Endymion* 27½ inches long and 8½ inches high. These are described in Appendix J:I with Wedgwood's notes, and added information based on recent research. Appendix J:II shows details of those uncatalogued bas-reliefs, principally subjects modelled in Rome between 1787 and 1790, which have been identified as having been first produced during Josiah's lifetime.

The jasper tablets were of special importance to Wedgwood & Bentley because they hoped, through the production of this new collection, to acquire a different market. It was no accident that the colours developed in jasper resembled so closely those made popular for interiors by Robert Adam and James Wyatt; and Bentley must have been even more aware than Wedgwood of the colossal sums exacted by fashionable architects from their patrons in the name of interior decoration. The 'contempt for money' that Mrs Montagu thought she discerned in 'Athenian'

[*]See p. 76.
[†]The exact number is not recorded, but 222 are listed in the 1779 Catalogue.

116. *Solid blue and white jasper oval plaque of* Feast of the Gods *(see Appendix J:I.4) after Guglielmo della Porta. Oval 6¼" × 9¼" (16 × 23.5 cm). Mark:* WEDGWOOD. c.1790. *The reverse is pierced with sixteen firing holes.* Brooklyn Museum, Emily Winthrop Miles Collection

116

117

118

119

117. *Pair of solid blue and white jasper oval plaques of* Silenus and Boys *and* Bacchanalian Boys at Play *after Duquesnoy (Fiammingo), probably from casts supplied by Mrs Landré in 1769 (see Appendix J:I.14 and 13). Oval 5½″ × 7½″ (14.0 × 19.0 cm). Mark:* WEDGWOOD & BENTLEY. *c.1778.* Dwight & Lucille Beeson Collection, Birmingham Museum, Alabama

118. *Solid blue and white jasper medallion of* Jupiter and Danaë. *Oval height 3¼″ (8.3 cm). Mark: Wedgwood & Bentley. c.1776. This subject is usually catalogued as 'Jupiter and Io', and Jupiter's disguise certainly appears more like a cloud than a shower of golden rain. Neither subject appears in the Ornamental Ware catalogues, but* Jupiter and Danaë *is one of two subjects thought by Bentley to be 'too warm' for his market in 1769, and Josiah's expressed admiration for the medallion may have induced him to make a few specimens of it in jasper. It is possible even that the subject omitted at no. 92 in Class II in the catalogues (see Appendix J:I) is* Jupiter and Danaë, *removed at Bentley's request.* Brooklyn Museum, Emily Winthrop Miles Collection

Stuart,[121] and which caused her to prefer him to Adam for the building of Montagu House about 1775, was rare, if not unique, among architects.

Wedgwood had supplied white terracotta biscuit and encaustic-painted basaltes tablets for chimneypieces as early as 1772,[*] and had written at the time: 'I suppose it is very much in Mr [Robert] Adams's [*sic*] power to introduce our things into use & am glad to find he seems so well dispos'd to do it – Sʳ John Wrottesley has promised me to introduce them into a Room he is furnishing – I told him the difficulties thrown in our way by the Architects, but he said they should not prevent his useing them.'[122]

Certainly Adam's decoration of such rooms as the Library (1770–1) and Drawing Room (1778) at Mellerstain in Berwickshire, the Dining Room (remodelled 1780–1) at Saltram in Devon, and the Etruscan Dressing Room (*c.*1775–6) at Osterley Park, Middlesex, might have seemed particularly suitable for the use of Wedgwood & Bentley plaques and tablets, but, although there is some indication that Adam may have

[*]Notably to Sir Watkin Williams Wynn for 20 St James's Square.

120

121

119. (Facing page) *Blue jasper dip circular plaque of* Marsyas and Young Olympus *(see Appendix J:I.61). Diameter 11 ¼" (28.5 cm). Mark:* WEDGWOOD. *c.1790–5. The blue dip, applied too thinly, allows the white jasper ground to show through it in parts, but the beautiful undercutting, illustrated by the shadows shed by both heads, the right index finger of Marsyas and Olympus's left arm, is typical of the best of eighteenth-century work.* Dwight & Lucille Beeson Collection, Birmingham Museum, Alabama

120. Solid blue and white jasper circular plaque of a Bacchanalian Figure *(see Appendix J:I.64–5). Diameter 12" (30.5 cm). Mark:* WEDGWOOD. *c.1790. The depth of relief and quality of undercutting are shown in the shadows behind the figure's foot and right arm.* Dwight & Lucille Beeson Collection, Birmingham Museum, Alabama

121. Green jasper dip circular plaque of a Centaur *(see Appendix J:I.57–9). Diameter 15⅞" (40.3 cm) in self frame. Mark:* WEDGWOOD. *c.1790. The reverse is pierced with six large and seven smaller firing holes. This subject is known also as* Centaur and Bacchante *or* Nessus and Deianeira, *both titles more informative than Wedgwood's.* Dwight & Lucille Beeson Collection, Birmingham Museum, Alabama

used unglazed enamelled biscuit plaques in 1772,[123] and he left a number of designs for chimneypieces* incorporating Wedgwood & Bentley encaustic-painted tablets, there is little evidence that he regarded jasper with favour. It appears to have been Josiah, rather than Robert Adam, who persuaded Lord Scarsdale to insert an oval jasper tablet into a chimneypiece originally designed with a plain rectangular marble centre.[124]

It was, no doubt, also at Josiah's request that his loyal patron Sir William Bagot 'sent his three pieces to Mr Wyat to be put into his (S^r W^ms) chimneypiece'.[125] Wyatt showed no enthusiasm for Wedgwood & Bentley's tablets, for the decoration of rooms or chimneypieces, and the attitude of Sir William Chambers was no more helpful. To Wedgwood's chagrin, the Queen, who visited the Greek Street showrooms in June 1779, did not order any tablets for her palaces. 'I am still persuaded', Josiah wrote to Bentley, 'the jasper tablets & pictures must sell, maugre all the good offices of our friends the architects, which I am sorry to find you have had a recent proof of in their persuading her majesty that our tablets were not fit for chimneypieces.'[126] Next month he added: 'If Sr Wm Chambers was as limited in his power over the *jasper tablets* as he is in the *Pearl White* we should have nothing to fear from him in that respect.'[127] It does not appear to have been only Wyatt and Chambers who failed to recommend the jasper tablets to their clients. 'We were', Josiah wrote, 'really unfortunate in the introduction of our jaspers into public notice, that we could not prevail upon the architects to be godfathers to our child. Instead of taking it by the hand & giving it their benediction, they cursed the poor infant by bell, book & candle, & it must have a hard struggle to support itself, & rise from under their maledictions.'[128] James Stuart was – at least for Mrs Montagu's house – an exception. Josiah wrote to congratulate Bentley on 'the conversion of the Athenian', trusting that it might lead to 'a more abundant harvest'.[129] His earlier hope that 'Jews, & Infidels & architects' were to be 'converted to the true belief – in our tablets'[130] was dashed; at least in respect of architects.

*Now in the Soane Museum, London.

122. *Solid blue and white jasper medallion of* Night *(see Appendix J:I.77), known also as* Venus and Cupid, Night shedding Poppies *and* Ceres and Triptolemus. *The original model is attributed to John Bacon senior. Oval height 6½" (16.6 cm). Mark:* WEDGWOOD & BENTLEY. *c.1777.* Wedgwood Museum

123. *Solid blue and white jasper medallion of* Day *(see Appendix J:I.78). Oval height 6½" (16.6 cm). Mark:* WEDGWOOD & BENTLEY. *c.1777. The pair to the medallion illustrated in Plate 122. Sometimes identified as the* Muse Erato. Wedgwood Museum

124. *Solid blue and white jasper medallion of* Hercules Farnese *(see Appendix J:I.157). Oval height 7¼" (18.2 cm). Mark:* WEDGWOOD & BENTLEY. *c.1777. The figure is derived from the Graeco-Roman statue in the Louvre, itself a fairly faithful replica of* Heracles at Rest *by Lysippus.* Wedgwood Museum

125. *Solid blue and white jasper medallion, the subject unidentified but probably* Sacrificing Figure *(see Appendix J:I.158), which is described on the 'Arbury' list (no. 5) as 'A male figure wearing only a cloak over the shoulder'. Oval 5⅞" × 4¼" (15.2 × 10.8 cm). Mark:* Wedgwood & Bentley. *c.1777. (Cf. Plate C25.)* Metropolitan Museum of Art, New York, Rogers Fund, 1914

122   123

124   125

The setback was temporary, but as Alison Kelly has pointed out,[131] it lasted until after Bentley's death, and the scarcity of references to tablets in the Wedgwood & Bentley letters between July 1779 and December 1780 has led to a general belief that they were permanently a costly failure. On the contrary, records of more than 115 suites of tablets and plaques for chimneypieces – all comprising bas-reliefs for tablets, friezes* and blocks (making up the entablature), and some the additional jambs† – have been located by Miss Kelly,[132] and it is evident that this figure gives a far from complete picture of Wedgwood production of these sets. Nor does it appear to be correct, as Miss Meteyard has stated,[133] that those suites of tablets sold in the Christie & Ansell‡ auction of 1781 were disposed of at substantial discounts from prices currently charged at the London showrooms.

*Usually the horizontal band of sculpture filling the space between the architrave and the cornice. On chimneypieces, friezes are long rectangular tablets positioned in the entablature between the centre tablet and the blocks at each end, or a composition of ovals to fill the same space.
†Upright tablets for the sides.
‡Now Christie Manson & Wood Ltd, King Street, London.

Tablets, plaques and medallions were not produced only for the decoration of chimneypieces. Listed by subject in Class II of the 1779 Catalogue, they are described as available either in 'the *black Basaltes*, which has the Appearance of antique Bronze, or in the blue *and white Jasper*'* and suitable for application as 'Cabinet Pictures, or ornamenting Cabinets, Book-Cases, Writing-Tables &c'. 'Cabinet Pictures' or, as they were also called, 'large Cameo-Pictures' were, to judge by the invoices of the period and the quantity sold in the 1781 auction sale, a useful part of the business. It is significant that no mention is made under Class II of the 1779 Catalogue of any jasper colour but blue, and marked Wedgwood & Bentley tablets or plaques of any other colour are extremely rare. Jasper 'Pictures' could be supplied in frames of gilded metal or wood, or occasionally, and in spite of Josiah's reservations about them, with moulded jasper frames of contrasting colours (usually black or white).

If the disapproval of the architects had been as influential as some writers have suggested,[134] and the production of jasper tablets and plaques the failure that is assumed to have resulted from criticism, it is unlikely that Josiah would have persevered in their production. It is even less probable, under such circumstances, that he would have indulged in the expense of commissioning tablets from Flaxman and Stubbs, or of setting up his own studio of artists in Rome specifically to model bas-reliefs from the antique. In fact, it is clear that some, at least, of the architects were won over to the use of jasper tablets and plaques in their designs for decoration. Both Wyatt and Henry Holland are thought to have bought suites of plaques for chimneypieces in the 1781 sale,[135] and invoices for 1784–7 show that Wyatt ordered five groups of plaques of sizes large enough to be suitable for interiors.[136] A far more important customer for large plaques appears to have been found, through orders probably placed indirectly by the architect Charles Cameron, in the Empress Catherine of Russia. The evidence that several rooms in the extension of the palace at Tsarskoe Selo, three suites of which were designed by Cameron, were

*A further note adds that they are available also in the cheaper terracotta.

126. *Rare green jasper dip head of Ceres, probably the head catalogued as Summer (Appendix J:I.115), one of four heads of the Seasons invoiced by Flaxman in 1777. Diameter 7¾" (19.1 cm). Mark: WEDGWOOD. c.1785. Wedgwood's Ornamental Ware catalogues list the dimensions as 10" × 8", indicating that the subject was produced on a rectangular or oval ground. Manchester Museum*

126A. *Reverse of the circular plaque in Plate 126 showing the arrangement of large firing holes behind the head. This particular plaque, from the Jesse Haworth Collection, was illustrated by Eliza Meteyard (Choice Examples of Wedgwood Art, 1879, Frontispiece) and erroneously described as marked 'Wedgwood & Bentley'.*

126B. *Black-painted plaster of the head of Ceres (Plate 126) on a circular ground. Diameter 9⅛" (23.0 cm). Unmarked. Apparently the original plaster cast supplied to Etruria as a model. Wedgwood Museum*

126

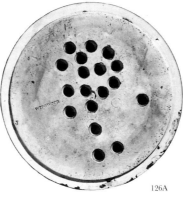
126A

126B

127. *White jasper portrait medallion of Mark Antony, attributed to Hackwood (see Appendix G, Class V, and cf. Plate 66). Oval height 7" (17.8 cm). Mark: Wedgwood & Bentley. c.1778.*
Kadison Collection

128. *Superb 'solid' white jasper plaque of* The Gladiators. *10½" × 11½" (26.5 × 29.0 cm). Mark: Wedgwood & Bentley. c.1778. The plaque is of outstanding quality, semi-translucent and pierced at the back with six firing holes. Unlike most of Wedgwood's plaques and medallions of this period, this piece was press-moulded in one piece and undercut instead of being ornamented with sprigged reliefs.*
Kadison Collection

decorated with jasper plaques of unusually large size, comes from photographs and the accounts of visitors to the palace, which was totally destroyed during the 1939–45 War. Documentary evidence has not yet come to light, but there is good reason to believe that some of the plaques required may have been obtained from the 1781 auction sale.[137]

Part of the objection to the use of Wedgwood & Bentley's plaques for interior decoration was due to the colours of the grounds. Josiah's friend and patron, Lord Gower, and the architect 'Capability' Brown had both disliked the blue and green grounds, preferring some closer imitation of a natural stone, or a plain white.* The latter choice was probably based on the then common misapprehension that classical sculpture was uncoloured. A few plaques of the white jasper, or 'fine white porcelain' with a 'glossy' surface, have survived, and it is not difficult to understand Brown's preference (Plates 127 and 128).

More encouragement came from old friends, and particularly at this early stage in the development of decorative jasper from Sir William Bagot of Blithfield, Staffordshire. Wedgwood described to Bentley his visit there to view a chimneypiece:

Sr Williams new room is hung round with Correggios, Raphaels, Guerchinos, Bassan[o]s & many more masters. . . . Amongst other great works of art S^r W^m particularly pointed out the chimney piece to my attention, assuring me at the same time that he esteemed it the best piece in his room. . . . You know the pieces in Homer & Hesiod for the tablet, & the Muses for the frise. . . . In looking at the tablet I was lamenting a little chip off the edge, which misfortune I suppose had befalen it in the hands of the workmen. Misfortune you call it

*See above, p. 86.

says S^r W^m? We esteem it a very happy accident. It shows the merit — the fine texture of the composition which might otherwise have pass'd for a painted surface.[138]

The 'Homer & Hesiod' to which Josiah referred was a new tablet (Plate 129), modelled by John Flaxman.[139] The source of the design was an engraving illustrated by d'Hancarville[140] of a scene from a bell krater in the Hamilton collection.* The subject, also known as 'A Victorious Citharist', was interpreted by Bentley as 'some Honour paid to the Genius of Homer';[141] and Sir William Hamilton, to whom Wedgwood had presented one of the tablets, went some way towards bestowing a new title upon the composition in his acknowledgement from Naples on 22

*Sold to the British Museum in 1772.

129

130

129. Solid pale-blue and white jasper tablet of Flaxman's Apotheosis of Homer *('A Victorious Citharist'), modelled in 1778 (see Appendix J:I.265). 7⅝" × 14½" (19.3 × 36.5 cm). Mark:* WEDGWOOD & BENTLEY. c.1779. *This tablet was mentioned by Josiah in his letter of 19 August 1778 (E25–18845) in which he listed to Bentley the tablets he was preparing 'for next winters show'. These included the cryptically described 'Etruscan, with Homer &c'. The source was a calyx krater in the British Museum (Hamilton Collection). Flaxman may have worked from the vase, painted in the style of the Peleus painter, c.440 BC, or from the engraving published by d'Hancarville (see Plate 130), and he made only slight alterations — most obviously in the provision of a chair for the seated figure on the left — to the original composition.* Wedgwood Museum

130. The Apotheosis of Homer *or* A Victorious Citharist, *Plate 31 from Volume III of P.F. d'Hancarville's* Collection of Etruscan, Greek and Roman Antiquities from the Cabinet of the Honble William Hamilton, *1767.* Photograph: Wedgwood

131. *White Carrara marble chimneypiece set with green and white jasper (probably dip) tablets of trophies, acanthus scrolls and Flaxman's* Apotheosis of Homer, *with circular medallions of Flaxman's* Medusa *in the blocks (above the jambs at the outer ends of the entablature). Chimneypiece 54¾" × 83½" (139 × 211.5 cm); length of tablets (Acanthus) 17½" (44.2 cm), (Apotheosis) 17" (43.0 cm). No visible marks. The chimneypiece was made for the Master of the Dublin Mint, c.1785.* Lady Lever Art Gallery, Port Sunlight

131

June 1779: 'I have the pleasure of receiving safe your Delightful Basrelief of the Apotheose of Homer, or some celebrated Poet indeed it is far super/ior to my most sanguine expectation.'[142] The choice of this subject was, no doubt, influenced from the first by its identification with Homer, vener/ated by scholars and travellers of the eighteenth century as the personifica/tion of all that was noble, and the supreme genius of the ancient world.

Josiah listed the tablet among those he was preparing for the winter show in 1778, but told Bentley he had made only two and would 'wait for orders'.[143] About seven years later, Flaxman designed and modelled a companion plaque *The Apotheosis of Virgil*,[144] and both bas/reliefs were later adapted to vases.*

Next in importance among Flaxman's bas/reliefs for Wedgwood is his model of *Hercules in the Garden of the Hesperides*. This was first men/tioned in his letter of 20 October 1785, in which he made it clear that he was working from a print.[145] This was certainly from d'Hancarville's sec/ond volume,[146] an engraving copied from the painting on a fifth/century red/figure hydria by the Meidias Painter, also the source of decoration on Wedgwood & Bentley's First Day's Vases of 1769.† Flaxman's practical knowledge of the jasper body is confirmed by his statement that he had modelled his bas/relief figures '5 Inches & ⅜^{ins} which allows one seventh for shrinking in the Bisque'.

In December he wrote again on the subject:

I shall take great pleasure in modelling Hercules in the Hesperian Garden & I think I can make it equal to Sr Wm Hamilton's Murrhin Vase if you are willing I should do my utmost but then I cannot set an exact price on it until it is finished. I should also be particularly

*See pp. 196–8 and Plates 262–4 and C49.
†See Plate 10.

obliged to you for instructions respecting the thickness – if it might be done as thin as the work on the before-mentioned Vase it would be the more perfect & the blue ground might shew thro' the thin parts of the drapery, which several Artists & other Persons of taste have remarked to me is a great advantage where it can be done.[147]

The bas-relief seems to have taken even longer to complete than Flaxman anticipated, for it was not invoiced to Wedgwood until August 1787, when it was priced at £23.0.0.[148]

Flaxman's allusion to Hamilton's 'Murrhin* Vase' was a reference to the 'Barberini' cameo-glass vase which had been purchased from him by the Duke of Portland the previous year.[†] Flaxman's preference for the transparent effect produced by thin modelling has already been noticed in his portrait medallions,[‡] but it made the application of sprigged ornament particularly difficult.

Of all Flaxman's work for Wedgwood, probably the most popular is the *Dancing Hours* bas-relief (Plates 132A–B) first mentioned in 1778 as 'intended as frises to the marr[iag]ᵉ of Cupid &c'. 'I have', Josiah added, 'made frises of Apollo & the muses to accompany the new tablet of Homer &c.'[149] No direct evidence has been found to prove Flaxman's responsibility for this exceptionally fine ornament, but long tradition is supported in this case by the fluid grace of the figures and confident free-dom of the modelling, the date at which it made its first appearance, and its association in Josiah's quoted letter with authenticated examples of Flaxman's skill. The source from which the design was adapted was either two engravings by Bartoli in his *Admiranda Romanorum*

---

*'Precious' (often of glass); made of murra.
[†]See pp. 215–36.
[‡]See p. 117.

132A

132B

132A–B. Pair of solid grey–blue jasper tablets, the grounds washed with a very slightly darker blue and ornamented with white jasper figures of the Dancing Hours, *attributed to John Flaxman junior, 1778 (see Appendix J:I.205). Each 5⅝″ × 18″ (14.3 × 45.7 cm). Mark:* WEDGWOOD & BENTLEY. c.1778. Wedgwood Museum

133. Greyish-white wax group of boys playing Blind-man's Buff, modelled on a slate ground by John Flaxman junior in 1782 'to decorate the sides of teapots' (see Appendix J:I.255). 4" × 14¾" (10.2 × 37.5 cm). Unmarked. c.1782. Comparison of this original model with the jasper reproductions shows that considerable alterations to Flaxman's figures were made in the cutting of the block mould, tidying the hair and changing the expressions on the faces, resulting in some loss of freedom in the modelling (cf. Plates 133A and C54). Wedgwood Museum

133A. Green jasper dip tablet of Blind-man's Buff *by Flaxman. The original composition has been extended and the groups separated to ornament a larger tablet, and the figures set above a rather clumsy white jasper 'ledge', the whole arrangement being fairly typical of mid-nineteenth-century disharmony. 6¼" × 18" (15.8 × 45.7 cm). Mark:* WEDGWOOD. c.1860. *(Cf. Plate C54.)* Dwight & Lucille Beeson Collection, Birmingham Museum, Alabama

134. Large grey–blue jasper with blue jasper dip medallion of the Marriage of Cupid and Psyche. *Oval 11" × 16¼" (29 × 41.0 cm). Mark:* WEDGWOOD & BENTLEY. c.1778–80. Manchester Museum

Antiquitatum,[150] in which similar figures described as 'Nuptiales Choreae' dance before an open colonnade, or a chimneypiece of marble and lapis lazuli installed by Sir Laurence Dundas, one of Wedgwood's patrons, in his house, Moor Park, in Hertfordshire. The chimneypiece, from the Borghese Collection (now in the Lady Lever Gallery, Port Sunlight), incorporates figures, 'Dancing Maenads', copied from a Graeco-Roman marble relief of the first century then in the same collection and now in the Louvre as *Les Danseuses Borgheses.*[151]

133

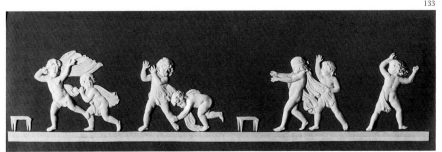

133A

134

135A

135B

135. Pair of solid grey–blue and white jasper medallions of
Marriage of Cupid and Psyche *and* Sacrifice to Hymen.
Oval length 3½" (8.9 cm). Mark: WEDGWOOD &
BENTLEY. *c.1777. The first of Wedgwood's copies of the
famous 'Marlborough gem', a sardonyx cameo of about the first
century AD by Tryphon, was made in 1771, possibly from a
cast supplied by Mrs Landré, though this is not clear (LHP 13
January 1771). A second version, evidently far larger than the
small medallion, 'the Copy from the D of M' Gem', and
modelled or cast from an ivory carving, is mentioned on 4
December 1774 (E25–18571). Neither of these is a close copy
of the gem: in the first, the amorino on the right lacks one
wing; and, in both, the original modelling of the bodies has been
lost, the legs of the bed or couch have been altered from round to
tapered square, the groundwork has been altered, and a number
of smaller changes have been made. Dr Lloyd Hawes was the
first to point out that all of these features occur in an engraving
by Theodorus Netscher published in P. de Stosch,* Pierres
Antiques Gravées, *1724, Plate LXX, a book listed seventh
in 'Books belonging to W&B the 10th of Aug' 1770' (Lloyd
Hawes, 'Nuptiae Cupidinis et Psyches' in* The American
Wedgwoodian, *Vol. I, No. 2, New York, January 1963;
Ms. 55–31201). A third, small and accurate version was copied
closely from a Tassie gem, itself a slightly amended copy of the
Marlborough cameo. Wedgwood's catalogue description (see
Appendix J:I.30) is not therefore strictly accurate.*

The Sacrifice to Hymen *medallion was modelled in time
to be included in the 1777 Catalogue, and has been regularly
assigned to Flaxman, but without supporting evidence. The
attribution appears to rest on the authority of Eliza Meteyard,
who credits Flaxman with this subject, and the best of the*
Marriage of Cupid and Psyche *medallions (Memorials
of Wedgwood, 1874, p. 168; Choice Examples of
Wedgwood Art, 1879, pp. 220 and 242, and Plates II and
XIII; Wedgwood Handbook, 1875, pp. 137 and 145); but
the evidence to which she refers is wrongly quoted in her Life of
Josiah Wedgwood, Vol. II, p. 485. Flaxman's invoice for 7
March–20 March 1781 (Ms. 1–205), of which there is a copy
or statement dated 26 May 1781 (Ms. 2–1330), was not for
'Cupid & Psyche' as stated by Meteyard, but for 'Two figures
of Cupid & Psyche', and the bill is receipted by John Flaxman
senior, probably indicating that the figures were plaster casts
rather than original work. Nevertheless, in spite of the lack of
manuscript evidence, the superiority of the modelling of the
largest plaques of this subject makes any other attribution less
satisfactory. If the finest plaques were modelled by Flaxman, he
must have completed them by 1780 at the latest, for several
examples of the highest quality are impressed with the
Wedgwood & Bentley mark (Plates 135 and 136; and cf.
Plate C20).*
British Museum

136. Solid grey–blue and white jasper medallion of the Marriage of Cupid and Psyche *with wash, or dip, of very slightly darker jasper on the upper surface, disguising the use of a coarser body for the tablet. Oval length 3¼"(8.2 cm). Mark:* WEDGWOOD & BENTLEY. *c.1778. The shadows cast by the figures and basket of fruit show the depth of the relief and the quality of undercutting.* British Museum

136A. *Reverse of the medallion illustrated in Plate 136, showing the arrangement of firing holes pierced beneath the relief, and the coarser jasper body undisguised by the wash of finer jasper applied to the front.*

136

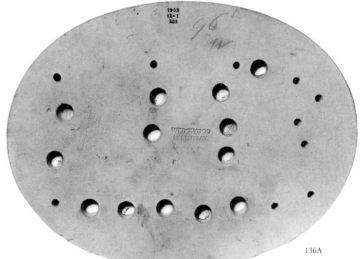

136A

137. *Berlin white stoneware medallion with deep blue ground, ornamented with the figures of Cupid and Psyche with an attendant amorino, from the Marriage of Cupid and Psyche. Oval 3⅞" × 3¼" (9.8 × 8.2 cm). Inscribed on reverse: 'No: Jx dx Berlin der 24 ⚹ Maey 1789 F G Kranich 14'. c.1789. This version of the subject follows very closely the remodelled Wedgwood edition (Plates 135 and 136), including the scattered lichen on the rocky groundwork, and was probably copied from it.* British Museum

137

The 'frises of Apollo & the muses to accompany the new tablet of Homer' in 1778 were also, at least in part, the work of Flaxman, but proof of their origin is not a simple matter. Some confusion arises from the fact that Wedgwood already owned a series of figures of Muses by Edmé Bouchardon; but he had some doubts about using them. 'They are not sufficiently finish'd for an unlearned modeler to copy,' he told Bentley.[152] He would have put Hackwood to work on them if he had not been already fully employed, although Josiah thought them probably poor copies of Bouchardon's original models.

Wedgwood had also an incomplete set in plaster, comprising Melpomene, Thalia, Terpsichore and Euterpe, with the companion figure of Apollo, which he had bought from John Flaxman senior in March 1775 for half a guinea each.[153] The bill for these was receipted by the younger Flaxman for his father, and it has been suggested that these 'are likely to be the earliest ceramic works' attributable to John Flaxman junior.[154] On 27 October 1777 Josiah wrote to Bentley: 'You may permit Mr Flaxman to proceed with the Muses of the size he had begun, they will be very useful to us. . . . we have Apollo, Melpomena [sic], Thalia & Terpsichore, so that we only want 6 more to complete our suite.'[155] From this it appears that the figure of Euterpe bought previously was either lost, mislaid or not identified among the stock of models. The last explanation seems most likely, for only two days later Josiah countermanded the order: 'Having laid all our bass-relief Goddesses & ladies upon their backs. . . . I instantly perciev'd that the Six Muses we want might be produc'd from this lovely group at half the trouble & expence they will be procur'd from Flaxman – & much better figures. For little more than 5/- each we can complete them very well. I hope you may not have order'd them to be model'd as I desir'd you would, but if you have, so be it, – it is only so much loss.'[156] Opinion is divided whether the order was rescinded in time or Flaxman completed the set.[157]

The attribution of models of the Muses to particular modellers is further complicated by the knowledge that Giuseppe Angelini (1742–1811) was paid for a set of models of the nine Muses in 1789.[158] This set, however, was probably copied direct and complete from the Sarcophagus of the Muses, then in the Capitoline Museum, Rome, and now in the

Jasper, 1774–1795

138. White jasper tablet of five figures of the Muses (Terpsichore, Melpomene, Calliope, Thalia and Urania) attributed to John Flaxman junior. 4⅞" × 6½" (12.4 × 16.4 cm). Mark: WEDGWOOD & BENTLEY. c.1778. Josiah wrote to Bentley on 13 November 1778 (E25–18861): 'I cannot resist the temptation of sending my dear friend a few things by the coach out of the last oven. The set of Muses in white Jasper are delicate to a degree. That is, to an extreme degree, & may serve as a specimen of what you may expect from us in white.' Wedgwood Museum

138

141

139

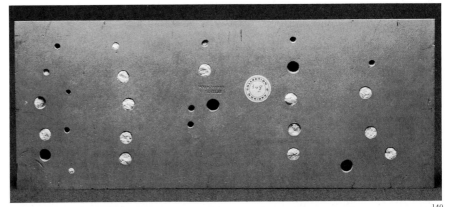

140

141

139. Solid blue and white jasper tablet of the Nine Muses *(Appendix J:I.203) attributed to John Flaxman junior.* 6½" × 25¼" *(16.4 × 64.2 cm).* Mark: WEDGWOOD & BENTLEY. c.1778–80. Brooklyn Museum, Emily Winthrop Miles Collection

140. Reverse of blue jasper dip tablet of Apollo and four of the Muses (Plate C21), showing the arrangement of sixteen large and eleven smaller firing holes, some of them filled with plaster from their being set into a chimneypiece. 6⅛" × 15¾" *(15.5 × 40.0 cm).* Mark: WEDGWOOD & BENTLEY. Kadison Collection

141. Four pale-blue and white jasper medallions with darker-blue jasper dip: (left to right) A Priestess *(Appendix J:I.167);* Euterpe, *attributed to Flaxman (cf. Plate 139);* Calliope, *attributed to Flaxman (cf. Plate 139);* Artemisia *(Appendix J:I.144). Ovals* 6⅛" × 4½" *(15.5 × 11.5 cm).* Mark: (all) WEDGWOOD & BENTLEY. 1775–80. Kadison Collection

Louvre. This marble funerary monument was already well known from the reproduction in Montfaucon's *L'Antiquité expliquée*[159] and was copied for part of the plasterwork decoration for the Library at Mellerstain, Berwickshire, when the room was designed for George Baillie by Robert Adam in 1778.

Fortunately, at least two sets of the Muses with Apollo Musagetes survive impressed with the WEDGWOOD & BENTLEY mark (Plates 139, C21 and C22). This rules out the possibility that any of the figures was modelled by Angelini, and only one, that of Polymnia, is an adaptation from the Sarcophagus of the Muses. Those of Erato and Urania were obviously modelled or chosen specially as 'end-pieces' to the composition.[160] The figures of Clio and Thalia are not, as has been stated, 'from the *Dancing Hours*' group,[161] though the similarity of style suggests the same source, if not the same modeller. Although the possibility that the group is a composition of the work of more than one modeller cannot be disregarded, none of the figures is inconsistent in style with Flaxman's work and it is generally accepted that all are his. Of the rest, those later figures which are reproductions from the Sarcophagus of the Muses may be assigned with some confidence to Angelini, leaving one or two – perhaps the best of the Bouchardon models, 'mended' by Hackwood – unattributed.

Flaxman's work for Wedgwood was so important, in quantity[*] as well as quality, that there has been a tendency to attribute to him all the finest bas-reliefs to the exclusion of less celebrated modellers. An exception has always been made, however, for George Stubbs, whose two bas-reliefs are too well documented to permit misappropriation. On 13 August 1780 Josiah first mentioned that Stubbs was to model a bas-relief. 'He has', Josiah wrote in some irritation, 'fixed upon his subject for modeling, the *lion & horse* from his own engraving.[162] He objected to every other subject so I gave it up, & he is now laying in the horse while I am writing a few letters this good Sunday morning.' Forgivingly, he added, 'He does very well so far, & with a little practice will probably be as much master of his modeling tools, as he is of his pencils.'[163] Only eight days later the tablet was finished, and Josiah promised to send Bentley a copy 'either in blue & white, or to save time, in one colour'.[164] A mould in the Wedgwood archives indicates that the original model included background details which are not found even upon the earliest models, perhaps because they were too thinly modelled for satisfactory reproduction as applied reliefs.[165]

[*]See Appendices H and J.

142. Solid pale-blue and white jasper medallion of Apollo Musagetes, sometimes attributed to Flaxman and probably the model supplied to Wedgwood by John Flaxman senior in 1775 (Appendix J:I.100). Oval 3⅛" × 3⅛" (9.9 × 8 cm). Mark: WEDGWOOD & BENTLEY. c.1776. *This figure is occasionally to be found as the principal ornament to a variegated vase. The ground shows some unevenness and slight blistering, sure indications of early solid blue jasper.* Wedgwood Museum

143. Solid blue and white jasper medallion of Apollo Musagetes. Oval 3⅛" × 3⅛" (9.9 × 8 cm). Mark: WEDGWOOD & BENTLEY. c.1775. *This figure appears as the principal ornament on variegated, basaltes and jasper vases. It is probably the model catalogued from 1773 on (Appendix J:I.44). The ground of the medallion (to the right of the figure) is impressed with a large letter 'B', thought to indicate that this was a trial or a reference piece.* Wedgwood Museum

Stubbs's second tablet, also his own choice of subject, was *The Fall of Phaeton* (Plate 144). Josiah wrote to Bentley on 28 October 1780:

> He [Stubbs] sleeps with us & wishes to employ some of his evenings in modeling a companion to his frighten'd horse, & has fixed upon one of his Phaetons for that purpose but cannot proceed till he has the print of this subject which he says may be had at some of the print shops, but he does not know which. There are two prints of Phaetons, in that which he would have the two *nearest* horses are fighting,[166] & in that which he would not have the middlemost, or farthest are fighting. . . . I have objected to this subject as companion to the frightened horse as that is a piece of natural history, this is a piece of un-natural fiction, & indeed I shou'd prefer something less hackney'd & shall still endeavour to convert him.[167]

On 12 November Josiah reported that the model of Phaeton was 'in some forwardness' and that Stubbs was working hard at it 'every night almost 'till bedtime'.[168] This superb tablet was probably never seen by Bentley, for he died two weeks later.

144. Solid blue and white jasper tablet, The Fall of Phaeton, *modelled by George Stubbs in 1780. 10½" × 19⅜" (26.6 × 49.0 cm). Mark:* WEDGWOOD *(twice). c.1785.* Lady Lever Art Gallery, Port Sunlight

145. Grey–blue and white jasper with darker-blue jasper dip tablet of An Offering to Flora. *8¼" × 19" (21.0 × 48.0 cm). Mark:* WEDGWOOD & BENTLEY. *c.1778. Josiah wrote to Bentley in September (?) 1778: 'The tablet Sʳ L. Dundass has boᵗ is a sacrifice [sic] to Flora which you have not yet seen. It is the largest we have yet made' (E25–18847 n.d.). The size of this tablet is precisely that of the tablet catalogued in 1779 (Appendix J:I.199).* Manchester Museum

144

145

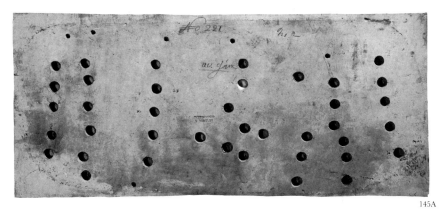

145A

146

145A. Reverse of the tablet, An Offering to Flora *(Plate 145), showing the pattern of thirty-nine large and six small firing holes, the largest being ½″ (1.27 cm). The thickness of the tablet is ⅜″ (0.95 cm).*

146. Solid blue and white jasper oval plaque, the subject uncertainly identified as Diomedes gazing at the Palladium. *Height 8″ (20.4 cm). Mark:* WEDGWOOD & BENTLEY. *c.1776. No subject of this name appears in the Wedgwood catalogues.* Diomedes carrying away the Palladium *and* Diomedes carrying off the Palladium *are listed from 1773 and 1777 respectively (Appendix J:I.34 and 169), but both are much smaller and are identifiable with a gem by Dioscorides (see Eliza Meteyard,* Memorials of Wedgwood, *1874, Plate VI and Carol Macht,* Classical Wedgwood Designs, *1957, Plate 19). Although it seems unlikely that so fine a model should have been omitted from the catalogues, no listed subject appears to resemble it in size and description.* Wedgwood Museum

William Hackwood's work on bas-reliefs is less clearly documented, and there is little that can be assigned to him with certainty. Two large groups only – *Birth of Bacchus* and *Triumph of Bacchus* (Plates C25, 147 and 148) – are mentioned in Josiah's letters to Bentley, both on 6 January 1776: 'Hackwood has nearly finish'd the two Tablets of the birth & Triumph of Bacchus, but I am afraid we shall not be able to make either of them in one continued Tablet. . . . We could make them fill a Frize very cleverly in separate pieces.'[169] Later this difficulty was overcome, for Josiah wrote on 21 February: 'The Birth of Bacchus, & 6 Figures in his Suite will at once shew you the state of Hackwood's Modeling, & the largest piece of Jasper we have yet made. We have now in the Oven a larger Piece – The Triumph of Bacchus – but this will not reach you in time to offer your vows to the Chinese Deity, the Protector of Porcelain, for its safety. Part of the 6 single Figures belong to the Triumph, but I hope you will dispose of them in many ways.'[170] This is the earliest reference to a practice which became common at Etruria: that of making medallions of single figures taken from a larger composition.

147. *Solid pale-blue and white jasper plaque,* Triumph of Bacchus, *modelled by William Hackwood in 1776 (Appendix J:I.201). Oval 7⅛" × 9⅝" (19.4 × 24.5 cm). Mark:* Wedgwood & Bentley *incised in script c.1776. Josiah wrote to Bentley on 6 January 1776: 'Hackwood has nearly finish'd the two Tablets of the birth & Triumph of Bacchus, but I am afraid we shall not be able to make either of them in one continued Tablet. . . . We could make them to fill a Frize* [sic, *of a chimneypiece] very cleverly in separate pieces,' and he included two sketches showing the figures separately arranged or as two tall ovals on either side of a larger (long) oval (E25–18641).* Dwight & Lucille Beeson Collection, Birmingham Museum, Alabama

147

148

148. *Blue jasper dip tablet,* Triumph of Bacchus, *modelled by William Hackwood in 1776 (Appendix J:I.201). 6⅜" × 12⅛" (16.2 × 31.0 cm). Mark:* WEDGWOOD & BENTLEY. *c.1778. This tablet illustrates Wedgwood's practice of making up the subjects of larger plaques and tablets from different sources. The principal group of Bacchus in his car accompanied by Silenus (Plate 147), which forms a satisfying composition by itself, has been augmented, without any artistic improvement, by two single figures: the first, a Bacchanalian figure with one hand raised above his head, is a sadly prettified version of a figure in B. de Montfaucon,* L'Antiquité expliquée et representée en figures, *1719, Vol. III, Pt 2, Plate CXXXIV; the second, a naked boy blowing a horn, is modelled in a more vigorous style and is evidently from a third, so far unidentified, source. Both appear as single figures on medallions of the same period.* Wedgwood Museum

149. *Grey–blue and white jasper with darker-blue jasper dip medallion of a 'Boy blowing a Horn'. Oval 5⅞" × 4¾" (14.9 × 11.1 cm). Mark:* WEDGWOOD & BENTLEY. *c.1778. This figure, one of two used to enlarge Hackwood's* Triumph of Bacchus *for use as a tablet at the centre of a chimneypiece entablature (Plate 148), does not appear in the catalogues of ornamental ware.* Dwight & Lucille Beeson Collection, Birmingham Museum, Alabama

149

146

150

150. Grey–blue and white jasper with slightly darker-blue jasper dip tablet, Sacrifice to Bacchus *(Appendix J:I.200). 8″ × 19⅜″ (20.2 × 49 cm). Mark:* WEDGWOOD & BENTLEY. *c.1778. This subject shows every sign of being a composition from several different sources. Although previously attributed to Flaxman, it seems more likely, from the disparity of the styles of the figures and the modelling, to be the work of Hackwood.* Manchester Museum

The *Birth of Bacchus* was, as Dr Carol Macht has shown,[171] inspired by an antique Parian marble vase signed by the Athenian sculptor Salpion. The composition, evidently adapted from more than one source, is well modelled but lacks cohesion, and the single figures are more effect-ive as separate medallions (e.g. Plate 125). The same defect is less obvious in the second group (Plates 147 and 148), in which the left hand figure, adapted from Montfaucon[172] and prettified on the way, is out of character with the rest. *The Judgement of Hercules* (Plate 151), said to have been mod-elled by Hackwood in 1777, is more satisfying: the quality of the model-ling is excellent, and the design was evidently conceived as a whole.

Little, if any, of Hackwood's work for tablets and plaques was origi-nal. His special talent was for remodelling and 'mending' plaster moulds and models, and adapting and converting to bas-relief existing designs in other media. In July 1776, Sir Roger Newdigate invited Wedgwood to take casts from the plasters and marbles he had brought home to Arbury Hall* from the Grand Tour. The task was given to William Bedson, who returned early in July with 'upwards of 30 Molds from Bassreliefs'[173] which Josiah listed to Bentley later in the month.[174] These included two casts from which the *Offering to Flora* (Plate 145) was composed, and part of the *Sacrifice to Bacchus*, both tablets attributed to Hackwood, and a number which Josiah misleadingly described as 'Statues', which appear in eighteenth-century jasper examples both as single figures on rectangu-lar, circular or oval grounds, and as additions to groups that were required to be enlarged.† With the arrival of the Arbury Hall moulds, Hackwood and Bedson had as much 'modeling, & repairing, absolutely upon the stocks as would last them two years.'[175]

On 16 June 1787 Josiah wrote to his old friend and patron Sir William Hamilton: 'unfortunately I must lose the advantage of Mr Flaxmans assistance, as he is preparing to go to Italy for two years. My own modeller also, Mr Webber, who was recommended to me by

---

*Sir Roger's Warwickshire mansion, Gothicised in a manner even grander than that of Horace Walpole's Strawberry Hill.
†Such composite designs, using figures modelled by both Flaxman and Hackwood, are sometimes facetiously described as the work of 'Flackwood'.

151. Grey–blue and white jasper with very slightly darker-blue jasper dip oval plaque, Judgement of Hercules *(Appendix J:I.69). Oval 9⅞″ × 13″ (25.0 × 33.0 cm). Mark:* WEDGWOOD & BENTLEY. *c.1778. The figure of Hercules is 7″ (17.8 cm) high and the relief is ½″ (1.28 cm) deep at the shoulder. The ormolu frame may be from Matthew Boulton's Soho (Birmingham) workshop.* Wedgwood Museum

151

152. Blue jasper dip on grey–blue jasper tablet, Birth of Bacchus *(Appendix J:I.206). 9⅜″ × 20½″ (23.2 × 52.0 cm). Mark:* WEDGWOOD & BENTLEY. *c.1779. A large and very rare tablet modelled by Hackwood.* Manchester Museum

152

153. Deep-blue jasper dip plaque, Birth of Bacchus. *Oval length 11⅝″ (29.5 cm). Mark:* WEDGWOOD. *c.1785. Modelled by William Hackwood in 1776 as a companion piece to his* Triumph of Bacchus, *and originally produced in this form because 'The Birth of Bacchus, & 6 Figures in his Suite' (Plate 152) could not be made in one piece.* Nottingham Castle Museum

153

148

154

155

154. *Pale-blue jasper dip portrait medallion of Sir Joshua Reynolds PRA. Height 3¼" (8.2 cm). Mark:* WEDGWOOD. *c.1790. (See Appendix H:I.)* Nottingham Castle Museum

155. *Lilac jasper dip saucer dish, engine-turned and ornamented with a leafage border and a centre group of* Infant Academy *(Appendix J:I.254). Diameter 8" (20.3 cm). Mark:* WEDGWOOD 3 B. *c.1785–90. Probably modelled by Hackwood, after Reynolds (Plate 156), from Francis Haward's stipple engraving published in 1783.* Holbourne of Menstrie Museum, Bath

156

156. The Infant Academy, *oil painting on canvas by Sir Joshua Reynolds, 56" × 45" (142.2 × 111.4 cm), 1782. In this work, which is closely related to Boucher's for Madame de Pompadour and even more closely to Van Loo's* Allegory of Painting *(Fine Arts Museum, San Francisco), Reynolds comments humorously on the art of the fashionable portrait painter, depicting children playing at the serious activities of adults.* The Iveagh Bequest, Kenwood

157. *Dark-blue jasper dip plaque,* Music, *modelled by William Hackwood in 1785 as a companion piece to* Infant Academy *(Appendix J:I.254). Oval 3¾" × 5¾" (9.5 × 14.6 cm). Mark:* WEDGWOOD. *c.1785–90.* Wedgwood Museum

157

158

159

Sir Joshua Reynolds & Sir William Chambers as the most promising pupil in the Royal Academy [Schools], is going with my eldest son [John] to spend the winter in Italy. . . . Mr Flaxman has promised to employ for me all the time he can spare in Rome, & to superintend a modeller, whom I have engaged to accompany him & to employ the whole of his time for me at Rome. Mr Webber is to do the same.'[176]

In the event, Flaxman found little time for work on Wedgwood's behalf, completing only one large bas-relief in wax of *The Birth of Bacchus*, and a small portrait of Victor Amadeus III at the request of John Wedgwood.[177] He did, however, send Wedgwood occasional and favourable reports on the progress of John de Vaere, the modeller hired to work full-time for him.[178] Reproved by Josiah for the infrequency of his letters, Flaxman gave as his excuse 'the Laberinth of fine things by which I am surrounded' and added: 'My Good Sir, my situation is somewhat similar to that of Brutus who declared he did not kill Caesar because he loved him less, but because he loved Rome more.'[179]

De Vaere's work in Rome included *The Rape of Proserpine*, 'after an Antique in the Barberini Palace', a composition of twelve figures with horses 'finished in the most beautiful manner'; bas-reliefs from the Borghese Vase; and the *Discovery of Achilles* (Plates 158 and 159), 'a sufficient evidence of his attention & improvement . . . full of the sentiment of the fine Antique'.[180]

Henry Webber was employed in Rome at the same salary as he received at Etruria (£250 per annum), and all expenses 'for the purpose of making Models, Drawings and other improvements in the Arts of Modelling and Designing for the benefit and advantage of the said Josiah Wedgwood'.[181] No evidence of any modelling he did there has been found, and it is clear that he delegated to the Italian modeller, Angelo Dalmazzoni (*fl.*1787–95), commissions for much of the work required and a good part of the administration that went with them.[182] This was, no doubt, a practical arrangement inspired by Webber's inferior understanding of the country and its language, and Dalmazzoni's knowledge of local artists and their work. It appears that Webber's time may have been rather less profitably spent in bear-leading John Wedgwood until his return home in 1789.

The existence, among the Mosley Collection of manuscripts in the Wedgwood archives, of notes of letters and accounts passing between Dalmazzoni in Rome and Wedgwood at Etruria[183] provides useful pointers to the sources of some of the bas-reliefs, and to the identity of the artists who copied them.* The models by Camillo Pacetti (1758–1826), though he was described by Dalmazzoni as 'a proud imperious fellow',[184] were especially approved by Josiah. They included 'the whole life of Achilles, from his mother Thetis in childbed, to his triumph over Hector' (Plates 160–7); 'Priam kneeling before Achilles, begging the body of his son Hector'; 'The fable of Prometheus', which does not appear to have been reproduced in jasper, though some of the figures described were probably used separately or to complete other compositions; 'Diana, the triform goddess' (Plate 169); 'Aesculapius and Hygeia' (Plate 170); and 'Endymion on Latmos' (Plate 171).[185] The quality of the last, alone, is sufficient evidence of Pacetti's ability.

*See Appendix J:II.

160

161

162

160. *Red wax model on slate,* The Birth and Dipping of Achilles, *modelled by Camillo Pacetti, 1789 (see Appendix J:II.17). 6½″ × 10½″ (16.5 × 26.6 cm).* Lady Lever Art Gallery, Port Sunlight

161. *Red wax model on slate,* Thetis delivering Achilles to Centaur, and Achilles on the back of Centaur hunting the Lion *(see Appendix J:II.17). 6½″ × 10½″ (16.5 × 26.6 cm).* Lady Lever Art Gallery, Port Sunlight

162. *Red wax model on slate,* Achilles dragging the body of Hector round the walls of Troy *(see Appendix J:II.17). 6½″ × 21″ (16.5 × 53 cm).* Lady Lever Art Gallery, Port Sunlight

163. Pen and wash drawing on lined paper, Achilles on the back of Centaur hunting the Lion *(cf. Plate 161) probably by Camillo Pacetti, 1789. 3″ × 8¼″ (7.6 × 20.8 cm). A highly finished drawing by Pacetti, or possibly by Flaxman, done perhaps to show how the rather crude and weathered carving on the Luna disc might be translated into an attractive subject for reproduction in jasper.*
Wedgwood Museum

164. Olive-green jasper dip tablet, The Birth and Dipping of Achilles. *6⅛″ × 18″ (15.5 × 45.6 cm). Mark:* WEDGWOOD. *c.1910–28. (Cf. Plate 160.)*
Dwight & Lucille Beeson Collection, Birmingham Museum, Alabama

165. Olive-green jasper dip tablet, Thetis delivering Achilles to Centaur, and Achilles on the back of Centaur hunting the Lion. *6⅛″ × 18″ (15.5 × 45.6 cm). Mark:* WEDGWOOD ENGLAND. *c.1910–28. (Cf. Plate 161.) (For further discussion of olive-green jasper, see p. 271.)*
Dwight & Lucille Beeson Collection, Birmingham Museum, Alabama

166. Dark-blue jasper dip tablet, Achilles dragging the body of Hector round the walls of Troy. *7½″ × 19½″ (19.1 × 49.5 cm). Mark:* WEDGWOOD. *c.1790–5. (Cf. Plate 162.)*
Mr & Mrs David Zeitlin Collection

163

164

165

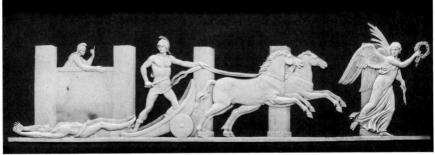

166

167

168

169

169A

167. Green, lilac and white jasper dip oval medallion, Achilles dragging the body of Hector round the walls of Troy. *Oval 3″ × 4⅝″ (7.6 × 11.8 cm). Mark:* WEDGWOOD O. *c.1790–95. A second version of this subject, remodelled to face in the opposite direction, and with a number of important alterations to the figures and composition. Sometimes attributed, without evidence, to Flaxman. (Cf. Plates 162 and 166.)* Manchester City Art Gallery

168. Brown wax model of Achilles in Scyros among the Daughters of Lycomedes, *attributed to Pacetti, 1788, and copied from the same source as his* Priam kneeling before Achilles begging the body of his son Hector *(the so-called sarcophagus of Alexander Severus and Julia Mammaea). 8″ × 18¼″ (20.3 × 46.5 cm). This subject is constantly described as 'The Sacrifice of Iphigenia', an error for which the first responsibility seems to be Meteyard's. It has been frequently repeated in spite of Dr Carol Macht's definitive correction (*Classical Wedgwood Designs, *1957, p. 26). (See Appendix J:II and cf. Plate C26.)* Lady Lever Art Gallery, Port Sunlight

169. Green jasper dip plaque, Triform Goddess (Diana, Luna, Hecate), *by Camillo Pacetti, 1788. Height 9¼″ (23.7 cm). Mark:* WEDGWOOD. *c.1790. (See Appendix J:II.37.)* British Museum

169A. Pink wax model on slate, Triform Goddess, *modelled by Camillo Pacetti in 1788. Height (figure) 9″ (22.9 cm); (slate ground) 10″ (25.4 cm).* Wedgwood Museum

153

170

170A

170. *Solid blue jasper plaque,* Aesculapius and Hygeia, *by Camillo Pacetti, 1788. 9½" × 8⁵⁄₁₆" (24.1 × 21 cm). Mark:* WEDGWOOD O. *c.1789–90. (See Appendix J:II.41.) This example of the plaque is particularly notable for the 'marbling' of the pillars. Note that the pillar second from the left does not reach the ground.*
Dwight & Lucille Beeson Collection, Birmingham Museum, Alabama

170A. *Pink wax model on slate,* Aesculapius and Hygeia, *modelled by Camillo Pacetti in 1788. 9¾" × 7¾" (24.8 × 19.0 cm).*
Lady Lever Art Gallery, Port Sunlight

171. *Pink wax model on slate,* Endymion sleeping on the Rock Latmos, *modelled by Camillo Pacetti, 1788. (See Appendix J:II.53 and Plate 410, for a fine twentieth-century jasper example by 'Bert' Bentley.)*
Lady Lever Art Gallery, Port Sunlight

171

In addition to the nine Muses, Angelini modelled 'Pluto carrying off Proserpine' (Plate 172), the 'Banquet' from the Sarcophagus of the Muses (Plate 173) and a number of smaller pieces. Also employed were Michelangelo Mangiarotti and Angelino Fratoddi, who supplied 'cameos in shells'; and a collection of '140 pieces of Marbles' was obtained for 14 zequins* from one Manzolini. Giuseppe Cades[†] (1750–99) was paid 5 zequins for '5 pastes backed with Cornelians'. One of these may have been the 'Sale of Erotes' copied by Wedgwood either from a mural painting now in the Naples Museum or from Cades's signed gem which was inspired by it.[186]

Some of these bas-reliefs, and many of those reproduced earlier from moulds supplied by Hoskins & Grant, Mrs Landré and others, were in part 'repaired' or even invented by the modellers. Few of the carvings which they used as sources of designs were in anything approaching original condition, and the replacement of missing heads, limbs, figures or groups was at the discretion of the modellers. Some of the source material was deliberately 'improved' in the model: Pacetti's 'whole life of Achilles', for example, is a beautifully classicised version of some rather dumpy late Roman carving (c.400–800) of the Luna marble disc in the Capitoline Museum.[187] Such models cannot accurately be described as 'copies' from the antique: some are more classical in composition and technique than their sources; in others the adaptation is so clearly neo-classical as to seem entirely eighteenth century in portrayal and classical only in theme.

The preservation of classical themes was important, for the foundation of the fashion for neoclassical art – indeed one of the essential elements of the style itself – was an education that made allusions to classical history and mythology instantly recognisable to all but the illiterate. During the last ten years of Wedgwood's life, however, he followed

*About 30 English shillings.
[†]Cades was a sculptor and gem engraver who was partly responsible for eighteenth-century decoration to the Borghese Palace, Rome.

172

173

172. Red wax model, Pluto carrying off Proserpine, *modelled by Giuseppe Angelini in 1789, and described in Dalmazzoni's lists as No. 55 'Pluto carrying off Proserpine, preceded by Hercules, a victory & Mercury; then Minerva, Jupiter, Juno & Venus & finally Ceres in her car in quest of Proserpine'. This is perhaps the 'Rape of Proserpine' finished by De Vaere (see Appendix J:II.55).* Lady Lever Art Gallery, Port Sunlight.

173. Dark-blue jasper dip tablet, Reclining Figures *(known also as 'Roman Banquet') by Giuseppe Angelini, 1789 (see Appendix J:II.26). 3¼" × 17¾" (8.3 × 45.0 cm). Mark:* WEDGWOOD. *c.1790.* Sotheby's, London

fashion again to the extent of commissioning work in the Romantic style, much of it showing a marked sentimentality of concept and design. In retrospect it seems strange that such work should have been commissioned simultaneously with the classically inspired bas-reliefs modelled by artists employed in Rome; but art concerned with the expression of emotion, and thus not subject to rules of mathematical proportion, has often in history existed side by side with classical art, which was generally governed by those rules. In the latter part of the century there was a reaction against what was seen as the distant austerity of classical design in favour of more sentimental and modern domestic subjects. Of these, the most obvious examples are the bas-reliefs of *Charlotte mourning at the tomb of Werther* (see Plate C28), inspired by Goethe's best-selling romance, *The Sorrows of the Young Werther*, published in 1774, and *Poor Maria* and *The Bourbonnais Shepherd* (see Plate C2) from Laurence Sterne's *Sentimental Journey* of 1768: both designed by Lady Templetown[188] about 1787.

With the production of such subjects as these, Wedgwood was appealing predominantly to female taste, an increasingly important aspect of his business, and it is not surprising to find that the artists who designed them were women. The first of them was Elizabeth, Lady Templetown (1747–1823).[*] On 27 June 1783 Josiah drafted a letter to her, addressed in unusually obsequious terms:

> Mr W. presents his most respectful comp[ts] to Lady Templeton [*sic*] & is very happy to learn by his nephew Mr Byerley that his attempt to copy in bas relief the charming groups of little figures her ladyship was so obliging as to lend him has met with that approbation which he durst not flatter himself with, & is sensible he owes much to Lady Templetons politeness on this occasion. Mr Wedgwood is afraid to trespass farther upon the goodness he has already experienc'd & is sensible that nothing but experience could justify his expressing a wish to be indulged in copying a few more groups. . . .[189]

[*]Elizabeth, daughter of Shuckburgh Boughton, of Poston, Hereford, married in 1769, Clotworthy Upton, who was raised to the peerage as Baron Templetown in 1776.

174. Portrait of Elizabeth, Lady Templetown, by John Downman ARA (1750–1824). Pencil, crayon and watercolour washes. Signed and dated 1790. 7¼″ × 5¾″ (18.5 × 15.0 cm). Author's collection

175. Green jasper dip medallion, Study, *modelled by Hackwood from a design by Lady Templetown. Oval 3½″ × 4½″ (8.9 × 11.4 cm). Mark:* WEDGWOOD. c.1790. *(See Appendix J:1.250.)* Mr & Mrs David Zeitlin Collection

174

175

A letter written some two years later to Charles James Fox makes clear the nature of the 'charming groups', which were 'modelled from some beautiful cut Indian paper',[190] and a bill from Hackwood dated 30 April 1785 indicates that it was probably he who transformed some, if not all, of them.[191] Fourteen bas-relief subjects can be assigned to Lady Templetown[192] on the evidence of Josiah's own notes to the 1787 Catalogue,[193] and these are listed in Appendix J. Several, including *Poor Maria* and the *Bourbonnais Shepherd*, were freely copied by other potters (Plate 51).

The designs produced by Miss Emma Crewe (*fl.1787–1818*) are identified only by the brief descriptions in the 1787 Catalogue, and it is possible that this short list of three bas-relief subjects[194] is incomplete. One, *Domestic Employment*, shares its title with another by Lady Templetown and the identification of either is unsure. It appears that the styles of these two artists are similar. Emma Crewe was the daughter of the Whig hostess, Frances Crewe, and it was her brother who was the subject of Hackwood's first portrait medallion.*

Like Lady Templetown, Lady Diana Beauclerk (1734–1808), daughter of the third Duke of Marlborough, is acknowledged in the 1787 Catalogue for her 'exquisite taste', but those of her designs for Wedgwood that have been identified are unlike Lady Templetown's or Miss Crewe's. She appears to have been a more accomplished draughts-man than either of them,[195] and her 'bacchanalian boys' have a vigour and humour about them which, at least in the clay versions, is attractively unsentimental. The first reference to her work occurs in Josiah's letter, quoted above, to Fox, dated 23 July 1785: 'Mr Wedgwood presents his most respectful compliments to Mr Fox, and a thousand thanks for the exquisite drawings he has receiv'd – and will be much obliged to Mr Fox if he will be so good to signify to Lady Diana Beauclere [*sic*] how much he esteems himself for this flattering mark of her Ladyships notice.' He enclosed a number of bas-reliefs modelled after Lady Templetown's 'cut Indian paper' designs to show the manner in which he would 'attempt to copy the drawings'.[196]

*See p. 109.

176

176. Solid green and white jasper plaque, An Offering to Peace, *modelled by Hackwood from a design by Lady Templetown. Oval length 9" (23.0 cm). Mark:* WEDGWOOD. *(See Appendix J:1.238.) This subject, not immediately identifiable with its catalogue title, forms the central group of a larger rectangular composition which includes a sacrificial altar. A third, elongated version, with a second altar and additional figures, is illustrated in Eliza Meteyard's* Memorials of Wedgwood, *1874, Plate XXIV.* British Museum

177. *Portrait of Lady Diana Beauclerk by Sir Joshua Reynolds. Oil on canvas 50″ × 40″ (127 × 102 cm). c.1764–5. The ewer in the background was designed by Jacques Stella* (Livre de Vases, *c.1667, Plate 10) and was copied, without the bas-relief figures round the body but with a satyr's-head terminal to the handle, in Wedgwood's basaltes c.1770. (See T. Clifford, 'Some Ceramic Vases and Their Sources, Part I', in English Ceramic Circle* Transactions, *Vol. 10, Pt 3, 1978, p. 165, and Plates 73 c and d).* Iveagh Bequest, Kenwood

178. *Watercolour drawing by Lady Diana Beauclerk of* amorini *playing in a woodland setting. 8½″ × 9⅝″ (21 × 24.5 cm). c.1785. This drawing was engraved by Mariano Bovi (Mrs Steuart Erskine,* Lady Diana Beauclerk, Her Life and Work, *1903, p. 63).* Author's collection

179. *Coloured stipple engraving by Francesco Bartolozzi after a watercolour drawing by Lady Diana Beauclerk. This group was copied by Wedgwood as* Group of Three Boys *(Appendix J:I.241) and widely used, alone and with others of Lady Diana's figures, for tablets, plaques and medallions, and as ornament for teawares and other pieces. (See Plates 180, 181 and C27.) Reproduced from Mrs Steuart Erskine,* Lady Diana Beauclerk, Her Life and Work, *1903.* Photograph: Wedgwood

177

178

179

181

180. *Green jasper dip tablet of ten figures of boys, composed from groups and a single figure after designs by Lady Diana Beauclerk. 6½" × 24" (16.5 × 61 cm). Mark:* WEDGWOOD o . A *(incised). c.1795. Wedgwood's 1787 Catalogue descriptions (Appendix J:I.241–3) do not account for more than one group of two boys, and it is clear that there were at least three of these in addition to the four single figures and the group of three listed. The composition of this tablet, which appears unfinished on the right, suggests that it was the left-hand side of a pair (cf. Plate C27, which shows the same feature).* Dwight & Lucille Beeson Collection, Birmingham Museum, Alabama

181. *Satinwood commode mounted with three blue and white jasper (dip?) medallions of boys after designs by Lady Diana Beauclerk. Commode: 38" × 64½" × 22½" (96.5 × 164.0 × 57.0 cm). Medallions: height (left to right) 5¾" (14.7 cm), 5⅛" (13.0 cm), 6" (15.2 cm). No marks visible. c.1785–90.* Lady Lever Art Gallery, Port Sunlight

Lady Diana's work is listed in the 1787 Catalogue,[197] and consisted at that date of three groups of figures – 'three boys', 'two boys' and 'Four boys single' – and a composite 'Bacchanalian tablet' of six boys 'under arbours, with panthers' skins in festoons', made up from the 'six preceding articles'. This last was varied to suit the space for which it was intended, and might consist of almost any combination of groups and figures (Plates 180 and C27) to form a long tablet or two plaques.[198]

Josiah's letter to Fox leaves little room for doubt that Lady Diana Beauclerk's drawings were not translated into bas-reliefs until August 1785 at the earliest. There is, however, evidence that some of her designs had been used for Wedgwood tableware some eight years before that date. In the second edition of Horace Walpole's *Description of Strawberry Hill*, published in 1784, the small number of Wedgwood pieces listed includes twelve plates of 'ware' decorated with 'cameos of brown and white and blue festoons' and a pair of flower vases with similar decoration from designs by Lady Diana dated 1777. None of these pieces has been traced, but it is possible that some have survived, unrecognised, in a private or public collection.

Towards the end of his introductory remarks to Class II of the 1787 Catalogue, Josiah wrote: 'These bas-reliefs, chiefly in jasper of two colours, are applied as cabinet pictures, or for ornamenting cabinets, book cases, writing tables, in the composition of a great variety of chimneypieces, and other ornamental works. With what effect they are thus applied, may be seen in the houses of many of the first nobility and gentry in the kingdom.' Sadly few of these early Wedgwood ornaments remain in their original settings. The mania for collecting has led to the mutilation of many a fine cabinet, commode or chimneypiece, and plaques and tablets have been overpainted in response to fashion.

182. Green jasper dip tablet, Sacrifice to Love *(Appendix J:1.208). 9¾″ × 24⅞″ (24.7 × 63.1 cm). Mark:* WEDGWOOD. *c.1790. The source of this subject has not been identified.* Dwight & Lucille Beeson Collection, Birmingham Museum, Alabama

183. Solid pale-blue and white jasper tablet, Volumnia, Wife of Coriolanus. *6″ × 9⅛″ (15.4 × 23.3 cm). Mark:* Wedgwood. *c.1785. This subject is generally catalogued as 'Penelope and her Maidens', but was described by Carol Macht* (Classical Wedgwood Designs, *1957, p. 118) as 'Volumnia, Mother [sic] of Coriolanus'. The source is an engraving published by P.F. d'Hancarville* (Collection of Etruscan, Greek and Roman Antiquities from the Cabinet of the Honble William Hamilton, *1767, Vol. II, Plate 26).* Metropolitan Museum of Art, Bequest of Mary Clark Thompson

183A. Volumnia, Wife of Coriolanus, *Plate 26 from Volume II of P.F. d'Hancarville's* Collection of Etruscan, Greek and Roman Antiquities from the Cabinet of the Honble William Hamilton, *1767.* Photograph: Wedgwood

182

183

183A

COMMEMORATIVE MEDALLIONS

Although Josiah had commissioned portrait medallions to celebrate contemporary heroes of the hour, such as Keppel's in 1779, the thought of
producing medallions to commemorate events does not seem to have
occurred to him until 1786, when he decided to celebrate the new
Commercial Treaty with France in this manner. He discussed the proposal with Flaxman, who sent him a drawing. Josiah acknowledged this
on 2 November 1786 in a letter which nicely illustrates his method in
commissioning work from an established artist with whom he was on
good terms:

> Nothing in my opinion can more properly or more forcibly express
> the ideas we wish to bring forward, than the group of figures you
> gave me, and which I now include, but as it will be necessary to have
> them divided into two parts in order to make a *pair* of medallions,
> that circumstance will call for a little alteration in the disposal of the
> figures. The three middle figures will make one medallion, which I
> will call No. 1. The burning of the implements of war, and the fig-
> ure of Peace, must then form another group for Medallion No. 2.

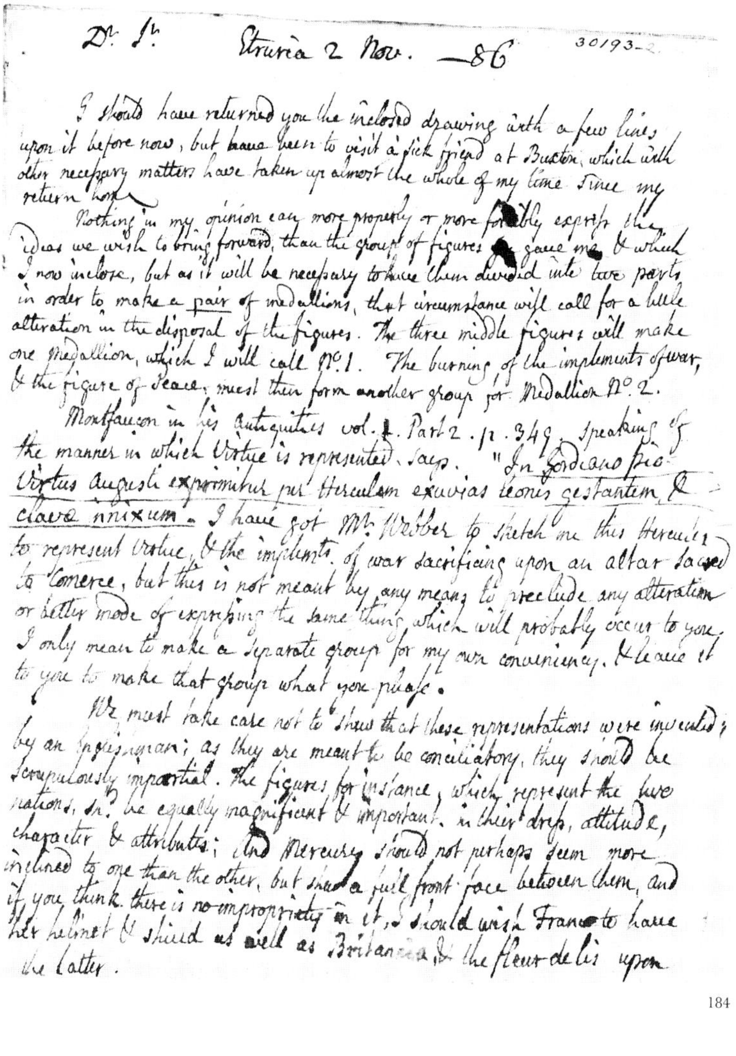

*184. Josiah Wedgwood's
letter of 2 November 1786
to John Flaxman junior,
commenting on his design to
commemorate the
Commercial Treaty with
France (Ms. 2–30193).
Wedgwood
Manuscripts, Keele
University Library*

184

185. *Solid blue and white jasper plaque,* Commercial Treaty with France *(Appendix J:1.256 or 257), usually catalogued as 'Mercury Uniting the Hands of Britain and France', designed by John Flaxman junior in 1786–7, and modelled by him in wax. 9″ × 9⅝″ (23.0 × 24.5 cm). Mark:* WEDGWOOD. *c.1787. Flaxman's pen-and-wash drawing is illustrated in D. Bindman (ed.),* John Flaxman RA, *1979, Plate 52a, with the wax model on slate invoiced in March 1787 (Plate 52b). The drawing is evidently not Flaxman's original design, for the figure of France holds a shield emblazoned with fleurs-de-lis, an alteration specifically requested by Josiah in his letter. The wax model shows further alterations, including the removal of France's shield in favour of a spear, and less complex and fragile designs for the crests of the helmets, which would be less vulnerable in firing.* Christie's, London

185

186. *Solid blue and white jasper plaque,* Commercial Treaty with France *(Appendix J:1.256 or 257), usually catalogued as 'Peace preventing Mars from breaking open the Gates of the Temple of Janus', designed by John Flaxman junior in 1786–7 and modelled by him in wax (illustrated in D. Bindman, (ed.),* John Flaxman RA, *1979, Plate 51a). 9″ × 10½″ (23.0 × 26.6 cm). Mark:* WEDGWOOD. *c.1787.* Christie's, London

186

186A. Earthenware biscuit block mould for Flaxman's Commercial Treaty with France *(Plate 186).* *Height 8⅝" (22.0 cm).* *1787.* Wedgwood Museum

186A

Montfaucon in his Antiquities vol.1. Part 2. p.349, speaking of the manner in which Virtue is represented, says, '*In Gordiano pio Virtus Augusti expromitur per Herculam exuvias leones gestantem, and* [sic] *clave innixum*'. I have got Mr Webber to sketch me this Hercules to represent Virtue, and the implements of war sacrificing upon an altar Sacred to Commerce, but this is not meant by any means to preclude any alteration or better mode of expressing the same thing, which will probably occur to you. I only mean to make a separate group for my own conveniency, and leave it to you to make that group what you please.

We must take care not to shew that these representations were invented by an Englishman; as they are meant to be conciliatory, they should be scrupulously impartial. The figures for instance, which represent the two nations, should be equally magnificent and important in their dress, attitude, character and attributes, and Mercury should not perhaps seem more inclined to one than the other, but shew a full front face between them, and if you think there is no impropriety in it, I should wish France to have her helmet and shield as well as Britannia, and the Fleur de lis upon the latter.

The figures must be modeled 8 inches high, and you know upon this occasion expedition is of great consequence, so I will detain you no longer than whilst I beg your pardon for this exercise of your patience. . . .

In a postscript he added: 'I have some doubt about Hercules being a proper representation of Virtue. A female figure may perhaps be better, but this is left to your better judgement.'[199]

Josiah's doubts in this respect, perhaps shared by Flaxman, persuaded them to choose a different subject for the second group, and both were described in a letter to William Eden: 'I have [had] modeled two bas-relief representing the commercial treaty with France. One of them consists of three figures, Mercury as the god of commerce, uniting the hands of England and France. On the other bas relief is represented the temple of Janus shut, and the door bolted by two caducei; Mars in a violent rage is going to burst the door open with his spear, but Peace arrests his arm and says, or seems to say, that the door so bolted is not to be broke open.'[200] Both bas-reliefs, reproduced in rectangular form in jasper (Plates 185 and 186), were the work of Flaxman, who invoiced wax models of them on 12 January and 26 March 1787 for fifteen guineas ('Mars') and thirty guineas ('Mercury') respectively,[201] and they are listed in the Ornamental Ware Catalogue for the following year.[202]

The French Revolution provided Josiah with another event that he could sincerely celebrate, and he lost no time in producing some suitable portrait medallions for sale on both sides of the Channel.* The fall of the Bastille also was commemorated in a pair of medallions (Plate 187). Just how quickly this was done is shown by an invoice dated 3 November 1789 charging for 'Box No. 248, Novr 3rd 29 rd Cameos Bastille Prison with motto @ 12/–, £17–8–0, 2 broke'. A further note added on the following day reads: 'Box 249, 6 rd Cameos Bastille Prison & Motto @ 12/–, £3–12–0'.[203] This date of November 1789 is of special interest as it coincides with the production of the Sydney Cove medallion.†

*See Plate 16.
†See Plate 190.

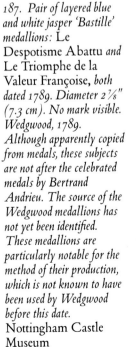

187. Pair of layered blue and white jasper 'Bastille' medallions: Le Despotisme Abattu *and* Le Triomphe de la Valeur Française, *both dated 1789. Diameter 2⅛"* *(7.3 cm). No mark visible. Wedgwood, 1789. Although apparently copied from medals, these subjects are not after the celebrated medals by Bertrand Andrieu. The source of the Wedgwood medallions has not yet been identified. These medallions are particularly notable for the method of their production, which is not known to have been used by Wedgwood before this date.* Nottingham Castle Museum

187

188. Blue jasper dip medallion celebrating the French Revolution. The design follows closely the suggestions made by Josiah II in July 1789, and was evidently drawn, and probably modelled, by Henry Webber. It shows France, holding a staff or spear surmounted by the Phrygian cap of liberty, greeting Minerva as goddess of war, before an altar inscribed 'FIDEL. PUBL.' on which stands the figure of Faith. Diameter 2¼" (5.7 cm). Mark: WEDGWOOD. c.1789. Wedgwood Museum

189. Blue jasper dip medallion celebrating the French Revolution. Diameter 2½" (6.4 cm). No mark visible. Wedgwood, c.1789. The design of this medallion is copied, with only slight amendments, from Henry Webber's 'Sydney Cove' medallion (cf. Plates 190 and 192). The figure of Hope has been given a staff surmounted by the Phrygian cap of Liberty, and in the background a shield emblazoned with fleurs-de-lis, representing the King, hangs discarded upon an Ionic column. Wedgwood Museum

In the production of the Bastille medallions, a new ornamenting technique appears to have been used by Wedgwood for the first time. The clouds, and the lettering and date of the 'Motto', are of such delicacy that to apply them by hand would be almost impossible and certainly uneconomic. A close inspection of the medallions, and comparison with other examples of the same subject, reveals that the lettering and the ground, with the central scene, have been formed in the same mould. The technique is most obvious in the uneven and unbalanced spacing of the lettering, common to all examples, and the regular pattern of clouds through which the blue ground adds irregular shading. Such effects could be produced only by pressing white jasper or jasper slip into the intaglio pattern of the mould, removing the excess clay, and then adding layers of blue jasper and white jasper, in that order, to make a laminate resembling jasper dip.[204]

This same technique was used in the production of the Sydney Cove medallion, which is unexpectedly linked with another of the medallions issued to celebrate the French Revolution. On 28 July 1789 Josiah II wrote to his father: 'Do you choose to have anything modelled . . . which should relate to the late revolution in France & to the support given to public credit by the national assembly? What do you think of Public faith on an altar & France embracing Liberty in the front? Mr Byerley says we ought to do something & that quickly. I will get Mr Webber to make a sketch & send it to you tomorrow.'[205] The next day he sent Josiah a sketch of the proposed medallion: 'The figure on the altar with the Caduceus in one hand & the Cornucopia in the other is Public Credit or Faith & instead of the caduceus on the Altar there ought, I think, to be the words Fid.Pub. for fides publica, the godess of liberty with the cap of liberty in her left hand takes hold of France in her right. . . . The story appears to me to be well told & to make a good composition' (Plate 188). He added: 'The figure of hope in the Botany bay medal would come in exceeding well for this figure of liberty,'[206] and it is plain that this suggestion was followed, not only for this medallion but also for a second (Plate 189) which is strikingly similar in composition to the Sydney Cove medallion.

190. Buff biscuit 'Sydney Cove' medallion, designed by Henry Webber, 1789. Diameter 2⅜" (6.0 cm). Mark: WEDGWOOD. 1789. (Cf. Plate 189.) Wedgwood Museum

191. Blue jasper dip medallion celebrating the French Revolution. Diameter 2½" (6.4 cm). Mark: WEDGWOOD. The medallion shows an interesting combination of pressed relief (the Latin inscription) and applied ornament. Peace (or perhaps Concordia), with her staff surmounted by the Revolutionary Phrygian cap, stands beneath an arch, against which lies a discarded shield emblazoned with fleurs-de-lis, representing Louis XVI. Wedgwood Museum

The success of these commemorative pieces encouraged the production of more, and in 1790 a series of cameos was designed for sale in Germany. Most of the subjects are concerned with celebrating the accession and virtues of the Emperor Leopold II, who had succeeded his brother Joseph II in January. The precise number of subjects is not known. Seven are listed on an invoice dated 11 September 1790 for ware sent to Frankfurt:

Fame inscribing Vase to the Memory of Elizabeth [favourite niece of Joseph II, who died in February 1790] Upright oval 1⅞" or bent oval [for shoe buckles &c] 1⅛"

Leopold the Lawgiver supported by Wisdom & Benevolence 1⅞" or 1⅜"

The Genius of Empire holding the bust of Leopold while a priestess is officiating at an altar Round 2⅛" Diam.

Germany in the character of Minerva presents Leopold with a Civic band as a reward for his code of laws 2⅛" Diam.

Mars presenting a Crown to the Genius of Germany to be placed upon the bust of Leopold which stands on an altar Round 2⅛".

Turkey and Russia — the two belligerent powers consulting upon peace, & Germany the mediator between them Round 2⅛" diam

Coronation of Leopold Oval upright 2"[207]

At least four others have been recorded, three identifying Minerva with the spirit of Germany,[208] and a fourth showing a two-headed eagle surmounted by the imperial crown. One of these is yet another adaptation of the all-purpose design by Webber for the Sydney Cove medallion, already adapted once to suit the French Revolution. In addition, a small portrait of Leopold II, the head surmounted by the imperial crown (Plate 194), was produced,[209] though this is hardly to be compared in quality with the earlier portrait of his brother Joseph (Plate 195).

166

192. *Eight blue jasper dip 'German cameos':* (top) *'Coronation of Leopold II',* oval height 2″ *(5.1 cm);* (upper left) unidentified, diameter 2³⁄₁₆″ *(5.3 cm);* (upper right) *Germany in the character of Minerva encouraging Art and Labour with Peace to work for the prosperity of the Empire* (cf. Plates 189 and 190), diameter 2⅛″ *(5.4 cm);* (centre) *'Turkey and Russia – the two belligerent powers',* diameter 2³⁄₁₆″ *(5.3 cm);* (lower left) *the figures of Germany and Turkey with* amorini *grieving for Elizabeth, diameter 1¾″ (4.4 cm);* (centre right) *seal of the Empire, oval height 1″ (2.5 cm);* (lower right) *'Mars presenting a Crown to the Genius of Germany', oval height 2″ (5.1 cm);* (bottom) *'Leopold the Lawgiver', oval height 1⅞″ (4.8 cm).* Mark: (all) WEDGWOOD. c.1790. Dr & Mrs Alvin M. Kanter Collection

193. *Three blue jasper dip commemorative cameos: 'Fame inscribing a Vase to the Memory of Elizabeth', oval height 1⅞″ (4.8 cm); French Revolution cameo ornamented with the staff and Phrygian cap of Liberty with the cornucopia of Fortune and the olive branch of Peace entwined, diameter 1″ (2.5 cm); and French Revolution cameo ornamented with the caduceus of Peace and the cornucopias of Concord (representing the Crown and the State) encircling two clasped hands, diameter 1″ (2.5 cm).* Mark: (all) WEDGWOOD. c.1790. Christie's, London

194. *Small blue jasper dip portrait medallion of the Emperor Leopold II, with the Imperial crown. Oval height 1¾" (4.4 cm). Mark:* WEDGWOOD. *c.1790. (See Appendix H:II.)*
British Museum

195. *Green jasper dip portrait medallion of the Emperor Joseph II. Oval height 4½" (11.4 cm). Mark:* WEDGWOOD. *c.1786. The style of modelling – particularly the upright stance and thinness of relief at the bridge of the nose – suggests the work of Flaxman. The source was an ivory carving belonging to Earl Cowper (see Appendix H:I).*
Wedgwood Museum

196. *Dark-blue jasper dip medallion ornamented with a sarcophagus surmounted by an urn and flanked by palm trees set on rocks over a rushing stream. The sarcophagus is inset with a black and white jasper dip cameo of the Muses of painting and poetry mourning over an altar on which is a tiny portrait medallion of Solomon Gessner, the Swiss poet. Oval height 4⅝" (11.8 cm). Mark:* WEDGWOOD. *c.1790. This medallion was modelled after a design by Michel-Vincent Brandoin (1735–1807), a Swiss émigré painter working in England, who had designed also the monument to Gessner in Zürich. Josiah wrote to Brandoin about Gessner's portrait medallion. (Appendix J:II) and this medallion in January 1790.* Dwight & Lucille Beeson Collection, Birmingham Museum, Alabama

195

194

196

197

197. *Dark-blue jasper dip medallion of Fame inscribing a tablet, which is hanging from a rose-garlanded pillar with accompanying scroll, lyre and olive branch. Similar medallions were produced to commemorate Elizabeth, niece of the Emperor Joseph II, and to celebrate the recovery of George III in 1789. This medallion evidently commemorates a poet, perhaps Gessner (cf. Plate 196). Oval height 4¾" (12.0 cm). Mark:* WEDGWOOD. *c.1790. The source of this subject is the 'Arbury' medallion (Appendix J:I.163 and see Plate 198).*
Dwight & Lucille Beeson Collection, Birmingham Museum, Alabama

198

199

198. *Solid pale-blue and white jasper medallion, Fame, No. 10 on the list of subjects moulded in 1776 from Sir Robert Newdigate's collection at Arbury Hall (see Appendix J:I.163). Oval height 4½" (11.4 cm). Mark:* WEDGWOOD & BENTLEY. *c.1777.* Mr & Mrs David Zeitlin Collection

199. *Blue jasper dip medallion of Fame inscribing a tablet,* 'HEALTH IS REST[ORED]', *beside a pillar surmounted by a bust of George III. A commemorative medallion celebrating the recovery of the King in 1789. Oval height 2⅝" (6.7 cm). Mark:* WEDGWOOD. Wedgwood Museum

200. *Pair of Sèvres solid blue and white biscuit porcelain octagonal plaques of Neptune and Venus. Height 7½" (19.2 cm). No visible mark. Sèvres, c.1810. The plaques, in imitation of Wedgwood's jasper, show readily identifiable signs of undercutting, particularly at the ends of the folded draperies, in facial features and under Venus's left arm and leg and Neptune's left hand.* Victoria & Albert Museum, London

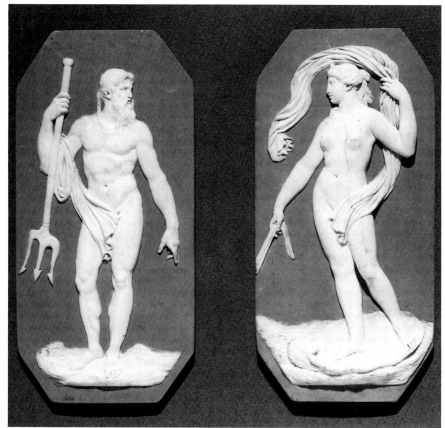

200

201. *Ilmenau white biscuit porcelain medallion with a pale-blue slip ground in the Wedgwood style, ornamented with a 'Sacrifice' group probably after Clodion. Oval length 6" (15.2 cm). Unmarked. Made at the Ilmenau (Thuringia) factory owned by the Duke of Weimar and leased to Christian Nonne. The Ilmenau biscuit porcelain shows a dull gloss. Bas-relief subjects included classical and mythological figures and groups, and contemporary portraits, and production lasted from 1792 to about 1808.* Kestner-Museum, Hanover

201

TABLEWARES

No mention of jasper teaware was made in the 1779 Wedgwood & Bentley Catalogue, and no examples are listed in the 1781 Christie & Ansell sale catalogue. These two pieces of negative evidence have given rise to the general assumption that none was made until after Bentley's death. The alternative possibility – that teaware might have been considered as 'useful' ware and thus outside the Wedgwood & Bentley partnership agreement – is scarcely worthy of consideration in view of the inclusion of black basaltes teawares in the partnership[*] and the widely accepted belief that jasper teawares were intended as cabinet pieces and not for use.[†] It is all the more surprising to read Josiah's 'Memorandum Nov[r] 23 1777 Jasper Composition',[‡] which gives detailed instructions for the making of jasper teacups 'of a fine polished white within and blue on the outside'. Not only does this memorandum indicate that jasper teacups could be made in this early period, but it specifies the 'jasper dip' process, which was certainly introduced some three years after the first solid jasper was made. It is not likely that the production of jasper dip teaware preceded that of teaware in the solid body. Nor is it sensible to suppose that the production of vases, which is believed to have begun in 1781,[§] preceded that of teaware, which must surely have been used to gain experience of applying jasper ornaments to curved surfaces.

In fact, jasper teaware was probably in production about twelve months before the memorandum was written. On 28 September 1776 Josiah promised Bentley: 'You shall have some Tea ware as soon as we

[*]This applied also to cane and rosso antico teaware.
[†]It is understood that, whatever the original intention, some of these pieces were used.
[‡]See pp. 87–91.
[§]See p. 195.

can get the Models and ware ready, & I will take the Dejuniers [*sic*], & their furniture* into immediate attention.'²¹⁰ The context of the letter leaves no doubt that he was writing of jasper, and at this period, before the development of jasper dip, he was certainly referring to solid colour jasper. In spite of the lack of material evidence in the form of marked specimens, it must be concluded that a small, perhaps only experimental, quantity of teaware was produced, both in solid jasper and jasper dip, before 1780.

Déjeuner sets, whose orthography consistently defeated Josiah, were composed of a tray (usually oval or round) with a small teapot and stand (or coffeepot or chocolate-pot), cream jug, sugar dish, and one or two teacups and saucers. A milk jug, tea canister and jam-pot might also be included. Such a set was known also as a *Cabaret*, *solitaire* or *à deux*, or *tête-à-tête*, according to the number of cups. Josiah often referred to trays as 'dejuniers'.

202

203

202. Solid pale grey-blue jasper 'Cabbage' or 'Leafage' teapot. Height 5" (12.8 cm). Mark: WEDGWOOD (placed between the spout and the foot in order to avoid spoiling the moulded base). c.1783. Moulded teapots of this type, without applied ornament, were among the simplest to be made in jasper, but no record of this particular shape appears before February 1783. Wedgwood Museum

203. Solid pale-blue and white jasper custard set of four covered cups and a rectangular tray, with acanthus leaf ornament and shell terminals to the handles. The interiors to the cups are lapidary-polished. Tray 6" × 6" (15.4 × 15.4 cm). Mark: WEDGWOOD 3. c.1786–90. The marks 'o' and '3' impressed occur only on pieces of particularly fine quality and are thought to be associated with a craftsman (or craftsmen) of the highest skill. The solid blue and white jasper oval tray with ribbon and ivy border measures 11" × 15¾" (28.0 × 40.0 cm). Mark: WEDGWOOD. c.1785–90. Wedgwood Museum

204. *Fine solid pale-blue and white jasper déjeuner set or* cabaret à deux *with an unusually large circular tray, diameter 15½" (39.5 cm). All pieces are ornamented with acanthus scrolls and classical figures and groups. Mark:* WEDGWOOD. c.1786–95. *The production of trays was always 'very hazardous', and even more so in jasper than in Queen's ware.* Christie's, London

204

205. *Solid pale-blue and white jasper déjeuner set or* solitaire, *ornamented with reliefs of* Poor Maria, amorini, *and groups from the* Domestic Employment *series by Lady Templetown and Miss Crewe. All the pieces (except the tray) are decorated with a band of engine-turning at the foot. Tray 11" × 13¾" (28.0 × 35.0 cm); teapot height 4½" (11.4 cm). Marks: (all except cream jug)* WEDGWOOD; *(cream jug)* Wedgwood. c.1786–95. Wedgwood Museum

205

206. *Solid pale-blue and white jasper set of eight eggcups on a footed tray. Height of cups 2¼" (5.7 cm); tray diameter 8¼" (21 cm). Mark:* WEDGWOOD. *The eggcups have lapidary-polished interiors. A very rare set on a tray which must have caused considerable problems of production. c.1790.* City Museum & Art Gallery, Stoke-on-Trent

206

207

207. *Turner solid blue~grey jasper teapot of ovoid shape with ribbed loop handle with leaf terminals, acanthus~moulded spout and engine~turned lid and band to foot, ornamented with two figures copied from Lady Templetown's* Sportive Love *(Appendix J:I.271). The shape, too, is Wedgwood's (cf. Plates C28 and C31). Height 5¾" (17.7 cm). Mark:* TURNER. *c.1785–90.* Temple Newsam House, Leeds

208

208. *Solid pale~blue and white jasper: covered sugar bowl ('sugar box'), bowl and cream jug, all engine~turned and ornamented with groups of* amorini *or figures after Lady Templetown's designs, and the first two pieces with feet inlaid with bands of white jasper. Diameter: (box) 3½" (9.0 cm); (bowl) 4⅞" (12.5 cm). Height (jug) 3" (7.5 cm). Marks: (box)* WEDGWOOD 3; *(bowl and jug)* Wedgwood. *c.1785–90.* Christie's, New York

209

209. *Solid pale~blue and white jasper teapot with ribbed loop handle with leaf terminals, acanthus~ moulded spout and ball knop, ornamented with floral scrolls and a decorative band of leaves above the turned foot. Height 3½" (8.9 cm). Mark:* WEDGWOOD 3. *c.1785.* Author's collection

210. *Adams of Greengates solid blue and white jasper tea canister, with bands of floral scrolls and figures of* Ulysses staying the Chariot of Victory *(a group apparently identical to the model attributed to Hackwood for Wedgwood),* Cupid and Psyche *and* Priam begging the body of Hector from Achilles. *Height 6" (15.2 cm). Mark:* ADAMS. C.1795. Temple Newsam House, Leeds

211. *Solid pale-blue and white jasper tea canister with flattened knop, ornament of* Poor Maria *above engine-turned fluting and a white jasper inlaid foot. Height 5½" (14.0 cm). Mark:* WEDGWOOD. C.1785–90. Manchester City Art Gallery

212. *Solid pale-blue and white jasper tea kettles:* (left) *with engine-turned lid and foot, ornamented with* Charlotte at the Tomb of Werther *after the design by Lady Templetown (Appendix J:1.272) and fitted with a mahogany and Sheffield Plate Handle;* (right) *with engine-turned foot, bail handle and Cupid knop, ornamented with the* Dancing Hours. *Height:* (left) 5¾" (14.5 cm); (right) 8¼" (20.9 cm). *Marks:* (left) WEDGWOOD; (right) WEDGWOOD M. *Both c.1785–95. Wedgwood was making tea kettles in black basaltes for fitting with wicker handles as early as 1773 (E25–18457 14 April 1773).* Dwight & Lucille Beeson Collection, Birmingham Museum, Alabama

210   211

212

By 1787, jasper teaware was evidently well established. Wedgwood wrote of Class XIII 'TEA *and* COFFEE EQUIPAGES' in his Catalogue that 'Tea pots, coffee pots, chocolates, sugar dishes, cream ewers, with cabinet cups and saucers' were 'now made in the *jasper* of two colours' besides in '*bamboo* [cane] and *basaltes*'. The jasper pieces were 'polished within (not glazed) like the natural stone, ornamented with bas-reliefs and very highly finished'. To emphasise the quality of the ware, he included a full-page mezzotint, printed in blue, of an engine-turned jasper dip coffee cup showing the transparency of the jasper body. In June of the previous year Josiah had sent a gift of his first set of jasper teaware 'polished within' to William Eden's wife, describing the lapidary polishing as 'in the manner in which agate and other stones are polished; a new improvement. . . . This is the first set.'[211]

213

213. *Solid pale-blue and white jasper covered broth bowl or écuelle and saucer with lotus knop, ornamented with rose garlands and aquatic plants. Height 4½" (11.4 cm); diameter of saucer 7" (17.8 cm). Mark: (bowl)* WEDGWOOD O; *(saucer)* WEDGWOOD 3 S. *c.1786–90.* British Museum

214

214. *Drum-shaped solid pale-blue and white jasper salt cellar, ornamented with the* Dancing Hours. *Lapidary-polished interior. Height 2⅛" (5.4 cm); diameter 3" (7.6 cm). Mark:* WEDGWOOD 3S. *c.1786–95. An identical pair of salt cellars, with the same mark (also on the écuelle in* Plate 213*) is in the British Museum.* Wedgwood Museum

215

215. *Engine-turned solid pale-blue and white jasper covered butter dish (normally supplied with a circular stand), and a large solid pale-blue and white jasper footed bowl with lapidary-polished interior, both ornamented with groups of* amorini *and* Bacchanalian Boys *at play, the butter dish with the figure of* Poor Maria *also. Bowl height 5" (12.8 cm); diameter 8⅞" (22.5 cm). Mark:* WEDGWOOD. *c.1786–95. The footed bowl is described in a Shape Book (Ms. 54–30028, c.1790) as a punch-bowl, made in quart or pint sizes.* Wedgwood Museum

Among the earliest teaware pieces in jasper were probably the 'leafage' teapots and stands (Plate 202), of which examples are known in white, solid grey–blue and solid grey–green. These moulded pieces would have required no applied ornament and may have been used to test the performance of hollowware shapes in drying and firing. No Wedgwood & Bentley marked pieces have been found, but examples are recorded bearing the eighteenth-century 'Wedgwood' mark impressed.[212] Ornamental solid jasper pieces must have followed shortly, some with engine-turned decoration and lapidary polishing (Plates 215, C29 and C30); and the jasper dip process, understood as early as 1777, was probably developed within a year or so. From examination of early examples, it appears that some of the smaller tea bowls and handled cups were made wholly of the fine jasper body rather than, as the memorandum suggests, of the coarser body with a dip of fine jasper, and it is possible that the process was too laborious and costly to be worthwhile for small teaware pieces. Size was not, however, the deciding factor, for some of the smallest cameos were made of the coarser body; but a further consideration would have been the quality required of fine cabinet pieces so that they would display the beauty of the translucent jasper body.

Later still, about 1786, came the introduction of three-colour jasper, at first by the simple use of different coloured ornaments in the form of swags, bands and cameos, and then by applying 'dice' of a second colour alternated with quatrefoils of a third. The diced or chequered pattern was

216. Solid lilac and white jasper oval basin with everted edge, the outside fluted and ornamented with husk festoons, the interior rim ornamented with aquatic plants and a bead-and-reel edge. 11" × 13" (27.0 cm × 33.0 cm). Mark: WEDGWOOD *and 1 (incised). c.1785–95. A rare piece in a rare colour.* Dwight & Lucille Beeson Collection, Birmingham Museum, Alabama

217. Extremely rare solid blue and white jasper monteith ornamented with garlands of vine suspended from paterae and a band of inverted grasses near the foot, the applied handles in solid white jasper. 5⅜" × 13½" (13.6 × 34.3 cm). Mark: WEDGWOOD *and* ∨ *(incised). c.1785–95.* Dwight & Lucille Beeson Collection, Birmingham Museum, Alabama

216

217

soon more economically produced by the use of the rose-engine-turning lathe to cut the 'dice' through dip, leaving the spaces to be ornamented as before.

218

219

220

221

218. *Solid lilac and white 'tear'- or 'pear'-shaped custard cup with applied lattice-work ornament. Height 2" (5.2 cm); length 2½" (6.3 cm). Unmarked. Wedgwood, c.1785–90. The sprigging-on of this trellis or lattice ornament without distortion required particular dexterity on the part of the ornamenter.* Wedgwood Museum

219. *Solid yellow and white jasper custard cup and cover ornamented with trellis or latticework, the cover intricately pierced. Height 2½" (5.2 cm). Mark:* WEDGWOOD. *c.1785–90. (Cf. Plate 218.) Examples of solid yellow jasper of this period are rare.* Wedgwood Museum

220. *Solid bright-blue and white jasper sweetmeat basket, pierced in a trellis pattern all over with 'wicker' edges, applied laurel swags, and scroll and bead border to the raised foot. Height 5¼" (13.4 cm). Mark:* WEDGWOOD. *c.1790.* Lady Lever Art Gallery, Port Sunlight

221. *Solid pale-blue and white jasper inkstand with central taper stand in the form of a broken column, flanked by an inkwell and covered sander in an oval base. Length 6½" (26.5 cm). Mark:* WEDGWOOD. *c.1785–90. This shape appears in the London Pattern Book for 1787 (Ms. 61–30635).* Dwight & Lucille Beeson Collection, Birmingham Museum, Alabama

222. *Pale-blue jasper dip teapot ornamented with floral scrolls and the sign of the zodiac for Cancer. Height 5⅜" (13.5 cm). Mark:* WEDGWOOD. *A rare form of ornament, perhaps created for a birthday present. c.1790.* Merseyside Museums

223. *Pale-blue jasper dip tea canister with flattened stopper, ornament of* Domestic Employment *modelled by Hackwood from designs by Lady Templetown above a wide band of engine-turned fluting, and a spreading turned foot. Height 5½" (14.0 cm). Mark:* WEDGWOOD. *c.1785–90.* Temple Newsam House, Leeds

224. *Blue jasper dip fluted chamber candlestick and snuffer with applied flowers and oak border. Height 3" (7.6 cm). Mark:* WEDGWOOD. *c.1790.* Manchester City Art Gallery

225. *An extremely rare lilac and white jasper dip flower- or bough-pot ornamented with reliefs of seven* amorini *playing musical instruments beneath a border of wreathed masks. The pierced cover, which should be of white jasper, is a painted metal replacement. Shape 348. Oval length 8¾" (22.2 cm); height 7" (17.8 cm). Unmarked. Wedgwood. c.1790. The bas-relief subject is usually attributed to Flaxman but no evidence has been found to substantiate this and the original wax model (Plate 225A) does not resemble his work either in the modelling technique or in the wax composition used.* Lady Lever Art Gallery, Port Sunlight

222

223

224

225

225A

225A. *Dark-brown wax model of amorini playing musical instruments and dancing beneath a border of wreathed masks. 6″ × 15″ (15.4 × 38.0 cm). The subject is copied from an octagonal cinerary urn, formerly in the Albani Collection and now in the Capitoline Museum and would almost certainly have come to Wedgwood from the atelier in Rome, and, since the original carvings on the urn were intended to represent the hope of life after death (Carol Macht,* Classical Wedgwood Designs, *1957, p. 61), may perhaps be identified with* Several Geniuses representing the Pleasures of the Elysian Fields, *modelled by Giuseppe Angelini in 1787 (Appendix J: II.57). Meteyard and others have identified the subject as 'Sacrifice to Hymen'. The Wedgwood version, which appears also without the border of wreathed masks and was extensively copied by Adams of Greengates, differs from the wax model by the removal of the drapery from the figure second from the left and the addition of unconvincingly attached drapery to hide the nudity of the others.*
Lady Lever Art Gallery, Port Sunlight

226

226. *Translucent white jasper chocolate-pot ornamented with ivy festoons in green and lilac, laurel and rosette borders in green, and two cameos in blue and white. Height 6¼″ (16.0 cm). Mark:* WEDGWOOD. c.1790. *A rare and fine example of four-colour jasper.*
Lady Lever Art Gallery, Port Sunlight

179

227. Small lidded cream jug of solid pale-blue jasper with engine-turned dicing and an applied pattern of running oak and quatrefoils in white and green jasper. Height 4⁷⁄₁₆″ (11.2 cm). Mark: WEDGWOOD H H. c.1790. An extremely unusual example of 'blind' dicing in three-colour jasper. Manchester Museum

228. Solid green and white jasper helmet-shape cream jug with inlaid foot and ornament of putti at various pursuits above a wide band of engine-turned vertical fluting. Height 4⅞″ (12.4 cm). Mark: Wedgwood. c.1785. Dwight & Lucille Beeson Collection, Birmingham Museum, Alabama

229. (Left) solid blue and white jasper teapot with acanthus-moulded spout, ornamented with amorini at play above a band of engine-turned vertical fluting. Height 4⅝″ (11.7 cm). Mark: Wedgwood. c.1785. (Cf. Plate 209.) (Right) tricolour jasper teapot: blue and white jasper dip, diced and ornamented with green jasper quatrefoils. Height 4½″ (11.4 cm). Mark: WEDGWOOD 3 3. c.1785–90. Dwight & Lucille Beeson Collection, Birmingham Museum, Alabama

230. Tricolour jasper teapot: lilac and white jasper dip ornamented with green jasper quatrefoils on a diced ground. Height 4½″ (11.4 cm). Mark: WEDGWOOD. c.1790–5. Dwight & Lucille Beeson Collection, Birmingham Museum, Alabama

227

228

229

230

231

232

232A

233

234

231. *Lidded jug and teapot of tricolour jasper; bright blue jasper dip with engine-turned dicing ornamented with green jasper quatrefoils. Height 5½" and 4" (14.0 and 10.2 cm). Marks: (jug)* WEDGWOOD 3; *(teapot)* WEDGWOOD 3 O. *c.1790.* Manchester Museum

232. *Green jasper dip cream jug with engine-turned dicing, and ornament of yellow jasper quatrefoils and white jasper floral scrolls with figures of Cupid among the scrolls, between borders of oak and scrolls. Height 3⅛" (7.9 cm). Mark:* WEDGWOOD. *c.1790. Both the Cupid and scroll ornament and the oak border are extremely unusual.* Merseyside Museums

232A. *Detail of the ornament on the cream jug illustrated in Plate 232.*

233. *Tricolour jasper coffee cup and saucer of green jasper dip with engine-turned dicing, yellow quatrefoils and white jasper Cupid and scroll ornament. Height 2⅞" (7.4 cm), diameter of saucer 4⅞" (12.3 cm). Mark:* Wedgwood N H. *c.1790.* Merseyside Museums

234. *Blue jasper dip miniature cream jug, the body engine-turned and ornamented with yellow strapwork and white beads and leaves, mounted in Sheffield Plate. Height 4½" (11.4 cm). No mark visible. c.1795. The body of the jug is formed from an oval bell pull, a shape used also for scent bottles (cf. Plate 60).* Wedgwood Museum

181

235. *Lockett black and white dip stoneware tea kettle in imitation of Wedgwood's jasper, ornamented with groups of Cybele, Cupid and Lion, Venus and Cupid with Eagle, and Venus and Cupid with Sea Monsters between borders of acanthus and vine. Height 10¼"* (26.1 cm). *Mark:* J. LOCKETT *impressed.* c.1790. *J. & G. Lockett were potters in Burslem in 1786, subsequently (from 1802) at Lane End.* British Museum

236. *Blue and white biscuit porcelain teaware in imitation of Wedgwood's jasper made at Gotthelf Greiner's factory at Groszbreitenbach, Thuringia, c.1790. This ware is of the type known in Germany as Wedgwoodarbeit, a name that Josiah may have found more flattering than the quality of the ware it described.* Kestner-Museum, Hanover

235

236

About that time, when some especially fine large teapots and jugs were being made, a technique for roughening the surface of jasper to produce an 'orange-peel' effect was introduced. This 'dimpled' or 'granulated' finish added variety and a textured ground for ornament (see Plate C38) contrasting with borders of smooth jasper. Solid blue teawares were made regularly until about 1790.[213] Both solid green and solid lilac examples are known, but their rarity indicates that quantities of these colours were never large. By 1790 at the latest jasper teawares were in regular production in jasper dip of five colours — black, dark blue, pale blue, green and lilac — with many variations of shade in each, and it is possible that trials were made in yellow and grey.

Many of the finest teawares of the period, both solid jasper and jasper dip, bear the impressed marks 'o' or '3' (sometimes both) in addition to the factory mark. Since these marks were impressed rather than incised, there is some suggestion that they may have had some greater significance than workmen's marks, perhaps indicating pieces of special quality.

Though they appear unimportant beside the grandest tablets or more spectacular vases, the best of the eighteenth-century tablewares display fine potting and the quality of Wedgwood's jasper body as few other examples do, and the 'cabinet' cups and saucers, in particular, are notable for their translucency.

BUSTS AND FIGURES

A few jasper busts, all in miniature and in plain white jasper affixed to socles of black basaltes, were made in the Wedgwood & Bentley period. These are listed in the 1779 Catalogue, Class XII, as Homer, Bacchus, Ariadne and Voltaire (all 4½ inches high), and Montesquieu, Rousseau,

237

237. Three miniature busts: (left) Aristophanes, white jasper on a black basaltes socle, height 4" (10.2 cm); (centre) Pindar, black basaltes, height 4" (10.2 cm); (right) Homer, glazed white terracotta on a black basaltes plinth, height 3⁹⁄₁₆" (9.0 cm). Marks: (left and centre) Wedgwood and Bentley (on bust and base) with names impressed on the busts; (right) WEDGWOOD (on plinth only). The two Wedgwood & Bentley busts are c.1779; the glazed terracotta bust may be earlier, c.1777, on a later plinth, perhaps attached unnecessarily to an unmarked but perfectly authentic Wedgwood & Bentley bust. Kadison Collection

238. Two miniature busts of white jasper on black basaltes pedestals ornamented with masks and drapery swags: (left) Ariadne; (right) Bacchus. *Height 5½" (14.0 cm). Mark:* Wedgwood & Bentley *(below truncation; both socles unmarked but with the number '6' incised).* c.1778–9.
Manchester Museum

238

238A. Biscuit stoneware busts of Ariadne and Bacchus. Height 5¾" (14.6 cm). Mark: WEDGWOOD *(Bacchus only).* c.1785.
Wedgwood Museum

238A

Pindar, Aristophanes and Voltaire (4 inches high). Their availability in jasper is not mentioned in the 1779 Catalogue, and knowledge of them relies chiefly on examples that have survived. The original idea for white busts, which he wanted 'large as life', came from Bentley in July 1774,[214] when he would certainly have been referring to their production in white terracotta biscuit. Josiah was doubtful 'how our white Bodies will stand in such large masses'. Four months later he wrote: 'We are making some of the very small Busts, Voltaire &c & shall send them soon. These, & larger[215] may be made of the white composition I believe.'[216] No evidence of white busts having been made at this period has been discovered, but in December 1778, just over six months after Voltaire's death, Josiah sent Bentley 'a head of Voltaire in white Jasper upon a Basalte Pedastal [*sic*] richly ornamented with the *disconsolate muse*, her Lyre unstrung at her feet & other suitable insignia, upon the death of so great a man'.[217]

The 1787 Catalogue contains mention of 'Small busts with emblematic terms',[*218] which were probably available in both black basaltes and jasper (Plate 239).

Also catalogued for the first time in 1787 were Wedgwood's jasper figures. In the introduction to Class XI Josiah wrote: 'A small assortment of the figures is now made in the jasper of two colours, the effect of which is new and pleasing.' This 'assortment' was probably confined to Numbers 36–41 in the list – Cupid, Hebe, Mars, Venus, Jupiter and (No. 38) 'small statues' – all described as 'on pedestal'. The five named figures have been identified from surviving examples, but the 'small statues' are less readily recognisable. None of these pieces is known to have been made during the Wedgwood & Bentley partnership, and no

*In this context the word 'term' is used to denote a square pillar. Correctly, 'term' (*terminus*) describes the whole object – a human bust or torso ending in a pillar or pedestal of square section.

239. *Four white jasper miniature busts on solid blue socles, mounted on blue jasper dip tapering pedestals ornamented with trophies. These are evidently four of the 'Small busts with emblematical terms' listed but not fully described in Class XI Section II of the 1787 Catalogue (Appendix L.42). Those illustrated are tentatively identified as (left to right) Jupiter, Venus, Mars and Cupid. Height ('Mars') 5¾" (14.6 cm). Marks: ('Jupiter' and 'Venus') Wedgwood; others unmarked. c.1787. These miniature busts are extremely rare: five examples – identified as Diderot (?), Minerva, Ariadne (wrongly described as 'Omphale') and Endymion – are in the Royal Collection at Windsor Castle (A. Dawson, 'Creamware, Cameos and Coffee Cans: Wedgwood in the Royal Collection', in* Country Life, *5 September 1985, Plate 4), and another, Aristophanes, is in a private collection in America (David Buten,* Eighteenth-Century Wedgwood, *1980, Plate 157).*
British Museum

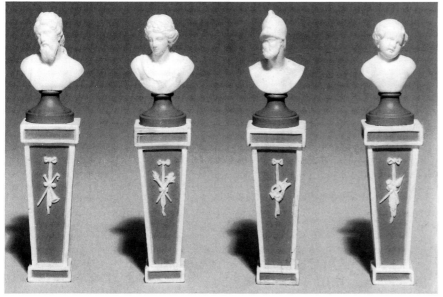

239

240. *Two Turner white jasper busts of* (left) *John Locke and* (right) *John Milton on black basaltes socles. Height 10⅜"* (26.5 cm) *and 10"* (25.5 cm). *Mark:* TURNER. *c.1800. John Turner of Lane End and his sons, who succeeded him in 1787, made fine-quality jasper and black basaltes comparable to Wedgwood's and often similar in style. Josiah Wedgwood and John Turner were on friendly terms and joined in leasing clay mines at Redruth and St Austell, undertaking a journey of exploration in Cornwall together in 1775.* Christie's, London

241. *Pair of grey-blue jasper pedestals, covered with a darker blue dip, with four feet composed of rams' heads and feet joined by strips of moulded laurel, the concave sides ornamented with figures of Cupid representing the seasons* (Appendix J:I.231–4). *Height 3⅛"* (8.0 cm). *Mark:* Wedgwood & Bentley. *c.1779. These are pedestals for the jasper figure of Venus (see Plate C41). Aileen Dawson, who published them in* Masterpieces of Wedgwood in the British Museum, *1984, p. 50 and Figure 37, correctly comments on the 'poor quality' of the grey-blue jasper, where it is visible on the undersides of the pedestals, suggesting that this may indicate that they were experimental pieces. In fact they are instructive examples of the use of the coarse jasper body, concealed on the upper surfaces by a finer jasper dip (see pp. 87–9).* British Museum

242. (Facing page) *Solid white jasper figure of Mars. Height 7"* (16.6 cm). *Mark:* WEDGWOOD. *c.1785. Apart from their brief descriptions in the 1787 Catalogue* (Appendix L.36–7 and 39–41) *little is known about Wedgwood's jasper figures. There is a possibility that one of these figures or the 'small statues'* (Appendix L.38) *may have been in the experimental stage as early as November 1777 (see caption to Plate C41), but this is uncertain. Some, at least, were in production by 1780, but all examples are rare. This figure would have been mounted upon a drum pedestal (cf. Plate 244).* Merseyside Museums

240

241

evidence of their existence before 1787 has been found. The figure of 'Venus rising from the sea, upon a pedestal richly ornamented with figures representing the seasons' appears in the 1779 Catalogue, but without any indication that it was available at that time in jasper. The existence of a Wedgwood & Bentley marked example (Plate C41) suggests that this subject may have been the first ornamental figure to be made in the blue jasper body. Josiah's frequent use of the words 'figure' and 'statue' to describe bas-reliefs has given rise to much confusion on the subject.

242

243

244

245

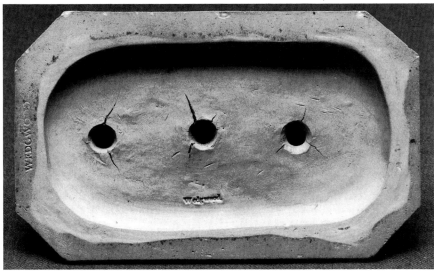

245A

243. *Solid white jasper figure of Venus with Cupid and a dolphin. Height 6⅝" (16.0 cm). Unmarked. (See caption to Plate 242 and cf. Plates 244 and C41.)*
Merseyside Museums

244. *Solid white jasper figure of Jupiter on a solid pale blue and white jasper drum pedestal ornamented with flower swags, paterae and trophies. Height 10¼" (26.0 cm); base only 2⅜" (6.0 cm). Mark:* WEDGWOOD. *c.1785. All three figures illustrated show signs of crazing, particularly noticeable in the body, cloak and base of the Jupiter figure.*
City Museum & Art Gallery, Stoke-on-Trent

245. *Tricolour jasper figure of a Sleeping Boy after Fiammingo, the figure in white and the sheet solid green on a solid lilac base. 3⅞" × 5⅛" (9.8 × 13.2 cm). Marks:* WEDGWOOD *and* Wedgwood *(see Plate 245A). c.1785–90.*
Kadison Collection

245A. *Marks on the base of the Sleeping Boy illustrated in Plate 245. The double-marking of jasper and black basaltes was frequent, but marking with two different stamps — in this case the 'upper case' and the 'upper and lower case' — is most unusual. The base has evidently been cut away and pierced by hand, and some firecracking has occurred around the firing holes.*

246. *Pen and ink and wash drawing for a chess set on lined paper, signed 'J Flaxman Inv^t et Delin^t.'. By John Flaxman junior c.1785. 6⅞" × 20⅜" (17.5 × 51.8 cm). Part of Flaxman's invoice dated 30 October 1783 reads: 'A figure of a fool for chess £1:5:0' (Ms. 2–1339). Such a price indicates an original model, almost certainly in wax, and this assumption is supported by the existence of wax models for some of the pieces in the Wedgwood Museum. The drawing makes use of fine modelling and chiaroscuro to give the* trompe l'œil *effect of the pieces displayed upon a shelf, and was probably commissioned by Wedgwood so that customers might make their choice from the different models of kings and queens, and between bishops and fools. (See Plate C42.)*
Wedgwood Museum

247. *Solid pale-blue jasper figure of a king from the Flaxman chess set. Height 3⅜" (8.5 cm). Unmarked. Wedgwood, c.1784. The three figures of kings are traditionally supposed to have been based on the actor John Philip Kemble in various Shakespearian roles (at least one as Macbeth). (Cf. Plate 248 and see also Appendix H:II.)*
Wedgwood Museum

248. *Solid white jasper figure of a queen from the Flaxman chess set. Height 3½" (9.0 cm). Unmarked. Wedgwood, c.1784. The three figures of queens are traditionally supposed to have been based on the actress Sarah Siddons, two of them showing her in the character of Lady Macbeth. The strong similarity of features between these small figures and those of the portrait medallion modelled by John Flaxman junior in 1782 (see Appendix H:I and Plate C17) lends some credence to the belief. Sarah Siddons was John Philip Kemble's sister.*
Wedgwood Museum

249. *Solid white jasper figure of a bishop from the Flaxman chess set. Height 3⅛" (8.0 cm). Unmarked, Wedgwood, c.1784. The three separate pieces illustrated in Plates 247–9 are all on bases of a smaller diameter than those of later editions and may be trial pieces.*
Wedgwood Museum

CHESSMEN

Flaxman's chessmen could not accurately be described as 'figures', though they are collected now more for their decorative qualities than for play. His bill dated 30 October 1783 charges £1.5.0 for 'A figure of a fool for chess', probably a model in wax, and three guineas is charged on the same bill, but dated more than a year later, for 'Three days employed in drawing bas-relief vases, Chess-men &c'.[219] On 5 February 1784 Flaxman wrote to Josiah: 'I return you many thanks, for the liberal praise you bestow on my chess figures.'[220] As the Oven Book for 1783 shows,[221] they were already in production in December, and in 1785 Flaxman pro-duced a remarkable *trompe l'oeil* drawing in pen and wash, showing the eighteen different pieces* arranged on two shelves (Plate 246). This draw-ing, for which he charged six guineas,[222] may have been intended for use in the Greek Street Showrooms, but there is also the possibility that, although not sold until 1785, it was originally executed in 1783 to give Josiah a clear idea of the proposed designs. It would have been invoiced later, when Josiah decided to keep it.

Chessmen were made in solid colours, and in white jasper with blue, green or lilac dip bases (Plate C42). According to Barnard, as many as 130 sets were sold between 1785 and 1795.[223] Their design is a remarkable example of eighteenth-century Gothick, seldom seen in ceramics.

CANDLESTICKS AND CANDELABRA

Some of Wedgwood's finest figure work is to be found in the jasper candlesticks. Triton and griffin candlesticks had been made in black basaltes some years before the invention of jasper,† but both models eventually translated well into the new body (Plates 250, 251 and C43). Candlesticks and inkstands were among the earlier articles to be made in jasper, examples of both being sent to London on All Fools' Day 1775,[224] but it is unlikely that these included anything so ambitious as figure candlesticks. Josiah had, in fact, much the same reservations about the suitability of ceramic bodies for candlesticks as he had about pottery frames for medallions.‡ He wrote to Bentley on 4 November 1778:

> Your favor of the 29th is before me with the sketches of candlesticks &c which shall be duly attended to, but I really despair of the article in pottery of any kind. In black it is too dismal. In pebble *of any kind* it will be *pitcher – the ware*, & in any other glazed ware it will be vulgar. Something pretty might be made in blue & white Jasper, but would not that vulgarize the material? . . . If one may confess a disagreeable truth upon the subject, it seems to me that *metal* is the only proper candlestick material. Clay serves only to satisfy caprice or poverty.[225]

*Eight pawns, castle, knight, bishop, fool (to replace the bishop for the French market), three Queens and three Kings.
†Both are listed in the 1773 Catalogue.
‡He deplored their 'Pott appearance.'

250. *Detail of the head of a triton from a solid blue and white jasper triton candlestick (see Plate C43). c.1785.*
Brooklyn Museum, Emily Winthrop Miles Collection

251. *Solid pale-blue and white jasper Griffin candlestick. Height 13¼" (33.5 cm). Mark: WEDGWOOD. c.1790. The jasper griffin candlestick differs from the basaltes examples by having a candleholder of the same material as the figure, but these pieces appear to have been made in both black basaltes and jasper with candleholders of either metal or stoneware. Josiah had some doubts about the suitability of his materials for candlesticks: 'I really despair of the article in pottery of any kind,' he wrote to Bentley on 4 November 1778 (E26–18859). 'Something pretty might be made in blue & white Jasper, but would not that vulgarise the material? ... If one may confess a disagreeable truth upon this subject, it seems to me that metal is the only proper candlestick material.'*
British Museum

250

251

252

252. *Lilac jasper dip candlestick in the form of an Egyptian sphinx with raised wings supporting a lotus candleholder, on a rectangular base ornamented with oval rosettes. Height* 5⅜" (13.4 cm); length 6⅝" (17.0 cm). *Mark: WEDGWOOD. c.1785. The large firecracks apparent at the left elbow and back leg, the neck and the junction of the* candleholder and the wing, *are evidence of the difficulty experienced in firing jasper even as late as 1785, when vases were in regular production.*
Merseyside Museums

It certainly was not to gratify poverty that Josiah made such candle-sticks as the tritons, griffins and sphinxes; nor the pair of 'rustic' candle-sticks attributed to Hackwood (Plate C44), the Ceres and Cybele candlesticks (Plates 253 and 254) or the Diana and Minerva candelabra (Plate 255). The earliest jasper candlestick designs incorporating human figures were probably those mentioned in Josiah's letter of 5 October 1780: 'The figure candlesticks are in hand & shall be sent with all speed when finished.'[226] A letter of 28 October is rather more specific: 'The fig-ure candlesticks with the blue plinths & nossels will be sent today.'[227] This description most clearly fits the single female figures[228] grasping candleholders in the form of cornucopias (Plate 256).

The Ceres and Cybele candlesticks were certainly in production by 1786, when Byerley recorded Josiah's comments on them in his Memorandum Book.[229] Josiah was critical of the candleholders which, he thought, 'should be straight & not bent as a Cornucopia'. He added that modelling was 'a very tedious & expensive work indeed – A pair of fig⁵ of that sort will cost near 20 guineas.' The figures of Diana and Minerva have been attributed to Henry Webber,[230] but no evidence has been found to support this theory, which rests on the similarity of style between the figure of Minerva and that of Britannia on the 'Naval victories' group,* and John Bacon's monument to the Earl of Chatham in Westminster Abbey (1779).† If these candlesticks were Webber's work, they must have been among his first models for Wedgwood, for he joined the firm at Etruria on 2 July 1782[231] and the Oven Book entry for 21 December reads: 'Minerva and Luna a branch candlestick 2 nosols in fine white 15 Ins'.[232]

*See Plate C59.
†Webber was Bacon's pupil.

253. Solid blue and white jasper candlestick in the form of a figure of Ceres holding a torch, the moulded flames forming the candleholder. Height 12½" (31.8 cm). Mark: WEDGWOOD and ℍℍ (incised). c.1785–95. Tom Byerley recorded Josiah's comments on this and the companion model of Cybele (Plate 254) in his Memoranda Book on 23 March 1786 (Ms. 45–29110): 'Ceres being represented in most antiques with a lighted torch in her hand as going in search of her daughter Proserpine, was what gave the idea of a flame for the nozzle of the Candlestick she bears . . . but as a new torch the handle should be straight & not bent as a Cornucopia.' Wedgwood Museum

254. Solid blue and white jasper candlestick in the form of a figure of Cybele with a lion, holding a cornucopia which supports a moulded candleholder. The companion piece to the Ceres candlestick illustrated in Plate 253. Height 12½" (31.8 cm). Mark: as Plate 253. Josiah described this piece as 'Cybele representing the Earth, and being accompanied by a tame lion to shew perhaps that cultivation will subdue all things' (Ms. 45–29110). Wedgwood Museum

253

254

255. *Pair of solid blue and white jasper two-branch candlesticks in the form of figures of Minerva and Diana. Height 13¾" (35.0 cm). Mark:* WEDGWOOD, *c.1783–95. These superbly modelled figures have been attributed to both Flaxman and Webber, but no sound evidence has been found to substantiate either claim. If they are Webber's, they must have been ambitious early work for Wedgwood for he did not arrive at Etruria until 2 July 1782 and these models are recorded as being fired during 1–8 December. Byerley's Memoranda Book for 23 March 1786 records Josiah as saying. 'I will endeavour to make two other figure Candlesticks to correspond with Ceres & Cybele & their nozzles shall spring from Palm Branches – but I find modeling a very tedious & expensive work indeed – A pair of fig⁵ of that sort will cost near 20 Guineas.' Since these cannot be the Minerva and Diana candlesticks, it appears that the models were never produced. The pair illustrated are extremely rare examples of tricolour jasper using two shades of solid blue – the palm branches being blue (sometimes described as 'deep blue') and the bases pale blue – with solid white jasper figures.*
Christie's, London

255A. *Earthenware biscuit example of the Minerva candlestick, showing the quality of the modelling. Height 13" (33.0 cm). Unmarked. Wedgwood, c.1783.*
Wedgwood Museum

255

255A

256

256. Pair of solid pale-blue and white jasper candlesticks in the form of female figures grasping cornucopias which support (replacement) candleholders. Height 11¼" (28.6 cm). Mark: WEDGWOOD.
c.1790–1810. These figure candlesticks appear to have been made for the first time towards the end of 1780 (see p. 191). They have frequently been catalogued as representing Cybele and Ceres (see Plate 254) but their wreaths of fruit and corn suggest a more likely pairing of Pomona and Ceres.
Metropolitan Museum of Art, New York, Friedsam Collection

257

257. Pair of solid grey–green and white jasper vases formed of well-modelled figures of Cupid with a bird's nest and Psyche with a butterfly, perhaps representing Spring and Summer. Height 8½" (21.6 cm). Mark: WEDGWOOD. c.1785–95. No evidence has yet been discovered to identify the modeller of these vases, but they are usually attributed either to Webber or to Flaxman. (Cf. Plate C47.)
Dwight & Lucille Beeson Collection, Birmingham Museum, Alabama

258

259

258. Pair of solid pale-blue and white jasper flower holders or bough-pots in the form of figures of Zephyr and Flora resting against sarcophagi. Height 5½" (14.0 cm); base measurements 4¹⁵⁄₁₆" × 8" (12.6 × 20.2 cm). Mark: WEDGWOOD. *The figures are attributed without evidence to Webber. The shapes of the small vases placed in front of the sarcophagi were varied (cf. Plate 259 and see David Buten,* Eighteenth-Century Wedgwood, *1980, Plates 173 and 174).* Dwight & Lucille Beeson Collection, Birmingham Museum, Alabama

259. Solid pale-blue and white jasper flower holder in the form of the figure of Flora resting against a sarcophagus. Height 5⅞" (15.0 cm). Mark: WEDGWOOD. *(Cf. Plate 258.)* Kadison Collection

VASES

On 12 November 1780, in his last recorded letter to Bentley, Josiah wrote: 'I am contriving some vases for bodies, and bodies for vases.'[233] Just two weeks later, Bentley died, and within twelve months Josiah was faced with the liquidation of the entire stock of ornamental wares produced before 26 November 1780 by auction sale. A letter written by Byerley to Josiah II nearly twenty-seven years later reveals that there was some speculation among Wedgwood's customers whether Bentley's death would have an adverse effect on the quality of Wedgwood ware.[234] 'When Mr Bentley died', Byerley wrote,

> a great many discriminating people were so captivated by his intelli-
> gence & animated conversation that they believed & propagated the
> opinion that he was the origin of all the fine works of taste & all
> which they saw exhibited in our rooms – without reflecting that he
> could not be spending his day in social intercourse with them and at

the same time sitting down at the Workmen's benches for days together directing them in the production of beautiful forms and inventing new modes of decoration. . . . He had some merit as a Culler and an index to works of antient art, but unfortunately less even in this way than has been imputed to him. It was however to be feared that this mistake would lead to a notion that with him would die away the whole of the art – and to counteract this it was determined to open the rooms after the public sale of W&B with works of original merit & quite dissimilar to anything before seen. At this period Jasper Vases were first introduced and answered the intention.

Wedgwood's experience of firing large vases with sprigged ornament in black basaltes and terracotta (crystalline) bodies, and the perfecting of the jasper body in 1777–8, might have permitted the production of jasper vases earlier than 1781, but he had constantly to balance the desire to stay ahead of his rivals against the need to sell existing stock. The over-hasty introduction of jasper vases might have made much of his stock of basaltes and variegated vases at least temporarily unsaleable. The auction at Christie & Ansell of the whole of his ornamental ware stocks gave him an unexpected and unique opportunity to introduce a new and exciting range of vases without risk to established lines. Josiah would certainly not have compromised the success of the auction by marketing jasper vases until the sale was completed on 17 December 1781.

When, at last, the jasper vases were released, they were an immediate success. If he hoped, as he had once told Bentley, to 'ASTONISH THE WORLD ALL AT ONCE', 'to amuse, & divert, & please, and astonish, nay, & even ravish the ladies',[235] and finally to become 'Vase maker General to the Universe',[236] it was the jasper vases that could make his hopes realistic. Many of the shapes produced were variations, principally in handles,

260

260. Bell hookahs: (left) cane ware ornamented with figures of the Muses after Flaxman, height 7 ½" (19.1 cm). Mark: WEDGWOOD Z. c.1800; (right) blue jasper dip ornamented with 'Acanthus and Bell' and floral scroll reliefs, height 10 ¼" (26.1 cm), diameter 14" (35.6 cm). Mark: WEDGWOOD. c.1800. Wedgwood and Bentley made their first attempt on the Turkish market as early as 1773, when Josiah reported that he had been 'setting our people at the ornamental works of making a few each of the Turkish articles' and it is not unlikely that Sir Robert Ainslie supplied Wedgwood with models of hookahs in 1777. References to the production of tobacco bowls occur in the Oven Books in the early 1780s (e.g. Ms. 53–30014 10 and 17 March 1781), but no specific mention of the bell hookah has been found earlier than May 1800 (Ms. 53–30018.2). A memorandum from Etruria to the London showrooms dated 21 April 1800 reads: 'You order Chillums . . . we don't know what these are unless you mean what we have heretofore call'd Hookers [sic]' (Ms. 138–27946). Wedgwood Museum

261. *Earthenware biscuit tulip-vase with three tiers of spouts or tubes each to hold a single tulip. Height 18½" (47.0 cm). Unmarked. c.1786. Vases of this type with up to eleven tiers of spouts around a cylindrical or pyramidal centre and set on a deep pedestal or plinth were made in tin-glazed earthenware in England, France, Germany and Italy, and most notably in Holland. Porcelain tulip-vases were produced in China for export to Europe, and at Vienna. Wedgwood's were apparently made in jasper, and a 'Blue and white promide [pyramid] for flower things' was fired in January 1786 (Ms. 53–30015 7 and 14 January 1786). A drawing of the piece appears as shape no. 291 in the factory Shapes Book. It is unlikely that many of these vases were made, and none is known to have survivied in jasper. On the right of the illustration is a biscuit tartlett stand, coloured with a black slip, apparently designed as a centrepiece to display small tarts or pies containing sweetmeats or fruit. This piece, no. 605 in the Shapes Book, appears in the Oven Book entry for 31 January and 7 February 1800 (Ms. 53–30018 Vol. II), and was made in jasper, cane and white biscuit (probably terracotta). Both these examples were discovered in the Wedgwood archives and researched by Mrs Lynn Miller (see Lynn Miller, 'Oven Books: Oddities and Incidentals', in Wedgwood Society Proceedings, No. 11, 1982, pp. 163–72 and Fig 3).*
Wedgwood Museum

261

finials and ornament, of forms already popular in black basaltes, but throughout his last active years Josiah continued to introduce new shapes and to experiment with colours, jasper dip, ornament and the use of the rose-engine-turning lathe to produce different styles of decoration.

Much of the ornament used for vases was adapted from existing bas-reliefs first modelled for plaques or tablets. One of the most important of these was Flaxman's *Apotheosis of Homer*, and it is not surprising that Josiah should have chosen it for the vase which he valued most highly. The 'Pegasus Vase', as it has come to be known, was made in 1786, the first example being fired on 18 and 25 February, when 'two blue & white vases 23 Ins with palm tree angel temple &c' were recorded in the Oven Book.[237] These were presumably solid blue vases, but '2 fine white jasper vases 23 Ins diped [*sic*] Made, thrown, turned & finished & broke. . . . angels &c on' appear under the dates for 4 and 11 March.

The Minutes of the General Meeting of the Trustees of the British Museum for 27 May 1786 briefly record Josiah Wedgwood's presentation of a vase 'of his own manufacture' to the Museum,[238] and his letter of 24 June to Sir William Hamilton leaves no doubt as to its decoration: 'I lamented much that I could not . . . send a vase, the finest & most perfect I have ever made, & which I have since presented to the British Museum. I enclose a rough sketch of it: it is 18 inches high, & the price 20 guineas.' He added, at the foot of the page, 'the sketch of the vase could not be got ready for this post but shall be sent soon: Subject, the apotheosis of Homer.'[239]

262

263

262A

263. The reverse of the Pegasus vase illustrated in Plate C49, showing the figure of Minerva standing inside a temple (perhaps the Parthenon) beside a large palm tree the significance of which, unless it represents Fame, is not plain. This jasper dip vase shows signs of incipient blistering in parts, though the general quality is excellent. The interior fixing of the vase to its plinth is hidden by a white jasper dome about two inches in height, a feature not found in the British Museum specimen (Plate 262) but occasionally to be seen inside other jasper vases of this period. Height 18" (46.0 cm). Mark: WEDGWOOD. c.1790. Nottingham Castle Museum

262. A side view of the solid pale-blue and white jasper vase ornamented on the front with Flaxman's bas-relief, The Apotheosis of Homer, *and presented by Josiah Wedgwood to the British Museum in May 1786. The handles are formed of two snakes competing for a pale-blue jasper egg, the greater part of their bodies (and their fixing to the vase) hidden by a mask of Medusa evidently copied from the head attributed to Flaxman (see Plate 36). The cloud upon which the finial figure of Pegasus rides is also of pale-blue jasper. Height 18¼" (46.4 cm). Mark: see Plate 262A. 1786. This example of the 'Pegasus' or 'Apotheosis' vase is discussed in detail in Aileen Dawson's* Masterpieces of Wedgwood in the British Museum, *1984, pp. 102–11. Many later reproductions of this vase were made, though the complexity of its manufacture limited the quantity by price, through most of the nineteenth and the early years of the twentieth centuries. Their ornament varies slightly, and the grandeur of the accompanying plinths appears to have been altered according to fashion. The vase presented to the British Museum by Josiah is therefore specially important as a criterion of excellence. (Cf. Plate C49.)* British Museum

262A. Mark on the base of the 'Pegasus' vase illustrated in Plate 262.

264. *Black jasper dip
Pegasus vase ornamented
with Flaxman's bas-relief.*
The Apotheosis of
Virgil *(see Appendix
J:I.266). Height 23¾"
(60.0 cm) including
pedestal 6" (15.3 cm);
pedestal 10¼" (26.0 cm)
square. Mark:*
WEDGWOOD *(pedestal
only). c.1795–1820. This
well-finished vase with
altered border reliefs and set
on an ornate pedestal is
unlikely to have been made
in Josiah's lifetime, but is
attributable to the period
immediately following his
death.*
Dwight & Lucille
Beeson Collection,
Birmingham Museum,
Alabama

265. *Solid green jasper vase
dipped in a slightly darker
shade of green and
ornamented with figures of*
Apollo and the Nine
Muses. *Height 15"
(38.1 cm). Mark:*
WEDGWOOD. *c.1786.
The figures of the Muses
are neither Flaxman's
(Appendix J:I.214–23)
nor Angelini's (Appendix
J:II.26) but a hybrid set
partly from casts supplied
by John Flaxman senior in
1775 (see p. 141). The
solid white jasper plinth, a
feature of most early jasper
vases, was gradually
superseded after September
1786, when John
Wedgwood wrote to his
father: 'every lady calls for
plinths of the same colour as
the Vase with the ornaments
white. . . . It will be done for
the next Vases,' (W/M 6
10 September 1786).*
Lady Lever Art
Gallery, Port Sunlight

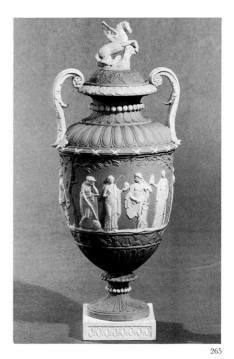

264   265

The design of the vase, in spite of the excellence of Flaxman's bas-relief, is not beyond criticism: the Medusa-head terminals to the snake handles are part-Flaxman and part-Montfaucon;[240] the Minerva figure is adapted from the Minerva Giustiniani in the Vatican Museum;[241] and the large palm tree appears to be filling a space rather than any design function. The total appearance of the vase is of some grace and elegance, and there is no doubting the quality of the examples in the British Museum and the Nottingham Castle Museum (Plates 263 and C49), the latter being a particular rare shade of greenish-buff jasper dip. As Aileen Dawson has pointed out, versions of this vase known to have been made in the nineteenth century lack the Minerva figure in the temple beside the palm tree.[242]

Flaxman's *Apotheosis of Virgil* bas-relief, believed to have been modelled about the end of 1785, was adapted to ornament a companion vase (Plate 264). Both bas-reliefs are listed in the 1787 Catalogue, and the 'Virgil vase' was probably produced by 1790. Wedgwood made no attempt to list or describe in detail his vases in the 1787 Catalogue, contenting himself with a good full-page illustration of a snake-handle vase ornamented with *Venus in her Chariot drawn by Swans* (Plates 276 and C50) after a design by Charles Lebrun. Of his 'VASES, TRIPODS, *and other ornaments, in the jasper with coloured grounds and white reliefs*' in Class XVIII of the Catalogue, he wrote with becoming modesty: 'As these are my latest, I hope they may be found to be my most improved work. Verbal descriptions could give but an imperfect idea of the delicacy of the materials, the execution of the artist, or the general effect; and I must therefore beg leave to refer those who wish for information in these respects, to a view of the articles themselves.'

One vase which would certainly have defied description was the extraordinary confection now known as the 'Prince of Wales' vase, in the Nottingham Castle Museum (Plate 277). This is reputed to have been made to celebrate the coming of age of George, Prince of Wales, later George IV, in 1783. The figures of Britannia and the lion and unicorn suggest Webber's hand, and it is possible that they are early examples of his work in jasper. The portrait medallion of the Prince, however, seems to show an older man, and the vase may have been produced for some later celebration, though, since his marriage was a disaster from the start, it is not easy to imagine what this might have been. Although it incorporates some good modelling, the total design of the vase is clumsy and bizarre. Perhaps fortunately, it appears to be unique.

266

267

268

269

266. *Solid lilac and white jasper vase ornamented with figures of* Apollo and the Nine Muses. *Solid white jasper plinth. Height 11¼" (28.6 cm). Mark:* WEDGWOOD. *c.1786. The vase is shape no. 1316. The figures of the Muses are the same hybrid group as were used to ornament the vase illustrated in Plate 265, but the figure of Apollo is from the medallion illustrated in Plate 143.*
Lady Lever Art Gallery, Port Sunlight

267. *Solid pale-blue and white jasper vase, Shape no. 1316, ornamented with Flaxman's figures of* Hercules in the Garden of the Hesperides *(see p. 136 and Appendix J:I.275). Height 13½" (34.5 cm). Mark:* WEDGWOOD. *c.1787. Flaxman modelled the subject in two parts, which he invoiced to Wedgwood in August 1787 for £23 (Ms. 2–1339). (Cf. Plate 266 which has the solid white jasper plinth in general use for vases until 1786.)*
City Museum & Art Gallery, Stoke-on-Trent

268. *Solid pale-blue and white jasper vase, shape no. 1316, ornamented with a framed figure of Apollo (cf. Plate 266) and laurel swags looped over circular paterae. Height 13⅛" (33.5 cm). Mark:* WEDGWOOD. *c.1787. A comparison of this vase with those of the same shape illustrated in Plates 266 and 267 reveals the very different effects achieved by varying the bas-relief ornament.*
Nottingham Castle Museum

269. *Solid blue and white jasper bulb vase with three laurel-leaf bulb holders fitted into holes pierced in the detachable flat grid. The body of the vase is ornamented with figures of* Apollo and the Nine Muses *(cf. Plate 265) above a band of trophies. The applied beads, which disguise the joint of the base of the vase with the spreading foot, are a feature of vases produced between about 1781 and 1810. Height 8⅞" (22.7 cm). Mark:* WEDGWOOD V. *c.1785–95.*
British Museum

270. *Solid pale-blue and white jasper vase on a tall cylindrical pedestal ornamented with swags of fruiting vine, medallions, lions' heads, ribbons and trophies. The vase is an adaptation of an antique marble vase formerly in the possession of the Borghese family in Rome and now in the Louvre. Five of the figures were supplied to Wedgwood by Flaxman or Mrs Landré in 1777 (Appendix J:I.126–30 and 153), but the whole composition was modelled again by John De Vaere while he was employed in Rome (see p. 150). A dark red wax model of the vase, height 8⅝" (21.9 cm) tentatively attributed to De Vaere is in the Nottingham Castle Museum collection. The subject was produced also as a tablet of ten figures, a rare example of which was illustrated in Meteyard's* Wedgwood and His Works, *1873, Plate V.3, mistakenly described as 'undoubtedly the tablet numbered 153 in the fourth edition of the catalogue, 1777', and assigned to Flaxman, who probably 'finished' De Vaere's model. Height 18¾" (47.5 cm); (pedestal) 12½" (32.0 cm). Mark:* WEDGWOOD *(vase only; pedestal unmarked).* c.1790.
Lady Lever Art Gallery, Port Sunlight

270

271. *Green jasper dip*
'tendril' vase, adapted from a
design by Edmé Bouchardon
and illustrated as Plate 8 of
Second Livre de Vases,
Inventé par Edmé
Bouchardon, *n.d. Height*
6½" (16.5 cm). Mark:
WEDGWOOD. c.1790.
Merseyside Museums

271

272. *Solid blue and white*
jasper footed bowl with
cover, ornamented with vine
festoons and groups of
Bacchanalian Boys *after*
Fiammingo, *the interior*
lapidary polished, set on a
solid blue and white jasper
pedestal ornamented with
bas-reliefs of the Seasons in
panels. Height 13"
(33.3 cm). Mark:
WEDGWOOD M. c.1790.
This is an imposing
adaptation of the punch-
bowl, illustrated in Plate
215 and usually supplied
without a cover.
Manchester City Art
Gallery

272

273. (Left) *solid pale-blue and white jasper square pedestal with loose grid pierced for flowers and fitted with a cup for a single bulb. Height (without grid) 7"* (17.8 cm). *Mark:* WEDGWOOD. c.1785. (Right) *solid dark-blue and white jasper square pedestal with grid fitted for use as a candlestick—cassolette. The front panel is ornamented with the French Revolution bas-relief adapted from Webber's Sydney Cove medallion (see Plates 189 and 190). Height (without grid) 7"* (17.8 cm). *Mark:* WEDGWOOD. c.1789. *These pedestals were used also for vases and flower holders. (Cf. Plate C48.)* Victoria & Albert Museum, London

274. *Solid pale-blue and white jasper ice pail or wine cooler, ornamented with figures of Boys after designs by Lady Diana Beauclerk (see Appendix J:1.243). Height 6¼"* (16.0 cm); *diameter 7½"* (19.0 cm). *Mark:* WEDGWOOD. c.1787. *The interior is lapidary polished.* Nottingham Castle Museum

273

274

275. *Green jasper dip snake-handle vase ornamented with* Sacrifice to Cupid, *an uncatalogued subject composed from figures from other bas-reliefs, on a solid white jasper plinth and a green jasper dip pedestal ornamented with rams' heads, medallions and winged beasts. Height 22½"* (57.5 cm). *Mark: (vase)* WEDGWOOD V: *(pedestal)* WEDGWOOD. c.1790. Christie's, New York

275

276

276. Solid blue and white jasper vase with tall loop handles, the body ornamented with Venus in her Chariot drawn by Swans, with attendant Cupids and Cupids watering the Swans (see Plate 293 and Appendix J:I.245–6) after designs by Charles Le Brun. Solid white jasper plinth. Height 15½" (39.5 cm). Mark: WEDGWOOD. c.1786. (See Plate C50 for the same vase shape with snakes entwined round the handles.)
Lady Lever Art Gallery, Port Sunlight

277

277. Solid pale-blue and white jasper vase ornamented with a portrait of George, Prince of Wales, in a laurel frame surmounted by the Prince of Wales's feathers, scrollwork on the body and lid, and a finial in the form of the figure of Britannia with shield and trophies. The vase stands upon a solid white jasper plinth ornamented with green jasper laurel festoons and the upper surface covered with greenish-brown jasper on which lie the white jasper figures of a lion and a unicorn (lacking his horn). The reverse of the vase is ornamented with a medallion of Fortuna with arabesque wreaths and shells. Height 14¾" (37.5 cm); width 13⅛" (33.6 cm). Unmarked. c.1783–95. (See p. 199.)
Nottingham Castle Museum

278A. Solid green and white jasper wine ewer ('Sacred to Bacchus') on white jasper plinth. Height 14½" (37.0 cm). Mark: WEDGWOOD. c.1785. Shape no. 236. This form of ewer was produced from models supplied by John Flaxman senior in 1775, (Cf. Plate C51.) Lady Lever Art Gallery, Port Sunlight

278B. Solid blue and white jasper water ewer ('Sacred to Neptune'). Height 15" (38.3 cm). Mark: WEDGWOOD. c.1786–90. (Cf. Plates 278A and C51.) Lady Lever Art Gallery, Port Sunlight

279. Three eighteenth-century jasper vases. (Left) solid blue and white jasper vase ornamented with festoons and medallions (Bacchus and Panther illustrated; cf. Plate 41), on a shaped octagonal plinth (the small cover is a replacement). Height 8⅛" (20.6 cm). (Centre) solid blue and white jasper vase with fluted neck and acanthus-moulded foot, ornamented with figures of cupids with a wreath and doves on a dimpled ground. Solid white jasper plinth. Height 8¼" (21.0 cm). (Right) solid pale-blue and white jasper vase ornamented with a Sacrifice subject on a dimpled ground. Height 7½" (19.0 cm). Marks: (left) WEDGWOOD. c.1790–5; (centre) Wedgwood. c.1785; (right) WEDGWOOD. c.1790. Dwight & Lucille Beeson Collection, Birmingham Museum, Alabama

278A

278B

279

280. *Solid pale-blue and white jasper inkstand in the form of a sarcophagus surmounted by two urns as inkwells, the body ornamented with shell corners and drapery enclosing an oval medallion of the* Marriage of Cupid and Psyche *(cf. Plates 134–6). Mark:* WEDGWOOD *(on back of sarcophagus). c.1790–5.* Dwight & Lucille Beeson Collection, Birmingham Museum, Alabama

281. *Solid green jasper hanging oil lamp with rounded gadrooned cover surmounted by three sibyls seated around a stoppered column. The lamp is ornamented with floral scrolls and leafage and three shell-shaped taper holders. Height 7½" (19.1 cm); diameter 7½" (19.1 cm). No visible mark. Wedgwood, c.1795. The three sibyl figures are the same models as were used for the 'Frog' service 'glaciers'. This lamp, then in the collection of Dr Braxton Hicks, was described by Eliza Meteyard in 1874 as 'comparatively modern' (*Memorials of Wedgwood, *1874, Frontispiece), but it was known to have been sold from the Marryat collection in 1867 and engraved in Joseph Marryat's* Collections towards a History of Pottery and Porcelain, *first published in 1850. It is most unlikely to have been made between 1810 and 1860. (See pp. 244–9 and cf. also plate C53.)* Lady Lever Art Gallery, Port Sunlight

280

281

282. Pair of solid pale-blue and white jasper bough-pot vases with solid white jasper pierced grids, the bodies ornamented with figures of gods and goddesses alternating with urns of flowers within moulded arches, the corners as caryatid and foliage supports on paw feet. Height 8⅝" (22.0 cm). Mark: WEDGWOOD. C.1790. Christie's, New York

283. Pair of solid blue and white jasper 'Quiver' vases, the domed lids ornamented with pairs of doves. The body of each quiver is ornamented with an unusual border of small shells, and with knotted drapery suspended from a ring. The joint of the foot with the circular plinth is largely hidden by rather clumsily modelled leaves. Height 8⅝" (22.1 cm). Mark: WEDGWOOD. C.1795. Dwight & Lucille Beeson Collection, Birmingham Museum, Alabama

282

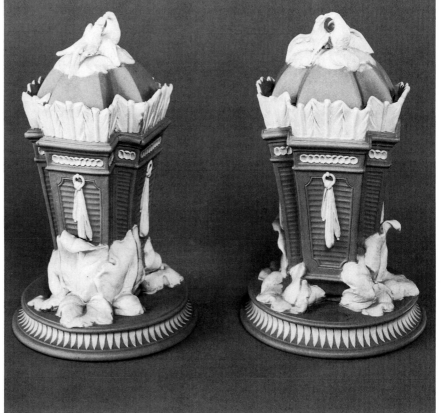

283

284. Solid pale-blue and white jasper vase ornamented with swan handles, inverted grasses and leaf borders, the lid surmounted by a finial in the form of figures of Leda and the Swan. Height 16⅞" (27.6 cm). Mark: WEDGWOOD V. c.1795. Dwight & Lucille Beeson Collection, Birmingham Museum, Alabama

285. Solid blue jasper vase with an almost imperceptible dip of the same colour, ornamented in white with festoons and medallions, with ram's-head handles. The neck is decorated with engine-turned vertical fluting and a ring of applied beads. Height 11¼" (28.6 cm). Mark: WEDGWOOD. c.1790. (Cf. Plate 279.) Manchester Museum

284

285

286

286. Garniture of three bright-blue and white solid jasper vases by Adams of Greengates. Height 9½" and 11½" (24 and 29 cm). Mark: ADAMS (and incised numerals). c.1800. Christie's, New York

287. Solid blue and white jasper 'ruined column' vase of three white jasper columns on a blue jasper base moulded with lichen, inscriptions and a central panel of figures evidently derived from A Roman Procession (see Appendix J:I.237). Height 9" (23.0 cm); base 12¾" × 4⁷⁄₁₆" (31.4 × 11.2 cm). Mark: WEDGWOOD ◠. c.1786–95. Dwight & Lucille Beeson Collection, Birmingham Museum, Alabama

287

288. Solid white jasper 'ruined column' vase. Height 8" (20.3 cm). Mark: WEDGWOOD. c.1786–95. These vases, which were made with one, two or three columns, reflect the contemporary fashion for ruins, grottos (sometimes with imported hermits), 'follies' and obelisks. Shape no. 1566 in the first Ornamental Ware Shape Book. Byerley recorded 'Prices rec'd from Etru' 29 June 1786. Ruin'd Vase 15/–, Single Columns 21/–, Double columns– 42/–. Triple columns – 63/–' (Ms. 45–29110.) (Cf. Plates 287 and 289 and C52.)
Wedgwood Museum

289. Blue jasper dip 'ruined vase', ornamented with figures, trees and a floral scroll. Height 6¾" (16.2 cm). Mark: WEDGWOOD. c.1786. (See caption to Plate 288).
Dwight & Lucille Beeson Collection, Birmingham Museum, Alabama

290. Lilac jasper dip flower-holder in the form of three bamboo canes embedded in a mound with scattered flowers. Height 10⅜" (26.3 cm). Mark: WEDGWOOD. c.1790.
Lady Lever Art Gallery, Port Sunlight

291. Solid blue and white jasper flower-holder in the form of three bamboo canes. Height 10½" (26.6 cm). Mark: WEDGWOOD. c.1790. (Cf. Plate 290.)
Wedgwood Museum

288

289

290

291

292

292. *Solid blue and white jasper vase with rope handles and principal ornament of* Psyche wounded and bound by Cupid *adapted from a gem illustrated by B. de Montfaucon* (L'Antiquité expliquée et representée en figures, *1719, Vol. I, Pt I, Plate CXV, no. 2). Height 6½″ (16.5 cm). Mark:* WEDGWOOD. *c.1786–90. This small vase is of exceptional interest and rarity, having the principal ornament and parts of the leaf borders applied in very pale-blue jasper, with the rest of the ornament in white. Josiah wrote to Bentley on 30 September 1776 of his intention to produce 'Bassrelief Figures of pale blue' for vases, and added: 'Would a Vase, the body of which was of our Black [basaltes] ware, unpolish'd, with Figures of our Jasper Body in white, or pale blue give you any ideas on Onyx?' (E25–18701). He was to find by experiment that the black basaltes and jasper bodies could not be reliably fused. The subject,* Psyche wounded, *is often catalogued as 'Venus bound by Cupid', an error arising from the removal of Psyche's wings during remodelling.*
Merseyside Museums

293. *Two black jasper dip vases with Etruscan scroll handles and bas-relief ornament of* Sacrifice to Pomona *and* Cupid watering the Swans *after a design by Charles Le Brun. Height: 10½″ and 12″ (26.6 and 30.5 cm). Mark: (left)* WEDGWOOD H; *(right)* WEDGWOOD. *c.1790.*
Wedgwood Museum

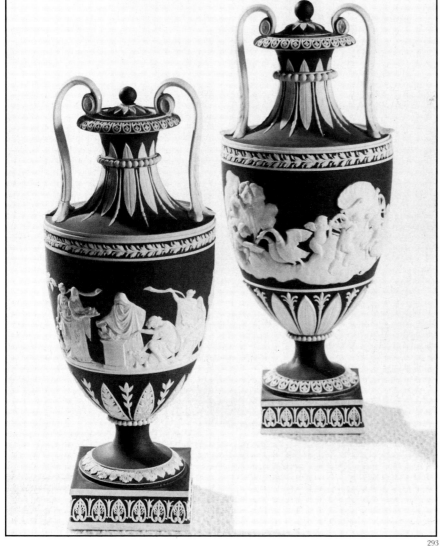

293

294. *Lilac jasper dip vase ornamented with bas-reliefs after a design attributed to Lady Templetown, on a solid white jasper plinth. Height 8⅞" (22.5 cm). Mark: WEDGWOOD. c.1785. This is a rare vase, being made in five pieces, the upper part above the turned rim lifting off with the small lid. The reason for this is not known, unless it was so that the lower goblet-shaped part might be used as a flower-vase or bough-pot, perhaps with a pierced grid. The vase is crazed all over, an unusual effect which may have been deliberately induced in imitation of some Chinese porcelain.* Manchester City Art Gallery

295. *Black jasper dip ewer of oenochoe form with serpent handle, ornamented with bands of classical groups in compartments and honeysuckle scroll above figures of the Muses (cf. Plate 265). Height 12⅜" (31.5 cm). Mark: WEDGWOOD. c.1790.* Lady Lever Art Gallery, Port Sunlight

296. *Fine pair of solid blue and white jasper ewers of oenochoe form with serpent handles and ornament of applied beads, acanthus leaves and bas-reliefs after designs attributed to Lady Templetown on a 'dimpled' ground. Height 10¾" and 10⅝" (27.3 and 27.1 cm). Mark: WEDGWOOD and 'T' (incised). c.1786–95.* British Museum

294

295

296

297. *Pair of Adams solid bright-blue and white jasper ewers ornamented with bands of acanthus, interlacing circles, and leaves and flowers and figures of the Muses Euterpe and Melpomene. Height 10¾"* (27.3 cm). Mark: ADAMS *impressed, 2 (incised).* c.1795.
Geoffrey Godden

298. *Black jasper dip pot-pourri vase with intricately pierced lid, the body ornamented with 'Torches', a series of flaming torches interlaced with plaited bands. Height 8⅜"* (21.3 cm). Mark: WEDGWOOD. c.1790–1800. Pot-pourri *was originally a liquid deriving its scent from decomposing flower petals and herbs. The English dry mixtures of flowers and herbs were more often used in open bowls. Pot-pourri vases, cassolettes and 'essence' vases became especially popular towards the end of the eighteenth century to disguise the odours of insufficiently aired rooms and their irregularly washed occupants. Wedgwood's incense burners were a slightly later introduction.*
Lady Lever Art Gallery, Port Sunlight

299. *Adams solid pale-blue and white jasper tripod candlestick-vase with reversible lid, the body with spiral fluting and ornament of leaves and tall flowers on a dimpled ground. Height (with candlestick top) 12"* (30.5 cm). Mark: ADAMS. c.1790. (Cf. Plate C45 *for almost identical shapes in Wedgwood jasper.*)
Temple Newsam House, Leeds

298

299

300. *Dark-blue jasper dip vase ornamented with 'blue–white' figures of* amorini *playing musical instruments beneath wreathed masks (see Plate 225). Height 15" (38 cm). Mark:* WEDGWOOD *(twice). c.1795. Eighteenth-century specimens of dark-blue jasper are rare and much prized. It was evidently a colour seldom used, probably because of problems of 'bleeding'.* Dwight & Lucille Beeson Collection, Birmingham Museum, Alabama

301. *Green jasper dip egg-shaped vase ornamented with a bold floral scroll and bands of anthemion and ribbon and ivy, the finial in the form of a figure of Cupid with his quiver. Height 8⅜" (21.2 cm). Mark.* WEDGWOOD H. *c.1795.* Dwight & Lucille Beeson Collection, Birmingham Museum, Alabama

300

301

302. *Pair of solid pale-blue and white jasper wine coolers, ornamented with 'blind' dicing and applied quatrefoils below a band of ribbon and ivy. The interiors are lapidary-polished to increase their impermeability. Height 6⅜" (16.1 cm); diameter at lip 7¼" (18.0 cm). Mark:* WEDGWOOD *and* ⌄ *(incised). c.1785.* Dwight & Lucille Beeson Collection, Birmingham Museum, Alabama

302

303

303. *Solid pale-blue and white jasper flower-*
pot and stand, ornamented with 'blind' dicing
and applied dots and quatrefoils below a border
of enclosed anthemion. Height 3⅝" (9.4 cm);
diameter of stand 4½" (11.7 cm). Marks:
(pot) Wedgwood; (stand) WEDGWOOD.
c.1785.
Manchester City Art Gallery

304

304. *Tricolour green jasper*
dip candlestick vase with
lotus finial and reversible lid,
the upper part of the body
diced and ornamented with
yellow jasper quatrefoils.
Shape no. 255. Height
9¾" (24.8 cm). Mark:
WEDGWOOD. *c.1790.*
(Cf. Plate C45 and the
Adams version of this
shape, Plate 299.)
Lady Lever Art
Gallery, Port Sunlight

305. *Pair of tricolour*
jasper flower-pots or
cachepots in black jasper dip,
diced and ornamented with
vertical floral scrolls and
green jasper quatrefoils. The
pots are pierced at the base
for drainage, and the stands
are ornamented with a band
of shells. Height 4¾"
(12.2 cm). Mark:
WEDGWOOD. *c.1790.*
Private collection
Photograph: Courtesy
of Buten Museum

305

306. (Left) tricolour lilac and white jasper dip flower-pot (lacking stand) engine-turned in stripes with 'interlaced' green jasper ornament in a basket-weave pattern. Height 3⁷⁄₁₆" (8.8 cm). Mark: WEDGWOOD Z. (Right) pair of tricolour lilac and white jasper dip bough-pots or flower holders, the bulbous bodies diced and ornamented with green jasper quatrefoils, and the loose grids pierced with one central hole, diameter ⁷⁄₈" (2.3 cm), surrounded by six smaller holes for flowers or foliage. Height 4¹⁄₁₆" (10.2 cm). Unmarked. Wedgwood, c.1790–1800.

307. Pair of tricolour blue and white jasper dip cassolette vases, the bodies and lids diced and ornamented with green jasper quatrefoils, and the lids pierced around the finials (left restored), on solid white jasper octagonal plinths. Height 11½" (29.3 cm). Mark: WEDGWOOD H. c.1790. These vases are made in five pieces – plinth, foot, body, open top and lid – to facilitate the filling and cleaning of the interiors. (See caption to Plate 298.)

308. Small tricolour pale-blue jasper dip flower-vase or bough-pot, the body and foot diced and ornamented with quatrefoils in a darker shade of blue, the top fitted with a pierced grid. Height 5⅛" (13.1 cm). Mark: WEDGWOOD. c.1795. Both the colour combination and the dicing of the foot are distinctive.

All Dwight & Lucille Beeson Collection, Birmingham Museum, Alabama

214

306

307

308

309

309. Similar vase in lilac dip. Dicing on the body and foot ornamented with green quatrefoils, and a scalloped gallery top. Height 6" (15.1 cm). Mark: WEDGWOOD O 3 c.1795. Dwight & Lucille Beeson Collection, Birmingham Museum, Alabama

310

311

THE PORTLAND VASE

Wedgwood's vases are generally of severely classical form with classically inspired ornament (except those with later 'Romantic' bas-reliefs after designs by Templetown, Beauclerk or Crewe), adapted from tablets and medallions. Many are ornamented with designs modelled by de Vaere, Pacetti and others in Rome, and some of the finest ornaments are from models by Flaxman. It appears to have been Flaxman, too, who first drew Josiah's attention to a vase in Sir William Hamilton's possession, formerly in the collection of the Barberini family, and later sold to the Duchess of Portland. 'I wish', Flaxman wrote on 5 February 1784, 'you may soon come to town to see Wm Hamilton's Vase, it is the finest production of Art that has been brought to England and seems to be the very apex of perfection to which you are endeavouring to bring your bisque & jasper; it is of a kind called "Murrina" by Pliny, made of dark glass with white enamel figures.* The Vase is about a foot high† & the figures between 5 & 6 inches, engraved in the same manner as a Cameo & of the grandest & most perfect Greek Sculpture.'[243] Josiah replied two weeks later: 'I am much obliged to you for the information you gave me respecting Sir Wm Hamiltons fine vase, & promise myself an exquisite treat when I do come to town, but the time is at present unavoidably uncertain.'[244]

*It was then a common misapprehension that the white figures were of some form of white enamel, but Flaxman plainly understood that they were examples of cameo-cutting.
†In fact 9¾ inches (24.5 cm) high and maximum diameter 7 inches (17.7 cm).

Although the vase is probably the most famous of all surviving Roman works of art, its history prior to 1600 is unknown. It is believed to have been made at Rome, perhaps by Alexandrians or craftsmen trained in Alexandria, centre of glass-making in the ancient world, about 27 BC to AD 14 (in the reign of Augustus). The vase is made of glass in two fused layers: the body, or foundation, in a dark blue, overlaid with almost opaque white. The bas-relief design was carved out of the white by *diatretii*, or gem engravers, and its meaning is still the subject of controversy. Most modern authorities are agreed that the decoration represents the myth of Peleus and Thetis, but the precise identification of episodes in the myth with the two sides of the vase is a matter for argument.[245] All are agreed, however, that it is a masterpiece of cameo-cutting.

The shape of the vase, on the other hand, is not original, and lacks the grace and balance of the amphora form, probably tapering to a point, in which it was originally made. The flat disc, on which the vase stands,[*] is a later piece of cameo glass of a much paler colour, cut from a larger composition and presumably attached when, at some unknown date, the foot of the amphora was broken. The decoration of the disc is thought to represent the head of Paris, son of King Priam, who awarded the golden apple to Aphrodite at the wedding feast of Peleus and Thetis. The co-incidence of themes of decoration on the body of the vase and the disc is unlikely to be accidental.[246]

The date of the disc is believed to be about fifty years later than that of the vase, but the repair could have been effected at any time between the first century and the end of the sixteenth century. The vase is first recorded as seen by Nicolas de Peiresc, the Provençal scholar and antiquarian, at the Palazzo Madama in the winter of 1600, when it formed part of the collection of Cardinal Francesco Maria del Monte (1549–1627). Correspondence between de Peiresc and Peter Paul Rubens[247] shows that the disc was already fitted to the foot by 1600. At some date during the next twenty years, the Cardinal granted the antiquarian Cassiano dal Pozzo, librarian to Cardinal Francesco Barberini, permission to publish a drawing of it, and such a drawing,[248] from the same collection, is now in the possession of Her Majesty the Queen. It provides additional proof that by that date the repair to the base of the vase had been completed. In 1627, on the death of Cardinal del Monte, the vase was bought by Cardinal Barberini and it remained in the possession of the family until 1780, when it was sold to settle the gambling debts of Donna Cornelia Barberini-Colonna, Princess of Palestrina and last of the Barberini family.

The purchaser was James Byres, a Scottish architect of marked entrepreneurial ability living in Rome, who had turned antiquarian and dealer.[†] Some three years later, after commissioning sixty plaster casts

[*]The disc is now displayed separately from the body of the vase in the British Museum.
[†]His first major purchase was a 'Picture of the Assumption by Poussin', now in the National Gallery of Art, Washington, for Lord Exeter; and his crowning achievement the acquisition and illegal export from Italy of Poussin's *Seven Sacraments*, sold to the Duke of Rutland. Byres died in 1817 at the age of eighty-three.

312. One of sixty copies of the Barberini Vase cast by James Tassie from the mould made by Giovanni Pichler, c.1782. Height 9¾" (24.8 cm). Tassie's copies in plaster were apparently commissioned by James Byres, but the motive of making casts that did so little justice to the original is not obvious. Tassie is not known to have made any reproductions of the vase in his glass paste body, though it would be surprising if he did not at least attempt to do so, and the only evidence of his further work on it is a number of glass paste medallions of separate figures and details. These are much in the style suggested in Wedgwood's letter to Hamilton dated 24 June 1786: 'cameos of two colors & polished grounds for rings, or the whole figures in separate pieces or groupes . . . for cabinets or pictures' (see p. 221).
British Museum

312

(Plate 312) to be made by James Tassie from a mould by Giovanni Pichler (1734–91), a gem-engraver, Byres sold the 'Barberini' vase to Sir William Hamilton for £1,000. On this occasion, Hamilton's zeal as a collector outstripped his discretion and his available means, and he was relieved to be able to sell the vase at the beginning of 1784 to the eccentric Duchess of Portland, 'a simple woman', according to Horace Walpole, 'and intoxicated only by *empty* vases'.[249] She died on 17 July 1785, and the vase was Lot 4,155 on the final day of the sale by auction of her extraordinary collection between 24 April and 7 June 1786. It was bought in by the third Duke of Portland, son and heir of the previous owner, for 980

313

guineas. Three days later it was in the hands of Josiah Wedgwood,[250] on loan from the Duke, who had given his permission (in return, it is said, for Josiah's agreement not to bid for it) for it to be copied in jasper.

Two weeks later, when he had given himself, and his modellers, time to examine the vase in detail, Josiah wrote at length to Sir William Hamilton for advice. 'When', he wrote, 'I first engaged in this work, & had Montfaucon only to copy,[251] I proceeded with spirit, & sufficient assurance that I should be able to equal, or excel if permitted, that copy of the vase; but now that I can indulge myself with full and repeated examinations of the original work itself my crest is much fallen, & I should scarcely muster sufficient resolution to proceed if I had not, too precipitately perhaps, pledged myself to many of my friends to attempt it.' Before asking for advice, he thought it necessary to give Hamilton an accurate idea of his capabilities. He had 'several modellers constantly employed . . . one of them [Henry Webber], who was recommended . . . by Sir Wm Chambers & Sir Joshua Reynolds . . . esteemed the first in his profession in England'. His material, jasper, he described as 'much harder than glass, nearly as hard as agate . . . & like the agate, it will bear to be cut, & take a polish, at the seal-engravers lathe. It has likewise a property peculiar to itself, which fits it perfectly for this imitation, – which is its taking a blue tint from cobalt, to any degree of strength.'[252]

As early as 1776 Josiah had been experimenting to produce 'Black blue grounds', but he had wasted time trying to unite blue or white jasper figures with black basaltes grounds.[253] Since then he had developed a black jasper, but its manganese base yielded a brown–black quite unlike the rich blue–black of the Portland vase glass. A new jasper mixture was required that would more closely resemble the original. Josiah was anxious, too, about the effect of light and shade achieved by the cameo-cutting technique: 'It is apparent, that the artist has availed himself very ably by the dark ground, in producing the perspective and distance required, by cutting the white away, nearer to the ground as the shades were wanted deeper, so that the white is often cut to the thinness of paper, & in some instances quite away, & the ground itself makes part of the bas-relief; by which he has given his work the effect of painting as well as sculpture.'[254]

He doubted that jasper bas-relief could ever be applied thinly enough to emulate this effect: 'it will be found that a bas relief with all the figures of one uniform white color upon a dark ground, will be a faint resemblance of what this artist has had the address to produce by calling in the aid of colour to assist his relief.' Josiah feared that his ornaments would display 'a disgusting flatness' and, acknowledging the need for an 'engraver' to finish the figures, was uncertain of being able to find one of sufficient skill to undertake the work who would be prepared 'to quit a lucrative branch of this profession, & devote half a life to a single work'.[255] He did not, in fact, ever succeed in applying the figures so thinly that the ground colour of the vase provided sufficient light and shade, and the loss of this transparency and 'perspective' had to be remedied by the application of a thin black slip over the white. Josiah II mentions this shading technique in a letter to his father dated 12 April 1791.[256]

The most serious of all the objections was that Josiah did not find the form of the vase satisfying. Although capable occasionally of producing combinations of shapes and ornament that were at best eclectic and at worst bizarre, Josiah had made a closer study of form – and especially of classical vase form – than all but a select few of his contemporaries. He had acquired a perceptive understanding of clay form, the result partly of his early experience as a thrower and partly of years of observation and study, and of the disposition and balance of decoration. The squat form of the Portland vase did not appeal to him, and he was honest enough in his opinions not to be overawed by the antiquity and fame of the vase.

Putting such thoughts in a letter to Sir William Hamilton required some delicacy. 'I suppose', he wrote, 'it is admitted that the form of this vase is not so elegant as it might be made if the artist had not been possessed of some very good reason for contenting himself with the present form.' He was hampered by the fact that neither he, nor anyone else in England at this period, understood that the base of the vase had been broken and repaired. He therefore continued to try to find excuses for its lack of formal beauty, supposing that 'the material made use of . . . that is, the body being made of one colour, & the surface covered over to a due thickness with another, was not capable of taking a form with those delicate parts on which its beauty as a simple vase would in great measure depend.'[257] From such uneasy comments it is plain that he did not recognise that the vase was not in its original state. His dislike of the form was instinctive, and aesthetically sound.

The beauty of the cameo-cut figures was never questioned, although their significance was imperfectly understood.[258] Josiah's reluctance to copy the vase as it stood is made clear in his letter to Hamilton: assuming that the reason for its lack of elegance is technical, 'I suppose', he wrote, 'you would still advise me to copy the form of the vase as well as the figures. But what I wish to ask you is, whether you would forbid me to apply these figures to any other form of vase, or with the addition of any borders, or other ornaments.' He had 'begun to count how many different ways the vase itself may be copied, to suit the tastes, the wants, & the purses of different purchasers'. Four types of copies were suggested:

The working artist would be content with a true & simple copy, a cast in one colour, of a durable material, with the price accordingly. Others, who could afford to proceed a step farther, would desire the addition of a blue ground, though painted only; & a third class would wish to have this addition in the composition of which the vase itself is made, & equally permanent, a fourth perhaps would pay for polishing this durable blue ground, & these two last would be my customers for Jasper copies; but whether any would be found with sufficient confidence in the abilities of our artists to order, or with patience to wait for, one of the highest order, finished by the engraver, or whether any artist would be found handy enough to engage in it, I have my doubts.[259]

Josiah reverted to the subject of using the figures: 'I would next beg your advice respecting the introduction of these figures in other works & forms, in which they might perhaps serve the arts, & diffuse the seeds of good taste, more extensively than by confining them to the vase only. For instance, many a young artist, who could not purchase any edition of the vase, would be glad to buy impressions of the heads of the figures, or the whole figures, in a durable material of one colour for studies.' This somewhat contrived appeal to Hamilton's desire to be regarded as an antiquarian was followed immediately by a frankly commercial proposal to produce 'intaglios of the heads of seals, & cameos of two colors & polished grounds for rings, or the whole figures in separate pieces or groupes, finished to any degree, for cabinet pieces or pictures. In tablets for chimney pieces, & many other purposes, I have some reason to believe they will be acceptable. . . . I should be glad to know if you see any objections to these proposed extensions & applications.'[260]

Somewhat surprisingly, Sir William had no objection to these proposals: 'You have', he replied in July, 'seen so well into the difficulties you will have to encounter, if you attempt an exact copy of this vase, that I have really nothing to add to the reflections you have made on the subject, and I much approve of your beginning with the most simple copies; and I much approve likewise of your making copies of single figures, and even of the heads; in short, you cannot multiply this wonderful performance too much.'[261] He approved, too, of Wedgwood's intention to restore, in his copies, 'surfaces partially decayed by time', and proposed that Flaxman might be employed in the task, 'for I must do him the justice to say, I never saw a bas-relief executed in the true simple antique style half so well as that he did of the Apotheosis of Homer'. Evidently Sir William had seen only the pale blue and white jasper, for he added: 'If you could instead of sky blue, make your ground look like an onyx, as in the vase itself, it would be better, for there is no natural stone of the sky-blue colour. Unless you hold up the Barberini Vase to the light, it appears to be of a real onyx, & was long mistaken for one.'[262] It was, in fact, widely believed to have been made from a natural stone until about 1750, although de Peiresc had identified it correctly 150 years earlier.[263]

For the first twelve months after he obtained the Portland vase on loan, Josiah concentrated on the reproduction of the figures. A cast of the entire vase was taken in plaster, and copies of all the figures were prepared in wax (Plate 314). Moulds taken from these waxes provided the matrices for block moulds, from which, in turn, working moulds were made.[264] This routine, first developed for the production of cameos,[*] was by now well established for all bas-reliefs copied from original models.

Never able entirely to delegate work of any importance, Josiah worked tirelessly on the vase himself, with Webber as chief modeller, and Hackwood and, probably, William Wood as assistants. On 16 June 1787 Josiah composed a letter to Sir William Hamilton, to acquaint him with the news that Flaxman was preparing to leave to spend two years in Italy, and that Webber would accompany John Wedgwood to Rome for the coming winter. 'But my great work is the Portland Vase,' he wrote. 'I have now finished a third & last edition of the figures, the two first being suppressed in hopes of making the third still more perfect; in this I have certainly succeeded, but how far I have done so upon the whole, with what success, others must determine.' He had already made some trials in applying the figures, probably at this early stage to jasper tablets:

[*]See p. 103.

314

315

My present difficulty is to give those beautiful shades to the thin & distant parts of the figures, for which the original artist availed himself of the semitransparency of the white glass, cutting it down nearer & nearer to the blue ground, in proportion as he wished to increase the depth of shade. But the case is very different with me. I must depend upon an agent, whose effects are neither at my command, nor to be perceived at the time they are produced, viz. the action of fire on my compositions: a little more, or a little less fire, & even the length of time employed in producing the same degree [of heat], will make a very material difference in this delicate operation. I am now engaged in a course of experiments for determining these points with as much precision as the nature of the case will admit of, and this is now the only thing that retards the completion of this grand object.[265] It was a happy coincidence that Wedgwood's pyrometer* had been brought to a state of such reliability that he was confident in presenting one to the King. Without such an accurate method of assessing high firing temperatures, the difficulties he experienced in reproducing the Portland vase in jasper might have proved insuperable.

On 24 March 1788 Josiah II wrote from Etruria to his father, who was visiting the London showrooms, to give him disappointing news: 'The Barberini vase I mentioned is come out this morning but the shoulder was turned† too thin & it is sunk in – The darker one will go in sometime next week.'[266] By this time, it is clear, Josiah was suffering from

*See p. 20.
†The Wedgwood Portland vase, like most other stoneware vases, was 'finished' on the lathe.

overwork, and Dr William Heberden,* his physician in London, pre-
scribed a holiday. Josiah replied that he would take one 'as soon as the
Portland Vase is completed'.[267]

In spite of his own reservations, and those expressed by Sir William
Hamilton, Josiah was determined to reproduce the Portland vase to the
best of his ability in jasper, and he had been encouraged by several of his
most valued patrons to make copies of the vase by subscription. He agreed
to this arrangement on condition that his customers should be at liberty,
when they saw their copies, to accept or refuse them; and on the understanding that orders would be completed, without time limit, in rota-
tion.[268] By 9 May 1790 he had received subscriptions for twenty vases. He
wrote to his second son, Josiah, from Greek Street:

> 2 trials of Barberini black. With respect to color, they are very much
> alike, & both very nearly the same as the vase I have with me. But in
> other respects, the total absence of cracks on the surface, that made of
> an equal mixture of blue & black, & then dipt in black, has the
> preference very greatly. It is indeed entirely free from cracks, which
> the other is not; & it seems to agree perfectly with both your whites,
> the yellow & the blue white,† I would have you proceed with that in
> order to lose no time, & be getting more raw materials prepared. I
> think Dan Hollinshead & his brother should be kept entirely on the
> vase. . . . But though I would have you be going on with this
> composition which we know will do, I wish you at the same time to
> be making trials with the blue clay, to make it take a black dip with-
> out cracking; perhaps a little 59 [dark-coloured Cornish moor-
> stone], or some ball clay, may have that good effect. The cracks are
> exceedingly minute, not visible when dry, even with a magnifying
> glass. . . . Some of the vases may be made with the white without any
> blue in it, & some with the yellow white, as I know that diff' people
> will have different tastes. The theory I proceed upon with respect to
> cracking is this, that the black diminishes more in burning than the
> blue, and therefore must crack if it keeps applied to the blue in every
> part. As 59 mixed with the blue will cause it to diminish in burning
> proportionably to its quantity, to a certain degree, there is a propor-
> tion which will make it diminish exactly the same with the black;
> that proportion is to be found out, & the cracking is cured. I con-
> gratulate you on the success you have had in making one body, the
> mixture of blue & black perfect in this respect.[269]

As this letter makes clear, bodies of two colours were mixed, and the
vase made in this mixture was then dipped in black. It has never been
obvious why Josiah should have chosen the jasper dip technique for the
Portland vase copies. The popular explanation has been that the

---

*William Heberden (1710–1801) FRS, FRCP, physician to Samuel Johnson and the poet
William Cowper, among others. The first to describe *angina pectoris*. His son, William, was
physician in ordinary to George III and Queen Charlotte.
†See p. 83.

316A

316A. *Black and white jasper (the body blue–black with a black dip) Portland Vase base disc. The ornament is identified as the head of Paris. Diameter 5 1/16" (12.9 cm). Unmarked. Wedgwood, 1790–3. The base disc of the original Barberini Vase measures 4 3/4" (12.1 cm) in diameter. The disc illustrated is on the base of the 'Hope' copy of the vase (Plate 318), and displays all the attributes of the finest of Wedgwood's 'first edition' Portland Vases: excellent undercutting, particularly obvious under the fingers, nostril and folds of the dress; careful shading of the leaves and cloak; and a precise reproduction of the original composition, including the abrupt curtailment of the elbow-joint where it is cut by the circumference of the disc. (These and other features of first-edition vases are discussed, in comparison with later editions, on pp. 232 and 288–98.)*
Wedgwood Museum

316B. *Interior view of a (detached) base disc from a first-edition jasper Portland Vase, showing how the base was made separately and attached to the thrown vase (from which the base would have been cut while in the clay state). Diameter 5 1/16" (12.9 cm). Unmarked. Wedgwood, c.1790–5. The vase, of which this disc is a part, was previously in the collection of Joseph Mayer, who was responsible for rescuing the Wedgwood and Bentley letters and many other important manuscripts from destruction (see p. 14 and n. 8).*
Merseyside Museums

316B

blue–black body would show, to some extent, beneath the black dip, giv-ing the vase that particular shade of blue–black that was scarcely visible, except by transmitted light, in the original vase. This was not a convin-cing explanation, and it is now seen to be false. The practical reason for this method of production was Josiah's ability to make a large vase in the coarser jasper body, while the same vase in the fine mixture would be too fragile for firing at the high temperature required. This problem had been solved in 1777 by the use of a dip of the finer mixture so that the whole body of the vase appeared to be of that quality. The discovery of the previously unpublished memorandum[*270] giving details of this technique has cast new light on much of Josiah's work in jasper.

In July 1789 Josiah wrote to Lord Auckland: 'You will perhaps wonder at your not having heard something of the Barberini Vase. I was always very sensible of the difficulty of attempting to copy so exquisite a piece of workmanship, but in the progress of the undertaking difficulties have occurred which nothing but practice would have discovered to me. The prospect, however, brightens before me, and, after having made several defective copies, I think I see my way to the final completion of it.'[271] Two months later he sent the first perfect vase[272] to his friend and 'favourite Aesculapius', Erasmus Darwin, with a caution not to show it to anyone except his family. Darwin, who could be relied upon to ignore all instruction but his own, replied in October: 'I have disobeyed you and shown your vase to two or three; but they were philosophers, not cogniscenti [*sic*]. How can I possess a jewel, and not communicate the pleasure to a few Derby philosophers?'[273] Later, he was to include a description of the vase, which he chose to regard as a 'mystic urn' whose decoration was symbolic rather than mythological, in his long poem *The Botanic Garden*, published in 1791. The illustration of the vase, to accompany the poem, was engraved by William Blake.[274]

It had been a long and arduous struggle, but Josiah was now sufficiently confident to show his vase to his most influential patron, Queen Charlotte. It seems most likely that she viewed a copy of the vase on 1 May 1790,[275] and later on the same day it was given another private showing at the house of a second old friend, Sir Joseph Banks. This was recorded in the *General Evening Post* and somewhat fancifully reported in the *Gazeteer and New Daily Advertiser* of 5 May:

On Saturday night last there was a numerous *converzationi* [*sic*] at Sir Joseph Banks's, Soho-square, when Mr Wedgwood produced the *great vase*, manufactured by himself, in imitation of that superb one about four years ago exhibited in the Museum of her Grace the Duchess Dowager of Portland. The vase is as large as the original; the ground colour that of an emerald [*sic*], embossed with white. It is most exquisitely finished, and allowed by all present, *in point of look*, to be at least equal to the original, which was valued at *two thousand five hundred pounds*. The whole of the above vase is a composition of the most beautiful transparency [*sic*], and does infinite credit to the artist. He has not yet, however, arrived at the *certainty of casting* them, as several cracked in the experiment. Beside Sir Joseph and a numerous company who attended on the above occasion, there were

[*]See pp. 87–9.

317. *Black and white jasper (the body blue–black with a black dip) Portland Vase traditionally believed to be Josiah I's own copy. Height 10 ⅛″ (25.8 cm). Unmarked. Wedgwood, c.1790. The obverse of the vase shows the figures identified as Thetis, resting in her rocky sanctuary, watched by Aphrodite and (left) Hermes. This copy of the vase has been described as being inscribed in manganese pencil with the number '25'* (Josiah Wedgwood: the Arts and Sciences United, 1978, no. 169), *but this inscription has not been found. Though the surface quality is fine, the shading accurate and the undercutting clearly visible, the vase is flawed by the failure of some of the reliefs permanently to adhere to the body. It is most likely that these lifted slightly in firing but did not break away until some time (even years) later. In 1776 Josiah told Bentley that tablets, which had been fired and allowed to cool without damage, had cracked later in transit or in stock (E25–18672 29 May 1776).*
Wedgwood Museum

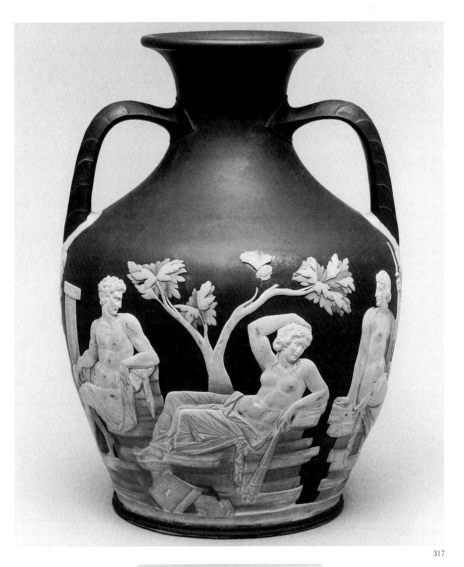

317

317A. *Reverse side of the Wedgwood jasper Portland Vase ('Josiah I's copy'), showing the figure of Peleus, encouraged by Eros and Doris (or her grandmother Tethys) and watched by Nereus (or Oceanus), stepping forward to greet Thetis.*

317A

226

present Sir Joshua Reynolds, Mr Locke,[*] the Hon. Horace Walpole and several members of the Royal and Antiquarian Societies.[276]

Two weeks later, Sir Joshua Reynolds, president of the Royal Academy, signed a certificate of approval, declaring Wedgwood's copy of the Portland vase to be 'a correct and faithful imitation both in regard to general effect, and the most minute detail of the parts'.[277] Sir William Hamilton, too, though he did not see the vase until the following summer, was 'much pleased' with it,[278] and wrote on 23 July 1791, some days after a visit to Etruria:

> I have accomplished one of my great objects which was the seeing of your wonderful Copy of the Portland Vase. I that am so well acquainted with the Original and the difficulties you must have met with, realy think it so. The sublime character of the Original is wonderfully preserved in your Copy & little more is wanting than the sort of transparency which your materials could not imitate. . . . in short I am wonderfully pleased with it, and give you the greatest credit for having arrived so near the imitation of what I believe to be the first specimen of the excellence of the Arts of the Ancients existing. . . .[279]

The approbation of the Queen, the presidents of the Royal Society and the Royal Academy, and of the distinguished and knowledgeable gathering at Sir Joseph Banks's house at the beginning of May, was quite sufficient to encourage Josiah to display the vase in Europe. He had always understood the need for patronage. Twenty years earlier he had written to Bentley: 'I need not tell you how much will depend on a *proper & noble* introduction';[280] and he believed firmly in the policy he enunciated to his son: 'begin at the Head first, & then proceed to the inferior members.'[281] Nor was he slow to take advantage of the good will of his patrons. In 1790, Lord Auckland, ennobled in the previous year, was in Holland as Ambassador Extraordinary to the Court at The Hague. This was clearly too good an opportunity to miss, and by the end of June 1790 the young Josiah II and Tom Byerley were on their way to Rotterdam at the start of a promotional tour of Europe that was to last until December.

The vase was shown to Lord and Lady Auckland on 3 July and, at Auckland's instigation, to the Prince and Princess of Orange at their summer 'house in the wood' on the 4th. 'The prince and princess', Josiah II told his father, 'both spoke very highly of the vase though I believe the latter only had much feeling for it. . . . The princess has the look of a very clever woman & I believe she is so.'[282] On the following day an exhibition was held in the morning at Lord Auckland's residence. Josiah II described it in breathless detail:

> About half after 10 Mr B & myself went over to Lord Aucklands and disposed all our chaise seat full upon 4 tables, one of which the collection of cameos filled. In this room there were upon the chimney

---

[*]William Locke (1732–1810), art amateur and collector.

318. *The 'Hope' copy of the Wedgwood Portland Vase, bought on 13 June 1793 for thirty guineas by the eccentric artist, patron and collector, Thomas Hope (see p. 229, fn), and perhaps the most perfect example of the first-edition vases yet identified. The black jasper dip surface is of silken smoothness and almost without a blemish, the figures and masks beneath the handles are beautifully undercut, and the shading has been added with unusual delicacy. Height 10⅛″ (25.8 cm). Unmarked. Wedgwood, c.1790–3. The inside of the lip bears a faint manganese pencil mark believed to be the number '2'. (See Plate 316A for an illustration of the base disc of this vase and Plates C57–8.)*
Wedgwood Museum

318A. *Reverse side of the 'Hope' copy of the Wedgwood Portland Vase. (See Plates 316A, 318 and C57–8.)*

318B–C. *Side views of the 'Hope' copy of the Wedgwood Portland Vase, showing the well-undercut and well-shaded masks of the goat-god Pan, hanging by their horns from the ridged handles. Wedgwood copied the shape of the handles with precision, but set them on a slant from upper left to lower right, whereas the original Barberini Vase (and, of course, the plaster casts by Tassie from Pichler's mould – Plate 312) shows them slanted from upper right to lower left. Most editions produced in the nineteenth and twentieth centuries were made with handles straightened towards the vertical.*

piece 7 jasper vases belonging to Ld Auckland so that altogether we cut a very respectable figure. We had some few cameos mounted very handsomely in necklaces, bracelets & ear drops which we also displayed. We had a thermometer [pyrometer] also which was much looked at & people seemed very inquisitive about it. In another room was the Vase by itself & in a third & 4th the company breakfasted.[283]

318

318A

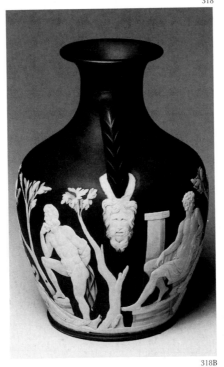

318B

318C

Princess Wilhelmina of Orange also left an account of the exhibition, writing of it to her son on 6 July:

> *Hier nous avons eu un grand déjeuné chez l'Ambassadeur d'Angleterre. Le but de cette fête étoit de voir les échantillons de la manufacture de Wedgwood que le fils de celui qui en est l'inventeur et d'après lequel la fabrique porte le nom, a porté ici et qu'il va montrer dans les principales villes d'Allemagne, afin de faire voir les progrès de la fabrique et établir des correspondences nouvelles. L'associé de son père étoit aussi avec lui. Ils avoient des choses charmantes; et la plus belle, la principale, sur laquelle toute l'attention devoit tomber, étant considerée comme le chef d'oeuvre de l'art, étoit un vase imité de l'antique . . . qui est connu sous le nom de Vase Barberini. . . . C'est un morceau superbe et dont il n'existe que cette seule copie, qui est parfaitement bien rendue à ce que disent les connois-seurs. Je crois, mon cher Fritz, que vous vous seriez amusé a ce déjeuner, d'abord à admirer toutes ces belles choses et ensuite à manger d'excellents fruits.*[284]

In spite of her enthusiasm, and the number of distinguished guests[285] assembled by Lord Auckland, no subscription order was taken for Wedgwood's Portland vase. The Princess bought a pair of bracelets for fourteen guineas.[286] Apart from mounted cameos to the ladies present, no other sale from the exhibition is recorded.

Josiah appears to have been pleased with his son's account, but he was anxious that the high cost of making the vase might have priced it beyond any accessible market. 'I shall be glad to know when you write next', he told Byerley, 'whether you think the price of the Barberini vase was any reason why you had no subscribers; & whether Ld Auckland took any notice of the price.'[287] Auckland's name appears on the list of subscribers,[288] though there is no record that the order was ever completed, as does that of Thomas Hope* of Amsterdam, who may have seen the vase a few days after the Prince of Orange.[289] In September the price was still not settled. Josiah wrote to his younger son, then in Frankfurt: 'With respect to the Barberini vases I do not yet know what to say about the price. I have not yet been able to make another good one. I have fired five more since you left us & not one near so good as that you have, nor indeed fit to show, so that unless we are more successful £50 is too little to save us from loss. Perhaps it would not be amiss to say this to some of the noblesse. . . . What encouragement is there for the moderns to attempt the production of such works if their patrons refuse to pay $\frac{1}{20}$ of what the ancients paid to their artists.'[290]

Letters written by Josiah II to his father in 1791 show that production of the vase was still slow and difficult.[291] On 9 April he reported trouble with blistering (Plate 315). Josiah had proposed the use of repairing cement for cracks, but this did not fire to the same colour as the vases. He

---

*Thomas Hope (1770?–1831), author, collector, designer of furniture in the 'Greek' and 'Egyptian' styles, and patron of such contemporary artists as John Flaxman junior, Thorvaldsen and Benjamin West. His copy of the Portland vase (possibly No. '2') is now in the Wedgwood Museum, Barlaston. (See Plates 318–318C).

then suggested a form of cement that did not require to be fired. On the 15th, three vases were brought from the ovens: one perfect, but on the other two 'the stain instead of being a bluish black is brown.' Supplies of 'Barberini black' clay had temporarily run out but, until fresh quantities could be made available, 'some blue ones' would be finished. While Josiah II contended with these difficulties, other potters, suffering from what he described as 'stagnation of trade',[292] were failing: Edward Bourne and Ralph Wedgwood 'tottering'; Joshua Heath and Ralph Mare unstable.

The Oven Book records list forty-three black 'Barberanean' vases (some made by Dan Hollinshead and 'finished' by Hackwood) fired between 27 May 1791 and December 1796. Of these, eleven are shown as having been broken; the number of faulty vases is not known.

There is no complete record of the total number of vases produced in the so-called 'first edition'* of Portland vases. The best estimate puts the

*'First edition' vases are those potted (if not finished and fired) during the lifetime of Josiah I. No further edition is known to have been attempted until 1845, though the possibility that single vases were made during the period cannot be ruled out. The Oven Books for part of this period are missing, so it may never be possible to be specific about the manufacture of Portland vases after Josiah's death. It seems most unlikely that Josiah II would have gone to the great expense of making vases while good examples of the first edition were still in stock.

319. Wedgwood's jasper Portland Vase No. 12 of the first edition, tilted to show the manganese pencil number inside the mouth of the vase. This example was acquired in 1969 from Sir Robin Darwin to whom it is believed to have been bequeathed by direct descent from his great-great-grandfather Erasmus Darwin, who received it as a gift from Josiah Wedgwood in 1789. Another example, on loan to the Fitzwilliam Museum, Cambridge, from George Pember Darwin (also a direct descendant of Erasmus Darwin) has a rival claim to be Josiah's gift to Erasmus. It is not likely that Josiah made two such extravagant gifts to the same friend, but not impossible that one of these two vases was bought by Erasmus, or that it is the copy known to have been bought by Dr Robert Waring Darwin in 1793, though the last is officially identified with the example transferred to the Victoria & Albert Museum from the Museum of Practical Geology, London, in 1901. While the provenances of these three vases may be controversial, their authenticity as examples of the first edition is not challenged. Dwight & Lucille Beeson Collection, Birmingham Museum, Alabama

319

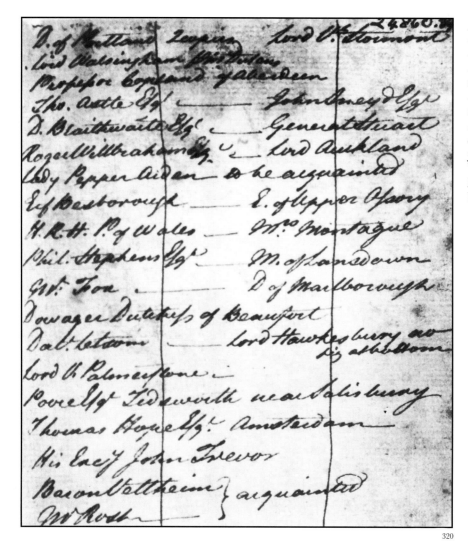

320. *The list of subscribers to Wedgwood's copies of the Portland Vase, from Tom Byerley's Notebook, 1789, including the names of the Prince of Wales, the Dukes of Marlborough and Portland, Lord Auckland and Thomas Hope (Ms. 33–24860).* Wedgwood Manuscripts, Keele University Library

figure at forty-five,[293] of which perhaps as many as thirty-one might have been considered of first quality. In a letter written in 1839 Josiah II stated, 'I believe my father never sold ten copies.'[294] Byerley noted '10 Portland Vases, 4 of them tolerably perfect, and 6 rather imperfect, having a leaf off or a few staines', remaining in the London showrooms in 1814.[295] The last of these may have been sold to Apsley Pellatt* in 1829. From this bare evidence, and taking into account the number of perfect vases that remained in the family or were presented to such friends as Darwin, it seems most improbable that the sales of the Portland vase ever repaid the development and production costs.

Some, perhaps all, of the first edition black vases were marked inside the lip of the vase with a number inscribed in manganese pencil (Plate 319). Solid blue jasper copies from the first edition do not appear to have been recorded by Byerley, probably because they were less highly finished

*Apsley Pellatt (1791–1863), manufacturer of decorative glass at Southwark (Whitefriars). He developed the *millefiore* and *crystallo ceramie* techniques for paperweights and other articles.

and cheaper, and thus considered of less importance. Their weight appears to be slightly less than that of the black copies, and they are also slightly smaller in height by about a quarter of an inch (two and a half per cent).[296] One of these (Plate C58) was presented to the British Museum by Josiah's eldest son, John, in 1802.

None of the jasper copies of the Portland vase made during Josiah's lifetime was impressed with the Wedgwood trademark, and the identification of examples from the first edition rests, therefore, principally upon quality. Of the authenticated examples, probably the most perfect is the 'Hope' copy, indistinctly numbered, in the Wedgwood Museum, Barlaston (Plates 318 and C57). Illustrations of this vase show the quality aimed at rather than the standard achieved. There are, nevertheless, certain hallmarks of first-edition vases which may be most clearly observed in comparison with later examples. The black body is of silken smoothness, often with slight pitting around the edge of the base disc. The surface of some specimens is disappointingly dull, and sometimes slightly blistered, and it shows little, if any, sign of the blue cast[*] that Josiah tried so hard to achieve. The bas-relief figures are as smooth as the ground, and the 'blue–white' or 'yellow–white' tint is noticeable. All the figures have been carefully undercut, sharpening the outline and the features. A comparison of base discs reveals that the bas-relief on the disc of first-edition vases copies precisely the form of the disc on the original vase: the relief extends to the edge of the disc, with the elbow of the figure truncated above the joint. This was copied also on the 1877 (Northwood) edition;[†] but on other editions a tidy border is left around the bas-relief, allowing the shape of the elbow-joint to be completed outside the circle of the composition.[‡]

Attention has been drawn to slight differences of the positioning of the figures,[297] and these are discussed briefly in relation to nineteenth-century editions of the vase;[§] but they are the sort of variations that occur with all hand-ornamented pieces, and similar variations of placing may be seen on contemporary, and otherwise identical, copies of the *Apotheosis* or *Pegasus* vases. It would be unwise to place too much reliance on such differences as can easily be accounted for in the course of production. Most of the later editions show little or no 'shading' by painting; but by far the most reliable evidence of the first edition is visible in the undercutting, the quality and detail of which was never equalled (even when it was attempted)[¶] on any later edition.

---

[*]The colour is, however, a blue–black as opposed to the brown–black produced by manganese oxide.
[†]See p. 293.
[‡]See Plate 449A.
[§]See pp. 288–98.
[¶]Even the 'Northwood' edition (see p. 293), which came nearer to the first edition than any other, was less detailed, and the monogram signature and the Wedgwood impressed mark make the Northwood copies easily identifiable.

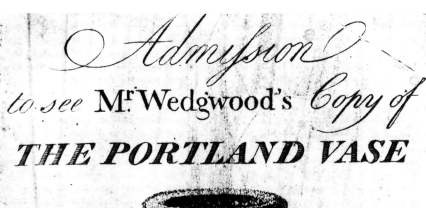

321

The original Barberini vase, broken at least twice[298] before it reached the hands of Josiah Wedgwood, was deposited on loan to the British Museum by the fourth Duke of Portland in 1810. There, in the Hamiltonian Ante-Room on 7 February 1845, a young Irishman, who subsequently gave his name as William Lloyd, smashed it again, using for the purpose an adjacent exhibit variously described as 'a Persepolitan monument of basalt' and 'a curiosity of sculpture'.[299] The culprit admitted the offence, claiming that he had been 'indulging in intemperance for a week before', and was suffering from 'nervous excitement'. Ludicrously, the wording of the Wilful Damage Act made it unlikely that a prosecution for damage to any article valued at more than £5.0.0 could be successful. 'Lloyd' (the name was probably 'borrowed' for the occasion) was therefore found guilty of breaking the glass display case in which the vase had been standing. After three days in gaol, he was released, on payment by a friend of a fine of £3.0.0.[300] The vase was purchased by the British Museum in 1945. It has been restored three times: in 1848, when more than two hundred fragments were patiently pieced together in no more than six months; in 1948, when some missing chips were incorporated; and in 1988–90, using slow-drying epoxy resin as the principal adhesive, when the last slivers of glass were replaced.

The finest of Wedgwood's first-edition copies of the Portland vase must rank among his greatest technical achievements as a potter. Whether it could sensibly be described as a work of art must be far more doubtful. However fine the quality of workmanship, there must be more to creation than copying, and an excellent craftsman's *tour de force* is rarely also a work of art. Wedgwood's Portland vases are copies in the wrong material, reproduced by entirely different techniques, of a vase which, as a

322. White stoneware copy of the Portland Vase by Neale & Co. Height 11½" (29.5 cm). Mark: NEALE & CO. c.1795. This travesty of the vase, with rope handles and the clumsiest of ornament (the male figures ludicrously emasculated by the addition of tiny fig-leaves) is typical of the debased copies, produced apparently without reference to the original or to Wedgwood's vases, that appeared, often in even less suitable materials than stoneware, during the hundred years following the distribution of the first jasper edition.
Christie's, New York

322

result of serious damage and not altogether sympathetic repair, had already lost much of its original grace. What is left derives its beauty from the colour and nature of its material – glass – and the exquisite artistry of the Alexandrian cameo-cutter. Neither of these qualities could be satisfactorily reproduced in stoneware.

By the side of the original, Wedgwood's jasper Portland vases look flat and dull, and the heavy appearance of the black and white jasper serves only to accentuate the squat and graceless form of the maimed original. It is as hard to believe that Sir Joshua Reynolds was sincere in his assessment of Wedgwood's vase as it is easy to understand why so few connoisseurs wished to buy it. It remains a triumph of perseverance and technique over human fallibility and the capricious nature of clay; a great labour that perhaps should not have been attempted, because true success was unattainable; a lasting reminder of Josiah's extraordinary ambition, and a tribute to his unending pursuit of excellence through experiment.

Some of the doubts and criticisms that have been applied to Wedgwood's Portland vases might be thought to be as relevant to the greater part of his work in jasper. Many of the shapes were not original, and most of the

323. 'Etruria', a sketch by Benjamin West for a painting of 'Genius calling forth the Fine Arts to adorn Manufactures and Commerce, and recording the names of eminent men in these pursuits'. Oil on canvas, 20 ¼" × 25 ½" (51.8 × 66.0 cm). Signed and dated 1791. Josiah Wedgwood's belief in his Etruria as the manufactory for the revival of the arts of antiquity is well expressed in this neoclassical painting, which illustrates also with what speed the fame of Wedgwood's copies of the Portland Vase had spread. Cleveland Museum of Art, Gift of the John Huntington Art and Polytechnic Trust

ornament was at least derived, if not copied, from earlier designs or bas-reliefs in different materials. Part of the answer to such criticism was given by Josiah himself in a letter to Erasmus Darwin written in 1789: 'I only pretend to have attempted to copy the fine antique forms, but not with absolute servility. I have endeavoured to preserve the stile and Sp[iri]' or if you please the elegant simplicity of the antique forms, & so doing to intro-duce all the variety I was able, & this Sir W. Hamilton assures me I may venture to do, & that is the true way of copying the antique.'[301]

Wedgwood's jasper vases, figures, bough-pots, tablets and medallions were an authentic expression of late-eighteenth-century taste, of the 'white world' of neoclassicism and the largely pastel world of the brothers Adam. It was, and is, legitimate to employ old sources of inspiration to create a style in art or decoration, particularly when those sources are also new in the sense that they have been lost or forgotten and are newly redis-covered. The imaginary classical world, much of it derived from objects excavated at Herculaneum and Pompeii, should be no more surprising, and at least as relevant, in the history of decoration as the imaginary orient which inspired European *chinoiserie*.

Much of Wedgwood's jasper has the qualities of elegance and simplicity that he hoped to emulate; little of it made during his lifetime, but much more after his death, was tastelessly over-ornamented and has no more artistic merit than the wedding cake it sometimes resembles. Josiah could not have foreseen the development of his material, nor could he have imagined the extent of the market it would eventually reach.

Jasper was not only the outstanding invention of Josiah Wedgwood's life as a potter, it was the paramount innovation in ceramic bodies since the discovery of porcelain. Without jasper or black basaltes, the pre-vailing style of the latter part of the eighteenth century would scarcely be represented in ceramics, for porcelain was not easily adapted to neo-classical design. Wedgwood's supremacy in the eighteenth century, in succession to Meissen and Sèvres, was founded upon Josiah's ability to adapt, or create, wares – particularly Queen's ware, black basaltes and jasper – for the ascendant fashion. As a technical feat the invention of jasper went far beyond Böttger's, which was a successful search for the secret of a ceramic body that was already available for study, and still ranks as one of the supreme achievements in ceramic history.

PART THREE

JASPER, 1795–1968

Towards the end of Josiah's I's life the popularity of jasper began to wane. It had never been so cheap that it could reach the sort of market that was dominated by Queen's ware, and even the smallest object had been beyond the reach of far the greater part of the population. As a taste for opulence and the exotic, shown in the developing demand for ornament in the 'Egyptian' style, *chinoiserie*, *japonaiserie* and Gothic, replaced the fashion for neoclassical design,[*] Wedgwood's ornamental wares began to look outmoded and dull. In December 1790 Jos was already telling Tom Byerley: 'We are in need of orders for our jasper men.'[1]

Nevertheless the Order Book for ornamental wares[2] shows substantial orders continuing to come in for a wide variety of objects and jasper colours during the first decade of the new century. These included cameos in lilac and white and black and white 'for Mr Vulliamy' and 'A set of ornaments for the front of a Harpsichord to drawing sent – blue ground' (cf. Plates 326–8).[3] The 'beehive' and octagon shapes are both recorded for 1801, as are pipe heads, 'heart shape', 'pear shape' and 'upright' network custards, 'Deep blue jasper sweetmeat baskets' and 'Yellow & white jasper baskets & stands [shape] 451' (Plate 331; and see Plates 219 and 220).[4] 'Hookah bottoms' and 'Chillums & Covers' in light blue, deep blue, lilac and green jasper appear in the orders for 1804 (see Plate 260)[5] and there was evidently no restriction on the production of vases or tablets. Yellow, brown and white jasper, three colours rarely found as grounds for ornament in the eighteenth century, appear regularly, though in small quantities, the white being ornamented with blue, green, lilac or black to make three-colour or four-colour combinations. 'Cane color Jasper' is mentioned for the first time in October 1805, but it was probably never in regular production and examples are extremely rare.

A deliberate attempt was made to give jasper a fresh appearance, by exploiting unfamiliar colours and introducing new shapes. An example of the latter is shown in Byerley's letter of 21 February 1801 to Mowbray at the York Street showrooms: 'You will receive this week four new ornaments in the form of Viol del Gamba [*sic*] or Violoncello for Musical Amateurs – to be used either as flowerpot, bulbous-root, or candlestick.

---

[*]Egyptian ornaments, successful on rosso antico, did not suit jasper.

324. Marble, bronze and ormolu clock by Benjamin Vulliamy (1747–1811), the base inset with a blue and white jasper medallion of 'Group of Three Boys' designed by Lady Diana Beauclerk (Appendix J.241). Height (clock) 18½" (46.8 cm); (medallion) 5¾" (14.7 cm). Mark: none visible. 1799. The details of this clock, which was delivered to a Mr R. Borough on 9 October 1799, are fully recorded in one of Vulliamy's workbooks now in the British Horological Institute Library, Ilbert Bequest (quoted by Hugh Tait, 'The Wedgwood Collection in the British Museum', Part II, Wedgwood Society Proceedings, No. 5, 1963, p. 37). The design of the clock has been cited as illustrating the combination of Egyptian sphinxes with neoclassical decoration (A. Dawson, Masterpieces of Wedgwood in the British Museum, 1984, p. 127) but the Egyptian sphinx was male, while those supporting the clock are endowed with the well-modelled breasts of the female Greek sphinx. (Cf. Plate 54.) The cameo inset in the base is an excellent example of undercutting. British Museum

324

They belong to a set intended to captivate musical people' (Plate 332).[6] 'Lyre Candelabras' were ordered through London in 1802 and 1803.[7]

Portrait medallions were also wanted, the most in demand being those of the King, Pitt, Fox and De Vaere's admirals, with some continuing requests for Wesley, Washington, Franklin and Solander.[8]

Wedgwood's by then traditional disregard for the niceties of design came in for some criticism when 'Lord V P—' observed of the 'Incence Vase 494 – with Lotus on the pedestal, and Egyptian figures on the band between the Sphynx heads . . . and the same figures repeated round the edges of the pedestal, instead of the key border' that 'it is *extremely inconsistent* to place a Grecian border on the pedestal of an ornament that in every other respect is perfectly Egyptian.'[9]

325

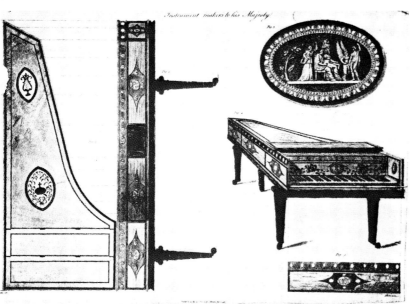

326

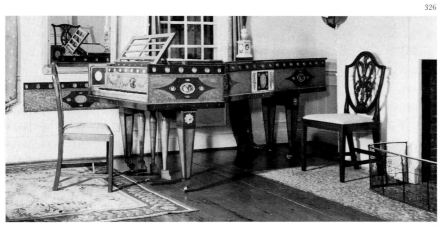

327

325. Ormolu and biscuit porcelain clock by Benjamin Vulliamy. The square ormolu pedestal, standing on an onyx and ormolu base, is inset with blue and white jasper medallions of Apollo and surmounted by an ormolu urn with enamel rotary dial. To the right of the urn stands the Derby biscuit porcelain figure (often described as 'Andromache') by John Deare after the earlier model by John Bacon. Height 17" (43.2 cm). Mark: signed VULLIAMY LONDON No 243 and dated 1800 (no Wedgwood marks visible). The Ornamental Ware Order Book for 7 November 1801 records cameos in black and white and lilac and white jasper 'for Mr Vulliamy'. (Cf. Plate 54.)
Lady Lever Art Gallery, Port Sunlight

326. Engraving, published by J. Barlow, 1796, of a design by Thomas Sheraton for a 'Grand Pianoforte . . . in a Satin Wood case ornamented with Marqueterie and with Wedgwood & Tassie's Medallions, manufactured by John Broadwood & Son in 1796 for Don Manuel de Godoy, Prince of the Peace, & by him Presented to Her Majesty the Queen of Spain'. (See Plate 327.)
Lady Lever Art Gallery, Port Sunlight

327. The Manuel de Godoy pianoforte now at the Heritage Foundation, Deerfield, Massachusetts. Photograph: Courtesy Miss Alison Kelly

328. Sheraton grand pianoforte by John Broadwood & Son, the panels above and beside the keyboard inset with three large Wedgwood blue and white jasper medallions of Muses and a griffin with musical instruments, and nine smaller medallions, c.1798. The Ornamental Ware Order Book for 16 May 1802 records an order for 'A set of ornaments for the front of a Harpsichord to drawing sent – blue ground'.
Albany Institute of History and Art, New York

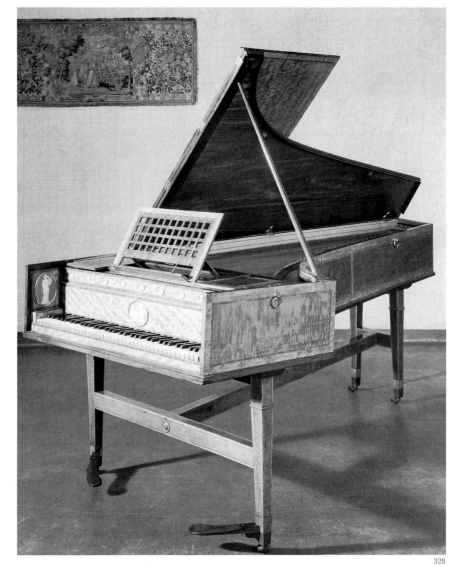

328

329. Rosewood collector's cabinet with ormolu mounts inset with six Wedgwood pale blue and white jasper cameos and medallions. The front of the cabinet falls to reveal five interior drawers. 20¾" × 14¼" × 8⅜" (53 × 36.2 × 21.2 cm). Mark: none visible. c.1795–1800. The choice of portraits of Michelangelo, Eustache Le Sueur, Correggio and Maratti (see Appendix H:I) to ornament the corners of the lid suggests that the cabinet may have been made for an artist.
Nottingham Castle Museum

329

330. *Deep-blue jasper dip clock case with solid white jasper figure and trophies representing the figure of 'Peace Destroying the Implements of War'. Height 16¾" (42.5 cm), width 17" (43.2 cm). Unmarked. Wedgwood, c.1802. The subject was first suggested to John Flaxman junior by Wedgwood in a letter dated 2 November 1786 proposing designs for a pair of medallions to commemorate the Commercial Treaty with France, and it is possible that this model was made at that date. A more likely date, however, seems to be 1802, when it would have been produced to celebrate the brief Peace of Amiens. The quality of the modelling suggests the hand of Flaxman or of Henry Webber.*
Merseyside Museums

330A. *Reverse of the clock case illustrated in Plate 330, showing the aperture for a cylinder clock in the French style. The slot in the base has been described as cut for a pendulum, leading to the assumption that the case is incomplete and was intended for mounting on a taller base (B. Tattersall,* Wedgwood at Woburn, *1973, p. 23). A French-style movement, however, would have had no pendulum, and it is likely therefore that the slot was cut to facilitate mounting on a marble or ormolu pedestal.*

330A

331. Solid blue and white jasper pierced sweetmeat basket with cover, ornamented with trophies suspended from floral swags and paterae, and scroll, twist, bead and floral borders, standing on four solid white jasper claw feet. Oval 5⅞" × 9" (15.0 × 23.0 cm), height 5¾" (14.5 cm). Mark: WEDGWOOD. c.1801. 'Deep blue jasper sweetmeat baskets' appear in the Ornamental Ware Order Book for 1 June 1801, and in various colours, including yellow and lilac during the following ten years. They were among the most fragile of Wedgwood's jasper pieces and few have survived.
Wedgwood Museum

332. Pale-blue jasper dip 'Viol del Gamba' [sic] vase, 'intended to captivate musical people'. Height 6½" (16.5 cm). Mark: WEDGWOOD. c.1801.
Wedgwood Museum

333. Lilac jasper dip portrait medallion, of Richard, first Earl Howe modelled by John De Vaere, 1798 (see Appendix H:III). Oval height 3⅞" (9.8 cm). Mark: WEDGWOOD. c.1800–10.
British Museum

334. Solid pale-blue jasper portrait medallion of Adam, Viscount Duncan of Camperdown modelled by John De Vaere, 1798 (see Appendix H:III). Oval height 4½" (11.3 cm). Mark: WEDGWOOD impressed; 'Duncan' inscribed. No firing holes. c.1870.
Victoria & Albert Museum

331

332

333

334

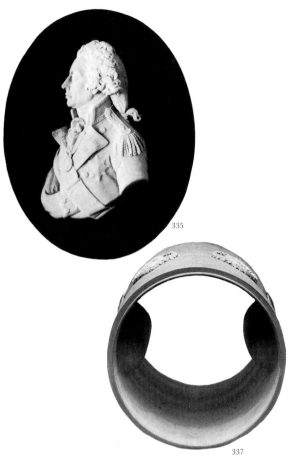

335

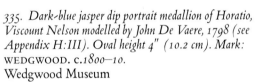

337

336

338

335. *Dark-blue jasper dip portrait medallion of Horatio,
Viscount Nelson modelled by John De Vaere, 1798 (see
Appendix H:III). Oval height 4″ (10.2 cm). Mark:*
WEDGWOOD. c.1800–10.
Wedgwood Museum

336. *Detail of the solid pale-blue and white jasper group
illustrated in Plate C59. The group shows the figure of
Britannia, her feet on the prostrate figure of France and a
spilled cornucopia, accompanied by a benign-looking lion.
Britannia holds a portrait of George III after the medal by
Burch (see Appendix H:I), and the pedestal is ornamented
with portrait medallions of the admirals Duncan, Howe,
Nelson and St Vincent's by De Vaere. The last of the
portraits was invoiced to Wedgwood on 24 December 1798,
so the most likely date for this rare piece, evidently
celebrating British naval victories, is 1799–1805.*
Beeson Collection, Birmingham Museum,
Alabama (group); Wedgwood Museum (pedestal)

337. *Interior of the cylinder-shape pedestal to the Britannia
group illustrated in Plate 336, showing the coiled-clay
method of construction and two strengthening lugs, one on
either side of the cylinder. This is one of two such pedestals
in the Wedgwood Museum collection.*

338. *Detail of Ackermann's engraving of the Wedgwood
& Byerley showrooms in York Street, c.1809, showing
the Britannia group inside a pillared and domed 'temple'.*
Photograph: Wedgwood

339. Blue jasper dip vase ornamented with Flaxman's Apotheosis of Homer, *the handles in the form of two snakes competing for an egg above the mask of Medusa, and the finial modelled as a figure of Pegasus riding on a cloud. Height 17¾" (45.0 cm). Mark:* WEDGWOOD ⁛ . *c.1802. (Cf. Plates 262, 263 and C49.)* Wedgwood Museum

339

The quality of the jasper being made at this time is illustrated by an order for '12 Transparent Jasper Vases. Washed blue – Swan necks, same shape as before made transparent white. Then to be turned as thin as they will stand & part finished with dancing hours as large as the vase will take.'[10] The wording of a message dated 18 June 1811 from York Street suggests that a new colour combination was being tried: 'Mr Wedgwood says the Yellow Jasper with blue ornaments of which you sent a can as patt[n] will do very well.'[11] Its period of production as a jasper dip was brief, but it was shortly to become popular as a combination of jasper dip and ornament on stoneware.

Throughout this period until about 1811 there is no indication that any difficulty was being experienced in the manufacture of jasper at Etruria. On the contrary, not only are there records of orders and produc‑ tion of eighteenth‑century models from vases to chessmen but there is ample evidence of the introduction of complicated new shapes and differ‑ ent colours. Most of these would have been as jasper dip and the wording of the orders indicates that this was the standard product, but there is no shortage of examples of the use of solid colour jasper, as in such pieces as sweetmeat baskets, 'network' custards and déjeuner trays. Diced jasper was used for vases and flower‑pots, and the comparatively difficult 'deep blue' colour appears in orders for both solid and dip pieces.[12]

It has been asserted, on the authority of Josiah IV, that the manufac‑ ture of jasper was 'discontinued in 1810'.[13] The 'O.W. Order Books' and surviving travellers' orders contain quantities of evidence to disprove this, but there is, nevertheless, plenty of material in them to show a rapid

340

341

340. *Small blue jasper-dip vase on a flat solid white jasper plinth fixed by a metal bolt and nut to a cylindrical pedestal. Height 6" (15.2 cm). Mark:* WEDGWOOD 2 FEB[Y] 1805. *A particularly rare example among recorded pieces (the majority of which are tripods) bearing this mysterious mark. (See Appendix B.)*
Mr and Mrs Samuel Laver Collection

341. *Dark-blue jasper dip beaker ('drinking can') ornamented with two lilac and white jasper cameos showing Neptune with his trident and the monogram 'HN' suspended from oak swags, the foot ornamented with 'Egyptian' reliefs. The inscription around the rim,* 'THE NAVY OF BRITAIN'*, is inlaid in blue. Height 3⅜" (8.6 cm). Mark:* WEDGWOOD. c.1801 *(Ms. 54–30024 26 June 1801). The unusual oak swags represent the oak timbers of the navy; Nelson's monogram and the use of Egyptian reliefs suggest a celebration of his victory at the battle of the Nile in August 1798.*
Manchester City Art Gallery

342

342. *Pair of pale-blue jasper dip figure candlesticks, probably representing Pomona and Ceres. Height 10⅞" (27.6 cm). Mark:* WEDGWOOD. c.1810. *(Cf. Plate 256.)*
Temple Newsam House, Leeds

245

343. *Black jasper dip portrait medallion of Frederick I, King of Württemberg. Height 5¼"* (13.2 cm). *Mark:* WEDGWOOD. *c.1797. Probably copied from a biscuit porcelain medallion produced by the Ludwigsburg factory, c.1775. (See also Plate 87B.)* Wedgwood Museum

344. *Dark-blue jasper dip portrait medallion of Arthur, Duke of Wellington, by John Henning, 1813, set in a solid pale-blue stoneware ribbon and laurel moulded frame. Oval height 3"* (7.6 cm). *Mark:* WEDGWOOD. *c.1860. Framed portraits of Wellington and others appear in R. G. Keeling's orders for 1844 (W/M 1637), but no solid colour jasper was then in production.* Wedgwood Museum

345. *Blue jasper dip portrait medallion of Sir Henry Paget, first Marquis of Anglesey by William Hackwood. Oval height 9"* (22.9 cm). *Unmarked. Signed 'W. Hackwood' on the truncation. c.1821. The lack of any Wedgwood impressed mark on the few examples of this medallion has cast some doubt on its provenance. It does not, however, appear likely that Hackwood would have produced this fine piece of work from any factory other than Etruria.* City Museum & Art Gallery, Stoke-on-Trent

346. *Rare plain blue and white jasper dip helmet cream jug, tea bowl and saucer and bowl. All but the cream have lapidary-polished rims. Cream height 4¾"* (12.0 cm); *tea bowl diameter 3¼"* (8.3 cm). *Marks: (cream)* WEDGWOOD ʃ *; (others)* WEDGWOOD 3. *c.1800–20.* Mr and Mrs Byron A. Born Collection

343

344

345

346

347. *Black jasper dip teapot ornamented with heavy fruit swags, medallions and trophies between borders of flowers and foliage, the handle in solid white jasper. Height 5½" (14.0 cm). Mark:* WEDGWOOD. ᴗᴗ *c.1810.* Dwight and Lucille Beeson Collection, Birmingham Museum, Alabama

348. (Right) *Adams solid blue and white jasper sugar box with swan knop, the body ornamented with sacrificing figures copied from Wedgwood's, width 6" (15.5 cm), c.1800; (left) Neale & Co. solid pale-blue and white jasper sugar box ornamented with boys at play above a wide band of moulded basketwork, width 4¾" (12.0 cm). c.1790. Marks:* (right) ADAMS; (left) NEALE & Co. Christie's, New York

347

348

349. *One of a pair of deep-blue jasper dip combined bough-pots and pastille-burners with solid white jasper handles and pierced grids, ornamented with classical figures in panels above a border of inverted bell flowers. Overall height 6⅝" (16.8 cm). Mark:* WEDGWOOD. c.1820. Dwight and Lucille Beeson Collection, Birmingham Museum, Alabama

349

decline in the making of larger pieces, such as vases, until, in the early 1820s, in spite of frequent experiments with the body, jasper was confined to such small and nondescript objects as upright cylinders (spill vases), flat taper candlesticks and caddy shells. Jos noted wearily: 'Very large pieces of ware were formerly made of jasper, but there was always much difficulty in it, the body for these purposes was coarsely ground.' He was trying to make a jasper body with a larger proportion of flint, and added: 'There is considerable loss in making bisque ware with jasper bas reliefs.'[14]

This note is of great interest: first, it confirms Wedgwood's loss of the ability to make large objects of jasper; second, it shows that Jos was aware that large pieces were made with a coarse-ground body; and third, it gives some indication of the steps taken to replace jasper by the 'bisque' or stoneware body, later called 'porcelain'.* Jos's perfunctory reference to the coarsely ground body is suggestive more of second-hand information passed on to him than of a first-hand intimacy with Josiah I's essential memorandum of 23 November 1777.† The subsequent failure to overcome the difficulties that had arisen strongly supports the implication that by about 1820 there was no longer anyone at Etruria who knew precisely how to make vases or other large pieces of jasper stand up in the fire.

It is not easy to imagine how such a situation could have been allowed to occur. One possible explanation might be that the memorandum, entrusted for safe keeping to Alexander Chisholm, in whose handwriting it has survived, was lost at the time of his death in 1805.[15] The next fifteen years or so were a period of change at Etruria, when many of the old craftsmen who had served the first Josiah retired from the firm. It is conceivable, however improbable it may seem, that the technique was lost, imperceptibly, without its loss being noticed until it was too late. Whatever may be the reason, lost the technique undoubtedly was, and no satisfactory substitute for it was discovered until 1845. Even when a new composition was found to withstand the fire, problems with cracking remained, and it was not until 1856 that Godfrey Wedgwood could write that the chief fault in his jasper was the quality of the surface.[16] In the meantime, no vases could be made in jasper, and it appears from Bateman's order sheets that, apart from a few caddy spoons, no solid jasper was made for sale between 1829 and 1844.[17]

Abner Wedgwood's notebook of 'Blendings' for 1807 to 1835 contains a number of recipes for jasper dip and ornaments, and records of many experiments with the jasper body, but no mention of trials with coarse or fine grinding. By February 1820 a blue jasper dip was already being used over white stoneware.[18] One of the more interesting of the recipes shows that green jasper dip was made by mixing nine measures of yellow dip with one of blue, and not by the use of either copper or chromium oxide.

---

*See below p. 282.
†pp. 87–9

In 1836 Frank Wedgwood was as mystified by failure as his father had been some fourteen years earlier:

> We formerly used to make large pieces of ware of jasper body, therefore am much surprised to find almost every piece that I attempt of any size dunt as soon as it comes out of BO [Biscuit Oven] whether in long continued or in a harty [*sic*] fire. It has been nothing to do with sudden cooling because they sometimes stand a day or two before they dunt. Can it depend on the grinding? The degree of grinding is certainly of the utmost importance in jasper body.[19]

He mentions the liability of his trials to 'fly in pieces' after coming out of the oven, and of the 'washes' or dip used on the jasper body to be covered all over with fine cracks.

Many trials were conducted to overcome the dunting and crazing, but they were unsuccessful, and the use of a jasper dip and jasper ornaments on stoneware was creating problems of its own: 'The difficulty of making jasper fig[ure]s or dip to agree with stone body is – that the additional proportion of flint in the jasper necessary to prevent cracking makes the body of which the figures are made so fusible that it will not bear the highest excess of fire without blistering.'[20]

In his travels in the eastern and south-west territories between 1826 and 1844, Jesse Keeling did not take a single order for jasper.[21] This confirms all the other existing evidence contained in the orders from Bateman and from the London showrooms, and in the 'Pottery Memos', that, except for a very small quantity of caddy shells and cylinders, no jasper was made between those dates.[*] No record of the production of jasper vases has been found between 1817 and 1845.

From Jos's and Frank's notes, and the frequency of trials for different jasper bodies, it is obvious that the more the composition of the body was altered, the further it deviated from Josiah I's successful formula and the less likely it became that the problems in firing it would be solved.

Jos's response to this problem is made clear in a note, written in 1817: 'Our Stone body has lately been used washed over with jasper slip & with jasper reliefs which seem to agree very well.'[22] This practice – of disguising a strong body, inferior in appearance, with a dip or wash of jasper and ornamenting it with jasper bas-reliefs – was strikingly similar in principle to Josiah I's, and it must be considered surprising that the required solution was not found by experiments in grinding the jasper body. However, the stoneware body decorated with jasper was an acceptable substitute for ordinary pieces but, for either aesthetic or manufacturing reasons, it does not appear to have been thought suitable for ornamental vases until 1839, when the first of many small Portland vases[†] were produced in it.

---

[*]Bateman's orders indicate that even the cylinders disappeared from production after June 1828.
[†]See below p. 288.

351

350

350. *White Stoneware vase dipped in bright blue jasper, engine-turned and painted with a band of scrolling thistles in enamel colours and gilded lines. Height 4⅛" (12.4 cm). Mark: WEDGWOOD ᵍ. c.1818. This style is evidently an early attempt to find a decorative alternative to bas-relief ornament. The only documentary evidence of it to be found so far is contained in Bateman's order dated May 1818 (18–16560). Wedgwood Museum*

351. *White stoneware flower-pot (lacking stand) dipped in pale-blue jasper and ornamented with spiralling 'leaf and flower between' reliefs. Height 6¼" (16.0 cm). Mark: WEDGWOOD. c.1820–30. The spiral relief was introduced about 1810–15. Merseyside Museums*

352. *Teapot, sugar box and cream jug in white stoneware, dipped in pale-lilac jasper and ornamented with a vine border in blue. Teapot length 7½" (19.0 cm). Mark: WEDGWOOD ~ ~. c.1820. Christie's, New York*

352

As a separate body, white or stained with colours usually associated with jasper, the stoneware ('porcelain') composition became a useful ornamental ware body, which is discussed in some detail below;[*] as a 'support' for jasper dip and ornament it filled a gap left by the jasper body until 1845 and then lasted, for some vases and cameos and in the production of 'Basrelief Ware', particularly for teawares and other pieces that might be put to some practical use (Plates 350–2), until the 1939–45 war. It was one of the many bodies finally discarded when the move to Barlaston was completed.

[*]See below pp. 282–7.

353A

353B

After years of unsuccessful experiment, the true jasper body was rein-troduced in 1844. In September R.G. Keeling's orders change abruptly from 'Blue & white basreliefs' to 'Blue & white jasper', and next month he celebrated its return with orders for vases as large as 12 inches high.[23] There was evidently some continuing difficulty with the production of black-and-white jasper* but this was overcome by November 1847, when vases in all colours were again available and the London orders included Sphynx candelabra and 354 teapots of various shapes for one customer.[24]

So certainly was the jasper body restored to production that William Evans published what he believed to be its composition in 1846:

WEDGWOOD'S BEAUTIFUL JASPER

Cauk stone, 168; blue clay, 91; cornish clay, 60; flint, 40; raw plaster, 8.

> N.B. It is better to make this ball clay before mixed, 1 grain of calx to 1 lb. of clay. To prevent Jasper from sticking take 8 or 12 of alum to 1 of charcoal; the alum must be well roasted before mixed with charcoal: then mix it well, and put it in a vessel at the top of a biscuit oven: when calcined pound it, put it in a vessel, and pour hot water upon it repeatedly, to take out the salt, then grind it in a stone dish, and use it.[25]

This may be compared with Wedgwood's recipe for 1849 of 50 parts cawk to 25 of Blue clay, 15 of China clay, 12 of flint and 2 of boiled plas-ter, a composition continued in use until 1854, when the proportion of China clay was increased to 17 parts.[26]

*See below p. 292.

Godfrey Wedgwood noted on 15 February 1856: 'The chief fault now is want of sharpness & a certain want of smooth waxy surface. I think they are both caused by over fusibility.' These were minor faults compared with what had already been overcome, but some of the old problems, often suggesting contradictory solutions, persisted. Godfrey noted that 'Flint causes vitrification & therefore running in in firing – also running in in cooling probably. . . . Cawk does not cause running in in firing but does in cooling'. Gypsum produced the same effects as cawk and caused 'haircracks but not gaping cracks', while chalk, 'put in to prevent dunting because the stone body without it ran in so much more than jasper dip either in the firing or the cooling', caused gaping cracks. Trials continued through 1856–9. Meanwhile, all jasper continued to be jasper dip.

354

354. Reading candlestick in white stoneware with blue jasper dip in the style described as 'blue white lines' introduced about 1843 (W/M 1637). Height 3⅝" (9.2 cm). Mark: WEDGWOOD. *This plain style, without ornament except lines or bands turned through the dip, is similar to the entirely plain jasper dip produced some forty years earlier (Plate 346), but the quality of the dipped stoneware is markedly inferior to that of the jasper.* Author's collection

355. Pair of white stoneware pillar candlesticks ornamented in blue with 'wreathed laurel', and a white stoneware vase dipped in yellow jasper ('yellow porcelain') and ornamented with the four seasons in panels and bands of foliage in 'light blue'. Height (candlesticks) 6¾" (17 cm); (vase) 5" (12.5 cm). Marks: (candlesticks) WEDGWOOD RK, c.1835; *(vase)* WEDGWOOD, c.1850 ('OW' Order Book 2 November 1850). Christie's, New York

355

356

356A

356. *Staite's patent pipe and stand of white stoneware dipped in blue jasper and ornamented with various classical cameos ('Aurora', 'Bellerophon watering Pegasus', 'Sacrifice to Aesculapius', 'Three Graces') and bands of foliage. Height 6⅛" (15.5 cm); base diameter 4⅜" (11.1 cm). Marks: (stand)* WEDGWOOD No 21; *(pipe)* WEDGWOOD STAITES PATENT. *c.1849. The '1843' Price Book (uncatalogued) contains details of prices for pipes of several patterns, including Staite's patent, on 28 December 1849 and an entry for 'Stand No 1 & large pipe to it 5/4d'.*
Author's collection

356A. *Staite's patent pipe and stand, shown separately to illustrate the construction of the pipe, which included a form of diaphragm to separate the tobacco juice and provide a drier smoke. It is notable that the Price Book entry for 28 December 1849 mentions 'Staite's Patent' although the patent was not registered by William Edwards Staite until the following year.*

357

357. *White stoneware teapot dipped in deep-blue jasper and ornamented with acanthus leaf and bell flower ('leafage with flower between') reliefs. Height 4⅛" (10.5 cm). Mark:* WEDGWOOD. *c.1840.*
Temple Newsam House, Leeds

358. *Spode white stoneware teapot with blue dip, ornamented with* Charlotte at the Tomb of Werther. *Height 4⅜", (11.1 cm). Mark:* SPODE. *c.1820.*
Norwich Castle Museum

358

253

359. *White stoneware teapot dipped in blue jasper and ornamented with* A Sacrifice to Hymen. *Height 5¼" (13.3 cm). Mark:* WEDGWOOD ENGLAND 24. *c.1895. A typical example of Etruria bas-relief ware, production of which continued until 1940. It is easily recognised by the difference in colour between the stoneware body, where it is undipped, and the applied ornaments, the former being a distinct grey-white, often with a brownish tint.*
Wedgwood Museum

360. *Pale-blue and white jasper dip ovoid vase with cherub finial, ornamented with 'Aurora' within a lilac and white circular frame of Signs of the Zodiac. Height 13⅜" (34.0 cm). Mark:* WEDGWOOD. *One of a pair: one vase inscribed 'Septr 1857'.*
Christie's, London

361. *White stoneware biscuit barrel with silver-plated mount and lid, and circular box, both dipped in blue jasper with white jasper ornaments (bas-relief ware). Height: (barrel) 5" (12.7 cm); (box) 2¾" (7.0 cm). Marks: (barrel)* WEDGWOOD; *(box)* WEDGWOOD BVQ. *c.1855 and 1862 respectively.*
Author's collection

362. *Solid blue jasper flower-pot ornamented with mixed leaves and bullrushes on a ground moulded all over with leaves and branches. Height 6" (15.2 cm), diameter 8½" (21.6 cm). Mark:* WEDGWOOD. *c.1860–5.*
Wedgwood Museum

359

360

361

362

In 1860 the jasper composition was sufficiently stable for an important change to be made: the reintroduction of solid colour jasper in pale blue, green and lilac.[27] Next year the London cabinet-makers Wright & Mansfield were supplied with 'Oval slabs' 7⅜ inches by 5¾ inches at twelve shillings and sixpence each and 'Long square slabs' 10¾ inches by 4¼ inches at seventeen shillings and sixpence in solid pale-blue and white jasper and some similar plaques in black basaltes for mounting in furniture.[28] Some of these were no doubt used for the fine cabinet exhibited by Wright & Mansfield in the London Exhibition of 1862 (Plate 363).

The return of solid jasper was not made without difficulty. Laurence Wedgwood noted in 1866 that dark blue and all the other jasper colours

363. Important cabinet in the Adam style with ormolu mounts, ornamented with framed Wedgwood medallions, made by Wright & Mansfield for the 1862 Exhibition.
Victoria & Albert Museum

363

364. *Cabinet mounted with Wedgwood medallions of assorted shapes and sizes exhibited by 'Mr Lamb, Cabinet Manufacturer of Manchester' in the 1862 London Exhibition. It is described in the Art* Journal Catalogue *of the exhibition as 'of inlaid woods, very beautiful in design, of admirable proportions, and unsurpassed as an example of good workmanship'. The Wedgwood plaques used in this supremely over-decorated piece include a large octagonal tablet of Lady Diana Beauclerk's groups of boys under arbours of panther skins (cf. Plate C27).*
Photograph: Wedgwood

364

except pale blue, green and lilac were still made as 'jasper wash or dip on a Stone body', and lilac also was produced in that manner when the pieces were 'too big to stand in the heat'.[29] Some light-blue jasper dip was again produced on stoneware in 1863–5 and trial medallions were made in stoneware in 1867, but otherwise all were made in solid jasper in spite of heavy losses in plaques made for the chimneypiece shown at the 1867 Exhibition.[30]

Laurence made notes also of two practical tips for the production of jasper lids:

To prevent jasper covers from sticking to jasper it is washed with non-sticker – Alum & charcoal mixed & fired GO [Glost Oven] & then made into a wash. . . . If the lids of jasper jars etc happen to be to [sic] large when fired they are rubbed on a stone till they will fit the jar, it is very useful and not easy work.[31]

About 1866 Frank recorded some important information about the modern production of jasper, which included partly coded recipes cover-ing a period of nearly ninety years:

We have made a good deal of jasper since we began making solid Jasper again – it is not so good as the old has not such a waxy surface & is not so sharp & yet dryer so that it soils & when the soiling is well rubbed in a nailbrush & soap will not get it out – it seems that the surface is full of little broken bubbles which hold the dirt. An old piece I had which had a very nice waxy feel had the same dirty specks but much smaller.

We only grind the figure clay 7 hours whereas we grind the blue body 48 – the consequence is the body is very often (generally I think) fired up when the figures are still porous. . . .

Our jasper mixtures have been:

			♁ [cawk]	♀ [flint]	gyp[sum]
3615 Cherokee					
about 40			48	8	2 my grandfathers*
3681 Bl[ue] Cl.	26				
Ch[ina] Cl.	14		48	8	2
Before 1840 26	14		48	8	2
1840	25	15	50	12	2 –boiled I think
1851	25	15	50	12	2
Now (1866) 25	17		50	12	1½ boiled[32]

Evidently Godfrey suggested to his father that more colours should be added to the range, and proposed that a chemist[†] might be employed to develop them. Frank replied to him on 23 February 1866:

As to Jasper – it is so exclusively almost blue or black that I do not think the public would buy anything else – if they wanted variety they would not neglect lilac & green & yellow so completely as they do – nevertheless a new color or two would no doubt be an advantage if one knew how to lay hold of it – but the objection to a chemist is that he would be absolutely ignorant and we should have to pay him while he was learning.[33]

*Frank had noted about 1823 that 'two arkfuls' of Cherokee clay were still in the round house at Etruria (60–32823 Pottery Memos).
[†]William Burton was employed as chemist in 1887.

365

366

365. Large white stoneware pot-pourri vase dipped in bright blue jasper with solid white jasper rope handles and bird finial, boldly ornamented with flowers and leaves. Height 15½" (39.5 cm). Mark: WEDGWOOD. c.1850. Merseyside Museums

366. White stoneware oval basin dipped in lilac jasper and ornamented with solid white jasper lion-mask handles and alternating acanthus leaf and bell flower ('leafage and flower between') reliefs, mounted on a Carrara body base modelled in the form of three scantily clad nymphs and attendant fauns on a cruciform plinth. Height 17½" (44.5 cm). Mark: WEDGWOOD. c.1866. A sketch of the bowl appears in an uncatalogued book of workers' measurements, described as a 'Lamp Tray'. Large bowls were always particularly vulnerable in firing, and Laurence Wedgwood noted in 1866 that the larger pieces of lilac dip were still being made at that date in the stone body owing to firing difficulties. The base group is included in the 1859 Carrara price list as 'Supporting Group' by Carrier de Belleuse. It appears also in the '1878' Ornamental catalogue as a Majolica 'Satyr Centre'. Christie's, London

No new colours were introduced until the 1870s, but trials were continued and both yellow and lilac dip were in use in 1869. Laurence wrote of the yellow: 'The colour is the nicest on the Jasper cameo, on the Stone cameo it is a dirtier greener yellow.'[34] This evidence of cameos being made of jasper-dipped stoneware is confirmed by a note dated 11 June 1869 which mentions trials with stone cameos dipped once or twice in green, black or white jasper. A later note shows that pale blue, dark blue and black dip were also being used in this manner, the dip being 'the old JW's mixing'.[35] The dark-blue dip proved difficult:

> For some year or more [Laurence wrote] we have not been able to get the real old Dark blue we used, which is a purplish and clear blue. Instead of this we have had nasty black & gray blues; but F[rank] W has got the right colour again by using the Carb. of Barytes instead of Sulphate in mixing the jasper.[*36]

In 1863 'Clock fittings', which included dark-blue and white jasper cameos, were made for Saglier of Paris, and 'clock slabs' were among the unusual goods supplied to Blumberg & Co., a firm that first approached Wedgwood in 1867 with an order for lamp vases in jasper and Majolica.[37] The lamp vases, of a footed ovoid shape with 'loose top', were modelled especially for Blumberg's, and the first six in light-blue jasper dip on 'Best White Stone' with figure ornaments were completed in November 1869.[38] Later orders for this firm included lamp vases 13 inches high in pale-blue and white jasper with and without Cupid and Psyche ornament, dark blue and white with 'Muses' and 'Sacrifice', sage green and white with 'Medallion & Festoon', lilac and white and black and white, priced from one guinea to thirty-five shillings each.[39] Blumberg's were supplied also with inkstands and candlestick fittings that were exclusive to them for three years from 9 April 1869. 'Clock slabs', made for the face and two sides of the clock, were ornamented with Cupid and Psyche figures.[40]

Throughout the 1870s both solid and dip jasper were made in large quantities, and many of the finest eighteenth-century models were reproduced. Much diced jasper was produced on the engine-turning lathe and the ornaments of some of the best vases were undercut.[41] Large jasper plaques were no longer impossible to fire and solid green-and-blue jasper reproductions of the 'Herculaneum pictures' (usually described as 'Pompeian figures') and the Clodion bacchanalian tablets were successfully produced, as were solid blue jasper déjeuner trays.[42]

Laurence noted towards the end of 1871: 'All Jaspers except Dark Blue dip contain Anderson's Cawk, Newcastle on Tyne at 44/—p.ton less 2½% for cash.' Plain solid pale blue cost nine shillings and sixpence a hundredweight, using one pint of stain to two hundredweight of clay. Dark-blue dip cost two shillings more.[43]

---

*This last comment demonstrates how far the jasper body had been changed from Josiah I's composition.

367

367. (Left and right) pair of lilac dip vases on drum pedestals, height 16¼" (41.0 cm). Mark: WEDGWOOD and date code for 1867. (Centre) solid pale-blue jasper vase on matching jasper-dipped pedestal, height 21" (53.5 cm). Mark: WEDGWOOD. c.1866. At this date some of the largest shapes made in one piece (such as the shaped pedestal) were still being made in dipped stoneware. Christie's, New York

368

369

368. Blue jasper dip coffee cup and saucer heavily ornamented with fruit swags and lilac and white cameo subjects. Height 2¾" (6.9 cm). Mark: WEDGWOOD and date code for 1869. A useful comparison may be made between the quality of this piece and that of the similarly ornamented teapot of some sixty years earlier (Plate 347). Sotheby's, London

369. Pair of blue dip pear-shape tea bowls ornamented with various classical groups, including Sacrifice to Aesculapius and Dipping of Achilles, in panels. Height 2½" (6.4 cm). Mark: WEDGWOOD A[?]Z. 1871. Author's collection

370. *Solid pale blue and white jasper medallion of Euterpe. Oval 6½" × 4¾" (16.5 × 12.0 cm). Mark:* WEDGWOOD. *The back is pierced with five firing holes (see Plate 87C) and the top of the medallion is slotted for hanging. c.1870.*
Author's collection

371. *Solid blue and white jasper medallion, Hercules and Cerberus. Oval 9" × 6¼" (22.9 × 15.9 cm). Mark:* WEDGWOOD. *c.1870. Some undercutting is visible under the hound's left foreleg and Hercules' left hand, but the general quality of both the body and the ornament is poor.*
Christie's, New York

370

371

372

372. *Solid blue and white jasper tablet,* Achilles in Scyros among the Daughters of Lycomedes. *3⅝" × 8½" (9.2 × 21.8 cm). Mark:* WEDGWOOD. *c.1870. The unusual feature of this tablet is the display of Victorian prudery in draping the originally nude male figures (cf. Plate C26).*
Norwich Castle Museum

373. *One of a pair of electroplated nickel silver girandoles mounted with solid pale-blue and white jasper plaques and candle-holders. Height 13⅝" (34.6 cm). No marks visible. For many years these pieces were erroneously catalogued and displayed in the Wedgwood Museum as late-eighteenth-century pieces with Sheffield plate mounts. Recent research by the Museum staff ('Wedgwood in London' Exhibition Catalogue, 1984, O47) has revealed that they were made for the 1871 International Exhibition.*
Wedgwood Museum

373

374. *Large solid pale-blue jasper table centre, reputedly owned by President Harding and given by him to his secretary. Height 15¼" (38.7 cm); oval width 21½" (54.6 cm). The colour of this piece connects it with the 'extra pale blue jasper' made in 1872 for 'a large table centre', though existing sketches suggest that there may have been more than one design produced. Laurence Wedgwood recorded the use of 'non-dunting' clay for this centre (60–32834 25 February 1872). Mark:* WEDGWOOD *(on base of one candlestick only).* Buten Museum

A more important development in the composition of jasper was recorded in February 1872. Although large pieces had been made successfully during the previous year, there had been occasional losses from dunting and the appearance of 'threading cracks in the plaques . . . [which] go through the ornaments to the body'.[44] To obviate the former, a special 'non-dunting' clay was created. Towards the end of February, pieces for candelabra and a large table centre (Plate 374) were made in an 'extra pale blue jasper and fired easy first fire which is the best way of getting awkward pieces straight & free of cracks and to avoid dunting'. 'I am', Laurence added, 'using non dunting Portland vase clay.'[45] The recipe for this was recorded for the first time the previous day:

Pale Light Blue Jasper for Portland vases &c Non Dunting
6 half bushels 6 quarts No 2 Jasper
8 pints 8 oz Green Glaze fritt
12 oz VQ stain

This is accompanied by a recipe for 'Quaker Grey' jasper, a mixing of No. 2 jasper body with calcined chromate of iron in proportions of twenty to one.[46]

The non-dunting body does not seem to have been invariably satisfactory: 'large heads of Priestley in non dunting blue' made on 24 November 1874 were both cracked, and another fired on 2 February 1875 dunted. Laurence made a note to 'make no more'. Five years later, however, the problems had been overcome and more were made.[47] It is clear that by the end of 1874 there was little that could not be made in all colours without much loss. Yellow dip and solid black were reintroduced, and chocolate-brown jasper plaques were fired in December 1875.[48] 'Large black &

white vases Pegasus ['Apotheosis' vases] with Griffin pedestals' fired on 7 December 1875 were 'very good'.[49] Yet another colour, oddly described as 'Grey or Maroon Jasper', was added in March 1879. From the recipe, which is identical in ingredients and proportions (though not in quantities) to that given in 1872 for 'Quaker Grey', it appears likely to have been more obviously grey than maroon in colour.

Frederick Schenck, a modeller engaged at a daily wage of five shillings, was employed at Etruria for about eight months from 3 August 1872. No record of his work was kept before 2 January 1873. Between that date and 5 April he repaired or remodelled two bas-reliefs, 'Satyr & two Bacchantes' and its companion piece by Clodion, and a bas-relief of Diana; produced models of a companion plaque to 'Flying Figures with Torch', a plaque with two figures entitled 'Vanity' and its companion 'War', and '4 Seasons', drawn and modelled 'out of a frieze from a Vase'; and modelled 'Minerva as companion to Jupiter', and figures or groups representing 'Utility', 'Beauty', 'Hector & Andromache', 'Poetry', 'Homer Muse' and 'Science'.[50] After this burst of industry, he left to join George Jones & Sons as a modeller of pâte-sur-pâte.

375. *Pale-blue jasper dip vases ornamented with lilac medallions, the finials, rims to lids, handles, stems and feet of ormolu. Height 11″ (27.9 cm). Mark:* WEDGWOOD. *c.1870–80.* Christie's, London

376. *Green jasper dip tablet,* Diana visiting Endymion *(Appendix J.274). 13¾″ × 30¼″ (34.9 × 76.8 cm). Mark:* WEDGWOOD. *c.1875. The size of this tablet, and its good quality, almost without firecracks, clearly demonstrate Wedgwood's restored ability to produce even the most vulnerable pieces of jasper from about 1875.* Wedgwood Museum

376

377

378

379

380

377. *One of a pair of black and white jasper dip vases, shape no. 1, ornamented with figures of the Muses. Height 15" (38.1 cm). Mark:* WEDGWOOD s66. *c.1875. By the last quarter of the century, solid jasper vases and all the dip colours could be made without much difficulty, and the quality of the body was better than at any time in the previous sixty years.*
Author's collection

378. *Black jasper dip Apotheosis of Homer vase with Pegasus finial, on octagonal pedestal raised on four feet and ornamented with griffins at the corners. Height 24½" (62.2 cm). Mark:* WEDGWOOD *on foot and pedestal. c.1875–85. (Cf. Plate 339 and Plates 262–4.)*
Christie's, New York

379. *Black jasper dip pot-pourri vase with pierced cover on a tall waisted pedestal ornamented with solid white jasper rams' heads at the upper corners. Height 23½" (59.0 cm). Mark:* WEDGWOOD. *c.1875–85.*
Christie's, New York

380. *Black jasper dip vase ornamented with bands of engine-turned diced pattern and yellow jasper quatrefoils. Height 14½" (37.0 cm). Mark:* WEDGWOOD. *c.1875.*
Christie's, New York

381. *Three-colour jasper teawares, ornamented with swags of vine and classical cameo subjects in lilac and green on a solid white jasper body. Mark:* WEDGWOOD. *c.1875–80.*
Christie's, New York

382. *Solid white jasper vase, shape no. 381, ornamented with green jasper festoons and lilac cameos. Height 8¼″ (21.0 cm). Mark:* WEDGWOOD *impressed,* 'T. LOVATT' *incised. c.1876. Thomas Lovatt (1850–1915) was chief ornamenter at Etruria, and a number of pieces, including Portland vases, made by him in jasper are signed by him in full or with his initials (see p. 294 and Plates 446–8). Vases of this colour combination are recorded as among Wedgwood's exhibits in 1862.*
Wedgwood Museum

383. *(Left and right) pair of three-colour jasper vases, the solid white grounds ornamented with four lion's masks, pilaster and paw feet suspending flower swags with medallions between, with borders of ribbons and ivy in lilac and green. (Centre) similar vase with almost identical ornament, the body dipped in lilac and the reliefs in green and white. Height 5¼″ and 7½″ (13.3 and 19.0 cm). Mark:* WEDGWOOD. *c.1875–85.*
Christie's, London

381

382

383

384. *Solid blue jasper rectangular plaque,* Raising an Altar to Bacchus, *probably adapted from the design by Alphonse Lechevrel, a French engraver and medallist employed by Benjamin Richardson at his glassworks at Wordsley, near Stourbridge. 9½″ × 12½″ (24.1 × 31.2 cm). Mark:* WEDGWOOD. *c.1878. The subject appears on a glass vase cameo-cut by Lechevrel between 1877 and 1879, when he left Richardson's service.* Mr and Mrs David Zeitlin Collection

384

385

385. *Black jasper dip oval plaque,* Venus and Cupid. *Oval 9⅛″ × 6⅛″ (23.1 × 15.5 cm). Mark:* WEDGWOOD. *c.1875–80. This version of the subject is not identifiable among eighteenth-century models, but it appears on stoneware wine coolers from about 1830. It is, perhaps, the work of William Theed.* Author's collection

386. Ovoid bright blue jasper-dip vase ornamented with ferns, flowers and butterflies. Height 10″ (25.5 cm). Mark: WEDGWOOD D impressed; 141 incised. c.1876–86. The modelling of these reliefs (see also Plates C64 and C65) suggests the work of a modeller both newly employed to work on jasper and skilled in the technique of building ornament directly on to the surface of a vase. Charles Toft's experience of pâte-sur-pâte modelling, about which Godfrey Wedgwood made a point of asking in his letter of 19 December 1876 (Godfrey Wedgwood Private Letter Book 1872–81), would have qualified him especially well to execute such work. Sotheby's, London

387. Pair of lilac jasper dip vases ornamented in a style similar to that illustrated in Plate C65 and probably by the same modeller. Height 7¾″ (19.7 cm). Mark: WEDGWOOD S. c.1876–86. Christie's, London

Charles Toft,[*] a fine modeller employed by Minton's, particularly in the manufacture of Henri Deux inlaid ware, was engaged by Godfrey Wedgwood in November 1876 at a salary of £350 a year rising to £370 over five years. 'We think', Godfrey told him, 'there is an opening for fresh figure (basrelief) models and shapes of vases in our jasper ware.'[51] Toft was instructed to visit the current exhibition of 'Old Wedgwood' at Phillips's to 'observe the effect of the reliefs . . . how the figures are disposed and lightness obtained without sacrifice of vigour'. One of his first assignments was a portrait medallion of William Ewart Gladstone (Plate 388) for which he was to seek the advice of William Theed the younger, whose father had worked for Wedgwood at the turn of the century and modelled the portrait medallion of Thomas Byerley (see Plate 18). Toft was employed as principal modeller from 1876 to 1888 and, in addition to his work in pâte-sur-pâte and inlaid wares, completed a number of models for jasper, including the 'Seven Ages of Man' after designs painted on a vase by Walter Crane, 'Four Ages – Youth, Adolescence, Autumn and Winter', and the large 'Peace and War' vase made for the 1878 Exhibition (Plate 390).[52] Four of these vases were fired in November 1880.[53]

In 1880 some new experiments were begun for the manufacture of large busts in jasper. On 5 October a trial was made: 'Best white jasper Shakespeare bust pressed (would not cast). Fired easy, it is nearly fired up & freer of cracks than I expected but it opens a little at the seams & this seems rather permanent. This trial is preparatory for FR's [Frederick Rathbone's] bust by Boehm.' The explanation of 'FR's bust by Boehm' appears in an undated note in the same manuscript:

[*]Charles Toft (1832–1909) was the father of the well-known sculptor and modeller Albert Toft, and the painter Joseph Alfonso Toft, both of whom were employed by Wedgwood while their father was at Etruria.

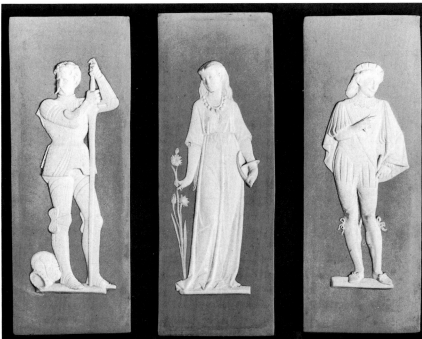

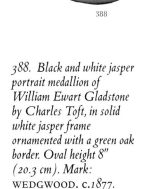

388. *Black and white jasper portrait medallion of William Ewart Gladstone by Charles Toft, in solid white jasper frame ornamented with a green oak border. Oval height 8"* (20.3 cm). *Mark:* WEDGWOOD. c.1877. Christie's, New York

389. *Three solid blue and white jasper plaques ornamented with figures modelled by Charles Toft,* c.1878. *Each* 9 1/2" × 3 5/8" (24.2 × 9.3 cm). *Mark:* WEDGWOOD. Manchester City Art Gallery

390. *Impressive solid black and white jasper vase, 'War and Peace', designed and modelled by Charles Toft for the 1878 Exhibition. Height* 24 1/2" (62.2 cm). *Mark:* WEDGWOOD. *Solid black had been reintroduced in 1874–5. A large oval plaque of 'War' was sold as Lot 275 of the Oster Collection at Sotheby's, London,* 30 *November* 1971. Manchester Museum

391. *Portrait medallion of Chaucer modelled by Charles Toft,* c.1880. *Replica in solid pale-blue and white jasper,* c.1950. Wedgwood Museum

Boehm's Bust of Gladstone is to be made of the greeny gray Artists Jasper as it will not cast the busts must be pressed & the seams carefully fettled in the green state. Bust must be fired once or twice as we find [by experiment] most successfully. Bust of jasper 4⅜ high shrinks in 2 fires to 3⅞ therefore a 12[-inch] Bust when fired, must be modelled 13⅝ as FR has noted. The Bust is to be 12 in without pedestal & FR means to sell them in celadon jasper BW [Best White] Jasper & B[asaltes] Black clay.[54]

From this it appears that Frederick Rathbone had commissioned a bust of Gladstone from the celebrated portrait sculptor Joseph Edgar Boehm* for reproduction in Wedgwood's jasper and black basaltes. The choice of the pale green Celadon jasper created especially for this piece was evidently Boehm's. The recipe for the new colour is given in a note dated 1 December 1880 headed 'Celadon Jasper for Busts':

5 pints Best white Jasper 28 oz to pint
4 oz Extra Pale Blue Jasper 28½ . . . .
1 pint Green Jasper slip 29 . . . .

The sculptor's preference is made clear by the accompanying note: 'this is what Boehm likes.'[55] This bust (Plate 392) has been described as of tinted Parian,[56] but no evidence has been found to show that it was produced in that body. An example in black basaltes is in the Buten Museum.[57]

*Sir Joseph Edgar Boehm (1834–90), lecturer on sculpture at the Royal Academy and Sculptor in Ordinary to Queen Victoria; appointed baronet in 1889.

392. 'Celadon' jasper bust of William Ewart Gladstone by Sir Joseph Edgar Boehm, commissioned by Frederick Rathbone in 1879. Height 11¼" (28.6 cm). Mark: see Plate 392A. c.1880. British Museum

392

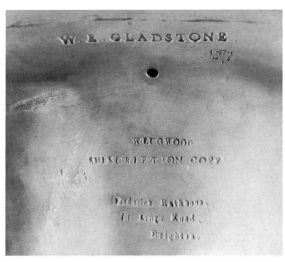

392A

392A. Impressed marks on the back of the bust of Gladstone illustrated in Plate 392: W. E. GLADSTONE. WEDGWOOD SUBSCRIPTION COPY. Frederick Rathbone, 71 King's Road, Brighton. Inscribed 'J. E. BOEHM fecit'. 1879. In comparison with black basaltes busts of the eighteenth century, this bust is notable for the single firing hole in the back.

Another new green jasper was introduced in 1882. On 5 October Clement Wedgwood sent his cousin George Darwin a sample of 'our peach green colour'. 'This', he wrote, 'is the colour that Mr Ricardo has been using so largely lately in decorating Lord Dysart's house at Buckminster & suits present style of furniture very well.'[58] The architect Halsey Ricardo was a leading proponent of the Arts and Crafts Movement, and later, under W.R. Lethaby, one of the distinguished group of teachers at the Central School of Art.

Buckminster Park, in Leicestershire, had been built by Samuel Saxon[*] for Sir George Manners, and the style of the interior, with its fine proportions and detail, showed a reticent elegance which was no doubt echoed in the chimneypieces. These were all removed in the early 1880s and replaced by Ricardo's designs, in which, to judge by a surviving photograph (Plate 395), both proportions and elegance were sacrificed to an imposing and overweight display of 'classical' columns and cornices. The house was demolished shortly after the 1939–45 war and its decorations are believed to have been dispersed in the United States.[59] Ricardo's chimneypieces[†] for Buckminster were all inset with Wedgwood medallions and tablets, and most of the overmantels were furnished with a clock face, all in the new 'Peach' or 'Dysart' green jasper.

[*]Samuel Saxon (1757–?) had trained at the Royal Academy and in the offices of Sir William Chambers. The gardens at Buckminster were laid out by Humphry Repton, with whom Saxon worked on Courteenhall, Northamptonshire, in 1791–3.
[†]Ricardo designed at least twelve chimneypieces for bedrooms in the house, as well as a complete scheme of redecoration for the dining room.

393. *Pair of pale-blue jasper dip vases, 1316 shape, with solid pale-green jasper handles and ornaments of Apollo and the Muses with garlands of flowers and stylised flower and foliage borders. Height 11½" (29.2 cm). Mark:* WEDGWOOD. *c.1880. The pale-green jasper body used for the handles and ornament of this vase appears to be the 'Celadon' jasper created for Boehm's bust of Gladstone (Plate 392).*
Wedgwood Museum

393

394. *Solid pale-blue and white jasper Trophy plates, heavily ornamented with borders of stylised flowers, ribbons and wreaths of fruit enclosing cameo subjects, the centres with 'Venus Bound' and 'Venus and Cupid', mounted in carved and gilt wood frames. Height 16½" (42.0 cm); plates diameter 8¾" (22.2 cm). Mark:* WEDGWOOD. *c.1880. Trophy plates, which continue to be produced in the 1980s, are often ornamented with as many as 170 separate reliefs. Apart from displaying the skill of the ornamenter, there seems to be little to recommend them.*

Christie's, New York

394

395. *Chimneypiece designed by Halsey Ricardo for Buckminster Park, inset with five large plaques, including a clock face, and smaller tablets and medallions in the new 'peach green colour' jasper, formally named 'Dysart' green after the owner of the house.*

Photograph: Courtesy Miss Alison Kelly

395

The composition of the peach colour is recorded in an undated recipe book of about 1882 as four parts of yellow jasper dip to three of sage green mixed in equal weights. Another rare colour noted at the same time is a 'Blue Grey Dip' made by mixing pale-blue and sage-green dip.[60] The turquoise dip was produced a few years earlier, and in 1883 a 'Mustard coloured dip, specially made' was tried as a ground for plaques. Most of them were either 'a brown shade' or had a 'speckled black appearance', and the experiments were abandoned. Clement noted that 'All large plaques have to be left in the oven for a day after the rest is taken out so that they cool gently & not dunt or the white figures crack by being brought suddenly into the cold air.'[61]

Ricardo's work was evidently thought to be a success, and his designs had certainly made the maximum use of jasper plaques. This gave Clement the idea that he might commission some sketches of jasper plaques 'chiefly of non-classic origin' from Ricardo, 'worked into chimneypieces with strips and tiles' for travellers to use as samples from which to take orders.[62] Although the sketches were produced and approved, and there was even a proposal that they might be reproduced in colour by chromolithography, nothing seems to have come of any plan to promote the sale of jasper for chimneypieces.

The nineteenth century saw some remarkable changes in Wedgwood's jasper. At the beginning of the century there had been no difficulty in making almost anything that might be required. Within thirty years the technique had been lost and production of all jasper, unless as a slip on stoneware, had been abandoned. It was about fifteen years before jasper returned and another fifteen before the solid colours could be made with any certainty. Not until the 1870s could the whole range of eighteenth-century models, including large vases and plaques, be reproduced, and the surface quality of it was never again what it had been before 1810.

The principal developments in the twentieth century have been in colour and, after the Second World War, in the 'reinvention' of the body. Crimson and a dark olive green were introduced as dips in 1910. Both 'bled' so badly into the white reliefs that their period of production was short. An attempt was made to reintroduce the crimson between 1925 and 1935 and, as a dip on stoneware ('Basrelief Ware'), it was less liable to bleeding, but the fault was still too severe to allow economic production. An exhibition at the Mortimer Museum, Hull, in July 1932 lists examples of pale-blue, sage-green, crimson and yellow 'Wedgwood Ware' (dip on stoneware) and pale-blue, dark-blue, sage-green and yellow (three-colour) and black jasper dip. A yellow–buff jasper with black ornaments was made in small quantities from 1929 to 1932.

The production of jasper and of the stone body for bas-relief ware was halted in 1941, and the jasper body only was not made again until 1948. Its reintroduction owed much to Norman Wilson, who developed a composition that was suitable for the firing methods at the new Barlaston factory. He succeeded in creating a body that could be manufactured reliably and economically in solid colours, but was adaptable to the production of jasper dip when the special effects obtainable by the use of engine-turning, such as two-colour fluting and dicing, were required. Pale-blue, green and black jasper were made for the first few years, and lilac was added from 1960 to 1962. A new jasper colour, solid orange—red terracotta similar in colour to rosso antico, was made between 1957 and 1959 with either black or white reliefs. Trials of solid grey and solid white were made in 1960, but neither was put into regular production. A 'Royal blue' jasper colour was created to commemorate the coronation of Queen Elizabeth II in 1953.

Since the war, the range of pieces made has been reduced, and the number of different shapes of vases has been restricted. Modern prices, and modern wages, have brought the smaller pieces to a wider public than ever before, and the consequence has been that the character of jasper has been changed from that of an exclusive ornamental ware into a popular giftware. Nevertheless, because of the skill required in the application of bas-reliefs, the production of jasper has, unlike most ceramic giftwares, never been uncontrolled, and the separation of more highly finished 'prestige' pieces has helped to maintain the reputation for quality of craftsmanship.

In 1960–1 an attempt was made to introduce a new style of jasper by inviting Lucie Rie to make prototypes of teaware pieces. A small quantity of blue and white jasper was supplied to her, some tea cups and coffee cups were made in her studio, and she subsequently visited the Barlaston factory. Sadly for all concerned, her technique of inlaying decorative lines of jasper was not considered suitable for modern methods of controlled quality and quantity production and the project was scrapped.[63]

396. White stoneware and pale-blue jasper dip water purifier, labelled 'SPENCER'S PATENT MAGNETIC PUREFYING FILTER'. Height 15″ (38.1 cm). Mark: WEDGWOOD. c.1887. Buten Museum

397. Green jasper dip clock case ornamented with the motto 'TEMPUS FUGIT' and relief figures of 'Father Time' and children from the 'Domestic Employment' series. Height 8″ (20.3 cm). Mark: WEDGWOOD. c.1885. Wedgwood Museum

396

397

398. Pair of small vases in
pale-blue jasper dip,
ornamented with figures of
the Muses. Height 5"
(12.0 cm). Mark:
WEDGWOOD CDT S
impressed; 1053 inscribed;
1529 printed in black. 1891.
Wedgwood Museum

398

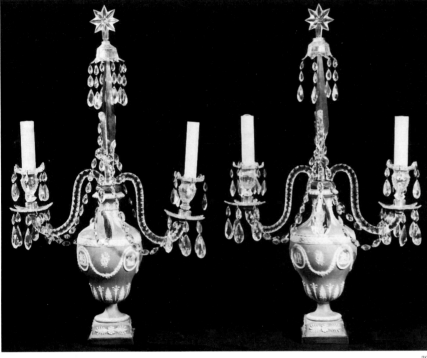

399. Pair of cut-glass
candelabra on solid green
and white jasper vase bases.
Height 26½" (67.3 cm).
Mark: WEDGWOOD
ETRURIA ENGLAND.
c.1895.
Christie's, London

399

400. Three pieces of jasper
ornamented by Harry
Barnard: (left) twice-
dipped trial spill vase —
dark-blue dip over crimson
on white — with sgraffito
and trailed slip ornament
and inscription, 'H B trial
5.2.98', height 2½"
(6.3 cm); (centre) deep-
blue dip rectangular box
ornamented with flowers
and leaves in modelled slip,
2½" × 7" (6.3 ×
17.8 cm); (right) pale-blue
dip mug ornamented with
flowers and leaves in
modelled slip, height 6"
(15.2 cm). Marks:
WEDGWOOD ENGLAND
and incised script signature.
Spill vase 1898; box and
mug 1898–1902.
Buten Museum

400

401. *Deep-blue jasper dip vase with sgraffito and modelled slip decoration by Harry Barnard. Height 11 ¾" (29.8 cm). Mark:* WEDGWOOD ENGLAND *and incised script signature. 1898–1902.*
Wedgwood Museum

402. *Blue jasper dip circular plaque ornamented with a profile portrait of King Christian IX of Denmark and Norway within a hexagonal frame of laurel and oak surmounted by the royal crown and the inscription '*MED GUD FOR AERE OG RET 1818 8 APRIL 1898*'. Diameter 7 ⅛" (18.0 cm). Mark:* WEDGWOOD ENGLAND *impressed; printed inscription '*WEDGWOOD EXPRESSLY MADE BY HAND FOR GOLDSCHMIDT MAGAZIN COPENHAGEN DENMARK*'. The quotation for this piece is recorded in the O[rnamental] W[are] Net Price Book (uncatalogued) for 1897–8. A charge of £10 was made for modelling.*
Mr and Mrs David Zeitlin Collection

403A–B. *Pair of solid pale-blue and white jasper dip circular plaques,* Apotheosis of Homer *and* Apotheosis of Virgil *by John Flaxman junior (cf. Plates 129 and 130) presented to Henry Brownsword on his completion of fifty-four years' service at Etruria, 1903. Diameter 12 ½" (32.0 cm). Mark: none visible. (Cf. Plate 404.)*
Wedgwood Museum

401

402

403A   403B

404

405

404. *Meissen green dip biscuit porcelain circular plaque,* Apotheosis of Homer *after the model by Flaxman. Diameter 12¾" (32.4 cm). Mark: Meissen crossed swords painted in blue. c.1810. This plaque was presented to the British Museum with the Franks Collection in 1887.*
British Museum

405. *Solid pale-blue and white jasper portrait medal of John Paul Jones. Diameter 2" (5.8 cm). Mark:* WEDGWOOD. *1906. Cast from a medal by Augustin Dupré, struck in 1779, and produced to the order of Frederick Rathbone in 1906 ('OW' Net Price Book).*
Dwight and Lucille Beeson Collection, Birmingham Museum, Alabama

406

406. *Pair of silver menuholders mounted with small medallions of Cybele and 'Poor Maria'. Mark:* WEDGWOOD X. *The silver holders bear the Chester hallmark for 1907–8.*
Kadison Collection

407

407. *Pair of solid black and white jasper portrait medallions of Edward VII and Queen Alexandra above inscribed and dated ribbon scrolls within olive and flower-head garlands. Oval height 8½" (21.5 cm). Mark:* WEDGWOOD. *1902. The modeller of these portraits, simply recorded as 'Watkin', has not been identified.*
Christie's, New York

408. *White stoneware mug, dipped in olive-green jasper and sparsely ornamented with 'Sacrifice' figures. The interior is glazed over a white jasper slip. Height 5⅜" (13.6 cm). Mark:* WEDGWOOD ENGLAND S. *c.1910.* Author's collection

409. *Solid green and white jasper liqueur bottle with stopper made for Humphrey Taylor & Co. Height 6¾" (17.1 cm). Mark:* WEDGWOOD *impressed and printed circular backstamp. c.1913.* Wedgwood Museum

408

409

410. *Solid pale-blue and white jasper rectangular plaque,* Endymion Sleeping on the Rock Latmos *by Camillo Pacetti (Appendix J:II.53). 13⅜" × 10" (34.0 × 25.4 cm). Mark:* ENDYMION on the ROCK LATMOS BB 46 1919. *A fine example of Bert Bentley's work and executed in a grey–blue jasper which is difficult to distinguish from the eighteenth-century jasper body. (Cf. Plate 171.)* Mr and Mrs David Zeitlin Collection

410

411A

411B

411C

411D

411A–D. Set of four rectangular tablets, 'Four Seasons', attributed to Bert Bentley, c.1921. Each 4" × 10" (10.2 × 25.4 cm). Mark: WEDGWOOD O. *The terms with trophies, which begin and end the groups of 'Spring' and 'Winter' respectively, indicate that this set was designed to be mounted as a single frieze. It is recorded in Bert Bentley's Work Book (uncatalogued), c.1921 with replicas of models by Toft, but the style and humour of the modelling suggest original work by Bentley.*
Wedgwood Museum

412. Three-colour jasper octagonal advertising cameo in yellow and black dip, ornamented with a caduceus and clasped hands of friendship between two cornucopiae within a moulded inscription, *JOSIAH WEDGWOOD & SONS ETRURIA ENGLAND. 1⅝" × 1⅝" (4.2 × 4.2 cm). Mark:* WEDGWOOD. c.1900. Christie's, London

413. *Pair of lustres in the eighteenth-century style with cut-glass and brass fittings on yellow dip and black jasper drums. No mark visible. Wedgwood, 1929–32.* Sotheby's, London

414. *Three yellow-buff jasper dip vases ornamented in black. Height 7" and 10¼" (17.8 and 26.1 cm). Marks:* WEDGWOOD ENGLAND. *1929–32. (Cf. Plate C67.)* Christie's, New York

415. *Bas-relief ware (blue jasper dip on stoneware) tea cup and saucer, ornamented with a specially designed relief of birds on a branch and an olive border commissioned by Caperns of Bristol. The interior of the tea cup is glazed. Tea cup height 2½" (6.3 cm); saucer diameter 5⅝" (14.3 cm). Mark:* WEDGWOOD *(sans-serif)* CAPERNS LIMITED BRISTOL MADE IN ENGLAND 3. c.1930–4. Wedgwood Museum

416. *Blue dip bas-relief ware coffeepot, 129 shape, ornamented with figures of Diana and Peace. Height 8" (20.3 cm). Mark:* WEDGWOOD *(sans-serif)* MADE IN ENGLAND. c.1935. Wedgwood Museum

412

413

414

415

416

417. Japanese solid blue and white stoneware cigarette box and ashtray (showing base) ornamented in imitation of Wedgwood's jasper. The coarseness of the shape, body and ornaments illustrates the difficulties inherent in imitation by methods of unskilled mass-production. Mark: 'MADE IN OCCUPIED JAPAN' printed in black. c.1950. Wedgwood Museum

417

418. Modern solid pale-blue and white jasper teapot, 146 shape. The body, created by Norman Wilson to be suitable for quantity production by modern methods of continuous firing, is more granular than earlier jasper compositions and closer in quality to the stoneware on which jasper was used as a dip. This change in texture is especially evident in the ornaments, although they are still applied by hand as they have been since the invention of jasper. Photograph: Wedgwood

418

419. Solid blue and green dip engine-turned jasper teaware made in 1955, showing the attractive quality of production still attainable with modern materials and compositions and by modern, but more costly, methods of manufacture. Mark: WEDGWOOD (sans-serif) MADE IN ENGLAND 3W. 1955. Wedgwood Museum

419

PLATES FROM THE '1878' ILLUSTRATED CATALOGUE OF ORNAMENTAL SHAPES

420. Plate 20. Blue and White Garden Pots (bas-relief): Bell; No. 317; No. 1060, Bordered; No. 1061, Bordered; Louis XV, Jardiniere; No. 1058 Wine Cooler. Jugs: Upright; Doric; Tankard.

420

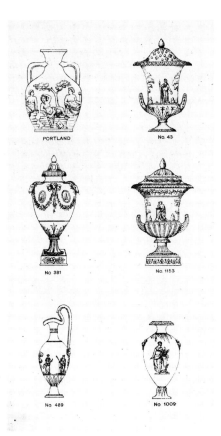

421. Plate 21. Blue and White Vases: Portland; No. 43; No. 381 (cf. Plate 382); No. 1153; No. 489; No. 1009.

422. Plate 22. Blue and White Vases (bas-relief): No. 495; No. 1110; No. 393; No. 1015; No. 384; No. 352; No. 1202; No. 130; No. 350; No. 496; No. 1010.

421

422

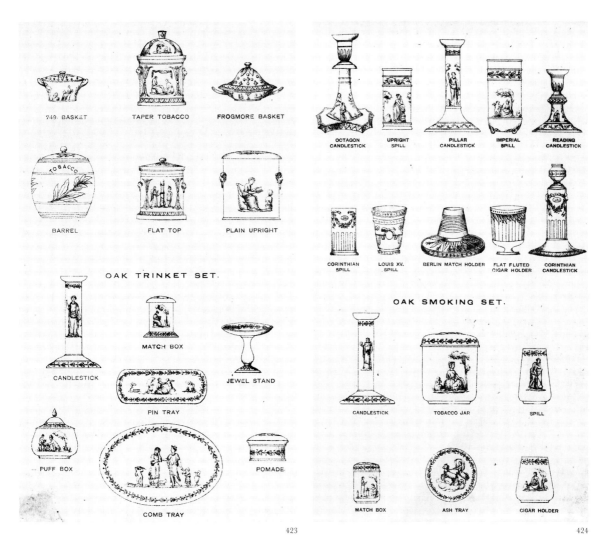

423. **Plate 23.** Tobacco Jars and Baskets: 749 Basket; Taper Tobacco; Frogmore Basket; Barrel; Flat Top; Plain Upright. Oak Trinket Set; Candlestick; Match Box; Jewel Stand; Pin Tray; Puff Box; Comb Tray; Pomade.

424. **Plate 24.** Blue and White: Octogon [sic] candlestick; Upright Spill; Pillar Candlestick; Imperial Spill; Reading Candlestick; Corinthian Spill; Louis XV Spill; Berlin Match Holder; Flat Fluted Cigar Holder; Corinthian Candlestick. Oak Smoking Set: Candlestick; Tobacco Jar; Spill; Match Box; Ash Tray; Cigar Holder.

425. *White stoneware jug with granulated ground, the body ornamented on both sides with different moulded scenes of two men, one in military uniform, drinking at a table, between borders of foliage, decorated in underglaze colours of blue, green, brown and orange. Height 6⅛" (15.7 cm). Mark: see Plate 425A. c.1800. The Etruria Oven Book for June 1800 (53–30018, Volume II) contains an entry for white stoneware jugs 'with a group of Dutch figures on the front' accompanied by a marginal sketch of a jug with a similar, but not identical, handle. Neither the figures nor the demi-floret border appear on any other Wedgwood ware, and the leafage borders do not accord with Wedgwood's. Almost identical marked jugs are in the Yorkshire Museum and the Victoria & Albert Museum, and an unmarked, undecorated, translucent version is in the author's possession. It is probable that this model, which bears a striking similarity to ware produced at Castleford and to work associated with the Pratt family, was made by several factories, those pieces bearing the impressed* WEDGWOOD *mark coming from Ralph Wedgwood's factory at Ferrybridge. (For a more detailed discussion of these jugs see John and Griselda Lewis,* Pratt Ware, *1984.)*
Photograph: Courtesy John and Griselda Lewis

425A. *Impressed mark on the jug illustrated in Plate 425. The irregular spacing of the letters reveals this as certainly not the mark of the Etruria factory.*

425

425A

5. WHITE STONEWARE

The early production of Wedgwood's white stoneware body is not well recorded. It appears that it was closely related to the development of the white terracotta stoneware body, which it superseded, the principal difference being that, in its final form and potted thinly, the stoneware body was slightly translucent. It was no doubt this quality that suggested the change of its name to 'white porcelain'.

This name was already in use by 1810, when orders were being taken for 'White bisque porcelain' jugs in the basketwork shape with blue edges.[64] The range of pieces made at that stage appears to have been small: principally jugs in various shapes and several sizes, and garden-pots of the type previously made in terracotta. In 1817 trials were made with this so-called porcelain body to imitate jasper dip. Josiah II noted: 'Our Stone body has lately been used washed over with jasper slip & with jasper reliefs which seem to agree very well.'[65]

In 1819 the recipe for the stone body was:
300 lb Cornwall Stone
140 lb   ,,   Clay
150 lb Blue ball clay
 50 lb Flint

This was whitened by the use of '4½ pints of stain, wet 22 ozs to the pint (11½ oz when dried)', and a further note shows that this was a blue–white stain to counteract the yellowish cast of the clay.[66] Two years later the recipe was altered for a 'new' stone body by a reduction of ten per cent in the quantity of Cornwall stone and the substitution of wet flint for dry. By the end of 1821 the blue ornaments for all white stone were being made of a composition that was about ninety-five per cent jasper shavings.[67]

The most popular shape for jugs was the 'Hunt' jug, ornamented with foxhunting scenes of which almost identical versions were made also by Davenport, Spode and Turner, among others, and on bone china at New Hall.[68] Wedgwood's 'Hunt' jugs with brown slip necks were still being made in five sizes in the 1850s.[69]

By 1818 the range had been extended to include the 'beehive' shape, banded ornaments of blue or white grape and bas-reliefs of bacchanalian boys; and teapots, sugar boxes, cream jugs, honey-pots, toy tea sets, wine coolers and oval violet baskets with covers had been added to the list of pieces made. Smear glaze was in use by 1815, and the 'white porcelain' was produced either 'bisque' or smeared from about that date. Reliefs were either plain white, blue or green. In May 1818 enamelled border decoration in green and purple was tried, but it was evidently unsuccessful and does not appear in later orders (see Plate 350).[70]

New ornaments were introduced in the 1820s, including 'Emblems' in blue and green in 1820–1, probably in celebration of the coronation of George IV;* arabesque with 'dog top'; 'fern', 'cameo subjects', 'wreathed laurel with flower between', 'border sunflower', 'embossed Chinese flowers', 'cymbals', and group of flowers;[71] and 'blue rose, thistle and shamrock' appeared in 1830. Gothic jugs were ordered by Bateman between 1828 and 1832,[72] and 'artichoke' teapots were available as late as 1845.

The most important function of the white porcelain body was as a replacement for jasper during the years when the jasper body could not be made to stand up in the fire. As well as being ornamented in colour, it could be dipped in jasper or stained to colours associated with jasper.† Its versality is illustrated by its use for such diverse objects as Flaxman's chessmen (Plate C70), figures of Psyche and Ariadne, Triton candlesticks, Portland vases and 'tubes' in five sizes, 10 to 18 inches long with ¾-inch to 1-inch bore for pharmaceutical use.[73] There is little evidence that any difficulty was ever experienced in its manufacture, and it was still in production with a jasper dip and reliefs in 1941, when it and jasper were discontinued for the duration of the war.[74] Unlike jasper, the white porcelain body was not reintroduced for post-war production, though some trials were made with plain white jasper.

---

*Ware to commemorate this event was made also in black basaltes.
†The colours were generally brighter.

426. White biscuit 'porcelain' (stoneware). (Left) mug with moulded bamboo handle and foot, the body ornamented with 'Borghese' figures. Height 5" (14.7 cm). Mark: WEDGWOOD. (Centre) handled basket with engine-turned decoration and basketwork moulding. Height 5" (14.7 cm). Mark: WEDGWOOD ٬٬. (Right) engine-turned and basketwork-moulded flower-pot and stand decorated with blue enamel lines. Height (and stand diameter) 5" (14.7 cm). Mark: WEDGWOOD ◡◡. c.1811. 'White bisque basket work blue edge' appears in the London Order Book from July 1811. Wedgwood Museum

426

428. White 'porcelain' jug with brown slip neck, ornamented with Flaxman's Blind Man's Buff (cf. Plate 133) on a granulated ground. Height 5½" (14.0 cm). Mark: WEDGWOOD D ◡. c.1820. Jugs with blue or brown slip necks ornamented with figures of boys or hunting subjects were made in white biscuit or smear-glazed porcelain from about 1818 to 1855. Wedgwood Museum

427 One of a pair of white biscuit stoneware wine coolers ornamented with acanthus-leaf paterae. Height 10" (25.4 cm). Mark: WEDGWOOD. c.1810–20. Author's collection

427

429. Smear-glazed 'porcelain' Club jug with bright blue slip neck, ornamented with a band of fruiting vine and groups of boys by Lady Diana Beauclerk (cf. Plates 179 and 180). Height 6½" (16.5 cm). Mark: WEDGWOOD. c.1820. Wedgwood Museum

428

429

430

431

432

433

430. *Smear-glazed white 'porcelain' teapot in the Gothic style. Mark:* WEDGWOOD. *c.1830. 'White porcelain Gothic' shapes appear regularly in the London and travellers' orders from 1828.*
Dr and Mrs Jerome Mones Collection

431. *Pair of white 'porcelain' vases, 384 shape with pierced grids, ornamented in green with borders of paterae, meander and foliage, and a candlestick–bough-pot with arched handles terminating in rams' heads, ornamented in green with a wide arabesque border. All with glazed interiors. Height 4½" and 6½" (10.5 and 16.5 cm). Marks: (pair)* WEDGWOOD ⌣⌣; *(bough-pot)* WEDGWOOD RK ⌒⌒. *c.1820.*
Dwight and Lucille Beeson Collection, Birmingham Museum, Alabama

432. *(Left) white biscuit 'porcelain' soap cup with lid, ornamented with bands of blue rose, daisy and vine relief. Height 5" (12.2 cm). Mark:* WEDGWOOD ◯. *(Right) small white biscuit porcelain vase with spiral olive relief. Height 4" (10.3 cm). Mark:* WEDGWOOD ✓. *c.1820–30.*
Wedgwood Museum

433. *Davenport smear-glazed white stoneware teapot ornamented in blue with a band of interlaced circles and flowers. Height 4" (10.5 cm). Mark: anchor trademark and $\frac{81}{203}$ ○ S impressed.*
Norwich Castle Museum

434. *Documentary smear-glazed white porcelain 'scent box' with pierced lid and thumb-scoop handle, ornamented in blue with quatrefoils and floral borders. 3⅝" × 4¾" × 1⅛" (9.2 × 12.0 × 4.8 cm). Mark:* WEDGWOOD *impressed; printed inscription (see Plate 434A). The order for a set of four of these objects was taken by Bateman direct from the Duke of Portland on 25 May 1824 (18–16859):* 'blue cymbals [sic] or group of flowers – 4 long square scent boxes, pierced cover the holes to be a little larger than the pattern and a small notch as thumb part cut in the cover to take it up by'.
Buten Museum

434A. *Impressed and printed marks on the Portland scent box.*

435. *Smear-glazed white stoneware:* (left to right) *pair of small vases on ribbed feet, ornamented in bright blue with 'leaf and flower between'; height 4¾" (12.0 cm). Mark:* WEDGWOOD G ～～; *combined bough-pot and pastille-burner ornamented with fruiting vine in brown, showing the solid inner plate 'for the pastilles to lie on', height 7" (17.8 cm), diameter 13" (33.0 cm). Mark:* WEDGWOOD; *small vase, 384 shape, ornamented in bright blue with figures between borders of flowers and vine, height 4" (10.2 cm). Mark:* WEDGWOOD KK ～～; *Club vine jug, the body moulded with an all-over relief of fruiting vine, height 5" (12.7 cm). Mark:* WEDGWOOD. All c.1820–40.
Author's collection
286

434

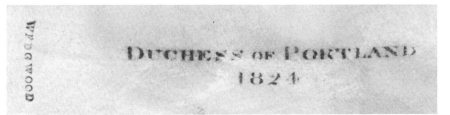

DUCHESS OF PORTLAND
1824

WEDGWOOD

434A

435

436

436. Smear-glazed white
'porcelain' crocus basket
with overhead bow handle
and convex pierced grid, the
pierced body dipped and
diced in bright blue. Height
9½" (24.1 cm). Mark:
WEDGWOOD ∼∼.
c.1830. Blue and white
diced 'Bowhandle crocus
pots and stands' appear in
the 'OW' Order Book as
late as 22 November 1850.
Buten Museum

437. White stoneware
cream jug, 146 shape,
ornamented with Priam
begging the body of
Hector, the exterior
covered with 'silver-plating'.
William Burton, chemist at
Etruria 1887–92, outlined
the method of this decoration
in an undated memorandum,
c.1890 (48–29422): 'A
solution of platinum in aqua
regia was slowly poured
with careful stirring, in
about three times its bulk of
an oily menstruum, such as
balsam of sulphur or spirits
of tar. This forms an oily
pigment which can be
applied to a piece of glazed
pottery. . . . When the oily
coating has become tacky by
drying, a film of finely
divided platinum, obtained
by charring ammonium–
platina–chloride, is dusted
upon it, and when the ware
is fired again at a low heat,
say 700–800°C., a
brilliant metallic deposit of
platinum is found fixed to
the glaze.'
Buten Museum

437

7. PORTLAND VASES

On 28 May 1798 Richard Lovell Edgeworth wrote on behalf of Dr Thomas Beddoes to ask the value of the Portland vase which had been given to him. Tom Byerley noted at the foot of the letter: 'Those . . . free from blemish all sell for 30 guineas. We have a few not quite so perfect but with no fault that subtracts from the general merit of the work nor with any disgusting to the eye and they are 25 guineas.[75] Sixteen years later there were still ten copies of the Portland vase in stock in London.[*]

According to a note from the Duke of Portland's steward, the original Barberini or Portland vase was lent to Wedgwood for a second time in October 1800.[76] The motive for this loan is not apparent. There is no record of any production of jasper Portland vases at this period, and, since there were at least ten from the first edition still remaining in stock, there could be no good reason for producing more. It is possible that the loan was connected with the presentations of a jasper Portland vase to the French Republic[77] and of a solid blue jasper copy to the British Museum in 1802.[†] John Wedgwood would certainly have wished to present the best available copies, and he may have wished to compare his remaining vases with the original before making his final choices. The production of '4 Wᵗ Bisket barberanum vases' recorded in the Oven Book for 13 and 20 January 1801[78] could scarcely have justified such an application to the Duke.

In November 1822 Bateman ordered 'White bisque E'ware glazed inside 4 Vases shape & size of the *Portland vase*' for a 'good customer',[79] but there is no evidence of any Portland vases being made in jasper until 1836, when William Adams is recorded in the Potters' Book as having made three Portland vases, '1 Green 2 White jasper'.[80] This entry is as surprising for its description of colours as it is for the apparent contradiction of both Jos and Frank Wedgwood's complaints that they could not make large pieces of jasper.[‡] The explanation must be either that these pieces were trials, of which many were carried out during this period in the hope of making jasper that would stand the fire, or that they were made of 'porcelain' with a jasper dip and jasper ornaments.

The same manuscript shows that twenty-six 'Portland vases Green jasper' were made on 26 May 1839. Others in green, lilac or blue made between 26 June 1839 and 6 November 1840 are all described as 'bas-relief', and it seems most probable that all were of jasper-dipped stone. Bateman's orders for 1839 to 1842 contain several for 'Barberini' vases in sizes varying from 4 inches to 9 inches in height, but none is described as jasper and it is clear from later orders that all were of the dipped stone or porcelain body.[81]

[*]Four were noted as 'tolerably perfect'.
[†]Plate C58.
[‡]See above pp. 248 and 249.

438A

438A–B. *Portland vase inherited by the composer Dr Ralph Vaughan Williams, great-grandson of both Josiah Wedgwood II and Dr Robert Waring Darwin. The detailed provenance of this vase is not certain, but its authenticity as an example of the first edition is not doubted. Unmarked. 1790–5. Apart from the quality of the jasper dip, the most evident features of the first-edition vases are undercutting of the figures, delicacy of the shading (particularly noticeable on the wings of Cupid) and the balanced spacing of the reliefs. The reverse of the vase (A) illustrates these attributes especially well, and it provides a useful point of reference in judging later examples.*
Wedgwood Museum

439

438B

439. *Base disc of the Hope copy of the Portland vase (Plates 318 and 318A). The base disc of the first edition is notable for two features in particular: the continuation of the relief to the extreme edge of the disc, cutting off the joint of the elbow; and the space between the index finger and the lip. All later editions, including the Northwood copies, are different in respect to one or both of these details.*
Wedgwood Museum

440. *White jasper vase of approximately the form of the Portland vase with glazed plaited handles terminating in masks, the exterior of the body covered in a stippled dark-green slip. Height 4¾″ (12.0 cm). Mark:* WEDGWOOD ⌣ ⌣. *c.1817. Since no solid jasper vases are recorded between 1817 and 1845, this extraordinary object is likely to have been an unfortunate experiment.*
Wedgwood Museum

440

441. *Black jasper dip on stoneware Portland vase of the type made in 1846. Height 8″ (20.3 cm). Mark:* WEDGWOOD ETRURIA V. *c.1846. An example of the 'Draped' version of the vase, a distressing travesty of the original, which persisted in the smaller sizes throughout the nineteenth century. The form of the vase is noticeably altered, the texture of the body, most often of stoneware with a coarse dip, is poor, and the modelling of the figures is deplorable. On those vases which have not been cast in one piece, the figures have been applied in lumps, without undercutting or shading, apparently from moulds of low quality. There are even more bashful examples on which the Cupid figure, already emasculated in the draped version, has been remodelled with his right leg crossed over his left.*
Sotheby's, London

441

442. White stoneware and dark-blue jasper dip 'Portland' jug, ornamented with draped figures. Height 6¼" (15.9 cm). Mark: WEDGWOOD impressed, ⌒ incised. c.1846. All the criticisms of the 1846 vase (Plate 441) may be applied with even greater justification to the jug. Portland jugs, 'blue with white basreliefs', are listed in the '1843' Price Book on 31 January 1846 and appear to have continued in production throughout the rest of the century. The shape was made also, cast in one piece, in 'self colours'. Wedgwood Museum

442

443. Samuel Alcock & Co. porcelain imitation of the Portland vase, the figures outline-painted in black against a blue enamelled ground. Height 10" (25.5 cm). Mark: S.A. & Co printed. c.1845–50. Christie's, London

444. Portland vase, black dip on stoneware with stoneware reliefs. Height 9½" (24.1 cm). Mark: WEDGWOOD (on foot rim). c.1850. A copy of low quality, without shading or undercutting, and of interest principally as an example of stoneware ornaments. Wedgwood Museum

443

444

The first traveller's order for jasper Portland vases is R.G. Keeling's of 17 February 1845, which includes also jasper vases no. 43 shape with pedestal. By that date, as Keeling's order of 23 October 1844 shows, jasper was again freely available for vases.[82] There seems still to have been some trouble in making black-and-white jasper vases. Frank Wedgwood wrote in March 1845:

> If we could make Portland vases white upon black we might just sell them now. . . . Try to get the Felspar body they are now made of [*sic*] stained black for the ground & lay the figs on in the same body but unstained – we might make the figs then lay them in the moulds now used to make the vases all at once then put a bat in & bat it in upon the figs.

On 12 March he attempted to make vases with jasper, drab stone and white stone with various stains. Experiments were continued between May and 8 October 1845, when a successful jasper trial produced a vase described by Frank as 'nearest in color to my P vase & whitest fig – would do I think'.[83]

It appears that the problem was no longer one of making a jasper body that would withstand the fire, but one of obtaining a suitable black colour for the jasper ground. Frank's memorandum is particularly interesting for its mention of 'moulds now used to make the vases all at once', indicating that stoneware Portland vases had, for some time past, been cast in one piece instead of thrown and turned and ornamented by hand. This is confirmed by a detailed list of 'prices sent to M[r] Phillips May 18 1846', which includes Portland vases in six sizes, from 4 inches to 10 inches in height. Notes show '9 ins not made at all'; '4, 7 & 10 inch Portlands are cast [complete with reliefs] – others laid on'; and the same sizes were made 'with head at bottom, 5, 6 and 8 ins without'. The vases are offered in four colours: 'Blue dip white basreliefs', 'White stone enamel black or matt blue ground', 'Plain white Stone' and 'Mazarine Blue', and the largest size only is available 'draped' or 'no drapery'. This is the first record of the 'draped' version of the Portland vase, on which the male figures that were originally nude were modestly covered so that they should not offend Victorian sensibilities. Prices ranged from five guineas for the draped mazarine blue vase to two shillings and threepence for the 4-inch draped version in white stone. Plain black basaltes vases without moulding or ornament were available in the 8-inch size at five shillings each.[84]

It is notable that this list does not include any vases in black and white, but a 10-inch 'Black & white Basrelief shaded Portland' was ordered by Keeling on 3 May 1845 at a price of thirty-five shillings, so it may be assumed that this colour was available in the dipped stoneware if not in jasper.[85] London orders for November 1847 include black-and-white jasper Portland vases in five sizes, but the largest is 8 inches high and it may be that there was a recurring problem in the production of the largest size in the jasper body.[86]

445

There is evidence of further difficulty with the jasper body in 1849, gaping cracks appearing in the body and haircracks like crazing in the applied figures. There was much trouble also with bleeding of the colours.[87] Almost continuous trials were made until 1860, when solid colour jasper was reintroduced, and Portland vases in the solid body are listed in three sizes, including the 10-inch vase, in April 1860.[88] Four 10-inch white porcelain vases dipped in white jasper and ornamented with white jasper reliefs were produced in November and December 1850.[89]

Not until 1871 were solid black-and-white jasper Portland vases produced with ease and in quantity. In 1876 John Northwood completed the first cased glass copy of the Portland vase, using a blank provided by Philip Pargeter. The work of cameo-cutting had taken him three years. Next year Wedgwood engaged him to finish the reliefs of a new edition of the jasper Portland vase, and Godfrey Wedgwood's copy was sent to London to be tinted, using the first-edition vase on display in the London showrooms as a model.[90] Thirteen copies by Northwood were sold by Philips, all being marked with Northwood's monogram incised above the Wedgwood impressed mark.

445A

446

446. Thomas Lovatt, chief ornamenter at Etruria during the latter part of the nineteenth century, and one of the few ornamenters to sign his work, using his monogram or his initial and name impressed. He ornamented an unknown number of Portland vases about 1880 which he signed on the base rim with his name or initials and a horizontal line or dash.
Photograph:
Wedgwood

447. Solid black and white jasper Portland vase, signed by Thomas Lovatt and mounted on a metal display stand originally fitted with a circular mirror to reflect the image of the base disc. Height 10″ (25.4 cm). Mark: WEDGWOOD T. LOVATT – on base rim. c.1880. The ornaments applied by Lovatt show some shading, but this is due to 'bleeding' of colour into the white and not to shading by tinting. On the base disc, a thin margin has been left around the relief design, but the elbow has not been completed outside the circle as it has been on other copies, including the Bellows edition (Plate 449A).
Christie's, London

447

Pale-blue and white jasper vases were made in the 'non-dunting' composition in 1872[*] but this was not reliable enough to be taken into regular use. Trials were made in 1878 to make a blacker body more closely resembling that of the first-edition vases and in November a special edition was made for Phillips at £25 each, pricing the ornamenting at twenty-nine shillings instead of the ordinary price of three shillings and sixpence.[91] Of the thirteen vases fired, not one was 'fit to send to be polished'.[92] Nevertheless, the 'ordinary' jasper Portland vase – without undercutting or shading of the figures – continued to be fired in fair quantities. Some of these were ornamented by Thomas Lovatt (1850–1915), an ornamenter who signed his work on Portland vases with his initials incised (Plate 448). Laurence Wedgwood was often critical, complaining of 'Or[namen]ts bad in Lovatts work' and vases 'not nicely ornamented. I told Lovatt to slap his clay.'[93] In view of these comments, it is surprising that Lovatt should have been given permission to break with tradition and sign the jasper he had ornamented.

A limited edition was produced in 1914 for Charles Bellows. Although at least some of these vases were finished by Bert Bentley, the quality of the body was low and has an unattractive sheen. There was otherwise apparently some gap in the production of 10-inch black and

[*]See above p. 261.

294

448. *Solid black and white jasper Portland vase, signed with initials by Thomas Lovatt. Height 10" (25.4 cm). Mark:* WEDGWOOD TL. *c.1880. The reverse side of Lovatt's vase shows three features which appear to be common to all editions (except the Northwood) after the first: reduced undercutting to the eye, mouth and ear of Cupid; a loss of the division in the branch by his left hand; and a solid or near-solid knot in the trunk of the tree (cf. Plate 438A).*
Christie's, London

white jasper vases between about 1885 and 1919, when Harry Barnard* was instructed to make a new edition of the vase. By his own account, his experiments took him four years to complete. In 1923–4 he made thirteen vases, of which seven were good, and thereafter produced a steady flow until the bicentenary in 1930. At the end of the year he sent in his report: of 195 vases made since 1923 only thirteen had been bad, and most of the vases had been sold with a 'reflecting mirror stand' to show the base for twenty guineas or with a 'new special stand incorporating the four panels of the original sarcophagus in miniature' at twenty-seven guineas. At the time of writing his 'Memoir' in 1931 there were still fifteen vases left in stock.[94] Although it is clear, both from his own recollections and from the price charged, that the Barnard edition was of a finer quality than any since the Northwood copies of 1876, the reason for the long period of trial and experiment is not clear.

*Craftsman potter, designer and author (see Plate 450).

449. *Bellows edition of the Portland vase produced in 1914, showing the unattractive surface sheen typical of all examples of this type. Height 9¾" (24.8 cm). Mark:* WEDGWOOD *and inscription (see Plate 449A).*
Wedgwood Museum

449

449A. *Base disc of the Bellows edition Portland vase, showing the inscription: 'Executed for Charles Bellows at Etruria in 1913. No. 1'. Three features, in particular, are evident as changes from the original: the introduction of a 'tidy' rim around the relief composition, which is not extended to the circumference of the disc; the completion of the right elbow of the figure by extending it outside the circle of the composition; and the positioning of the index finger so that it touches the chin (cf. Plate 439).*

449A

450. *Harry Barnard (1862–1935) with one of his solid black and white jasper copies of the Portland vase displayed on a 'Sarcophagus' stand, which he designed. c.1930. Bert Bentley's Work Book records the production of two such stands, c.1921.* Wedgwood Museum

450

451. *Solid black and white jasper Portland vase of good quality. Height 10½" (26.5 cm). Mark:* WEDGWOOD *on rim of foot. c.1875. This example shows some undercutting, and the division of the branches beside Cupid's left hand is restored, but the lack of definition of eyes and mouths, in particular, establishes this as a late-nineteenth-century vase. Of those produced since 1817, only Northwood's copies, all of which are signed with his monogram, and the best of Barnard's are obviously of better quality.* City Museum & Art Gallery, Stoke-on-Trent

451

Throughout the whole of the period from about 1840, small Portland vases ranging in height from 4 inches to 8 inches were made in a variety of colours. Most of these were bas-relief ware – stoneware washed and ornamented with jasper – and their production continued until 1941.

Various small editions of the Portland vase have been made since the Second World War. The first, in 1953, was produced in solid green jasper for use in the stage and film production of Wolf Mankowitz's *Make Me an Offer*, the plot of which is constructed around the search for a unique green jasper Portland vase. A limited edition in the new Portland Blue jasper was made in 1973, and another limited edition in solid Royal Blue was made to celebrate the Silver Jubilee of Queen Elizabeth II in 1977.

The surviving evidence of production of Portland vases between 1800 and 1930 is – largely because it is incomplete – both confusing and contradictory, and a form of summary is therefore necessary. It is clearly inaccurate to write of any 'edition' of the Portland vase between 1800 and 1876, and no evidence has been found of the so-called '1839' edition on which much previously published information has been based.[95] The description of this edition coincides with that given in the '1843 Price Book' for vases priced in May 1846,[96] and it is not certain that any of these vases was solid jasper. None is listed as black-and-white jasper. Nor, as the same manuscript shows, is it correct that all the later vases except those of the 1876 and 1923–30 editions lack the base disc.[97] There is, in fact, no evidence of any 10-inch solid black-and-white jasper Portland vases made at Etruria between 1800 and 1845 and even those made at that date are listed as 'Black & white Basrelief' and are therefore most likely to have been made of the dipped stone body.

Apart from trial pieces, the first certainly recorded nineteenth-century Portland vases of this size in solid black-and-white jasper were made in 1870, though other solid colours were available ten years earlier.[98] The period, therefore, during which almost all nineteenth-century black-and-white jasper Portland vases were made was 1870–85, when they were produced in good quantities and with little loss. During this period there were evidently two different qualities in production, the lower quality being without shading or undercutting. The second period in which the vases were made in quantity was between 1923 and 1930, when Barnard's well-finished edition was issued. Most surviving vases of this size and colour belong to one of these two periods. Of the rest of the nineteenth-century black-and-white vases, the majority are of jasper-dipped stoneware ('porcelain').

Appendix A

The Wedgwoods
of Etruria and Barlaston
(Names in capitals are of those connected with the firm)

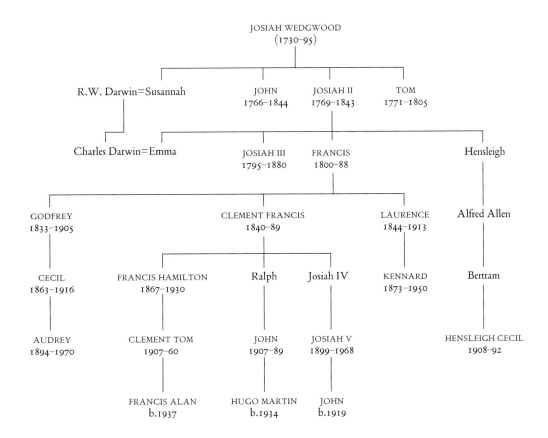

JOSIAH WEDGWOOD
(1730–95)

R.W. Darwin=Susannah   JOHN 1766–1844   JOSIAH II 1769–1843   TOM 1771–1805

Charles Darwin=Emma   JOSIAH III 1795–1880   FRANCIS 1800–88   Hensleigh

GODFREY 1833–1905   CLEMENT FRANCIS 1840–89   LAURENCE 1844–1913   Alfred Allen

CECIL 1863–1916   FRANCIS HAMILTON 1867–1930   Ralph   Josiah IV   KENNARD 1873–1950   Bertram

AUDREY 1894–1970   CLEMENT TOM 1907–60   JOHN 1907–89   JOSIAH V 1899–1968   HENSLEIGH CECIL 1908–92

FRANCIS ALAN b.1937   HUGO MARTIN b.1934   JOHN b.1919

APPENDIX B

Wedgwood Trademarks

During the first half of the eighteenth century trademarks were irregularly used on English porcelain and, apart from a handful of exceptional pieces, no marks appeared on Staffordshire pottery until Josiah Wedgwood began to mark his wares. Two features distinguish his marks from most others of the period: instead of being painted or printed, they were impressed in the unfired clay, which made them far less vulnerable to forgery; and the marks used were the name of the manufacturer, and not of the manufactory.

The earliest wares made by Josiah Wedgwood were unmarked. Certain pseudo-Chinese seal marks incorporating the letter 'W' have been attributed to Wedgwood but no sound evidence has so far been found to sustain these attributions. The first manuscript evidence of the use of trademarks occurs in a letter to Bentley dated 9 July 1771 in which Josiah writes: 'If we alter the large characters it must be by having new moulds. The letters are stamped with printers letters & we want a middle size betwixt those large ones & the least' (LHP). On 15 November 1772 he refers to the matter again: 'we are going upon a plan to mark the whole if practicable' (25–17420).

From both quotations it is plain that the marking of ware at Etruria was no innovation, but neither was it the rule before the end of 1772 that all ware should be marked. This rule was evidently put into effect for, in a letter to Bentley postmarked 6 November 1773, Josiah wrote of a Mr Edmond Radcliffe of Manchester who 'seems in earnest to do a great deal of business with us', but only on condition that the goods should not be trademarked. This customer had told Wedgwood: 'You may put a W upon them if you please but you are not to send your name in any of these transactions.' 'He adds', Josiah wrote, 'that if I send good things & behave with propriety to him (not making myself known to his correspondents I suppose he means) I may rest assured of the same treatment from him on all occasions, and our dealings will be considerable' (E25–18496). Somewhat surprisingly, Josiah was prepared to consider this arrangement, but no record has been found of further transactions so it is possible that Bentley advised against doing business on these terms.

The value that Josiah put on his trademarks is demonstrated by his insistence that even the smallest seals should be impressed (if not with the full 'Wedgwood & Bentley' mark at least with 'W & B') and his reluctance to see them set, as Boulton preferred, 'with a Pebble at the back'. 'This', he told Bentley, 'is bad for us in one respect as it hides *our name*' (E25–18474 21 June 1773, E25–18501 21 November 1773).

Some form of occasional marking seems to have been used by Wedgwood early in the 1760s and it is probable that Wedgwood began to mark his ware with some regularity from about 1766, when his royal appointment was confirmed. These first marks were either incised or impressed with stamps for individual letters. Early impressed marks of this kind were often stamped in a curve. The single stamp for the full trademark (1) appears to have been introduced in 1769, after the start of the Wedgwood & Bentley partnership. In 1877 Isaac Falcke, whose large and distinguished collection of Wedgwood was subsequently presented to the British Museum, wrote to Eliza Meteyard to deplore 'the forgery by [the] Wedgwood present firm of the Wedgwood & Bentley mark' (W/M 527 20 May 1877). Although forgeries of this mark have been noted, no evidence has been found to support the allegation that any such forgeries were perpetrated by the Wedgwood firm at any date, and it is not easy to imagine what benefit could have accrued to the firm from such a deception.

MARKS USED ON JASPER, 1774–1968

1. WEDGWOOD — Impressed in varying sizes, on 'useful' wares from 1769–80, and on all wares from 1780 onwards unless otherwise specified below.

2. Wedgwood & Bentley 356 — Impressed on small cameos and intaglios, 1773–80, with the Catalogue number.

3. W. & B. — Impressed on very small cameos and intaglios, 1773–80, with the Catalogue number. Sometimes the Catalogue number only was used.

4. Wedgwood & Bentley. — Rare oval impressed mark, found only on chocolate and white seal intaglios (usually portraits) made of two layers of jasper with polished edges.

5. Wedgwood & Bentley

WEDGWOOD & BENTLEY

WEDGWOOD & BENTLEY

WEDGWOOD & BENTLEY ETRURIA

— Impressed marks on plaques, tablets, medallions and other ornamental partnership wares, 1769–80. The addition of ETRURIA is uncommon.

6. Wedgwood. — Impressed mark, varying in size, on 'useful' wares c.1779–95 and on all types of ware c.1781–95. Known as 'upper and lower case' mark to distinguish it from 7.

7. wedgwood — Unusual 'all lower case' mark on 'useful' wares c.1780 and more rarely on ornamental wares 1781–5.

8. WEDGWOOD & SONS — Very rare impressed mark c.1790

9. JOSIAH WEDGWOOD Feb. 2nd 1805 — Rare dated mark. See below.

10. — So-called 'commas' or 'moustache' marks: two curved dashes, variously arranged, impressed on dry bodies, 1800–20.

11. FEQ

ENGLAND

MADE IN
ENGLAND

Impressed three-letter marks were used to date earthenware from 1860 to 1906. The first letter indicated the month, the second the potter, and the third the year. As may be seen from the table below, the third letter may indicate two possible dates for the years 1860–80 and 1886–1906. After 1891 the word ENGLAND was added to comply with the McKinley Tariff Act of 1890. The words MADE IN ENGLAND appear from c.1898 but were not in general use until about 1908. The example shown, FEQ, indicates two possible dates: February 1862 or 1888.

Code (first) letters for months:

January	J	
February	F	
March	M	(1860–3)
	R	(1864–1907)
April	A	
May	Y	(1860–3)
	M	(1864–1907)
June	T	
July	V	(1860–3)
	L	(1864–1907)
August	W	
September	S	
October	O	
November	N	
December	D	

Code (third) letters for years:

A	1872	1898	O	1860	1886
B	1873	1899	P	1861	1887
C	1874	1900	Q	1862	1888
D	1875	1901	R	1863	1889
E	1876	1902	S	1864	1890
F	1877	1903	T	1865	1891
G	1878	1904	U	1866	1892
H	1879	1905	V	1867	1893
I	1880	1906	W	1868	1894
J	1881		X	1869	1895
K	1882		Y	1870	1896
L	1883		Z	1871	1897
M	1884				
N	1885				

12. 3BS
    4BD

From 1907 the figure 3 was substituted for the first (month) letter. From 1924 the figure 4 was used. The last letter continued to indicate the year as shown below:

J(3)	1907	V	1919
K	1908	W	1920
L	1909	X	1921
M	1910	Y	1922
N	1911	Z	1923

O	1912	A(4)	1924
P	1913	B	1925
Q	1914	C	1926
R	1915	D	1927
S	1916	E	1928
T	1917	F	1929
U	1918		

From 1930 the actual date was impressed, at first as the last two figures of a mark including the month numbered in sequence and a potter's mark (e.g. 3B35 = March 1935) and later simply as two figures (e.g. 57 = 1957).

Workmen's errors occur in the numbers and letters of marks 11 and 12, and the letters are not always legible.

THE 2 FEBRUARY 1805 MARK

The most puzzling mark to appear on Wedgwood of any period is that which records, in various forms, the date of 2 February 1805. The several versions of this mark, which appears in both upper-case and upper-and-lower-case lettering, include the names 'Wedgwood' and 'Josiah Wedgwood' with the date given as 'Feb 2 1805', 'Feb 2d 1085 [*sic*]', '2 Feby 1805', '2nd Feby 1805' or 'Feby 2nd 1805' (Plates 453–8). The mark is usually found impressed, but stencilled and enamelled examples are known (Plates 454, 456 and 458). The differences

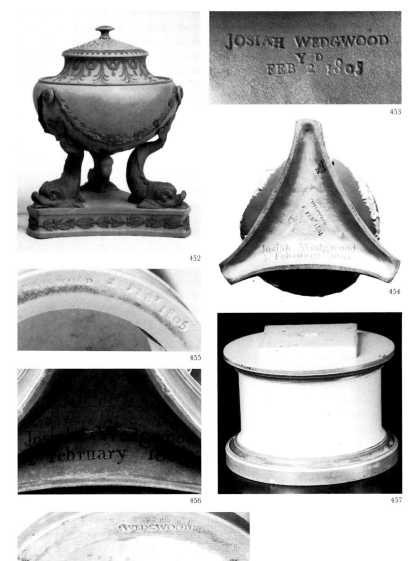

453

452

454

455

456

457

452. Rosso antico 'Dolphin' tripod pastille-burner with black ornaments of the shape most commonly found with the 2 February 1805 mark in its various forms. Height $5\frac{1}{2}''$ (14.0 cm). Kadison Collection

453. Mark from the pastille-burner illustrated in Plate 452: JOSIAH WEDGWOOD FEB[Y] 2[D] 1805. *Note the elongated capital J and uneven spacing and ill-alignment of 'JOSIAH' and the date, showing that each letter and figure was separately impressed.*

454. Base of a deep-blue jasper dip 'Dolphin' tripod (lacking pierced cover), height $4\frac{1}{2}''$ (11.4 cm), showing the two marks : WEDGWOOD 2 FEB[Y] 1805 *impressed and 'Josiah Wedgwood 2[d] February 1805' stencilled in grey.* British Museum

455. Base of the drum pedestal fixed to the miniature vase illustrated in Plate 340 showing the impressed mark : WEDGWOOD 2 FEB[Y] 1805. Mr and Mrs Samuel Laver Collection

456. Pearl ware 'Dolphin' tripod (lacking cover) handpainted with a border of flower scrolls in black and iron-red, the triangular base decorated with pink (gold) lustre. Mark : 'Josiah Wedgwood 2[d] February 1805' from the same stencil as that illustrated in Plate 454 Mr and Mrs Byron A. Born Collection

457. Pearl ware cylindrical (drum) pedestal with flat square plinth pierced with a central hole for the fixing of a vase (cf. Plate 340) decorated with bands of pink (gold) lustre. Diameter 3'' (7.6 cm). (See Plate 458.) Wedgwood Museum

458. Base of the drum pedestal illustrated in Plate 457 showing the WEDGWOOD *mark impressed on the foot rim and the enamelled inscription 'Josiah Wedgwood Feb[y] 2[d] 1805'.*

458

in the marks are readily accounted for by the necessity to impress all but the name 'WEDGWOOD' (or 'Wedgwood'), which would be immediately available as a one-piece metal stamp, in separate letters and figures, and the instruction to mark these pieces would have been carried out by different craftsmen in their own, sometimes eccentric, fashion.

The particular significance of this date is less easily explained. No documentary evidence of the application of the mark has been found, and the firing records (Oven Book) for this date, which might have cast valuable light on the problem, have not survived. One piece of evidence, however, appears to be relevant. This is contained in a report by Alexander Chisholm sent to Josiah II on 11 February 1805 with a covering letter from Josiah Byerley (Mss. 95–17608 and 11–2058). Chisholm's report deals at some length with suggestions made by Josiah II for the improvement of the Wedgwood pyrometers, in particular the composition of the stoneware used for their manufacture. Jos's letter, which Byerley notes as having been dated 2 February, has not been preserved.

Attention was drawn to this correspondence by Mrs Jean Gorely in 1942* and it has been suggested that the date of Jos's missing letter demonstrates some close connection between its contents and the production of pieces marked with the same date. This is unlikely. Unless it was misdated, or Byerley's reference to it is inaccurate, Jos's letter to the factory, written probably from Gunville in Dorsetshire, could not have arrived at Etruria in time to influence ware made on 2 February. Furthermore, ware stamped on 2 February would not have dried and been fired in time to influence Chisholm's report, which was dictated to Josiah Byerley on or before 11 February. It might seem then that the matching dates of Jos's letter and the mysterious marks are no more than coincidence and Chisholm's report has no relevance to this ware.

Such a conclusion is probably premature. The only certain evidence found so far exists in the ware which bears these marks, and some useful deductions may be made from it. The pieces identified are of four shapes:

1. Dolphin tripod pastille burner (Plates 452–4).
2. 'Egyptian' tripod pastille burner.
3. Tripod vase-candlestick lacking lid (Plate C45).
4. Small vase on drum pedestal (Plates 340 and 455 and see Plates 457–8).

The bodies used are jasper, black basaltes, Queen's ware and Pearl ware. The decoration is enamel, pink (gold) lustre, copper (gold) lustre and applied ornament.

The diversity and extreme scarcity of pieces marked in this manner are convincing grounds for assuming that they were trials, and the shapes and decorations chosen further suggest that they were trials of firing methods. Tripods are notoriously liable to warping, sagging and cracking in firing; and lustre, applied ornament and onglaze enamel colours are all types of decoration especially vulnerable to faulty firing. Together, these pieces make up a fair sample of the selection most likely to have been chosen for trials of a new kiln or of a pyrometer.

Chisholm's report makes it clear that a course of experiments had been carried out over a period, and probably begun some time before the receipt of Jos's letter of 2 February. Moreover, he writes of Jos's new proposals for a pyrometer as a project for the future, not one that has already been tried: 'The Pyrometer you propose appears to be unexceptionable in principle, and I am only afraid that it will be found too operose in adjustment and too incommodious in use. . . .' It appears most likely that these trials were inspired by the introduction of lustre decoration and the new techniques required for its firing. The addition of Josiah's name to the usual Wedgwood stamp would differentiate those pieces from normal production, and the particular trial of the new kiln would be confirmed by the date.

The suggestion that the eccentricity of the marking is to be explained by these pieces having been marked by the aged 'Chisholm, himself, with shaky hand'† does not bear serious examination. Nor can it be accepted that this unexpectedly early appearance of lustre decoration is to be explained by the use of old stock. Three examples are illustrated, one decorated with lustre, of pieces marked in ceramic colours (Plates 454, 456 and 458), and such marks are not likely to have been applied earlier than other onglaze decoration.

* *Old Wedgwood*, Wellesley, Massachusetts, 1942, pp. 98–101.
† *Ibid.*, p. 101.

Appendix C *Ornamenting*

459(1)

459(2)

459(3)

459(4)

459(6)

459(5)

459(7)

459(8)

459. ORNAMENTING.
(1) *A pug of clay being placed on top of a relief block mould to receive an intaglio impression.*
(2) *The clay being hammered on to the relief block mould.*
(3) *The block mould and the intaglio clay mould taken from it.*
(4) *Sharpening the details of a finished intaglio mould ready for use.*
(5) *Clay being pressed into a fired clay intaglio mould.*
(6) *The clay relief being lifted from the mould.*
(7) *Applying an acanthus relief ornament to a modern black basalt bowl. The surface is dampened to allow the relief to adhere. Firing completes the process of adhesion.*
(8) *Sharpening the detail of the relief ('undercutting') before firing.*

305

APPENDIX D

Engine-turning

The simple lathe, originally a development of the potter's wheel, has been used for turning (shaping and thinning) wood since the Bronze Age, when the pole lathe was employed, and the technique was later developed for turning metal. It does not appear to have been used for pottery until towards the end of the seventeenth century, and it was reputedly introduced to Staffordshire by the brothers Elers. Writing to Bentley on 19 July 1777 (E25–18772), Josiah stated: 'The next improvement introduc'd by Mr. E[lers] was the refining our common red clay, by sifting, & making it into Tea & Coffee Ware in imitation of the Chinese Red Porcelaine, by casting it in plaister moulds, & turning it on the outside upon Lathes. . . .'

The engine-turning lathe is similar in principle to the simple lathe, but the motion is eccentric, reciprocating in a horizontal plane while the shaft and the object being worked rotate. The cutting tool is held stationary, cutting flutes or more complex patterns as the reciprocating motion brings the object into contact with it.

Josiah Wedgwood claimed to have introduced the engine-turning process to the pottery industry in 1763 (Commonplace Book 39–28408, p. 35; draft for a history of the Staffordshire Potteries by Josiah Wedgwood, 1788, W/M 1858), and this claim, though not the date, is confirmed by a note in the Journal of Sir Joseph Banks for 18 December 1767: 'Mr Wedgewood [sic] has lately introduc'd into this manufactory the use of Engine Lathes which work upon the Clay with the greatest of Ease not requiring the tool to be fastned to the rest by a screw as is common but held fast by a finger of the workman on the top of the rest' (Cambridge University Library Add. Ms. 6294 Pt 2). The earliest mention of this technique in Josiah's own correspondence occurs in a letter to Bentley dated 28 May 1764 (E25–18057): 'have sent you a sample of one hobby horse (engine turning). . . . This branch hath cost me a great deal of time & thought & must cost me more. . . . I have got an excellent book on the subject in french & latin.* Have enclosed one chapter wch if you can get translated for me it will oblige me much & will thankfully pay any expense attend^g it. Tom Byerley is learning that language but I cannot wait his time.' In a letter to Tom Byerley dated 11 February 1765 (E25–18061) Josiah mentions 'Engin'd Teapots' in passing, evidently referring to engine-turned redware teapots which had been in production for some time.

On 6 July 1765 Josiah told his brother John: 'I shall be very proud of the honour of sending a box of patterns to the Queen, amongst which I intend sending two setts of Vases, Creamcolour engine turn'd, & printed.' This is the first reference to engine-turned creamware and to the application of the technique to the decoration of vases.

In 1767 Josiah made a series of important experiments with the twin aims of improving his lathe and exploiting its potential. On 16 February he wrote two letters (E25–18136–7) on the subject to Bentley, concerned principally with the use of the 'Rose' or 'Rosette' (edge cam) and the 'Crown' (face cam) which, with the 'Tudicle' (cam follower) locked in position, caused the shaft to move along its axis or laterally. The two cams could be used simultaneously, but the variations of fluting and other patterns made possible by combinations and placing of cams and followers were not immediately either discovered or mastered. 'We make constant use of both the Rose & Crown motion seperately', Josiah wrote, 'but have tryed very little what effects may be produced by combineing them, that is by useing them both at the same time, & upon the same piece of ware. . . . We sometimes fix the tudicle on the side of the rose next to the workman, & sometimes on the other side, & alter the spring accordingly, but I have no idea of continueing these two motions so as both of them to act at the same time.'

He was much troubled by what he described as 'tremulous motion' in the machine, producing 'chatter marks' on the ware. Bentley was able to make some useful suggestions as to how this might be overcome, though whether these came from his study of Plumier's book or from his own study of the problem is not clear. Josiah had many other questions to ask:

The *Twisted Columns* are very apropos to what I am now attempting, an Elegant Pillar, or Column Candlestick in which the Twisting wo^d I apprehend have an excellent effect, & I sho'd be glad to know on this subject

---

*J. Plumier, *L'Art de Tourner*, Paris, 1701.

460A. Engine-turning
lathe.

460B. Engine-turning the
base of a vase to produce a
pattern of vertical stripes.

460C. Engine-turning the
base of a vase to produce a
diced pattern.

460A

460B

460C

first whether you apprehend my Lathes can have the apparatus for twisting fixed to them? or the whole Lathe must be formed for the purpose – How far the Mandarin *may* be, or *requires* to be, thrown from the right to the left, & vice versa for this purpose. . . . What sort of *Rosetts*, or *Crowns*, or *slopes* or Tudicles are made use of, & how, & where are they fixed. Does it require the Lathe to be turned backward & forward, alternately, or will the twisted work be made with the Lathe being turned one way only. . . . every motion will be new to me in the art of Engine Turning, besides those produced by the *Rosetts* & *Crowns* used separately, & not compounded. . . . what I wish to know is, every other improvement that may be applied to Pott turning.

In May Josiah visited Matthew Boulton's factory at Soho, Birmingham, where he saw, as he told Bentley (E25–18147 23 May 1767), 'a Lathe executed upon the plan of that which is full of Rosetts, & every Rosett had a projection from the edge so ⁄⁄ & for a Crown motion, the whole was most completely finished, & the person for whom it was made hath at present no use for it, I am to spend a day or two with him (Mr Bolton) & intend to ask him if he wo^d like to part with it'. Later in the year Josiah showed his lathe to John Wyke, the Liverpool watch- and tool-maker who made metal punches and runners for Wedgwood, and they considered the possibility of Wyke's making a lathe (E25–18170 24 October 1767), but four months later he was proposing to make a lathe at Etruria. He wrote to Bentley (E25–18187 22 February 1768) asking for the return of Plumier's book:

which I want to look at, as I believe we shall make a Lathe or two here, & can do it better than at Liverpool – We have an ingenious & indefatigable smith amongst us, who has ever since Engine Lathes were first introduc'd here, been constantly employd in that business, & he promises me very faithfully that whatever improvements I may instruct him in, he will make them for no one else, but that you know is a superfluous engagement, as we have renounced those narrow, selfish views & are to let our improvements take a free course for the benefit of our *Brethren* & *Country*. Well then, that being settled, we have contriv'd a Lathe to work with 10 Rosets, & nearly as many *double* crowns, that is crowns with two edges, to be thrown with two springs to one, or the other, alternately, or as the nature of the work may require. The Rosets will likewise be thrown with great facility to a Tudicle behind as well as to one before, & the double motions, produced by the Rosett & Crown motions working together may have their full effects with the greatest simplicity of Machinery, all which will create variety ad infinitum as you will readily conceive. I shall set him about altering one of mine first, & if I approve of his workmanship in that tryal I think we cannot do better than employ him in making as a complete Lathe or two for our Ornamental work.

By the end of 1769 there were three lathes in operation at the ornamental works at Etruria, and Josiah admitted that he had 'committed a Sad Robbery upon my Burslem works to furnish it – We have not one Engine Turner left there now'. He added as a postscript to engine-turned 'useful' wares: 'Poor Burslem – Poor Creamcolour. They tell me I sacrifice all to *Etruria and Vases*' (E25–18269 19 November 1769).

Engine-turning is a highly skilled operation for both the turner and his assistant. Some of the patterns produced are so intricate that the lathe must be turned slowly by hand. The engine-turning lathe presently in use at Barlaston is little altered from the eighteenth-century prototype still preserved there in working condition except that it has been adapted to electrical motive power. The new machine was built in 1976 by Wedgwood's engineering staff and assembled by Arthur Ward, a fitter, and George Hughes, a pattern-maker, who between them had seventy-four years' experience at the Wedgwood factories at Etruria and Barlaston.

Appendix E

Cameos and Intaglios 1773–95

Class I

The information in this Appendix is reprinted from the Wedgwood Catalogue of 1787 with minor corrections where the original descriptions were obviously incorrect (e.g. cameo 1246 Antinous for 'Antonius'), and with additions from the reprinted Catalogue issued by Boardman in Liverpool in 1817. The italicised references to sources are Wedgwood's, as is the spelling. The dates, which have been added, refer to Wedgwood & Bentley or Wedgwood Catalogues in which the subjects were listed for the first time. Many of the cameos and intaglios were listed in successive catalogues from 1773 to 1787, and were continued in production for many years thereafter; some are still made; and many more could be reproduced from existing moulds at the Wedgwood factory. None of these subjects was made in jasper before 1774.

Cameos

Egyptian Mythology

Those marked with an asterisk * are heads, the others figures.

1. Osiris, or Apis, worshipped by the Egyptians under the figure of an ox, with Harpocrates his son, on the sacred bank of the Nile; from a black jasper   1773
*3. Isis, wife of Osiris, with the flower lotus on her head; from a green jasper, *in the possession of Mr T. Jenkins*   1773
*4. Another figure of Isis; from a cameo   1773
5. The same; from a sardonyx   1773
7. Isis with the sistrum; from a carnelian   1774
13. The temple of Isis; from a cameo   1773

*17. Harpocrates with the fruit and leaves of Persea upon his head; onyx   1774
19. Harpocrates standing in a bark   1774
36. The flower lotus; from a chalcedony   1774
42. An Egyptian sphinx with an ape; from a cameo, *cabinet of baron Stosch*   1773
1646. An Egyptian figure covered with hieroglyphics   1774
1690. Harpocrates, the god of silence   1777
1727. Horus sitting upon the lotus, with the sun and moon, and other hieroglyphics   1777

Grecian and Roman Mythology

47. Saturn holding a scythe, and an open book at his feet; from a carnelian   1773
52. The Corybantes striking their bucklers, to prevent the cries of the infant Jupiter from being heard by Saturn   1774
*53. Cybele; from a carnelian   1773
*54. The same; from a cameo   1787
*55. The same; from a carnelian   1774
*59. Jupiter with all his attributes; from a carnelian, *Mr Wood*   1773
**64. Jupiter and Isis   1777
*65. Jupiter Olympius; from a sardonyx, *cabinet of the king of France*   1774

*66. Jupiter with the diadem; from a cameo   1774
74. Jupiter Olympius sitting in the middle of the zodiac, with Mercury, Minerva, and Neptune; carnelian, *king of France's cabinet*   1773
83. Jupiter Conservator; carnelian   1774
87. Jupiter sitting on his chariot drawn by four horses, thundering upon the giants; Grecian workmanship, *cabinet of the king of Naples*   1773
94. Juno; carnelian   1774
99. Jupiter, in the form of a swan, caressing Leda; carnelian   1774

549. Two Cupids in a bark drawn by four dolphins; carnelian — 1774
*579. Æsculapius; carnelian — 1774
*583. The same; chalcedony — 1773
586. Æsculapius standing with a serpent; chalcedony — 1774
592. Hygiea standing with the serpent; chalcedony — 1774
628. Nemesis holding a flower — 1774
1600. Venus standing; carnelian — 1787
1601. Venus sitting; carnelian — 1787
1604. Neptune — 1774
1605. Ceres — 1787
1606. Bathing Venus — 1777
1607. Hercules gathering the golden apples in the garden of the Hesperides — 1774
1608. Apollo — 1779
1613. Minerva — 1779
1620. Æsculapius and Hygiea — 1774
1624. Young Hercules — 1774
1625. Hercules — 1774
1635. A Bacchanalian triumph — 1774
1639. Leander in the Hellespont — 1774
1640. A crouching Venus — 1774
1645. A deification — 1774
1672. Marriage of Bacchus and Ariadne — 1774

1674. Marriage of Cupid and Psyche; *duke of Marlborough* — 1774
1675. Beautiful Medusa — 1774
1677. The three Graces — 1777
1678. Justice with balance and cornucopia — 1777
1679. Hygiea — 1777
1681. Hygiea with a basket of flowers — 1777
1682. Hygiea — 1777
1697. Diana — 1777
1698. Niobe — 1777
1702. Young Bacchus — 1777
1705. Venus — 1777
1708. Young Hercules — 1777
1710. Fortune — 1777
1715. Hercules strangling the Nemean lion — 1777
1728. Neptune — 1777
1729. Mercury with a caduceus — 1777
1730. Contemplating Muse — 1777
1731. Hope — 1777
1732. The same; smaller — 1777
1733. Omphale with the club of Hercules — 1777
1750. Justice sitting — 1787
1751. Neptune standing — 1787
1752. Flora standing — 1787
1754. Venus belles-fesses (Callipyge) — 1787
1755. Venus de' Medici — 1787
1756. The same — 1787

SACRIFICES, &C.

598. A sacrifice; rock crystal, *high constable of Cologne* — 1773
603. The same; rock crystal, *duke Strozzi* — 1773
605. The same; carnelian — 1774
614. An enchantment; carnelian, *king of France* — 1774
615. A priest holding a patera; antique paste — 1787

616. A high priestess; sardonyx, *prelate Molinari* — 1774
1621. Hygiea, &c., a sacrifice — 1774
1622. An offering to Victory — 1774
1644. A sacrifice — 1774
1749. Offering to Minerva — 1787
1763. Sacrifice to Cupid — 1787

ANCIENT PHILOSOPHERS, POETS AND ORATORS

*654. Homer; chalcedony, *Mr Henri* — 1773
*655. The same; carnelian — 1773
*656. Plato; carnelian — 1773
*662. Socrates and Plato; granite — 1773
*664. Socrates; carnelian — 1774
*666. Socrates and Aristotle; sardonyx — 1787
*670. Epicurus, niccolo — 1773
*675. Æsop; carnelian — 1773
*676. Philemon; hyacinth — 1773
*677. The same; carnelian — 1787
*679. Euripides; ditto — 1773
*682. Aristides; ditto — 1773
*688. Antisthenes; ditto — 1773
*689. Aristophanes; carnelian, *king of Naples* — 1787
*690. Theophrastus; hyacinth — 1787
*692. Diogenes; cameo, *high constable of Cologne, at Rome* — 1787

*694. Diogenes disputing with Laïs; carnelian — 1787
*700. Pythagoras; engraved in gold — 1787
*701. Pythagoras sitting; carnelian — 1773
702. Anacreon; carnelian — 1773
*703. Hippocrates; carnelian — 1774
*704. Apollonius Tyanæus; green jasper — 1787
*705. Theon; niccolo — 1773
*706. Lucius Apuleius; carnelian — 1774
*707. Solon; chalcedony — 1787
*709. Pindar; opal — 1787
*711. Horace; emerald — 1773
*712. Periander; chalcedony — 1774
*715. Plautus; jasper, *king of Naples* — 1787
**716. Mago and Dionysius; plasma — 1773
*717. Charondas; sardonyx — 1773
*718. Democritus; carnelian — 1773
*724. Sappho; green jasper, *France* — 1774

*729. Ovid; sardonyx	1773	
*730. Virgil; hyacinth	1773	
*734. Seneca; chalcedony	1773	
*740. Hermes Trismegistus, with Mercury's caduceus; chalcedony	1774	
*1541. Livy; carnelian, *king of France*	1779	
*1656. Cicero	1773	

*1661. Cato of Utica	1787
*1688. Demosthenes	1777
*1700. Phocion	1779
*1701. Socrates	1777
*1707. Homer	1777
*1709. Phocion	1777
*1787. Seneca	1787

SOVEREIGNS OF MACEDONIA, &C.

*743. Alexander the Great; agate	1773
*749. Olympia, his mother; niccolo, *Dresden*	1774
*753. Lysimachus; crystal	1773
*756. Antiochus II, King of Syria; carnelian	1773
*762. Ptolemy, King of Cyrene; carnelian, *grand duke*	1774
*765. Juba; green jasper	1787
*767. Semiramis giving the command to her son; sardonyx	1774
*768. Masinissa, King of Numidia; chalcedony	1773
*769. The same; plasma	1773
*772. Alcibiades; porphyry	1773
*774. Hamilcar; agate, *Mr Edward Walpole*	1787
*775. Hannibal, with the Punic characters; amethyst	1773
*778. Phocion; cameo, *cardinal Alexander Albani*	1773

*779. The same; niccolo	1787
*783. Byzas, founder of Byzantium; agate	1773
*793. Cleopatra; *Grecian*	1787
*794. The same; carnelian, *king of France*	1787
*796. Ptolemy Soter, first King of Egypt; oriental granite, *grand duke*	1773
*797. The same, with his family; carnelian	1773
*799. Ptolemy Philadelphus, second King of Egypt; amethyst	1773
*800. Arsinoë, daughter of Ptolemy Soter; carnelian, *grand duke*	1773
*801. Ptolemy Euergetes, third King of Egypt; carnelian, *king of France*	1773
*804. Ptolemy Philopator, six King of Egypt	1774
*805. Ptolemy Euergetes, seventh King of Egypt; chalcedony	1773
*813. Ptolemy junior, thirteenth King of Egypt; carnelian	1773

FABULOUS AGE OF THE GREEKS

818. Prometheus forming a head	1773
823. Bellerophon taming Pegasus; carnelian	1773
828. Bellerophon conquering Chimæra; antique paste	1787
832. Medea rejuvenating the father of Jason; carnelian	1773
840. Œdipus; onyx, *Mr Robinson*	1787
*845. Theseus; carnelian	1773
847. The same; sardonyx; *Austrian cabinet at Vienna; Grecian*	1773
850. The same, raising the stone under which his father had hidden his sword; carnelian, *duke of Orleans*	1773
854. A centaur carrying a branch of a tree, and a cornucopia; carnelian	1774
861. Leander; chalcedony	1773
862. The same; carnelian, *countess Carusini*	1787

866. Cresphontes, Temenus and Eurysthenes, drawing lots for the cities of Messina, Argos and Sparta; carnelian	1773
871. Perseus; carnelian	1773
873. Perseus with the head of Medusa; aquamarine, *duke of Devonshire*	1773
874. Perseus with his armour; carnelian; *king of Naples; Grecian*	1773
876. Perseus and Andromeda; red jasper	1773
877. Bellerophon watering Pegasus at the bottom of Parnassus; carnelian	1787
878. Medusa; chalcedony; *Grecian, duke Strozzi*	1773
*884. Meleager; carnelian, *grand duke*	1773
887. The same, *baron Stosch*	1779
888. The same; chalcedony	1773
893. Dædalus; carnelian	1773

WAR OF TROY

*912. Priam; sardonyx, *duke of Devonshire*; *Grecian*	1774
*913. Paris, with the Phrygian cap; amethyst	1773

**921. Hector and Andromache; carnelian	1774
*927. Achilles; carnelian	1773
928. The infant Achilles carried by the centaur Chiron; carnelian	1773

929. Chiron instructing Achilles; sardonyx 1774
930. Chiron shooting with a bow; chalcedony, *Metastasio at Vienna* 1773
932. Achilles playing on the lyre; amethyst; *Grecian* 1787
939. Ajax and Teucer defending the fleet from the Trojans; carnelian 1774
*940. Ajax carrying the body of Patroclus; agate, *king of France* 1773
942. The same; carnelian, *grand duke* 1787
943. A soldier bringing the news of the death of Patroclus to Achilles; cameo, *countess Carusini* 1773
947. Hector dragged round the walls of Troy; carnelian 1774
948. Priam begging the body of Hector from Achilles; onyx, *lord Brudenell* 1773

949. The same; carnelian 1787
954. Achilles wounded in the heel; carnelian 1777
955. Ajax carrying the body of Achilles; niccolo 1773
956. Diomedes carrying the body of Achilles; niccolo 1787
957. Diomedes carrying away the palladium; carnelian; *Grecian* 1774
958. The same; carnelian, *duke Strozzi* 1777
960. The same; sardonyx 1774
961. The same; chalcedony 1774
963. Diomedes prevented by Apollo from pursuing Æneas; carnelian 1773
976. Laocoon; granite; *duke of Leeds*; from the statue in the Vatican 1773
1684. Ajax guarding the body of Patroclus 1777

Roman History

987. The goddess Roma, sitting with trophies; carnelian, *grand duke* 1774
998. Claudia, vestal virgin; carnelian, *king of France* 1774
999. A vestal; chalcedony 1773
1000. Tuccia, a vestal, carrying water in a sieve in proof of her chastity 1787
1001. Claudia, a vestal, drawing the loaded barge with her girdle in proof of chastity; carnelian 1787
1014. A chariot; cameo; *Grecian, king of Naples* 1787
1016. A chariot; carnelian, *king of France* 1787
1037. Dacia restituta; carnelian 1774
1038. Lucius Papirius, with his mother persuading him to reveal the resolutions of the senate; carnelian 1774
1044. A high priest kneeling, and making a treaty of peace; plasma 1774
1046. The Romans finding the books of the Sybils; white agate, *king of Naples* 1773
1047. Sophonisba taking poison, that she might not be led in triumph to Rome; plasma 1773
1048. Jugurtha delivered to Sylla; carnelian, *king of France* 1774
1049. Celia given as a hostage to Porsena; carnelian, *king of France* 1773
1052. Captive soldiers; sardonyx 1787
1053. Military charity; carnelian 1774
1054. A conquered province; carnelian 1773
1055. Naval engagement between Augustus and Antony; rock crystal, *king of Naples* 1787
1070. A soldier on horseback; onyx 1787
1071. Trajan fighting on horseback; antique paste, *prelate Molinari* 1787
1075. The death of Julius Cæsar; rock crystal, *abbé Fanchini at Sienna* 1773

1076. Nero in the habit of a muse; carnelian 1773
1078. Marcus Aurelius on horseback; cameo, from the bronze statue at Rome 1773
1079. Antonia, with the urn containing the ashes of her son Germanicus; carnelian 1774
*1083. Romulus; carnelian 1773
*1085. Numa Pompilius; niccolo 1787
*1086. Numa Pompilius as a priest; carnelian 1773
*1088. Ancus Marcius; niccolo 1787
*1089. Lucius Junius Brutus; white amethyst, *baron Stosch* 1773
*1095. Lucius Valerius Publicola; carnelian, *grand duke* 1787
*1096. Marcus Junius Silanus; carnelian 1787
*1097. Lucius Cornelius Sulla; carnelian 1787
*1100. Scipio Africanus; carnelian 1773
*1101. Regulus with the nail behind his neck; carnelian 1773
*1103. Cincinnatus; carnelian 1773
*1104. Cato of Utica; chalcedony 1773
*1106. The same; sardonyx 1787
*1107. Caius Marius; chalcedony, *baron Stosch* 1787
*1108. Albinus Postumius; chalcedony 1787
*1111. Marcus Claudius Marcellus; jasper 1773
*1112. The same; carnelian 1787
*1114. Caius Numonius Vala; carnelian 1787
*1115. Marcus Crassus; sardonyx 1787
*1117. Quintus Fabius Maximus; sardonyx 1787
*1118. Lentulus; carnelian 1773
*1119. Quintus Catulus; sardonyx 1787
*1122. Cato censor; carnelian, *king of France* 1773
*1123. P. Cornelius Nasica; amethyst 1777
*1125. Cicero; sardonyx, *king of France* 1787

*1126. The same; niccolo, *prince of Orange at the Hague* 1774
*1127. The same; cameo, *prince Odescalchi at Rome* 1773
*1128. Marcus Varro; carnelian 1787
*1130. Mæcenas; carnelian; *Grecian, king of Naples* 1787
*1138. Pompey the Great; carnelian, *countess Luneville at Naples* 1787
*1139. Cneius Pompeius, son of Pompey; chalcedony 1787
*1141. Sextus Pompeius; aquamarine; *Grecian, grand duke* 1787
*1142. The same; niccolo 1779
*1143. Marcus Junius Brutus with the dagger; sardonyx 1773
*1144. The same; black jasper 1777
*1146. A consular head; carnelian 1787
*1148. The same; carnelian 1787
*1149. The same; carnelian 1787
*1151. The same; red jasper 1787
*1153. The same; carnelian 1787
*1154. A Roman family; carnelian 1787
*1156. Julius Cæsar; crystal 1787
*1159. The triumvirate of Marc Antony, Lepidus and Augustus; carnelian 1787
*1160. Antony and Cleopatra; sardonyx, *Dresden* 1773
*1165. Augustus; cameo, *king of Naples* 1773
*1166. Augustus, and Livia his wife; carnelian 1787
*1167. Livia; carnelian, *lord Carlisle* 1773
*1170. Agrippa, son-in-law of Augustus; green jasper 1787
*1172. Caius and Lucius Cæsar; carnelian 1787
*1173. Caius Cæsar; carnelian 1787
*1174. Lucius Cæsar; carnelian 1787
*1175. The same; hyacinth 1787
*1176. Tiberius; carnelian *Mr Edw. Walpole* 1774
*1178. Tiberius; carnelian 1779
*1179. Tiberius, and Livia his mother; cameo, *grand duke* 1773
*1180. Drusus, son of Tiberius; chalcedony, *duke of Devonshire* 1787
*1181. The same; carnelian 1787
*1183. Nero Claudius Drusus, brother of Tiberius; hyacinth, *grand duke* 1773
*1184. The same; carnelian 1773
*1185. Antonia junior, daughter of Marc Antony; cameo 1787
*1194. Caligula, and his sister Agrippina; cameo 1787
*1195. Drusilla, sister of Caligula; carnelian 1787
*1198. Claudius; green jasper 1773
*1199. Messalina Valeria, wife of Claudius; carnelian 1787
*1200. Agrippina junior, wife of Claudius; sardonyx 1787

*1201. Britannicus, son of Claudius; carnelian 1787
*1202. The same; carnelian, *cabinet Capponi at Rome* 1787
*1203. Nero; cameo 1773
*1207. Poppæa, wife of Nero; carnelian 1773
*1210. Galba; oriental agate, *king of France* 1787
*1212. Otho; carnelian 1773
*1213. Vitellius; carnelian 1773
*1214. Vitellius; carnelian 1787
*1215. Vespasian; cameo, *grand duke* 1787
*1216. Vespasian; carnelian, *king of France* 1773
*1218. Titus; carnelian 1773
*1219. The same; cameo 1774
*1220. Julia, daughter of Titus; oriental sapphire; *Grecian, treasury of St Dennis, France* 1787
*1222. The same; hyacinth; *Grecian, Mons. Deringh* 1787
*1223. Domitian; cameo, *king of Naples* 1773
*1224. The same; niccolo 1787
*1230. Nerva; carnelian 1787
*1232. Trajan; carnelian 1773
*1233. Trajan, Plotina, Marciana, and Matilda; onyx, *king of Naples* 1773
*1235. Plotina, wife of Trajan; carnelian 1787
*1236. Marciana, sister of Trajan; carnelian 1773
*1239. Hadrian; carnelian, *king of Naples* 1773
*1241. The same; carnelian 1779
*1242. Sabina, wife of Hadrian; carnelian, *duke of Marlborough* 1773
*1243. The same; carnelian, *at Venice* 1774
*1244. The same; carnelian 1779
*1245. Sabina veiled; crystal, *prince of Waldeck* 1787
*1246. Antinous, the favourite of Hadrian; carnelian 1773
*1248. The same; carnelian 1787
*1249. The same; carnelian 1787
*1253. Ælius Cæsar, brother of Hadrian; amethyst, *countess Carusini* 1787
*1256. Antoninus Pius; amethyst, *grand duke* 1773
*1257. The same; amethyst, *king of Naples* 1787
*1258. Faustina, wife of Ant. Pius; carnelian 1787
*1260. The same; carnelian 1787
*1261. Faustina veiled; carnelian 1787
*1262. Galerius Valerius Antoninus, son of Ant. Pius 1773
*1263. Marcus Aurelius; sardonyx 1773
*1264. The same; red jasper 1773
*1265. The same; rock crystal 1773
*1266. Marcus Aurelius and Faustina; cameo 1773
*1270. Faustina junior, wife of Marcus Aurelius; carnelian 1787
*1271. Lucius Verus; antique paste 1787
*1272. The same; carnelian 1787

*1275. Commodus; hyacinth, *grand duke*	1787
1277. The same; amethyst	1787
*1280. Commodus and Ennius Verus, brothers; cameo	1773
*1281. Pertinax; carnelian	1773
*1282. The same; plasma	1787
*1288. Didia Clara; carnelian	1787
*1291. Pescennius; carnelian	1787
*1292. Albinus; chalcedony	1787
*1293. Septimius Severus; amethyst	1787
*1294. Septimius Severus; carnelian	1787
*1297. Sept. Severus, Julia Pia, Caracalla, and Geta; carnelian	1773
*1298. The same; carnelian	1787
*1299. Julia Pia, wife of Sept. Severus; hyacinth	1787
*1302. Caracalla; chalcedony	1773
*1303. The same; carnelian	1787
*1304. The same; carnelian	1787
*1306. Geta, brother of Caracalla; carnelian, *king of Naples*	1773
*1307. Macrinus; carnelian	1787
*1308. Diadumenianus; carnelian	1773
*1311. The same; niccolo	1787
*1317. Alexander Severus; carnelian	1773
*1320. Maximinus; plasma	1773
*1323. Gordianus Africanus; chalcedony, *baron Stosch*	1773
*1330. Sabinia Tranquillina, wife of Gordian; carnelian	1787

*1332. Philippus, Otacilla his wife, and Philippus junior his son; niccolo	1773
*1333. Trajanus Decius; niccolo	1773
*1335. Volusianus; carnelian	1787
*1336. Æmilianus; chalcedony	1787
*1340. Claudius II, Gothicus; lapis lazuli	1787
*1341. Quintillus; carnelian	1787
*1343. Probus; carnelian	1787
*1344. Allectus; carnelian	1787
*1345. Constantine the Great; carnelian	1774
1346. The same, on horseback; red jasper, *baron Stosch*	1787
*1348. Constantinus, his son; rock crystal, *grand duke*	1787
*1349. Julian the Apostate; sardonyx	1787
*1350. The same, with Flavia Julia Helena his wife; granite	1774
1609. Pompey the Great	1774
1610. The same; smaller size	1774
1614. Cæsar Germanicus	1787
1617. Lucius Junius Brutus	1774
1704. Sabina	1777
1711. Cleopatra	1777
1712. Marcus Aurelius	1777
1735. Continence of Scipio	1777
1753. Antonia standing	1787
1757. Sophonisba	1787
1758. Julius Cæsar	1787

MASKS, CHIMÆRAS, &C.

829. A chimæra; carnelian	1773
1351. A man putting on a mask; chalcedony, *baron Stosch*	1779
1355. Cupid masked; carnelian	1774
1356. The same; red jasper	1774
1357. Cupid dressing a mask; carnelian	1787
1363. An actor of comedy; carnelian	1773
1402. Two masks; carnelian, grand duke	1773

1408. A chimæra; emerald, *king of France*	1774
1409. The same; carnelian	1787
1449. A sphinx; carnelian, *duke Strozzi*	1773
1454. The same; carnelian	1774
1533. A basilisk drawn by four cocks; red jasper	1773
1618. Four masks	1773

ILLUSTRIOUS MODERNS

*735. Alexander Pope; chalcedony	1773
*1537. Mary, Queen of Scots; carnelian	1787
*1538. Oliver Cromwell; amethyst	1773
*1539. The Pretender; carnelian	1773
*1542. Baron Montesquieu; sardonyx	1787
*1543. Cardinal Alexander Albani; carnelian	1774
*1544. Antonio Correggio; cameo	1774
*1545. Raffaelle d'Urbino; carnelian	1773
*1546. Mich. Angelo Buonarroti; chalcedony	1773
*1547. Carlo Maratti; carnelian	1787
*1612. King George III	1773
*1619. Earl of Clanbrassill	1773

1658. Cervantes	1787
*1659. Voltaire	1787
*1660. Grotius	1787
*1662. Milton	1787
*1671. Sir John Fielding	1773
*1673. Pope Clement XIV	1773
*1676. Inigo Jones	1787
*1685. Sir Isaac Newton	1777
*1686. The same	1777
1687. The same, smaller, from his own ring	1777
*1689. Milton	1777
*1691. Henry IV, of France	1777
*1692. Duke de Sully	1777

*1693. Louis XV	1777	*1723. The same, by Marchant	1777
*1694. George II	1777	*1724. The same, by Kirk	1777
*1695. Joseph II, Emperor of Germany	1777	*1725. Dr Mead	1777
*1696. Oliver Cromwell	1777	*1726. The same, smaller	1777
*1699. Mr Blake	1787	*1736. Dr Franklin	1787
*1703. General Washington	1787	*1737. Lord Chatham	1787
*1706. Louis XIV of France	1777	*1738. General Honeywood	1787
*1713. George III	1779	*1739. George III and Queen Charlotte	1787
*1714. Queen Charlotte	1779	*1740. The same, smaller	1787
*1716. Duchess of Portland	1777	*1741. King of Prussia	1787
*1718. Mr Hamilton, of Bath	1777	*1742. Prince of Prussia	1787
*1719. Shakespeare	1777	*1743. William III, of England	1787
*1720. The same	1777	*1744. King of Naples	1787
*1721. Mrs Barbauld	1777	*1745. Queen of Naples	1787
*1722. Garrick, by Pingo	1777	*1746. King of Sardinia	1787

MISCELLANEOUS

1421. A man making a vase; carnelian, *king of France*	1774	1467. The same; carnelian	1773
1422. The same; carnelian	1779	1485. A sow; carnelian	1773
1423. The same; cameo, *king of Naples*	1773	1489. A bull; carnelian; *Grecian, king of France*	1773
1424. The same; carnelian	1773	1506. Two sea horses; carnelian	1774
1425. A vase; carnelian	1773	1623. A conquering hero	1773
1426. The same; carnelian	1773	1680. A man firing a rocket, in the character of Mars	1777
1434. The same; carnelian	1773	1747. Jesus Christ	1787
1457. A lion; carnelian	1773	1748. Virgin Mary	1787
1458. The same; carnelian, *duke Strozzi*	1787	1759. Brace of birds	1787
1462. The same; carnelian	1773	1760. A pointer dog	1787
1463. A lioness; carnelian	1787	1761. An elephant	1787
1464. A lion devouring a wild boar; carnelian	1787	1762. A horse	1787
1466. A lion devouring a horse; red jasper	1779	1764. A rattlesnake	1787

Intaglios

ANTIQUE SUBJECTS

Subjects numbered 1–290 are listed first in the 1774 Catalogue; those from 292 to 359 in the 1777 Catalogue; 376–9 in the 1779 Catalogue; and from 392 to 399 in the 1787 Catalogue.

1. A dancing Faun	*19. Sabina	*39. Ptolemy Philopator
2. Mars and Venus	*21. Lysimachus	*40. Sappho
	*22. Neptune	*41. An unknown queen, perhaps Cleopatra
4. Diomedes, Apollo, and Æneas	*23. Ceres	42. Minerva
*6. Young Hercules	*24. Æsculapius	*43. Theseus
7. A Victory	*25. Germanicus	*44. Charondas
8. A Vestal	27. Hygiea	*45. A philosopher
9. Hercules and Lion	28. Adonis	*46. Bacchus
*10. Neptune	*29. Horace	*47. Aristotle
*11. Apollo	*30. Cicero	*48. Hercules
*13. Medusa	33. A conquered Province	*49. Periander
*14. Homer	*34. Camillus	*51. Sappho
*15. Scipio Africanus	*35. Ceres	*52. Juba
*16. Socrates	*36. Socrates	*53. Young Hercules
*17. Marcus Aurelius	*37. Olympias	*54. Æsculapius
	38. A Faun	

317

*55. Perseus
*56. A Faun
57. A lioness
*58. Young Antinous
59. A lion in front
*60. Phocion
*61. Polyhymnia
62. Iöle
*63. Mercury
*64. Drusus
*65. Cicero
*66. Laocoon
*67. Plato
68. Atlas supporting the world
69. A lion devouring a horse
*70. Bacchus
*71. Æsculapius
*72. Neptune
*73. Demosthenes
74. Reposing Hercules
75. Cupid
76. A vase
77. Aristophanes
*78. Horace
*79. Solon
*80. Virgil
*81. Young Faustina
*82. Didia Clara, daughter of
Didius Julianus
*83. Neptune
*84. Hercules and Iöle
85. Contemplative Muse
*86. Sabina, wife of Hadrian,
in the character of Ceres
*87. Pompey
88. Cupid inflaming the mind
*90. Poppæa, wife of Nero
*91. Leander
*92. Britannicus, son of
Claudius
*93. Paris
94. Theseus raising a stone,
&c.
95. A Sphinx
97. Chiron shooting with a
bow
*99. Jupiter Ammon, small
101. Diomedes
*102. Venus
103. Venus and Cupid
104. A sow
105. A Sphinx
*106. Chiron, centaur
*107. Apollo
*108. Pan
*109. Lucius Junius Brutus
110. A figure from
Herculaneum

*112. Augustus Cæsar
*113. Lucius Verus
*114. Unknown
*115. Julius Cæsar and Livia
*117. Scantilla, wife of Didius
Julianus, small
118. Man making a vase
*119. Antinous
*120. Ceres, small
121. The centaur Nessus
122. Apollo standing with his
lyre
123. Juno upon an eagle
124. A Bacchante
125. Sacrifice
126. Cupid and Psyche
127. Mercury standing
128. The Three Graces
129. Mercury
130. Mercury sitting on a ram
131. Mercury, god of travellers
132. Mercury raising a dead
man by the hand
133. Mercury keeping the flocks
of Admetus
134. Cupid and Psyche
*135. Harpocrates
136. The same, standing in a
bark
137. The same, with
cornucopia
138. The same
139. Jupiter Conservator
140. The Three Graces
*142. Plutarch
143. A furious Faun
144. Julius Cæsar
145. Jupiter, Hebe and
Ganymedes
*146. Venus
147. Bacchanalian figures
148. Venus Victrix
149. An Egyptian figure
150. The Three Graces
151. Peace, or Union
152. Neptune with sea-horses
153. Pomona
154. Phæthon falling from
heaven
155. The lyre of Apollo
156. Thalia
157. Euterpe
158. Melpomene
159. Terpsichore
160. Apollo and lyre
161. Diana, huntress
162. Endymion with the Moon
163. Bacchus with a Faun

164. Bacchus sitting on a tiger
165. Hercules overcome by
Love
166. Venus and Cupid
167. The temple of Venus
168. Cupid
169. Æsculapius
170. Enchantment
*171. Æsop
172. Pythagoras, sitting
173. Hero and Leander
174. Perseus, standing
175. Meleager with a boar's
head
176. Claudia, vestal virgin
177. Castor and Pollux
178. Roman matron
179. Antonia and urn
180. Seneca in the bath
181. Constantine on horseback
182. A man putting on a mask
183. Cupid masked
184. Cupid dressing a mask
185. A Chimæra
186. A man making a vase
187. A vase
188. A cock with the diamonds
*189. Livy
194. Chiron the centaur,
playing upon the lyre
195. Semiramis giving the
command to her son
*196. Alcibiades
*197. Hannibal
198. Prometheus forming a man
199. Theseus killing the
Minotaur
200. Medea, &c.
*202. Jupiter Olympius
*203. Cicero
*204. Homer
205. Scævola, &c.
206. Hope
207. Venus and Cupid
208. Cupid and Psyche
*209. Iöle
211. Cleopatra
*213. Regulus, with the nail
*215. Jupiter with all his
attributes
216. Birth of Bacchus; Michael
Angelo's seal
217. A cow and calf
218. Ægle binding Silenus to a
tree
219. Sophonisba taking poison
220. Calliope
221. Diana, huntress

222. Papirius and his mother
*223. Marcus Junius Brutus
*224. Iöle
*227. Anacreon
*229. Agatho
*230. Ennius
*231. Apuleius
*232. Hermes Trismegistus
*233. Ovid
*234. Theocritus
*235. Pythagoras
*236. Socrates
*238. Medusa
*239. Seneca
*240. Alexander
241. Minerva
242. Marcus Aurelius on horseback
243. Iöle
244. Peace
245. Jupiter and Leda
246. Mars
247. Bacchanalian figures
248. Neptune standing in a shell
*249. Cicero
250. A Bacchante with a thyrsus
251. Bacchus and Ariadne on a tiger
252. Saturn with an encircled serpent
*253. Cybele
254. Saturn devouring a stone
*255. Cybele
256. The flower, lotus
257. Bellerophon watering Pegasus
*258. Isis with the sistrum
259. Canopus
260. Jupiter and Isis
*261. Isis with the budding horns
262. Ganymedes
*263. Virgil
*266. Madonna
268. Two Cupids
270. Mars and Venus, small
*271. Apollo, large
272. Venus
273. Conquered province, second size
274. Apollo
*276. Madonna
277. Mars

278. Venus
279. Hygiea
281. Venus
282. The Three Graces
*285. Britannicus
287. A priestess
288. Minerva
289. Hygiea
290. Diana of the mountains
292. Diana
293. Apollo and Daphne
294. Theseus killing the Minotaur
*295. Venus
296. Pomona
297. Saturn
299. Venus Victrix
300. Offering to Victory
301. Diomedes or Perseus
302. Agrippina. 4, 5, 6
303. A bull
*304. Hannibal
305. Neptune
306. Night shedding poppies
307. Nereides
308. Priam begging the body of Hector from Achilles
309. Æsculapius
310. Hygiea
311. A priest
312. Neptune
313. A sacrifice
314. Virtue
315. Justice
316. Neptune in peace with Minerva
317. Mucius Scævola before Porsenna
318. Ulysses stopping the chariot of Victory
319. A sacrifice
320. Diana
321. Ceres instructing Triptolemus in agriculture
322. Flora
323. Sophonisba taking poison
324. Plato
326. Hope with an anchor
327. Two sea-horses
328. A lion seizing a horse
*329. Pindar
330. Cybele giving Jupiter to be educated
331. A warrior

332. Hercules killing a bull
333. Mucius Scævola burning his hand, &c.
334. Diogenes disputing with Laïs
335. A sacrifice
*336. Neptune
337. A warrior
338. A warrior
339. A bird let fly
340. Hygiea
342. A Cupid
344. Offering to Victory
345. Perseus with armour, small
346. Venus Victrix
*347. Silence
348. Venus and Cupid
349. Cupid with a caduceus
350. A piping Bacchus and Cupid
351. A Cupid with a butterfly
352. Æsculapius, Hygiea, and Telesphorus
353. Three Cupids
354. Marriage of Cupid and Psyche
355. Two Cupids in a bark
*358. Zingara
*359. A gaping head
*376. Xenophon
*377. Flora
379. Female Fortune
*392. M. Brutus
393. Judgment of Hercules
395. Justice, standing
*396. Achilles
397. Offering to Minerva
*398. Virgil
399. Sacrifice to Cupid
†409. Hercules and Amazon
†418. Sophonisba taking poison
†425. Dying Adonis
†426. Male figure in a Grecian habit, holding the hand of a female who is covered by a veil
†429. Figure in a kneeling posture under a tree, with a pyramid behind her; another female figure standing, in one hand a dagger, in the other a cup
†445. Pan's pipes
†447. Chimæra
†**452. Sacrifice to Truth

The last eight subjects marked † do not appear in the Catalogues issued during the lifetime of Josiah I, and are listed only in the reprint issued by Boardman in 1817. They are, therefore, not dateable more precisely than 1788–1817, though all may belong to the eighteenth century.

MODERN SUBJECTS

Subjects numbered 3–286 are first listed in the 1774 Catalogue; those from 291 to 366 in the 1777 Catalogue; from 368 to 378 in the 1779 Catalogue; and from 380 to 394 in the 1787 Catalogue.

*3. Pope Clement XIV
*5. Oliver Cromwell
12. Alexander Pope
*20. Sir Isaac Newton
*26. George II
*31. George III
*32. Henry IV of France
89. A child with a cat
*96. Sir Isaac Newton, from his own ring
98. Oliver Cromwell, from a ring
*100. Alexander Pope
*111. Alexander de' Medici
*116. Alexander Pope
*141. Dr Mead, large
*190. Baron Montesquieu
*191. Correggio
*192. Raffaelle d'Urbino
*193. Carlo Maratti
*201. Louis XV of France
*210. Garrick
*212. Milton
*214. Emperor of Germany

*225. Henry IV of France
*226. Louis XIV
237. Portrait of a gentleman
*264. Dr Mead, small
*265. George II
267. Shakespeare
*269. Alexander Pope
*275. Dr Lucas
*280. Garrick
*283. HRH the late Duke of Gloucester
*284. Sir Isaac Newton
*286. Duke de Sully
*291. George III
325. A pointer dog
*341. George III
343. Alphabetic cyphers
*356. Lord Chatham
*357. Milton
*360. Mrs Barbauld
*361. Duke of Richmond
*363. Shakespeare
*364. The Bath washerwoman
365. A brace of birds

*366. Queen Charlotte
*368. Pope Pius VI
*369. George III and Queen Charlotte
*370. Cervantes
371. William III
*372. Garrick
*373. The same
374. The Masons' Arms
375. A horse taking a leap
378. Buchanan
*380. General Washington
*382. Voltaire
*383. Lord Keppel
*384. King of Prussia
*385. Prince of Prussia
386. A squirrel
387. An elephant
388. A rattlesnake
389. The three Swiss deliverers
*390. Dr Franklin
*394. John Wesley

The following subjects do not appear in the Catalogues issued during the lifetime of Josiah I and are listed only in the reprint issued by Boardman in 1817. The portraits of William I and the Queen of The Netherlands are likely to date from about 1790, when Josiah II and Byerley visited The Hague; that of Frederick William III of Prussia cannot have been made before 1797. It is probable, but not certain, therefore, that all numbers from 410 onwards were made after 1795.

400. A sportsman loading his gun
*401. Prince of Wales
*402. William I of the Netherlands
403. Queen of the Netherlands
404. Le diable emporte l'amour
405. Fide, sed cui vide
406. Letter; motto, 'Lisez et croyez'
407. Yours, &c.
408. A slave in chains; motto, 'Am I not a man and a brother?'
*410. Frederick William III of Prussia
*411. Frederick the Great of Prussia
*412. Unknown
*413. Music
414. King and constitution
415. God save the King

*416. Frederick II of Prussia
417. George III and Queen Charlotte
419. Queen Charlotte
420. John Wesley
421. Répondez vite
422. Unknown
423. Wafer seal
424. The same
*428. Unknown
*429. Doctor Priestley
*430. Charles James Fox, front face
431. The same, side face
*432. Henry Grattan
*433. Duke of York
*434. Frederick William III of Prussia
*435. A Druid
436. A shepherdess
437. A horse
438. A fox; motto, 'Tally-ho'

439. A cat
440. Arrow and motto
441. Anchor and heart
442. Maria
443. Je me porte bien
444. Prince of Wales's crest and motto
446. Padlock
448. Union flag, with motto, 'Pro patria'
449. Eliza
450. Elizabeth
451. Mary
453. Cupid led by a dog; motto, 'Fidelity my guide'
454. Cupid caressing a dog
455. Laurel leaf, with motto, 'Je ne change qu'en mourant'
456. Cupid on an ass, flogging it at full speed; motto, 'These are my subjects'

APPENDIX F

Medals 1773–95

CLASS VIII: HEADS OF THE POPES
CLASS IX: KINGS OF ENGLAND
KINGS OF FRANCE

Descriptions are from the 1787 Catalogue, with minor corrections and some additional reference material. Unless otherwise specified, all dates refer to Wedgwood & Bentley or Wedgwood Catalogues in which the subjects are listed for the first time. These medals were originally cast in one piece with their relief (without any sprigged ornament).

Medals were made first in black basaltes, occasionally bronzed, and were intended to be sold cheaply, in sets for collectors' cabinets. Although they were made in large quantities, they do not appear to have been much valued in the past and are now surprisingly hard to find. Jasper medals date from 1774–5.

HEADS OF THE POPES (CLASS VIII) 1773

Jesus Christ, A, B, C
St Peter, A, B

1. Linus	25. Felix	48. Gelasius	72. Theodorus I
2. St Anacletus	26. Eutychianus	49. Anastasius II	73. Martin I
3. St Clement	27. Caius	50. Symmachus	74. Eugenius
4. Evaristus	28. Marcellinus	51. Hormisdas	75. Vitalianus
5. Alexander I	29. Marcellus	52. John I	76. Adeodatus
6. Sixtus I	30. Eusebius	53. Felix IV	77. Domnus I
7. Telesphorus	31. Melchiades	54. Boniface II	78. Agathon
8. Hyginus	32. Silvester	55. John II	79. Leo II
9. Pius I	33. Marcus	56. Agapetus	80. Benedict II
10. Anicetus	34. Julius	57. Sylverius	81. John V
11. Soterus	*35. Liberius	58. Vigilius	82. Conan
12. Eleutherus	*35. Felix II	59. Pelagius I	83. Sergius I
13. Victor	36. Damascus	60. John III	84. John VI
14. Zephirinus	37. Siricius	61. Benedict I	85. John VII
15. Calixtus	38. Anastasius	62. Pelagius II	86. Sisinnius
16. Urban I	39. Innocent I	63. Gregory	87. Constantine
17. Pontianus	40. Zosimus	64. Sabinianus	88. Gregory II
18. Anterus	41. Boniface I	65. Boniface III	89. Gregory III
19. Fabianus	42. Celestine	66. Boniface IV	90. Zacharias
20. Cornelius	43. Sixtus III	67. Deusdedit	91. Stephen II
21. Lucius	44. Leo I	68. Boniface V	92. Paul I
22. Stephen	45. Hilary	69. Honorius I	93. Stephen III
23. Sixtus II	46. Simplicius	70. Severinus	94. Constantine
24. Dionysius	47. Felix III	71. John IV	95. Stephen IV

96. Adrian I	135. John XIII	176. Gregory VIII	216. Paul II
97. Leo III	136. Domnus II	177. Clement III	217. Sixtus IV
98. Stephen IV	137. Benedict VI	178. Celestine III or	218. Innocent VIII
99. Pascal I	138. Boniface VII	Cœlestin	219. Alexander VI
100. Eugenius II	139. Benedict VII	179. Innocent III	220. Pius III
101. Valentinus I	140. John XIV	180. Honorius III	221. Julius II
102. Gregory IV	141. John XV	181. Gregory IX	222. Leo X
103. Sergius II	142. Gregory V	182. Celestine IV	223. Adrian VI
104. Leo IV	143. Silvester II	183. Innocent IV	224. Clement VII
105. Pope Joan	144. John XVII	184. Alexander IV	225. Paul III
106. Benedict III	145. John XVIII	185. Urban IV	226. Julius III
107. Nicholas I	146. Sergius IV	186. Clement IV	227. Marcellus II
108. Adrian II	147. Benedict VIII	187. Gregory X	228. Paul IV
109. John VIII	148. John XIX	188. Innocent V	229. Pius IV
110. Martin II or	149. Benedict IX	189. Adrian V	230. Pius V
Marinus I	150. Gregory VI	190. John XX or XXI	231. Gregory XIII
111. Adrian III	151. Clement II	191. Nicholas III	232. Sixtus V
112. Stephen VI	152. Damasus II	192. Martin IV	233. Urban VII
113. Formosus	153. Leo IX	193. Honorius IV	234. Gregory XIV
114. Boniface VI	154. Victor II	194. Nicholas IV	235. Innocent IX
115. Stephen VII	155. Stephen IX	195. Celestine V	236. Clement VIII
116. Theodorus II	156. Benedict X	196. Boniface VIII	237. Leo XI
117. John IX	157. Nicholas II	197. Benedict XI	238. Paul V
118. Benedict IV	158. Alexander II	198. Clement V	239. Gregory XV
119. Leo V	159. Gregory VII	199. John XXII	240. Urban VIII
120. Christopher	160. Hildebrand	200. Benedict XII	241. Innocent X
121. Sergius III	161. Victor III	201. Clement VI	242. Alexander VII
122. Anastasius III	162. Urban II	202. Innocent VI	243. Clement IX
123. Lando I	163. Pascal II	203. Urban V	244. Clement X
124. John X	164. Gelasius II	204. Gregory XI	245. Innocent XI
125. Leo VI	165. Calixtus II	205. Urban IV	246. Alexander VIII
126. Stephen VII	166. Honorius II	206. Boniface IX	247. Innocent XII
127. John XI	167. Innocent II	207. Innocent VII	248. Clement XI
128. Leo VII	168. Celestine II	208. Gregory XII	249. Innocent XIII
129. Stephen VIII	169. Lucius II	209. Alexander V	250. Benedict XIII
130. Martin III,	170. Eugenius III	210. John XXIII	251. Clement XII
Marinus II	171. Anastasius IV	211. Martin V	252. Benedict XIV
131. Agapetus II	172. Adrian IV	212. Eugenius IV	253. Clement XIII
132. John XII	173. Alexander III	213. Nicholas V	254. Clement XIV
133. Leo VIII	174. Lucius III	214. Calixtus III	255. Pius VI
134. Benedict V	175. Urban III	215. Pius II	256. Pius VII

*35. This number was deliberately repeated in Wedgwood's catalogues. Felix II, Antipope (355–8), was chosen by the Arian party after the banishment of Liberius, but deposed three years later when Liberius was reinstated.

KINGS OF ENGLAND (CLASS IX, SECTION I) 1773

Sold only in sets, with or without wooden cabinets. From heads supplied by Thomas Astle FRS (1735–1803), antiquary and palaeographer (see E25–18517 26 February 1774).

William the Conqueror	Edward III	Edward VI	Queen Mary II
William Rufus	Richard II	Queen Mary	Queen Anne
Henry I	Henry IV	Queen Elizabeth	George I
Stephen	Henry V	James I	George II ⎫ two medals
Henry II	Henry VI	Charles I	Q. Caroline ⎭
Richard I	Edward IV	Oliver Cromwell,	George III ⎫ two medals
John	Edward V	Protector	Q. Charlotte ⎭
Henry III	Richard III	Charles II	
Edward I	Henry VII	James II	
Edward II	Henry VIII	William III	

(Section II)
'Another set of the Kings of England in high relief, including their present Majesties.'

MEDALS. KINGS OF FRANCE. (CLASS IX, SECTION III)

1. Pharamond	19. Childéric II	36. Robert	54. Louis XI
2. Clodion	20. Théodoric II	37. Henri	55. Charles VIII
3. Mérovée	21. Childéric III	38. Philip	56. Louis XII
4. Childéric	22. Pépin	39. Louis VI	57. François I
5. Clovis	23. Charlemagne	40. Louis VII	58. Henri II
6. Childebert	24. Louis	41. Philip II	59. François II
7. Clotaire	25. Charles the Bald	42. Louis VIII	60. Charles IX
8. Clotaire II	26. Louis II	43. Louis IX	61. Henri III
9. Charebert	27. Louis III and Carloman	44. Philip III	62. Henri IV
10. Clotaire II	28. Charles II	45. Philip IV	63. Louis XIII
11. Dagobert	29. Eudes	46. Louis X	64. Henri IV
12. Clovis II	30. Charles III	47. Philip V	65. Louis XIV
13. Clotaire III	31. Robert	48. Charles IV	66. Louis XV
14. Childéric II	32. Louis IV	49. Philip VI	67. Louis XVI and Marie-Antoinette
15. Théodoric	33. Lothaire	50. John II	
16. Clovis III	34. Louis V	51. Charles V	
17. Childebert III	35. Hugues Capet	52. Charles VI	
18. Dagobert III		53. Charles VII	

These were moulded by William Bedson from a set of heads in Lord Bessborough's collection (see E25–18615 9 August 1775). The last four medals were made in several versions and sizes, some of which were added after 1775.

APPENDIX G

Portrait Medallions : Antique Subjects

CLASS III: KINGS AND QUEENS OF ASIA MINOR, GREECE &C.
STATESMEN, PHILOSOPHERS AND ORATORS
POETS
GRECIAN HEADS OF LARGER MODELS
CLASS V: HEADS OF ILLUSTRIOUS ROMANS
CLASS VI: THE TWELVE CAESARS
THEIR EMPRESSES
CLASS VII: EMPERORS FROM NERVA TO CONSTANTINE THE GREAT

Descriptions are from the 1787 Catalogue, with minor corrections and some additional reference material. Unless otherwise specified, all dates refer to Wedgwood & Bentley or Wedgwood Catalogues in which the subjects were listed for the first time.

The medallions first listed in 1773–4 were originally cast in one piece in basaltes or terracotta, but many of these were subsequently remodelled for production in jasper, the heads being applied separately.

KINGS AND QUEENS OF ASIA MINOR, GREECE &C. (CLASS III)

The medallions of Alexander the Great and Lysimachus are listed in the 1774 Catalogue; the remainder do not appear in the Catalogues until 1777.

Ariadne
Helena
Polyxena, daughter of Priam
Iphigenia
Cassandra
Dido
Amyntas, King of Macedonia
Ariobarzanes Eusebes, King of Pontus
Mausolus, King of Caria
Artemisia, Queen of Caria
Alexander the Great
Alexander and Olympias
Alexander Epirota
Ptolemy Lagus, first King of Egypt
Seleucus Nicator, King of Syria
Antigonus, King of Asia

Demetrius Poliorcetes, King of Macedonia
Lysimachus, King of Macedonia
Arsinoe his widow
Nicomedes, King of Bithynia
Ariobarzanes, King of Pontus
Antiochus Theos, King of Syria
Antiochus Hierax
Antiochus Magnus
Ariarathes V, King of Cappadocia
Prusias, King of Bithynia
Ptolemy Euergetes, or Physcon, King of Egypt
Antiochus Cyzicenus, King of Syria
Antiochus Grypus and Cleopatra
Philippus Epiphanes, King of Syria
Ariarathes IX, King of Cappadocia

STATESMEN, PHILOSOPHERS AND ORATORS (CLASS III)

Minos	1777	Chilo	1774
Theseus	1777	Solon	1773
Lycurgus	1777	Thales	1773
Bias	1777	Heraclitus	1773
Pittacus	1774	Pythagoras	1773

Aristides	1773	Æschines	1773
Socrates	1774	Callisthenes	1773
Zaleucus	1773	Diogenes	1773
Herodotus	1787	Aristotle, two models	1773
Thucydides	1787	Xenocrates	1773
Xenophon	1787	Epicurus	1773
Lysander	1777	Euclid	1773
Antisthenes	1773	Theophrastus	1773
Thrasybulus	1777	Crates	1773
Aristippus	1773	Aratus	1773
Aristomachus	1777	Zeno, the Stoic	1773
Demosthenes	1777	Archimedes	1773
Epaminondas	1777	Chrysippus	1774
Mago and Dionysius of Utica	1774	Apuleius, rhetor	1773
Hippocrates	1773	Carneades	1773
Archytas	1774	Asclepiades	1773
Plato	1774	Posidonius	1773
Leodamas	1777	Apollonius Tyanæus	1774
Isocrates	1773		

POETS (CLASS III)

Pytheas, of Colophon	1774	Euripides	1774
Hesiod	1773	Sophocles	1774
Homer	1773	Aristophanes	1774
Alcæus	1774	Menander	1774
Sappho	1774	Posidonius	1777
Anacreon	1774	Theocritus	1774
Simonides	1777	Apollonius of Rhodes	1774
Pindar	1774	Moschus	1774

GRECIAN HEADS OF LARGER MODELS

4 inches by 3

		$3\frac{1}{2}$ inches by 2	
Minos	1777	Homer	1777
Cyrus	1774	Pittacus	1777
Lysimachus	1774	Alexander	1777
Alexander	1777		
Lycurgus	1777	*3 inches by $2\frac{1}{2}$*	
Plato	1777	Herodotus	1779
Demosthenes	1777	Thucydides	1779
		Xenophon	1779

ILLUSTRIOUS ROMANS (CLASS V)

2 inches by $1\frac{3}{4}$

		Sulla	1773
Romulus	1777	Pompey the Great; two models	1773
Numa	1773	Cicero	1773
Tullus Hostilius	1777	Cassius	1779
Ancus Marcius	1777	M. Brutus	1773
Junius Brutus	1773	Sallust	1779
M. V. Corvus	1777	M. Antonius	1773
Hannibal	1777	Cleopatra	1773
Scipio Africanus	1773	Varro	1773
T. Quintus Flaminius	1773	Virgil	1773
Terence	1777	Horace	1773
Marius	1773	Livy	1779

Ovid	1773	*4 inches by 3*	
Agrippina	1773	Junius Brutus	1777
Agrippa	1777	Scipio Africanus	1777
Persius	1777	Marius	1777
Seneca	1774	Sulla	1777
Julia, daughter of Titus, A, B	1773	Cicero	1777
Sabina	1777	Pompey	1777
Antinous	1774	Julius Cæsar	1777
Faustina	1774	Seneca	1777
L. J. Rusticus	1777		

3 inches by 2$\frac{1}{2}$

Marius	1777
Cicero	1777
Augustus	1777

THE TWELVE CÆSARS, four sizes, A, B, C, D. Their EMPRESSES, one size, 2 inches by 1$\frac{3}{4}$ (CLASS VI) 1777

1. Julius Cæsar and Pompeia
2. Augustus and Livia
3. Tiberius and Agrippina
4. Caligula and Antonia
5. Claudius and Messalina
6. Nero and Octavia
7. Galba and Lepida
8. Otho and Poppæa
9. Vitellius and Petronia
10. Vespasian and Domitilla
11. Titus and Julia, his daughter
12. Domitian and Domitia

SEQUEL OF EMPERORS FROM NERVA TO CONSTANTINE THE GREAT, INCLUSIVE (CLASS VII) 1773 unless otherwise dated

13. Nerva		39. Jul. Philippus	1777
14. Trajan		40. J. Philippus Fel	1777
15. Hadrian		41. Trajanus Decius	1777
16. Antoninus Pius		42. Q. Heren. Decius	1777
17. L. Verus		43. Gallus	
18. M. Aur. Antoninus		44. Volusianus	
19. Commodus		45. Æmilianus	
20. Pertinax		46. L. Valerianus	
21. Didius Julianus		47. Gallienus	
22. Pescennius Niger		48. S. Valerianus	1777
23. Septimius Severus		49. Postumus	1777
24. Clodius Albinus		50. Claudius Gothicus	
25. Caracalla; three models		51. Quintilius	1777
26. Geta; two models		52. Aurelianus	
27. Macrinus		53. Tacitus	
28. Diadumenianus	1777	54. Florianus	
29. Elagabalus		55. Probus	
30. Alexander Severus		56. Carus	
31. Maximianus I		57. Numerianus	
32. J. V. Maximianus II	1777	58. Carinus	1774
33. Gordianus I		59. Diocletianus	
34. Gordianus II		60. Maximianus	
35. Pupienus		61. Constantius	
36. Balbinus		62. Galerius Maximianus	
37. Gordianus III		63. Maximianus	1777
38. Valens Hostilianus	1777	64. Constantinus	

APPENDIX H

Portrait Medallions, Modern Subjects 1771–*1967*

*Jasper from 1774

This list is arranged alphabetically in two sections: portraits catalogued by Wedgwood up to 1788; and portraits believed to have been produced before 1795 but not listed in Wedgwood's Catalogues, either because they were modelled too late to be included, or because they were not for public sale, or because they were omitted in error.

Modellers' names given in capitals are those for which satisfactory evidence is available. Those in lower-case letters are attributions on such grounds as style or circumstantial evidence.

Descriptions 'To left' or 'To right' refer to profiles facing to the viewer's left or right.

'First Catalogue' dates are those of the earliest Catalogue in which the subject is listed.

The principal reference for the information in this Appendix is Robin Reilly and George Savage, *Wedgwood: The Portrait Medallions*, London, 1973, but the Appendix contains some additional references and a small number of important corrections to previously published material.

The following abbreviations have been used: 'BM' for British Museum, and 'V&A' for Victoria & Albert Museum.

Portraits marked * are illustrated in this Appendix; those marked † are illustrated elsewhere in the text.

Unless otherwise specified, all manuscript references are to manuscripts in the Wedgwood collection deposited at Keele University.

I: PORTRAITS CATALOGUED BY 1788

Description	First Catalogue	Modeller	Source	Ms. Reference	Remarks
Addison, Joseph (1672–1719), essayist. $\frac{3}{4}$-face	1773				Probably two versions
Adolphus Frederick, Prince (1774–1850). To right	1787	J.C. LOCHEE	Wax BM 87–12–16–29	2–939 30 April 1787	
Albani, Francesco (1578–1660), painter. $\frac{3}{4}$-face	1773				
D'Alembert, Jean le Rond (1717–83) encyclopaedist. To left	1779	Hackwood	Medal by Pesez	E25–18688 7 September 1776	
Amherst, Jeffery, first Baron (1717–97), soldier. To left	1787	Tassie			

Antoine de Bourbon (1518–62), King of Navarre. To right	1773				
Augusta, Princess of Wales (1709–72). To right	1773	ISAAC GOSSET	Medal by Kirk		
Augustus Frederick, Prince (1773–1843). To left	1787	J.C. LOCHEE	Wax BM 87–12–16–30	2–939 30 April 1787	
Averanius, Benedictus (1645–1707), Italian scholar. To right	1774		Medal 1708		Recorded with incorrect name 'CAR.MAZARINE' impressed
Baker, Sir George (1722–1809), physician	1773				No example of this portrait has been identified
*†Banks, Sir Joseph (1743–1820), naturalist. All to left	1779	J. FLAXMAN		E25–18617 25 July 1775; E25–18648 [Jan./Feb. 1776]; 1–206 21 August 1779; E26–18920 2 September 1779	Three portraits: the first by Flaxman, 1775; the second, based on the first and 'classicised' for the series of large portraits, 1779; the third, attributed to Flaxman, c.1779
Banks, Dorothea, Lady (1758–1828), wife of Sir Joseph. To right	1788	Flaxman		2–840 20 March 1782	
Barbauld, Anna Letitia (1743–1825), authoress. To left	1788	Joachim Smith	Wax	E25–18605 3 July 1775	First produced in 1775 but uncatalogued until 1788
Barnard, Sir John (1685–1764), Lord Mayor of London	1773				No example of this portrait has been identified
Barry, comtesse du (1746–1793), mistress of Louis XV. To left	1788		Medal by Pesez		A small medal portrait of this subject was listed in 1773
Beaumont, Francis (1584–1616), dramatist. To right	1779	Flaxman			Modelled for the 'English Poets' series
Berch, Charles Renold (1708–77), antiquary and historian. To right	1779		Medal, 1757	E25–18657 24 February 1776 E26–18905 3 July 1779	

Bergman, Torbern Olof (1735–1814), chemist and natural historian. To right	1787		Plaster by T. Sergel		Also extant in Tassie's glass paste
Birague, René (1507–83), Chancellor of France. To right	1773		Medal		No example of this portrait has been identified with certainty
†Blake, John Bradby (1745–73), naturalist. ¾-face.	1779	JOACHIM SMITH	Medal	E25–18659 3 March 1776; E25–18668 12 May 1776	Initials 'I.S.' on truncation
Boccage, Anne-Marie Fiquet du (1710– 1802), poetess. To left	1779		Medal by Pesez		
†Boerhaave, Hermann (1688– 1738), physician. ¾-face	1787	J. FLAXMAN	Wax	E26–18889 8 May 1779; 2–30187 8 July 1782	
Boileau-Despreaux, Nicolas (1636– 1711), critic and author. To right	1773		1. Ivory by D. Le Marchand 2. Medal		Two portraits: the first, after Le Marchand, of doubtful identity
Boucherat, Louis de (1616–99), Chancellor of France. To left	1773		Medal by Mollart		
Bouillon, Marie, duc de (1728–92), soldier	1787			2–847 24 January 1784; 1–209 29 September 1787	No example of this portrait been identified
Boyle, the Hon. Robert (1627–91), natural philosopher and chemist. To left	1779		Marble bust by Rysbrack c.1733	E26–18924 18 September 1779	Modelled for the series of large portraits
Bridgman, Charles (d.1738), garden designer and architect	1773				Listed in 1773 and 1788 as 'William Bridgeman'. So far unidentified
*Brunswick, Charles Ferdinand, Duke of (1735– 1806), soldier. To right	1788	Lochée	Wax	136–27207 8 November 1787	Two portraits: the first attributed to Lochée; the second from the same source as the Fürstenberg bust by Desoches, 1772
Buchan, William (1729–1805), physician and writer. To left	1787	J. FLAXMAN		2–1339 1783	

Burlamaqui, Jean Jacques (1694–1748), jurist. To left	1779		Probably medal by Pesez		
Butler, Samuel (1612–80), poet. To right	1773				Modelled for the 'English Poets' series
†Byres, James (1733–1817), art-dealer. To right	1788	J. TASSIE			Signed and dated 1779 on truncation
*Camden, Charles Pratt, Earl (1714–94), Lord Chancellor 1. To left. 2. To right	1779		Medal by T. Pingo, 1766	E25–18657 24 February 1776; E25–18737 10 July 1777	Two portraits: the first after the medal by Pingo; the second perhaps as late as 1782
Carracci, Annibale (1560–1609), painter. ¾-face	1773		Engraving by Pietro Aquila after Maratti		
†Catherine II of Russia (1729–96), Empress. To right	1787		1. & 2. Medals by T. Ivanov, 1762, 1774 3. Model by Maria Feodorowna 1782	E25–18669 15 May 1776; E25–18726 [14 December] 1776	Three portraits: the first two after Ivanov produced by 1779; the third, as Minerva, signed 'Marie F. 21 April 1782' on truncation
†Chambers, Sir William (1723–96), architect. To left	1788	C. PEART		2–931 29 March 1787	
Charles I (1600–49)	1788				No example of this portrait has been located
Charles II (1630–85) 1. To right. 2. ¾-face	1779		1. Medal by J. Roettiers. 2. Medal by P. van Abeele		Two portraits
Charles III, King of Spain (1716–88). To right	1787		Medal by T.F. Prieto, 1765	1–115 16 September 1776; E25–18669 15 May 1776; E25–18797 26 November 1777	
Charles XI, King of Sweden (1655–97). To right	1773		Medal		
*Charles XII, King of Sweden (1682–1718). 1. ¾-face. 2. To right	1773				Two portraits

Charles Emmanuel II, duc de Savoie (1634–75). ¾-length. To left	1773		Medal, 1673		Catalogued in 1773 as 'Charles Emmanuel XI'
*†Charlotte Sophia, Queen (1744–1814). Five to left; two to right	1773	ISAAC GOSSET, W. HACKWOOD	Wax	LHP. 7 September 1771; E25–18635 23 December 1775; E25–18673 6 June 1776; E25–18680 5 July 1776	At least seven portraits, of which two are by Hackwood after Gosset as pairs to portraits of George III. See also Mrs Kennicott
Châtelet-Lomont, Gabrielle, Marquise de (1706–49). To left	1779		Medal by Pesez		
†Chatham, William Pitt, first Earl of (1708–78). All to left	1779	J. FLAXMAN	Wax (1). Medal by T. Pingo, 1760 (3)	E25–28635 23 December 1775; E25–18657 24 February 1776; E25–18840 1 July 1778	Three portraits: one from an original wax by Flaxman; another from a medal by Thomas Pingo
Chaucer, Geoffrey (?1340–1400), poet. ¾-face	1773		Portrait in Occleve's *De Regimine Principum*, f. 91		Modelled for the 'English Poets' series. (Profile by C. Toft *c.*1880)
Chesterfield, Philip Dormer Stanhope, fourth Earl of (1694–1773), statesman. 1. To left. 2. To right	1779		Medal by J.A. Dassier, 1743 (1)	E25–18657 24 February 1776	Two portraits
Christina, Queen of Sweden (1626–89). To right	1779		Medal by Travany		
Christine, duchesse de Savoie (1606–63)	1773		Medal		Catalogued as 'Christia Francia'. No example of this portrait has been identified
Clairon de la Tudi, Hippolyte (1735–1803), actress. To right	1779		Probably Medal by Pesez		
Colbert, Jean-Baptiste (1619–83), statesman. To right	1779		Medal by T. Bernard, 1683		
*Coligny, Louise de, Princesse d'Orange (1555–1620). ¾-face	1787	Flaxman	Engraving by A. Schouman after Houbraken	44–28876 4 September 1781	The engraving sent by Veldhuysen

Condamine, Charles Marie de la (1701–74), scientist. To left	1779				
Condé, Louis II de Bourbon, Prince de (1621–86). To right	1773		Medal, 1660		
Congreve, William (1670–1729), playwright. $\frac{3}{4}$-face	1779				Modelled for the 'English Poets' series
†Cook, James (1728–79), navigator and explorer. 1. $\frac{3}{4}$-face. 2. To right. 3. $\frac{3}{4}$-face, large size	1779	Flaxman (1), J. FLAXMAN (2)	Portrait by W. Hodges (1). Original wax (2)	2–1339 1784	Three portraits: the first attributed to Flaxman, largely on grounds of style; the second, documented; the third, $9\frac{1}{2} \times 7\frac{3}{4}$ in. oval
Corneille, Pierre (1606–84), dramatist. To left	1779		Medal by Pesez		
Correggio, Antonio Allegri da (c.1489–1534), painter. To left	1779		Medal		
*Courland, Peter Biron, Duke of (1742–1800). To left	1779				
Cowley, Abraham (1618–67), poet. $\frac{3}{4}$-face	1779				Modelled for the 'English Poets' series
*Cowper, George Nassau, third Earl (1738–89). To left	1787	J. FLAXMAN		T. Byerley to Cowper 7 November 1786 Hertfordshire County Records Office D/EPF 310/18	
Coysevox, Antoine (1640–1720), sculptor. To right	1779		Medal		
Crébillon, Prosper Jolyot de (1674–1762), dramatist. To right	1779		Probably medal by Pesez		
Cromwell, Oliver (1599–1658), Lord Protector. 1. $\frac{3}{4}$-face. 2. To left. 3. To right	1773		Bust by Rysbrack (1). Engraving by Houbraken after Cooper (2)	E25–18657 24 February 1776	Three portraits

Dacier, Anne (1654–1720), writer. 1. To left. 2. To right	1773		Ivory by David Le Marchand (1). Probably medal by Pesez (2)	E25–18657 24 February 1776	Two portraits
Demoivre, Abraham (1667–1754), mathematician. To right	1779		Medal by J.A. Dassier		
De Noves, Laura †(c.1307–48), Petrarch's mistress. To left	1779				
†Descartes, René (1596–1650), philosopher. To right	1779		Medal by Pesez		
Déshoulières, Antoinette (1638–94), poetess. To right	1779		Medal by Pesez		
Diderot, Denis (1713–84), encyclopaedist. To right	1779		Engraving after bust by Houdon		
Dolben, William (1726–1814), member of parliament. To left	1787	J. TASSIE 1779			Signed 'T' and dated on truncation
Dryden, John (1631–1700), poet. $\frac{3}{4}$-face	1779				Modelled for the 'English Poets' series
Edwards, George (1694–1773), naturalist. To left	1779	ISAAC GOSSET			Cf. Engraving by I. Miller after Gosset, 1763
*Elizabeth I (1533–1603). $\frac{3}{4}$-face	1779		Possibly adapted from 'Armada medal'		
Erasmus, Desiderius (1466–1536), scholar and theologian. 1. $\frac{3}{4}$-face. 2. To right	1773		Probably adapted from medal by Schweiggers (1)	E25–18657 24 February 1776	
Ernest Augustus, Prince (1771–1851). To left	1787	J.C. LOCHEE	Wax. BM 87–12–16–28	2–939 30 April 1787	
Estrées, Gabrielle d', Duchesse de Beaufort (1573–1599), mistress of Henri IV. To left	1779		Medal by Pesez		

461. *Large solid blue and white jasper portrait medallion of Sir Joseph Banks. Oval height 10¼″ (26.0 cm). Mark :* WEDGWOOD & BENTLEY. 1779.
British Museum

462. *Solid pale-blue and white jasper portrait medallion of Charles Ferdinand, Duke of Brunswick. Oval height 3⅝″ (9.2 cm). Mark :* WEDGWOOD. c.1788.
British Museum

463. *Green jasper dip portrait medallion of Sir Charles Pratt, first Earl Camden. Oval height 3¾″ (9.5 cm). Mark :* WEDGWOOD. c.1786–90.
Wedgwood Museum

464. *Glazed creamware portrait medallion of Charles XII of Sweden. Oval height 4¼″ (10.8 cm). Unmarked. Probably a reference medallion for use by the ornamenters. Formerly author's collection*

465. *Solid pale-blue and white jasper portrait medallion of Queen Charlotte. Oval height 2½″ (6.4 cm). Mark :* Wedgwood & Bentley. 1776–80. Wedgwood Museum

466. *White terracotta body portrait medallion of Louise de Coligny, the ground enamelled chocolate-brown. Oval height 4 5/16″ (11.6 cm). Mark :* WEDGWOOD. c.1781. Royal Scottish Museum, Edinburgh

467. *Solid blue and white jasper portrait medallion of Peter Biren, Duke of Courland. Oval height 3¼″ (8.2 cm). Mark :* WEDGWOOD. c.1781–90. Wedgwood Museum

468. *Solid blue and white jasper portrait medallion of George Nassau, third Earl Cowper. Oval height 4½″ (11.4 cm). Mark :* WEDGWOOD. c.1785. Wedgwood Museum

469. *Solid pale-blue and white jasper portrait medallion of Queen Elizabeth I. Oval height 4″ (10.2 cm). Mark :* WEDGWOOD & BENTLEY. c.1779. Brooklyn Museum, Emily Winthrop Miles Collection

Fénelon, François de Salignac de la Mothe (1651–1715). To right	1779				
Finch, Lady Charlotte (1725–1813), royal governess. To left	1787	JOACHIM SMITH	Wax	E25–18550 30 July 1774; E25–18557 5 September 1774; E25–18648 [Jan./Feb.] 1776	
†Finch, Henrietta, daughter of Lady Charlotte. To left	1787	JOACHIM SMITH	Wax	E25–18555 30 August 1774	See also uncatalogued portrait of Matilda Fielding
Fletcher, John (1579–1625), dramatist. $\frac{3}{4}$-face	1779		Probably after engraving by G. Vertue, 1729		Modelled for the 'English Poets' series
Fleury, André Hercule de, (1653–1743), cardinal. To right	1779		Probably from medal by J. Dassier, 1734		
Folkes, Martin (1690–1754), antiquary and philosopher. To right	1773		Medal by A. Dassier, 1740		
Fontenelle, Bernard le Bovier de (1657–1757), writer. To left	1779		Engraving by St Aubin after bust by Le Moyne		
Fordyce, James (1720–96), doctor of divinity. To left	1787				Listed, in error, under 'Physicians'
†Forster, Johann Reinhold (1729–98), naturalist. 1. To right. 2. To left	1779	JOACHIM SMITH	Waxes	E25–18668 12 May 1776	Both moulds inscribed
Fothergill, John (1712–80), physician. To right	1779	Flaxman	Probably medal by L. Pingo	E25–18797 26 November 1777	
Fountaine, Sir Andrew (1676–1753), connoisseur. To right	1779		Medal by J.A. Dassier		
*Franklin, Benjamin (1706–90), statesman. All but one to left	1779	W. HACKWOOD (1) Hackwood (2)	From wax by Patience Wright (3). From bust by Caffieri (5). From terra-cotta by J.B. Nini, 1777 (6)	E26–18890 9 May 1779	Eight portraits: one in the series of large portraits made in 1779

*†Franklin, William (1731–1813), son of Benjamin Franklin. To left	1787	Flaxman			
*Franklin, William Temple (1760–1823), natural son of William Franklin. To right	1788	Flaxman		2–865 30 January 1783	
†Frederick Augustus, Duke of York (1763–1827). Two to left, two to right	1787	Lochée E. BURCH J.C. LOCHEE J.C. LOCHEE	Wax Wax (BM87–12–16–25) Wax	E25–18669 15 May 1776	Four portraits
Frederick Louis, Prince of Wales (1707–51). Both to left	1779	ISAAC GOSSET (1)	Wax V&A A55–1970		Two portraits
*Frederick II of Prussia (1712–86). Two to left, one to right	1779		Medal. Terracotta bust	E25–18809 4 February 1778; E25–18835 [11 May] 1778; E26–18888A 3 April 1779	Three portraits: the second reversed from the first. Ms. of 3 April 1779 refers to untraced large portrait, possibly for the 1779 series
*Frederick William II, King of Prussia (1744–97). All to left	1788		Probably from a medal (1 & 2). Wax after drawing by A. Poggi (3)	E26–18991 4 July 1790; 2–982 24 December 1789	Three portraits, including one of the largest made ($15\frac{1}{2} \times 13$ in.). The third was not modelled until 1788
Freind, John (1675–1728), physician and chemist. To left	1779		Medallion by F. de St Urbain, c.1726		
Galilei, Galileo (1564–1642), mathematician and astronomer. To right	1779		Medal by A. Simon		
†Garrick, David (1717–79), actor. Both to right	1779	W. HACKWOOD	Medal by T. Pingo, 1772	L1–112 December 1773; E25–18797 26 November 1777; E25–18805 22 December 1777; E26–18904 June 1779	Two portraits by Hackwood: the second a remodelled version of the first; and both after the medal by Pingo supplied by Hoskins & Oliver in December 1773

Gassendi, Pierre (1592–1655), philosopher and astronomer. To right	1779		Medal by Warin, 1648		
Gay, John (1685–1732), poet. To right	1773		Wax		Apparently adapted from a wax portrait of Matthew Prior (*q.v.*)
*George I (1660–1727). 1. $\frac{3}{4}$-face. 2. To left	1773	M. GOSSET	Wax: V&A A6–1931 (1) Wax (2)		Two portraits: the second signed on truncation
George II (1683–1760). To left	1779	M. Gosset I. Gosset	Wax Wax: V&A Bate.79		Two portraits: a wax of the first, attributed to Matthew Gosset sold Christie's 13 December 1966
†George III (1738–1820). Of ten portraits traced, nine face to right. Double portrait, to right	1773	ISAAC GOSSET W. HACKWOOD HENRY BURCH	Wax Wax Medal by E. Burch	E25–18440 30 January 1773; E25–18673 6 June 1776; E25–18635 23 December 1775; E25–18874 July 1777	At least ten portraits, of which no less than four are by Hackwood after Gosset. The rare double portrait of George III and Queen Charlotte dates from 1777
*George IV (1762–1830). Five to left, one to right	1787	Flaxman J.C. LOCHEE J. FLAXMAN	Drawing by E. Scott. Wax: BM 87–12–26–24 Wax		At least six portraits, all but one of which appear to have been modelled before 1790
George, Prince of Denmark (1653–1708)	1773				No example of this portrait has been identified
Gervais, Nicholas (*c.*1610–?1666), physician and poet	1788				Doubtful identity. Catalogued as 'Louis Gervaise' (untraced)
Gonzalez	1779				No clue has been found to the identity of this subject
Gordon, John (b.1708). To right	1773		Wax by J. Pozzo, 1728. V&A A8–1931		The same portrait, inscribed, exists in bronze, but the subject seems to be otherwise unknown

Gower, John (*c*.1325–1408), poet. To right	1773		Engraving by G. Vertue, 1727		Modelled for the 'English Poets' series
Grignan, Françoise Marguerite, comtesse de (1646–1705). To right	1779		Medal by Pesez		
Grotius, Hugo (1583–1645), jurist and theologian. To left	1773		Possibly the terracotta bust by Rysbrack	E26–18921 10 September 1779	
Guilford, Frederick, Lord North, second Earl of (1732–92), Prime Minister. To left.	1787	M. GOSSET	Medal by T. Kirk		Probably moulded from the medal, rather than from Gosset's wax
†Gustavus III, King of Sweden (1746–92). To right	1779	J. FLAXMAN Flaxman	Medallion by J.T. Sergel	E25–18771 17 July 1777; E25–18797 26 November 1777; 2–1339 23 November 1784	Two portraits, one documented as Flaxman's, the second attributed
Gyllenborg, Carl, Count (1679–1746), statesman	1773		Possibly medal by Enhörnying		No example of this portrait has been identified
Haller, Albrecht von (1708–77), physiologist. To right	1779	Medal by Moerikofer			
†Hamilton, Sir William (1730–1803), Ambassador to Naples. To left	1773	JOACHIM SMITH		E25–18355 17 February 1772; E25–18364 6 April 1772; E26–18890 9 May 1779; E26–18920 September 1779	Three portraits: the first modelled by Smith in 1772; the second remodelled from it; and the third, remodelled again and 'classicised' for the series of large portraits produced in 1779
Hanway, Jonas (1712–86), philanthropist. To left	1788		Engraving by Bretherton after T. Orde		
*Hastings, Warren (1732–1818), Governor-General of India. Full-face	1787	J. FLAXMAN	Portrait by J. Zoffany	Invoice of 14 January 1785 E.2–1339	
Hay, Elizabeth (*fl.c.*1690–1720). To right	1773				

470. *Solid pale-blue and white jasper portrait medallion of Benjamin Franklin. One of the series of large-size portraits produced in 1779. Oval height 11¾″ (27.4 cm). Mark:* WEDGWOOD & BENTLEY. *1779–80.* British Museum

471. *Pale-blue jasper dip portrait medallion of William ('Governor') Franklin. Oval height 4¼″ (10.5 cm). Mark:* WEDGWOOD. *c.1783–90.* British Museum

472. *Pale-blue jasper dip portrait medallion of William Temple Franklin. Oval height 4¼″ (10.5 cm). Mark:* WEDGWOOD. *c.1783–90.* Nottingham Castle Museum

473. *Blue jasper dip portrait medallion of Frederick II of Prussia. Oval height 5″ (12.7 cm). Mark: new F wash (incised)* WEDGWOOD. *c.1785.* Brooklyn Museum, Emily Winthrop Miles Collection

474. *Blue dip on buff-coloured jasper portrait medallion of Frederick II of Prussia. Oval height 2¾″ (7.0 cm). Mark:* WEDGWOOD & BENTLEY *and 'ım/lc/ı No. 1559/ı Dish flint in' (incised). 1778–80.*

475. *Green jasper dip portrait medallion of Frederick William II of Prussia. Oval height 3¾″ (9.5 cm). Mark:* WEDGWOOD. *c.1790.* Both Wedgwood Museum

476. *White terracotta body portrait medallion of George I, the ground and back enamelled in a deep red. Oval height 4⅜″ (11.1 cm). Unmarked Wedgwood, c.1775. Inscribed 'M* GOSSET *Fect'.* Formerly Eugene D. Buchanan Collection

477. *Pale-blue jasper with darker-blue dip portrait medallion of George, Prince of Wales by J.C. Lochée, c.1787. Oval height 3 11/16″ (11.0 cm). Mark:* WEDGWOOD. *c.1787–90.* Wedgwood Museum

478. *Blue jasper dip portrait medallion of Warren Hastings. Oval height 4½″ (11.4 cm). Mark:* WEDGWOOD. *c.1785–90.* Victoria & Albert Museum

*Heathfield, George Augustus Eliott, first Baron (1717–90), Governor of Gibraltar. 1. Full-face. 2. To left	1787	Peart	Medal. Engraving by W. Angus after G.F. Koehler		Two portraits, the first of which was in production by 1783
Hein, Pieter (1577–1629), naval commander. $\frac{3}{4}$-face	1787	Flaxman	Medal	44–28876 4 September 1781 (Veldhuysen to Wedgwood)	
†Henri IV, King of France (1553–1610). 1. To left. 2. To right	1773		Medal by G. Dupré	E25–18679 2 July 1776; E25–18714 28 October 1776	Two portraits, both in production by 1780
Henry Frederick, Prince of Prussia (1726–1802)	1779				No example of this portrait has been identified
†Hillsborough, Wills Hill, second Viscount (1718–93). To left	1787	C. Peart			
Hogerbeets, Rombout (1561–1625), lawyer. $\frac{3}{4}$-face	1787	Flaxman		44–28876 4 September 1781 (Veldhuysen to Wedgwood)	
Hood, Samuel, first Viscount (1724–1816). 1. to left. 2. to right	1787	J.C. Lochee (2)	Wax		Two portraits
John of Lancaster, Duke of Bedford (1389–1435), Regent of England and France. To left	1779		Bedford Missal		
John III Sobieski, King of Poland (1624–96). $\frac{3}{4}$-face	1773				
Johnson, Samuel (1709–84), lexicographer. 1. To left. 2. To right	1788	J. Flaxman	Engraving	2–1339 3 February 1784	Two portraits, the second unattributed
Jones, Inigo (1573–1652), architect. 1. To right. 2. $\frac{3}{4}$-face	1773		Bust by Rysbrack. Portrait by Van Dyck	E25–18657 24 February 1776	Two portraits
Jonson, Ben (1573–1637), poet and playwright. $\frac{3}{4}$-face	1779				Modelled for the 'English Poets' series

†Joseph II, Emperor of Austria (1741–90). 1. To right. 2. To left	1788	Flaxman	Ivory medallion	Byerley to Cowper 7 November 1786 Hertfordshire County Records D/EPF 310/18	
Kaempfer, Engelbrecht (1651–1716), traveller and writer	1787				No example of this portrait has been identified
Keder, Nicholas (1659–1735). To right	1779		Medal by Medlinger, 1733		
Kennicott, Ann (d.1830)	1787			E25–18709 October 1776	Unidentified portrait, but probably one of those identified as Queen Charlotte, to whom Mrs Kennicott bore a remarkable resemblance
†Keppel, Augustus, first Viscount (1725–86), admiral. 1. To left. 2. To right	1779	Hackwood		E26–18878/80/82/ 84 25 February– 14 March 1779; E26–18891 20 May 1779	Two portraits, the first often attributed, without evidence, to Flaxman, but more probably the work of Hackwood. The second possibly 1782
*Kortenaer, Egbert Meeuwszoon (d.1665), admiral. ¾-face	1787	Flaxman		44–28876 4 September 1781 (Veldhuysen to Wedgwood)	
*La Fontaine, Jean de (1621–95), fabulist. To right	1779		Medal by Pesez		
Lambertini, Giovanni, Prince (fl. c.1770–90). To right	1788				
Lamoignon, Guillaume de (1617–77), first President of Paris parlement	1773				No example of this portrait has been identified
Lansdowne, George Granville, Viscount (1667–1735), poet. ¾-face	1779				Modelled for the 'English Poets' series

La Rochefoucauld, Frédéric Jerome de Roye de (1701–57), cardinal	1788				No example of this portrait has been identified
Laud, William (1573–1645), Archbishop of Canterbury	1773				No example of this portrait has been identified
Le Fèvre d'Ormesson, Louis François de Roule, marquis (1718–79). To right	1779				Identification doubtful
L'Enclos, Anne ('Ninon de L'Enclos) (1616–1705), courtesan. To right	1779		Medal by Pesez		
Leopold I, Emperor (1640–1705). To right	1773				
Le Sueur, Eustache (1616–55), painter. To right	1779		Medal		
*Lever, Sir Ashton (1729–88), collector. To left	1787	J. FLAXMAN	Wax		
†Ligne, Charles Joseph, Prince de (1735–1814), soldier. To left	1788	J.C. LOCHEE	Wax	E2–939 30 April 1787; E2–970 21 November 1787	
†Linnaeus, Carolus (1707–78), botanist. To right	1779		Probably medal by W.S. Taylor or wax by Inlander	1–204 19 January 1775; E25–18748 19 April 1777; E26–18889 8 May 1779	Invoiced by Flaxman, on his father's behalf, for moulding from a medal and from a wax medallion, 1775
Liverpool, Charles Jenkinson, first Earl of (1727–1808). To left	1788	J. FLAXMAN	Wax	E2–1339 21 March 1784	
Locke, John (1632–1704), philosopher. To left	1779		Probably bust by Rysbrack		Two versions of the same portrait
Louis XIV, King of France (1638–1714). To right	1773		Ivory by M. Mollart. V&A. A44–1935		Four other portraits are known, but none is reliably identified
Louis XV, King of France (1710–74). To right	1773		Medal by Dassier. Medal by Duvivier	E25–18679 2 July 1776	Two portraits

†Louis XVI, King of France (1754–93). Two to right. One to left	1779	W. Hackwood	Medal by Duvivier. Medallion by Renaud	Three portraits
Louisa, Queen of Denmark (1724–51). To right	1773			No example of this portrait has been identified with certainty
Louvois, François Michel Le Tellier, marquis de (1641–91)	1773		Probably a medal	No example of this portrait has been identified
Maffei, Francesco Scipione di (1675–1755), man of letters. To right	1779		Medal by A. Dassier	
Magliabecchi, Antonio da Marco (1633–1714), bibliophile. To right	1773		Medal	
Mahomet II, Sultan of Turkey (1430–81). To left	1773		Medal	Incorrectly catalogued by Wedgwood as Amurath I, and impressed 'AMURAT I' below truncation
Mansfield, William Murray, Earl of (1705–93), Lord Chief Justice. To right	1787	J. Tassie		Tassie's glass-paste portrait signed and dated 1779
Maratti, Carlo (1625–1713), painter. To left	1773		Probably a medal by Gaab	
Maria Theresa, Empress (1717–80). To left	1773		Medal by Scure	
†Marie-Antoinette, Josephe Jeanne (1755–93), Queen of France. Two to left. One to right	1779		Terracotta medallion by J.B. Nini	Three portraits: one signed 'I.B. NINI F.1774' on truncation; the sources of the others unidentified
Marlborough, John Churchill, first Duke of (1650–1722), soldier. $\frac{3}{4}$-face	1773		Medal by J. Dassier, 1722	
Marmontel, Jean-François (1723–99), writer. To right	1779		Engraving	

Mazarin, Jules (1602–61), cardinal. 1. ¾-face. 2. To right	1773		Both from medals		Two portraits: the first sometimes found impressed 'Romano' below truncation. Mazarin's name is to be found impressed on portraits of Averanius and Fénelon
†Mead, Richard (1673–1754), physician. ¾-face	1779	Hackwood	Ivory carving by Silvanus Bevan; Wax inscribed 'J Flaxman'. BM 1957–12–6–1	E25–18860 8 November 1778	Though inscribed, the attribution to Flaxman of the wax portrait is open to doubt. Probably by Hackwood. See Chapter 12
Melanchthon, Philipp (1497–1560), religious reformer. To left			Medal	E25–18657 24 February 1776	
Melville, Henry Dundas, first Viscount (1742–1811). To left	1787	J. TASSIE	Wax by I. Gosset		
Michelangelo Buonarotti (1475–1564), painter and sculptor. To right	1773				
Milton, John (1608–74), Poet. Two ¾-face; one to left, one to right	1773		Medal by J.S. Tanner	E25–18657 24 February 1776	Two ¾-face portraits modelled for the 'English Poets' series; portrait to right after Tanner; to left probably nineteenth century
Molesworth, Richard, third Viscount (1680–1758), soldier. To right	1773		Medal		
†Molière (Jean Baptiste Poquelin) (1622–73), dramatist. To left	1779		Medal by Pesez		
Monckton, the Hon. Robert (1726–82), soldier. To right	1787	J. TASSIE			

Montagu, Edward (d.1775), husband of Elizabeth Montagu	1787			No example of this portrait has been identified
*Montagu, Elizabeth (1720–1800), 'bluestocking'. To right	1787		E25–18604 24 June 1775; E25–18605 3 July 1775; E25–18609 11 July 1775	One of the earliest portraits to be produced in blue and white jasper
Montagu, John, second Duke (1690–1749), Master-General of Ordnance. To left	1779	Medal by J.A. Dassier, 1751	E25–18657 24 February 1776	
Montaigne, Michel Eyquem, seigneur de (1533–92), essayist and philosopher. To left	1788	Medal by Pesez		Portrait impressed 'PESEZ' on truncation
Montespan, Françoise-Athenaïs de Rochechouart de Mortemart, marquise de (1641–1707), mistress of Louis XIV. To left	1779			
*Montesquieu, Charles de Secondat, baron de la Brède et de (1689–1755), writer	1773	Medal by J.A. Dassier, 1753	E25–18657 24 February 1776	
†More, Samuel (1725–99), secretary of Society of Arts. To right	1773		E25–18630 5 December 1775	
Meulen, Adam Frans van der (1632–1690), painter	1788			No example of this portrait has been identified
*†Newton, Sir Isaac (1642–1727), natural philosopher and mathematician. Two ¾-face, three to right	1773	Ivory by David Le Marchand	E25–18726. [14 December] 1776; E26–18890 9 May 1779; E26–18887 26 April 1779; E26–18893 30 May 1779	Apart from the ¾-face portrait either cast or modelled from the Le Marchand ivory carving, the sources remain unidentified. The second ¾-face portrait was modelled for the 1779 series of large-size portraits

Noailles, Louis Antoine de (1651–1729), cardinal	1773				No example of this portrait has been identified
Northumberland, Sir Hugh Percy, first Duke (1715–86), politician. To right	1787	J. TASSIE	Medal by T. Kirk, 1766		
Oldham, John (1653–83), poet. To right	1779				Modelled for the 'English Poets' series
Oldenbarneveldt, Jan van (1547–1619), statesman. To right	1779			E26–18921 10 September 1779	
*Orange, Royal House of 1. Frederica Sophia Wilhelmina, Princess (1751–1820). To right 2. William V, Stadtholder of Holland (1748–1806). To left 3. William George Frederick, Prince (1774–99). To right 4. Frederica Louisa Wilhelmina, Princess (1770–1819). To right 5. William I, King of Holland (1772–1843). To left	1788		Plaster relief portraits by J.H. Schepp	2–837 18 February 1782; W/M 1501 5 July 1782	Framed and supplied separately, and also, as in the fine example illustrated here (Plate 487), as a group on one plaque
Orford, Sir Robert Walpole, first Earl (1676–1745). 1. $\frac{3}{4}$-face. 2. To left 3. To right	1773		Sulphur cast supplied by Hoskins & Grant, 1774. Wax attributed to I. Gosset. Medal by L. Natter	E25–18632 10 December 1775	Three portraits
Orford, Catherine Countess of (d.1737). $\frac{3}{4}$-face	1779		Mezzotint by J. Simon after M. Dahl		
Otway, Thomas (1652–85), poet. To right	1773				Modelled for the 'English Poets' series

479. *Solid white jasper portrait medallion of Lord Heathfield. Diameter 3¼″ (8.2 cm). Unmarked. Wedgwood, c.1783.* Metropolitan Museum of Art, New York

480. *Light-blue jasper with darker-blue jasper dip portrait medallion of Henri IV of France. Oval height 4″ (10.2 cm). Mark :* WEDGWOOD & BENTLEY. *1778–80.*

481. *Solid pale-blue and white jasper portrait medallion of Egbert Meeuwszoon van Kortenaer. Oval height 3½″ (8.9 cm). Mark :* WEDGWOOD. *c.1781–90.* Both Wedgwood Museum

482. *Blue jasper dip portrait medallion of Jean de La Fontaine. Oval height 2¼″ (5.7 cm). Mark :* WEDGWOOD. *c.1781–90.* Wedgwood Museum

483. *Pale-blue jasper dip portrait medallion of Sir Ashton Lever. Oval height 4⅛″ (10.4 cm). Mark :* WEDGWOOD. *c.1785–90.* Brooklyn Museum, Emily Winthrop Miles Collection

484. *Blue jasper dip portrait medallion of Elizabeth Montagu. Oval height 2¾″ (7.0 cm). Mark :* Wedgwood & Bentley. *c.1776–80.* Wedgwood Museum

485. *Blue jasper dip portrait medallion of Montesquieu. Oval height 2¼″ (5.7 cm). Mark :* WEDGWOOD. *c.1781–90.* Wedgwood Museum

486. *Solid blue and white jasper portrait medallion of Sir Isaac Newton. Oval height 10⅞″ (27.5 cm). Mark :* WEDGWOOD & BENTLEY. *1779–80.*

487. *Five portrait medallions of members of the House of Orange on a pale-blue jasper dip ground. Diameter 8½″ (21.6 cm). Mark :* WEDGWOOD. *c.1782–90.* Both Brooklyn Museum, Emily Winthrop Miles Collection

Pascal, Blaise (1623–62), mathematician and writer. To left	1779		Medal by Pesez		
Paul I, Emperor of Russia (1754–1801). 1. To right. 2. $\frac{3}{4}$-face	1788	J. Tassie J. Flaxman	Engraving by J. Walker	2–1333 February 1782	Also small head to right as companion to portrait of Natalia Alexierna. After a medal by J.G. Jaeger, 1773
†Pemberton, Henry (1694–1771), physician and mathematician. To right	1779		Ivory by S. Bevan	E25–18860 8 November 1778; E26–18929 9 October 1779	
Pennant, Thomas (1726–98), antiquary and naturalist. To right	1779	J. Smith		E25–18668 12 May 1776	
†Peter I, Tsar of Russia (1672–1725) 1. To left. 2. To right	1773		Medal	E25–18354 [15 February] 1772; E25–18581 1 January 1775	Two portraits: the first, listed as a 'fine medallion 17″ × 14″', is probably the largest produced in the eighteenth century
Peter II, Tsar of Russia (1715–30). To right	1779		Medal		
Philips, Sir John	1787				Usually identified as 'General Sir John Phillips', though no officer of that name and rank served in the British Army in the eighteenth century
†Pitt, William (1759–1806) statesman. $\frac{3}{4}$-right	1787	J. Flaxman			Two other portraits have been erroneously identified: the first, in profile to right (Reilly and Savage, *Portrait Medallions*, p. 276), is of Lord Brougham and Vaux; the second, in profile to left and attributed to

					Lochée (David Bindman (ed.), *John Flaxman RA*, London, 1979, p. 68), remains unidentified
Pius VI (1717–1799), Pope. To right	1788		Portrait '*ad vivum*' by J.E. Mansfield, 1782		
Pompadour, Jeanne-Antoinette Poisson, marquise de (1721–64). To left	1779		Medal by Pesez		
Pope, Alexander (1688–1744), poet. To left	1773		Bust by Roubiliac		
Porter, Endymion (1587–1649), royalist. To right	1779		Medal by Warin		
*Préville, Pierre Louis Dubois de (1721–99), actor. To right	1779				
†Priestley, Joseph (1733–1804), dissenting minister and chemist. To right	1779	G. CERRACCHI Hackwood		E26–18887 24 March 1779; E26–18890 9 May 1779; E26–18893 30 May 1779	Two portraits: the first modelled in plaster by Cerracchi; the second remodelled, probably by Hackwood, for the series of large-size portraits, 1779
Prior, Matthew (1664–1721), poet. 1. $\frac{3}{4}$-face. 2. To right	1773		Bust by Antoine Coysevox (2). Wax: V&A A7–1931 (2)		Two portraits: the first modelled for the 'English Poets' series; the second, after Coysevox, apparently adapted for Wedgwood's portrait of John Gay (*q.v.*)
Racine, Jean-Baptiste (1639–99), dramatist. To right	1779		Medal by Pesez		
Raphael (1483–1520), painter. $\frac{3}{4}$-face	1773		Portrait by Maratti		

*Ray, John (1627–1705), naturalist. $\frac{3}{4}$-face	1779		Medal attributed to G.D. Gaab, 1705		
Reda von Redern, Sigismund Ehrenreich, Baron (1719–89), director of Berlin Academy of Sciences. To left	1788				Baron von Redern accompanied Josiah Wedgwood to Cornwall in 1782 to search for china clay
†Reynolds, Sir Joshua (1723–92), painter. To right	1788				Long attributed, but without evidence, to Flaxman
Rochester, John Wilmot, second Earl of (1647–80). $\frac{3}{4}$-face	1773				Modelled for the 'English Poets' series
Rockingham, Charles Watson Wentworth, second Marquis of (1730–82). To left	1787	J. Tassie			c.1787
Romano, Giulio (c.1492–1546), painter and architect. To left	1773		Engraving after the self-portrait		
Rousseau, Jean-Jacques (1712–78), philosopher. To right	1773			Glasgow City Archives TD 68/1 2 November 1790; E25–18657 24 February 1776; E25–18726 [14 December] 1776	
†Ruyter, Michel Adriaanszoon de (1607–1676), admiral. $\frac{3}{4}$-face	1787	J. Flaxman	Wax	2–1333 44–28876 4 September 1781 (Veldhuysen to Wedgwood)	
St Albans, Francis Bacon, first Viscount (1561–1626), philosopher. $\frac{3}{4}$-face	1773			E26–18924 18 September 1779	A second, large-size, portrait seems to have been planned, but no example has been traced
Saint-Evremond, Charles Marguetel de Saint-Denis, seigneur de (1613–1703). To left	1779			E25–18657 24 February 1776	

Sandwich, John George Montagu, fourth Earl (1718–92). To right	1787				
Sartine, Antoine-Raymond-Jean de (1729–1801), statesman. To left	1779		Medal by Pesez		
Saxe, Hermann Maurice, Marshall de (1696–1750), soldier. To left	1779		Medal by Fontenoy, 1748		Portraits of William Augustus, Duke of Cumberland, are known impressed 'Marshal Saxe'
Scudéry, Madeleine de (1607–1701), novelist. To left	1779		Medal by Pesez		
Sévigné, marquise de (1626–96), *écrivain.* ¾-face	1779		Medal by Pesez		
†Shakespeare, William (1564–1616), poet and playwright. 1. To left. 2. ¾-face with laurel twig. 3. ¾-face	1773	W. HACKWOOD (1)	Possibly wax by A. McKenzie. V&A (Bate Loan) 1.178	E25–18797 26 November 1777; E25–18805 22 December 1777; E25–18906 June 1779	At least three portraits during the eighteenth century, and two others assigned to the nineteenth century *c.*1864
Shannon, Henry Boyle, Earl of (1682–1764), politician	1779				No example of this portrait has been identified
Shipley, Jonathan (1714–1788), Bishop of St Asaph. To right	1787				Perhaps two versions
†Siddons, Sarah (1755–1831), actress. Two portraits to left	1787	J. FLAXMAN		2–1334 1782	The pose strongly resembles that of one of the queens in Flaxman's chess set. The identification of a second portrait is less sure
Sidney, Algernon (1622–83), republican. ¾-face	1779		Portrait by Justus van Egmont	E25–18809 4 February 1778; E26–18860 8 November 1778; E26–18862 21 November 1778	

Sidney, Sir Philip (1554–1586), poet. $\frac{3}{4}$-face	1773				Modelled for the 'English Poets' series
Sloane, Sir Hans (1660–1753), naturalist. 1. To right. 2. $\frac{3}{4}$-face	1779		Engraving by J. Smith, 1733 Ivory by Silvanus Bevan	E25–18860 8 November 1778; E26–18929 9 October 1779	Two portraits
†Solander, Daniel Charles (1736–82), naturalist. To right	1779	J. FLAXMAN		E25–18648 [Jan./Feb.] 1776; E25–18617 25 July 1775; E26–18920 2 September 1779; E26–18940 28 November 1779	Two portraits: the first modelled by Flaxman in 1775; the second 'classicised', probably by Hackwood, for the 1779 series of large-size portraits
Sorel, Agnes (1409–50), mistress of Charles VII of France. To right	1779		Medal by Pesez		Catalogued as 'Agnes Soreau'
Spenser, Edmund (?1552–99), poet. $\frac{3}{4}$-face	1779				Modelled for the 'English Poets' series
†Stafford, Granville Leveson-Gower, first Marquis (1721–1803), statesman. To right	1787				
Stanislas II, Augustus Poniatowski, King of Poland (1732–95). To right			? Cameo by Holzheusser		
Steele, Sir Richard (1672–1729), poet and man of letters	1773				No example of this portrait has been identified
†Stuart, James ('Athenian') (1713–88), architect. To left	1773				Two portraits. Catalogued, flatteringly, under Class XI 'Princes and Statesmen'
Stukeley, William (1687–1765), physician and antiquary. To right	1779		Medal, 1765		
*Sully, Maximilien de Béthune, duc de (1559–1641). 1. To left. 2. To right	1779		Medal 'of Severs Bisque'	E25–18696 September 1776	Two portraits

Surrey, Henry Howard, Earl of (1517–47), poet. ¾-face	1779			Modelled for the 'English Poets' series
Suze, Henriette de Coligny, comtesse de la (1618–73). To left	1779	Medal by Pesez		
Swieten, Gerhardt van (1700–1772), physician. To left	1779			
Swift, Jonathan (1667–1745), author. To right	1773			Modelled for the 'English Poets' series
*Temminck, Egbert de Vrij (1700–85), politician. ¾-face	1787			
Thomson, James (1700–48), poet	1773			No example of this portrait has been identified. Probably modelled for the 'English Poets' series (though a Scot)
Titian (Tiziano Vecelli) (c.1490–1576), painter. To right	1773	Etching by Van Dyck		
Turenne, Henri de la Tour d'Auvergne, vicomte de (1611–75), soldier	1788			No example of this portrait has been identified
Leonardo da Vinci (1452–1519), painter and sculptor. To left	1779	Probably medal by Hérard, 1669		
†Voltaire, Jean François-Marie Arouet de (1694–1778). 1. To right. 2. To left	1773	W. HACKWOOD (2)	E25–18657 24 February 1776; E25–18846 24 August 1778; E26–18889 8 May 1779	Two portraits: the second, signed by Hackwood
Waller, Edmund (1605–87), poet. To right	1773			Modelled for the 'English Poets' series
*†Washington, George (1732–99), President. Two to right; two to left	1779	Medal designed by Voltaire, 1777. Etching by Joseph Wright, 1789. Bust by Houdon	E25–18771 17 July 1777; E25–18772 19 July 1777	Four portraits, and a fifth remodelled from the first two

West, Benjamin (1738–1820), painter. To left	1788			
William III, King (1650–1702). To right	1779	E. BURCH		Signed on truncation
William Augustus, Duke of Cumberland (1721–65), soldier. To right	1773	ISAAC GOSSET	Medal by Kirk	Examples of this portrait exist impressed 'Marshal Saxe'
William, Duke of Gloucester (1689–1700)	1788			No example of this portrait has been identified
William Henry, Prince (1765–1837). Two to right; two to left	1787	J.C. LOCHEE		E2–954 30 June 1787	No new portrait was modelled after the Prince's accession as King William IV
William I, Prince of Orange (1533–84). ¾-face	1788		Engraving after portrait by Mierevelt	44–28876 4 September 1781 (Veldhuysen to Wedgwood)	
William IV, Stadtholder (1711–51). 1. To right. 2. To left	1773	Gosset	Engraving by Houbraken after Van Dyck. Wax. V&A A1060–1910 Medal		Two portraits
Witt, Cornelis de (1623–72), republican. ¾-face	1787	J. FLAXMAN	Wax	44–28876 4 September 1781 (Veldhuysen to Wedgwood)	
Witt, Jan de (1625–72), leader of republican party. ¾-face	1787	J. FLAXMAN	Wax	44–28876 4 September 1781 (Veldhuysen to Wedgwood)	
Woodward, John (1665–1728), natural philosopher. To left	1779	Hackwood	Ivory carving by Silvanus Bevan	E25–18860 8 November 1778	
†Wren, Sir Christopher (1632–1723), architect. 1. To right. 2. To left	1773		Ivory carving by D. Le Marchand. Perhaps the bust by Coignand	E25–18657 24 February 1776	Two portraits
Wyatt, James (1746–1813), architect. To left	1788				

488

490

489

491

488. Black basaltes portrait medallion of Pierre de Préville. Oval height $3\frac{7}{8}''$ (9.8 cm). Unmarked. Inscribed 'Preville' in script on reverse. c.1779. Author's collection

489. Pale-blue jasper dip portrait medallion of John Ray. Oval height $3\frac{7}{16}''$ (8.7 cm). Mark: WEDGWOOD. c.1781–90. Nottingham Castle Museum

490. Solid blue and white jasper portrait medallion of the duc de Sully. Oval height $4\frac{1}{2}''$ (11.4 cm). Mark: WEDGWOOD&BENTLEY.c.1776–80. Wedgwood Museum

491. Blue jasper dip portrait medallion of George Washington. Oval height $2\frac{1}{2}''$ (6.3 cm). Mark: WEDGWOOD. c.1781–90. British Museum

II: Uncatalogued Portraits Prior to 1795

Description	First Catalogue	Modeller	Source	Ms. Reference	Remarks
Alexander I, Emperor of Russia (1777–1825) and Constantine, Grand Duke (1779–1831). To left		Empress MARIA FEODOROWNA, 1791			Identical to the Tassie glass-paste medallion and probably supplied by him. Double portrait, the heads superimposed
Amalia, Princess of Orange (*fl.*1625–60). ¾-face			Horn medallion BM 89.7–6.2 John Osborn, 1626		Possibly produced in error as portrait of Elizabeth of Bohemia. Cf. Frederick Henry, Prince of Orange
Anne, Princess of Orange (1709–59). 1. To left. 2. To right		1. Gosset	Wax. V&A A1061–1910		Two portraits: the second doubtfully identified
†Auckland, William Eden, first Baron (1744–1814), statesman. To right		E.G. MOUNTSTEPHEN *c.*1789	Wax	E26–18997 14 November 1790	Original wax exhibited National Portrait Gallery 3 October 1973, No. 4a. Refer also letters A. Storer to Lord Auckland 28 September and 22 October 1790 (R.J. Auckland, third Baron, Bishop of Bath and Wells (ed.), *The Journal and Correspondence of William, Lord Auckland*, 4 volumes, London, 1862, Vol. II, pp. 371–3)
†Auckland, Eleanor Elliot, Lady (1758–1818). To left		E.G. MOUNTSTEPHEN	Wax	E26–18997 14 November 1790	
†Bailly, Jean Sylvain (1736–93), writer and astronomer. To right			Probably medal by Duvivier, 1789	12–11263 23 December 1791	Cf. engraving by Cook after Boizot, 1790

†Bentley, Thomas (1730–80), Liverpool merchant and partner of Josiah Wedgwood. Four portraits, all to right	J. SMITH Hackwood		1–112 December 1773; E26–18860 8 November 1778; Oven Book entries 12 and 19 October 1782	The first portrait, in Court dress, by Joachim Smith (initialled on mould); three others, more or less 'al antique', attributed to Hackwood. A fifth, 21 inches, recorded in Oven Book for October 1782 but no example traced
†Bevan, Silvanus (1691–1765), apothecary. With his second wife, Martha. Double portrait, profiles superimposed to right		Ivory by S. Bevan	E26–18860 8 November 1778; E26–18929 9 October 1779	
Bevan, Timothy (1704–86), apothecary. With his second wife, Hannah (d.1784). Double portrait, profiles superimposed to right		Ivory by S. Bevan	As for Silvanus Bevan	
†Black, Joseph (1728–99), chemist and physicist. To left	W. TASSIE	Wax		This, and Tassie's glass-paste portrait, signed and dated 1788 on truncation
†Bourne, Edward (fl.1770s), bricklayer at Etruria. To right	W. HACKWOOD		E26–18860 8 November 1778; E26–18862 [Rec'd] 21 November 1778; E26–18862 June 1779	
Brindley, James (1716–72), engineer	J. Smith		E25–18420 15 November 1772	No example of this portrait has been identified
*Buckingham, George Grenville, first Marquis (1753–1813), statesman. To left	J.C. LOCHEE	Wax	C. Peart to T. Byerley 26 March 1788	

*Buckingham, Mary Elizabeth Nugent, Marchioness of (1759–1812). To right	J.C. LOCHEE			
Burke, Edmund (1729–97), politician. To right				Doubtful identification
Camelford, Thomas Pitt, first Baron (1737–93). To right				First produced *c.*1779
Camper, Pieter (1722–89), physician. To right		Plaster by J.H. Schepp	W/M 1501 27 April 1784 (Veldhuysen to Wedgwood)	
Caroline of Ansbach, Queen Consort of George II (1683–1737). To right				
*Cats, Jacob (1577–1660), poet. ¾-face	Flaxman		44–28876 4 September 1781 (Veldhuysen to Wedgwood)	
Cervantes Saavedra, Miguel de (1547–1616), author and soldier. To left			E25–18846 24 August 1778	Catalogued in 1779 but only as an intaglio
Charles Edward Stuart, Prince (1720–88). To right		Wax by I. Gosset		
*Charlotte Augusta Matilda, Princess Royal (1766–1828). To left	Lochée		W/M 1460 2 April 1788 (Josiah Wedgwood II to Josiah I)	
Christian VII, King of Denmark (1750–1808)			2–834 6 August 1779	No example of this portrait has been identified
Conduitt, Catherine, Viscountess Lymington (?1721–50). To right		Medal by J.S. Tanner, 1729		Probably private commission. The subject is portrayed aged seven years
†Coote, Sir Eyre (1726–83), soldier. ¾-face	E.G. MOUNTSTEPHEN 1788	Marble bust by Nollekens, 1779	Invoice 1–1319 23 June 1788	Often erroneously catalogued as Ferdinand of Sicily by Flaxman
†Darwin, Erasmus (1731–1802), physician and poet. ¾-face	Hackwood	Painting by Joseph Wright of Derby, 1770	Oven Book 19 and 26 February 1780	

*Devonshire, Georgiana Cavendish, Duchess of (1757–1806). To left	Flaxman		Oven Book 10 August 1782	
Dieden, Baroness (fl.1750–90). Wife of Danish envoy to London. To left	J. Smith		E48–8864 1775	Perhaps reproduced from Joachim Smith's stock of waxes. Certainly an odd choice
Dürer, Albrecht (1471–1528), painter and engraver. To right		Woodcut self-portrait		Possibly a nineteenth-century addition
Dutens, Louis (1730–1812), writer and historiographer. To right	Flaxman		2–965 14 September 1787	
†Edgeworth, Honora Sneyd (d.1780), second wife of R.L. Edgeworth. To left	Flaxman	Silhouette by Mrs Harrington and miniature by J. Smart	LHP 10 May 1780 Oven Book 2 June 1781	Private commission
*Edward Augustus, Duke of Kent (1767–1820). To right	J.C. LOCHEE 1787 Flaxman	Wax by Lochée: V&A 87–12–16–27		Two portraits
*†Elers, John Philip (fl.1690–1730), potter and silversmith. $\frac{3}{4}$-face	W. HACKWOOD	Wax	E25–18734 25 January 1777; E25–18772 19 July 1777	Private commission from Paul Elers
Elizabeth, Princess (1770–1840), third daughter of George III. To left				Recorded only by Frederick Rathbone (Old Wedgwood, London, 1898, Plate XIX). No example identified, no mould located. Existence doubtful
Eugène, François, Prince de Savoie (1663–1736), soldier. To right		Medal		
Eyre, Charles Chester. To right		Ivory carving by D. Le Marchand inscribed, signed and dated 1700 V&A A19–1974		The Wedgwood portrait first identified by the author in 1984.

Eyre, Elizabeth. To left				Nothing appears to be known about this subject or of Charles Eyre (*q.v.*). Probably they are related and both were most likely private commissions.
Ferdinand I, King of the Two Sicilies (1751–1825). To left	J. FLAXMAN		Invoice 1781	
†Fielding, Matilda, daughter of Lady C. Finch. To right	JOACHIM SMITH, *c*.1774		E25–18555 30 August 1774	Cf. references for Lady Charlotte Finch and Henrietta Finch
†Flaxman, Anne (*fl.*1775–1820), wife of John Flaxman jnr. To right	J. FLAXMAN *c*.1790			
†Flaxman, John (1755–1826), sculptor. To left	J. FLAXMAN *c*.1771 (1) *c*.1787 (2)		E26–18886 20 March 1779	Two self- portraits: the first as a boy; the second as pair to the portrait of his wife
*Fox, Charles James (1749–1806), statesman. $\frac{3}{4}$-face	Flaxman			Probably after the portrait by Sir Joshua Reynolds, *c*.1790. Also in Tassie's glass paste
Frederick Henry, Prince of Orange (1584–1647). $\frac{3}{4}$-face		Horn medallion BM 89.7–6.1 John Osborn, 1626		Possibly produced in error as portrait of Frederick V of Bohemia. Cf. notes for Amalia
Gessner, Salomon (1730–88), poet. To right		Wax	E26–18991 23 January 1790	
*Gibbon, Edward (1737–94), historian. To left		Painting by Sir J. Reynolds, 1779		
*Goethe, Johann Wolfgang von (1749–1832). $\frac{3}{4}$-face	Flaxman			Produced *c*.1790
Gordon, Lord George (1751–93), leader of 'No Popery' riots of 1780. To right	J. TASSIE 1781	Painting by J. de Fleur		Jasper and glass paste portraits signed and dated

492. *Solid pale-blue and white jasper portrait medallion of the Marquis of Buckingham. Oval height 3¾" (9.5 cm). Mark:* WEDGWOOD. *c.1788. Wedgwood Museum*

493. *Solid pale-blue and white jasper portrait medallion of the Marchioness of Buckingham. Oval height 3¾" (9.5 cm). Mark:* WEDGWOOD. *c.1788. Wedgwood Museum*

494. *Solid blue and white jasper portrait medallion of Princess Charlotte Augusta. Oval height 3¾" (9.5 cm). Mark:* WEDGWOOD. *c.1787. Wedgwood Museum*

495. *Pale-blue jasper dip portrait medallion of Georgiana, Duchess of Devonshire. Oval height 4½" (11.4 cm). Mark:* WEDGWOOD. *c.1782–90. Nottingham Castle Museum*

496. *Solid blue and white jasper portrait medallion of Prince Edward Augustus, Duke of Kent. Oval height 3¾" (9.5 cm). Mark:* WEDGWOOD. *c.1787–90. Wedgwood Museum*

497. *Solid pale-blue and white jasper portrait medallion of John Philip Elers. Oval height 3⅜" (8.6 cm). Mark:* WEDGWOOD & BENTLEY. *1777–80. Brooklyn Museum, Emily Winthrop Miles Collection*

498. *Dark-blue jasper dip portrait medallion of Charles James Fox. Oval height 3 9/16" (9.0 cm). Mark:* WEDGWOOD. *c.1790. Wedgwood Museum*

499. *Solid pale-blue and white jasper portrait medallion of Edward Gibbon. Oval height 2 15/16" (7.4 cm). Mark:* WEDGWOOD. *c.1785. Wedgwood Museum*

500. *Green jasper dip portrait medallion of Goethe. Oval height 4" (10.2 cm). Mark:* WEDGWOOD. *c.1790. Wedgwood Museum*

†Griffiths, Ralph (1720–1803), publisher. To left				Produced *c*.1790
Hamilton, Captain Edward (*fl.*1750–80). To left	J. Smith *c*.1774			
Handel, Georg Friedrich (1685–1759), composer. ¾-face				
*Herschel, Sir William (1738–1822), astronomer. 1. To left. 2. To right	Flaxman (1) Lochée (2)		Oven Book, 1785	
Hulse, Sir Edward (1682–1759), physician. To right		Ivory carving by S. Bevan	E25–18860 8 November 1778	Probably one of the casts sent to Etruria by Samuel Moore in 1778
Ingenhousz, Jan (1730–99), physician. To right			Ingenhousz Account Book, 1778. Stedelijk Museum, Breda (No. 2054)	
Jacquin, Nicolas Joseph (1727–1817), naturalist. To right		Relief portrait by L. Posch		
*Kemble, John Philip (1757–1823), actor. To right	Flaxman *c*.1784			
†Lafayette, Marie Joseph Paul Roch Yves Gilbert Motier, marquis de (1757–1834). 1. To right. 2. To left		Medal by Duvivier (1)	12–11263 23 December 1791 Returns from Burley, Birmingham	Two portraits
Lamballe, Marie Thérèse Louise, princesse de (1749–92). To left	J.C. LOCHEE 1787		2–970 2 November 1787 LHP April 1788	
Lavater, Johann Kaspar (1741–1801), poet. To left			Oven Book 21 August 1779	
†Leopold II, Emperor (1747–92). To right				Often wrongly catalogued as Prince Charles Edward. Probably made with so-called 'German cameos' in 1790

Macklin, Charles (c.1697–1797), actor	J.C. LOCHEE, 1784			
†Maria I, Queen of Portugal (1734–1816). 1. $\frac{3}{4}$-face. 2. To right	J. FLAXMAN (1) Lochée (2)		Invoice E2–1339 1 June 1787 (1)	
Maria Leczinska, Queen of France (1703–1766). To left				
Mary I, Queen (1516–58). To left		Medal by Jacopo di Trezzo, 1555		
Matthews, John (1755–1826), physician and poet. To left				Doubtful identification
*Mecklenburgh-Strelitz, Prince Charles of (fl.1740–90), brother of Queen Charlotte. To left	J.C. LOCHEE, 1787		136–27207 8 November 1787; W/M 1460 2 April 1788	
†Meerman, Anna Cornelia Mollerus, Countess (1749–1821). To left	J. FLAXMAN, 1785		Invoice E2–1339 2 December 1785	
†Meerman, Johann, Count (1723–1815), author. To right	J. FLAXMAN, 1785		Invoice E2–1339 2 December 1785	
Mendelssohn, Moses (1729–86), philosopher. To left		Silver medal by A. Abrahamson	E25–18817 14 March 1778	
Middleton, Conyers (1683–1750), polemical writer and historian. To right		Medal by G.B. Pozzo, 1724	E25–18657 24 February 1776 W. Cox to T. Bentley	
†Mirabeau, Honoré Gabriel de Riqueti, comte de (1749–91). To right				Usually found in circular form with anthemion border matching those of other revolutionary heroes (see Bailly, Lafayette)
Moore, Dr John (1729–1802), physician. To left				Father of Sir John Moore. Probably a private commission

†Necker, Jacques (1732–1804), statesman. ¾-face		Both from medals	12–11263 23 December 1791 (Returns from Burley, Birmingham)	Two portraits: one commonly found in circular form with *fleur-de-lis* border
Noailles, Louis Marie de (1756–1804), general and politician. To right				
†Orléans, Louis-Philippe-Joseph, duc d' (Philippe Egalité) (1747–1793). 1. To right. 2. To left			LHP April 1788	Two portraits: the second commonly found in circular form with laurel border. Evidently produced too late for inclusion in 1788 Catalogue
Paul I and Natalia Alexierna Tsarevitch, late Paul I (1754–1801) and his first wife. Facing pair		Medal celebrating their marriage, by J.G. Jaeger, 1773		Produced separately and as facing pair on same ground
Penn, William (1644–1718), Governor of Pennsylvania. To right	Hackwood	Ivory carving by S. Bevan	E26–18929 9 October 1779	
Pole, Anne, Lady de la (*fl.*1770–90). To right	Lochée			
Poniatowski, Michel-Georges, Primate of Poland (1736–94)				
Raper, Matthew (1665–1745), silk trader. To right		Probably ivory carving by D. Le Marchand		Probably a private commission
Raper, Mrs Elizabeth (*fl.*1700), wife of Matthew Raper. To left		Probably ivory by Le Marchand		
Reynolds, Frances (1729–1807), sister of Sir Joshua. To right				Identification doubtful
Roupell, George (1726–94), Postmaster-General. To left			E26–18860 8 November 1778	

Seddon, John (1725–70), rector of Warrington Academy. To right				Identification doubtful
Smith, Adam (1723–90), political economist. To right	J. TASSIE			Signed and dated 1787 on truncation
Smith, John Christopher (1712–95), musician. To right				Sometimes erroneously catalogued as 'Bishop of St Asaph' (cf. Shipley)
Talleyrand Périgord, Charles Maurice de (1754–1838), statesman. To left				Known only in circular form, with anthemion border, matching those of other revolutionary heroes (cf. Bailly, Lafayette)
Temple, George (1750–1820), banker. To right	Hackwood	Wax by G. Leader, 1794		
Townley, Charles (1737–1805), art connoisseur. To left		Probably Tassie medallion, 1780		
Tromp, Cornelis (1629–91), admiral. $\frac{3}{4}$-face		Medal		
Tromp, Maarten Harpertszoon (1597–1653), admiral. $\frac{3}{4}$-face		Medal by O. Muller		
Victor Amadeus III, King of Sardinia (1726–96). To left	J. FLAXMAN, 1788		1–210 15 March 1788	Modelled in Italy at request of John Wedgwood
Vondel, Jost van den (1587–1679), poet and dramatist. $\frac{3}{4}$-face			E26–18889 8 May 1779; 44–28876 4 September 1781 (Veldhuysen to Wedgwood)	
†Voyez, Jean (c.1740–after 1790), modeller and sculptor. $\frac{3}{4}$-face	Voyez			
Walsingham, Sir William de Grey, first Baron (1719–81). To right				

501. Green jasper dip portrait medallion of Sir William Herschel. Oval height 4″ (10.2 cm). Mark: WEDGWOOD. c.1785–90. Wedgwood Museum

502. Green jasper dip portrait medallion of John Philip Kemble. Oval height 4½″ (11.4 cm). Mark: WEDGWOOD. c.1784–90. Wedgwood Museum

503. Blue jasper dip portrait medallion of Lafayette. Oval height 1⅞″ (4.8 cm). Mark: WEDGWOOD. c.1789–95. Author's collection

504. Pale-blue jasper dip portrait medallion of Prince Charles of Mecklenburgh-Strelitz. Oval height 3⅜″ (8.6 cm). Mark: WEDGWOOD. c.1787–90. Brooklyn Museum, Emily Winthrop Miles Collection

501

502

503

504

III: UNCATALOGUED PORTRAIT MEDALLIONS 1795–1967

This list is arranged alphabetically by subject. Since no catalogue of portrait medallions of this period has ever been issued, the principal sources of reference have been surviving moulds and known examples of finished medallions, with additional information from relevant manuscript letters and memoranda. During the late nineteenth and twentieth centuries it has been fairly common practice for the firm to make portraits to order, sometimes in very small quantities and of subjects whose names are no longer familiar. For this reason the list is probably incomplete.

Modellers' names in capitals are those for which satisfactory evidence is available. Those in lower-case letters are attributions on such grounds as style or circumstantial evidence.

Descriptions 'To left' or 'To right' refer to profiles facing to the viewer's left or right.

Portraits marked † are illustrated elsewhere in the text.

Unless otherwise specified, all manuscript references are to manuscripts deposited at Keele University.

A separate note referring to the medallions made for the Cameograph Company appears at the end of this Appendix. The relevant medallions are keyed §.

Description	Modeller and date	Reference
Albert I, King of the Belgians (1875–1934). To left	MARCEL GOUPY 1915	Inscribed mould
†Albert, Prince of Saxe-Coburg-Gotha (The Prince Consort) (1819–61). To right	J. A. HAMMERSLEY 1844	Inscribed mould
†Alexandra, Queen Consort of Edward VII (1844–1935). ¾-face	WATKIN 1901	Inscribed mould
Alice Victoria, Empress of Russia (1872–1918). To left		
Allardyce, Alexander (fl.1760–1800), member of parliament for Aberdeen. To right	JOHN DE VAERE 1798	Receipt 1–20 31 January 1798
†Anglesey, Henry William Paget, first Marquis (1768–1854), field-marshal. ¾-face	WILLIAM HACKWOOD c.1821	Signed. After engraving by J. Thompson, 1821
Beatty, David, first Earl (1871–1936), admiral. ¾-face		
Bismarck, Prince Otto Edward Leopold von (1815–98), Prussian statesman. To right	1896	Mould dated
Blücher, Gebhard Leberecht von (1742–1819), Prussian field-marshal. To left	c.1815	
Bright, H. M. (unidentified). To right		
Brougham and Vaux, Henry Peter, first Baron (1778–1868), Lord Chancellor. To right	JOHN HENNING 1813	3–2618 19 October 1813
Browning, Robert (1812–89). Poet	THOMAS WOOLNER 1856	W/M 1415 19 August 1866; 60–32834 7 March 1871
Brownsword, Henry (fl.1849–1903), modeller and painter at Etruria. To left		
Byerley, Thomas (1742–1810), Josiah Wedgwood's nephew. To left	WILLIAM THEED 1810	Inscribed mould
Byron, George Gordon, sixth Baron (1788–1824), poet. To left		
Cannero, Manuel (unidentified). To right		
Carlyle, Thomas (1795–1881), essayist and historian. To right	THOMAS WOOLNER 1855	W/M 1415 19 August 1866; 60–32834 7 March 1871
Caroline Amelia, Queen Consort of George IV (1768–1821). To left	1796	Mould inscribed '24th June 1796'. After drawing by Edmund Scott
Chamberlain, Joseph (1836–1914), statesman	1908	O.W. Price Book
Chaucer, Geoffrey (1340–1400), poet. To right	CHARLES TOFT c.1878	
Chodkiewicz, Jan Karol, Count (1560–1621), Polish general. Full-face	EDWARD J. KUNTZE 1869	Inscribed mould

367

†Christian IX, King of Denmark and Norway (1819–1906). To right	1897	O.W. Net Price Book, December 1897
Christian X, King of Denmark (1870–1947). To right		
Churchill, Sir Winston Leonard Spencer (1874–1965), statesman. To left	ARNOLD MACHIN 1945	
Clarke, Adam (1762–1832), Wesleyan minister. $\frac{3}{4}$-face	ENOCH WOOD c.1825	Two similar portraits, one signed 'E. WOOD'
Clemenceau, Georges (1841–1929), French statesman. $\frac{3}{4}$-face	JESSIE M. RIDING 1919	Inscribed mould
Czarniecki, Etienne (1599–1665), Polish general. $\frac{3}{4}$-face	EDWARD J. KUNTZE 1869	Inscribed mould
Danko, N. (unidentified). To left	1935	Inscribed mould
Darwin, Charles Robert (1809–82), naturalist. To left		
Dickens, Charles (1812–70), novelist. To left	A. H. ('BERT') BENTLEY c.1920	
†Duncan, Adam, Viscount (1731–1804), admiral. To left	JOHN DE VAERE 1798	Receipt 1–23, 24 December 1798
Edinburgh, Prince Philip, Duke of (b.1921). To right	ERIC OWEN 1953	
†Edward VII, King (1841–1910). (1) $\frac{3}{4}$-face, (2 & 3) to left	(1) WATKIN 1901 (2) HERBERT HAMPTON 1910 (3) HERBERT HAMPTON 1911	Inscribed mould· W/M 690 15 December 1910
Edward VIII, King (1894–1972). To left	Cameograph Co.§ c.1925	See note below
Elizabeth II, Queen (b.1926). To left	ERIC OWEN 1953	
Elizabeth, Queen Consort of George VI (b.1900) To left	Cameograph Co.§ c.1925	See note below
Foch, Ferdinand (1851–1929), French marshal. $\frac{3}{4}$-face	JESSIE M. RIDING	Signed on truncation
Franz Joseph I, Emperor of Austria (1830–1916). To right		
†Frederick William Charles I, King of Württemberg (1754–1816). To left	1797	Until 1971 wrongly recorded as Duke of Bridgewater
French, John, first Earl (1852–1925), field-marshal. To left		
George V, King (1865–1936). (1) To right, (2 & 3) to left	(1) HERBERT HAMPTON 1911 (2) HERBERT HAMPTON 1911 (3) Cameograph Co.§	W/M 690 15 December 1910. See note below
George VI, King (1895–1952). To right	Cameograph Co.§	See note below
George, Henry (1839–97), American economist. To left	1909	Dated mould
†Gladstone, William Ewart (1809–98), statesman. (1) To left, (2) $\frac{3}{4}$-face	CHARLES TOFT 1877	Godfrey Wedgwood Private Letter Book 1872–81
Grahame, James (1765–1811), Scottish author. To right	JOHN HENNING 1813	3–2618 19 October 1813
Haydn, Franz Josef (1732–1809), Austrian composer. To left	c.1810	
Hirzel, Hans Caspar (1746–1827), Swiss politician and administrator. To right		
Holland, Edward (unidentified). To left		
Holmes, Oliver Wendell (1809–94), American writer. $\frac{3}{4}$-face	1895	Dated mould
Hooker, Sir Joseph Dalton (1817–1911), botanist. To left		

Hooker, Sir William Jackson (1785–1865), botanist. To right	1867	'1843' Price Book
Horsley, George (unidentified). To left		Name inscribed on portrait
Howard, John (1726–90), prison reformer. To left	After T. Butler 1900	Cf. plaster in collection of Royal College of Physicians
†Howe, Richard, first Earl (1726–99), admiral. To right	JOHN DE VAERE 1798	Receipt 1–23 24 December 1798
Huth, C. F. (unidentified). To left	E. W. WYON 1892	Inscribed mould
Huth, Reginald (unidentified). To right	E. W. WYON	Inscribed mould
Jefferson, Thomas (1743–1826), third President of the United States. To left	ERIC OWEN 1951	
Joffre, Joseph Jacques Césaire (1852–1931), French general. To left	MARCEL GOUPY	Inscribed mould
†Jones, John Paul (1747–92), American naval commander. To right	1906 After medal by A. Dupré, 1779	O.W. Net Price Book, n.d. Cast for F. Rathbone, 1906 (each 7/-)
Kennedy, Jacqueline Lee Bouvier (b.1929). To left	ERIC OWEN 1962	
Kennedy, John Fitzgerald (1917–63), thirty-fifth President of the United States. To right	ERIC OWEN 1962	
Kitchener, Horatio Herbert, first Earl (1850–1916), field-marshal. To left	MARCEL GOUPY	Inscribed mould
Klaproth, Martin Heinrich (1743–1817), German chemist. To left		
Lane, Sir Hugh Percy (1875–1915), Irish art collector. To right	1888	Dated mould
Lincoln, Abraham (1809–65), sixteenth President of the United States. To left		
Lloyd George, David, first Earl (1863–1945). $\frac{3}{4}$-face	1919	Dated mould
Louis XVIII, King of France (1755–1824). To left		
Lyth, Thomas (1892–1965), Wedgwood Museum curator. To left	JESSE WILBRAHAM 1953	
McLeod, Sir Donald Friell (1810–72), Indian administrator. To right	A. B. WYON 1872	Signed and dated on truncation
Lady McLeod. To right	1872	
Mary, Queen Consort of George V (1867–1953). (1) To left, (2) to right	(1) HERBERT HAMPTON 1911 (2) Cameograph Co.§	Companion portraits to George V (1) and (3)
Mozart, Wolfgang Amadeus Chrysostom (1756–91), Austrian composer. To left	c.1810(?)	W/M 1287 n.d.
Napoleon I Bonaparte (1769–1821), French Emperor. (1) Classical bust to left, (2) to left	(1) From medal by Andrieu, c.1800	
Napoleon I and Empress Joséphine. Double portrait, profiles superimposed to left	From medal by Andrieu, c.1805	Portrait signed
†Nelson, Horatio, first Viscount (1758–1805), admiral. To left	JOHN DE VAERE 1798	Receipt 1–22 9 November 1798
Nicholas II, Emperor of Russia (1868–1918). To left		
Nicholas, Grand Duke (1856–1929), Russian general. To left		
Orlando, Vittorio Emmanuele (1860–1952), Italian statesman. $\frac{3}{4}$-face	1917	Dated mould
Palgrave, Sir Francis (1788–1861), historian. To left	THOMAS WOOLNER 1899	Inscribed mould
Peel, Sir Robert (1788–1850), statesman. $\frac{3}{4}$-face	c.1834	After the portrait by Sir Thomas Lawrence

Pitman, Sir Isaac (1813–97), inventor of shorthand system			
Pollock, Sir George (1786–1872), field-marshal. To left			
Roberts, Frederick Sleigh, first Earl (1832–1914), field-marshal. ¾-face			
Romilly, Sir Samuel (1757–1818), lawyer and law-reformer. To left	JOHN HENNING 1813	3–2618	19 October 1813
Roosevelt, Franklin Delano (1882–1945), thirty-second President of the United States. To right	ARNOLD MACHIN		
Rothschild, Emma Louisa, Baroness. To left	SIR J. E. BOEHM c.1885		
†St Vincent, Sir John Jervis, first Earl of (1735–1823), admiral. To right	JOHN DE VAERE 1798	Invoice 1–23	24 December 1798
Scott, Sir Walter (1771–1832), Scottish poet and novelist. To right	JOHN HENNING 1813	3–2618	19 October 1813
Stewart, Dugald (1753–1828), Scottish philosopher. To right	JOHN HENNING 1811 (supplied in 1813)	3–2618	19 October 1813. Portrait dated 181
Tennyson, Alfred, first Baron (1809–92), poet. To left	THOMAS WOOLNER 1866	W/M1415	19 August 1866
Victor Emmanuel III, King of Italy (1869–1947). To left	MARCEL GOUPY		
†Victoria, Alexandrina, Queen (1819–1901). (1) To left, wearing crown and Garter chain, (2) To left truncated at neck, (3) in widow's weeds	(1) c.1844 (2) J. A. HAMMERSLEY 1844 (3) c.1897	(2) Inscribed mould	
Washington, Martha (1732–1802). ¾-face	1903	Dated mould	
Wedgwood, Cecil (1863–1916). To right			
†Wedgwood, Doris Audrey (1898–1970). To right	1928	Medallion dated	
Wedgwood, Francis Hamilton (1867–1930). To right			
Wedgwood, Godfrey (1833–1905). To left			
Wedgwood, Hensleigh (b.1908)	JESSE WILBRAHAM		
Wedgwood, Josiah V (1899–1968). To left	ERIC OWEN and JESSE WILBRAHAM 1955		
Wedgwood, Phoebe (1893–1964). To left			
†Wellington, Arthur Wellesley, first Duke of (1769–1852), soldier and statesman. (1) To right, (2) full-face	(1) JOHN HENNING 1813 (2) After the portrait by H. P. Briggs 1837	3–2618	19 October 1813
Wilbraham, Jesse (1891–1963), modeller at Etruria and Barlaston. To left	Self-portrait 1953		
Wilhelmina, Queen of the Netherlands (1880–1962)	1898	Dated mould	
Wilson, Norman (1902–85), Wedgwood production director. To right	JESSE WILBRAHAM 1955		
Wilson, Thomas Woodrow (1856–1924), twenty-eighth President of the United States. ¾-face			
Wolseley, Garnet Joseph (1833–1913), field-marshal. To left			
Yale, Elihu (1649–1721), Benefactor. ¾-face	1898	Dated mould	
Zamojski, Jan (1541–1605), Polish grand chancellor. Full-face	E. KUNTZE 1869	Inscribed mould	

§The Cameograph Company of London specialised in the production of bas-reliefs and sculpture multiplied by the process of machine carving. Harry Barnard, who modelled fifty-four medallions and six busts for the Cameograph Company, described the process as 'wonderful . . . and quite satisfactory for a foundation, but in translating it into such a material as our Jasper it required much more work upon it, which was entrusted to me' (H. Barnard's unpublished 'Record', c.1931). Cameograph portrait medallions have a curiously flat appearance in comparison with those produced by traditional methods of modelling and casting.

Tablets, Plaques and Medallions 1769*–95

*Jasper from 1775

I

The information in the first column of this Appendix, including the original assignments of subjects to artists and modellers, is reprinted from the Wedgwood & Bentley Catalogues of 1773–9 and the Wedgwood Catalogue of 1787. No other previously published attributions have been repeated unless evidence has been found to substantiate them. The dates refer to the Catalogues in which the subjects are listed for the first time. Unless otherwise specified, all manuscript references are to manuscripts in the Wedgwood archives deposited at Keele University.

For subjects which have been discussed at greater length in the text, the principal manuscript references only have been quoted.

Subjects marked * are illustrated in this Appendix; those marked † are illustrated elsewhere in the text.

Modellers' names given in capitals are those for which satisfactory evidence is available. Those in lower-case letters are attributions on such grounds as style or circumstantial evidence. Hackwood's name in parentheses indicates work remodelled from original designs supplied by another artist.

Description	Modeller	Date	References	Remarks
1. *Birth of Bacchus* 6″ × 5″		1773		See also 118 and 206
2. *War of Jupiter and the Titans* Oval 6″ × 9″		1773		This, and the four following subjects,
3. *Destruction of Niobe's Children* Oval 6″ × 9″		1773		were copied or adapted from bas-reliefs by Guglielmo della Porta
†4. *Feast of the Gods* Oval 6″ × 9″		1773	LHP 3 March 1771	(d.1577), probably by way of plaster casts
5. *Marriage Feast of Perseus and Andromeda* Oval 6″ × 9″		1773		from bronze reliefs by Jakob Cornelisz Cobaert (d.1615)
6. *An Antique Boar Hunting* Oval 6″ × 9″		1773		
7. *Jupiter and Ganymede* Rectangular 3″ × 6″		1773		
8. *Apollo and Marsyas* Octagonal 3″ × 6″		1773	Invoice 1–56 [n.d.] 1769 (receipted 25 March	This, and the two following subjects,
9. *Apollo and Daphne* Octagonal 3″ × 6″		1773	1769)	were obtained as casts from Mrs Landré
10. *Apollo and Python* Octagonal 3″ × 6″		1773	As 8–9	
11. *Judgment of Midas* Octagonal 3″ × 6″		1773		
12. *Bacchanalian Triumph* Rectangular and oval 4″ × 6″		1773	Invoice 1–56 1769	Probably the 'Antique Bacchanalians' obtained from Mrs Landré for 7/6d

†13. *Bacchanalian Boys at Play* $6'' \times 8''$	1773		This, and the next, probably after
†14. *Silenus and Boys* $6'' \times 8''$	1773		Fiammingo, and among the pieces obtained from Mrs Landré in 1769
15. *Boys Dancing Round a Tree* Circular. Diameter $6''$	1773		
*†16. *Bacchus and Panther* Rectangular and oval $6'' \times 11''$ and sizes down to $5'' \times 6''$	1773	E25–18420 15 November 1772	
17. *A Head of Venus* Circular. Diameter $2''$	1773	(?) LHP 13 January 1771	This, and the next, are probably the 'heads from Mrs Laundre'
18. *A Head of Apollo* Oval $2'' \times 1\frac{1}{2}''$	1773		(*sic*) mentioned in January 1771
19. *Minerva* Oval $6'' \times 5''$	1773		
20. *Alexander* $2'' \times 1\frac{1}{2}''$	1773		
21. *Minerva* $2\frac{1}{2}'' \times 2''$	1773		
22. *Perseus* $4\frac{3}{4}'' \times 4''$	1773		
23. *Andromeda* $4\frac{3}{4}'' \times 4''$	1773		Pair to 22
24. *Young Hercules* $2\frac{3}{4}'' \times 2''$	1773		
25. *Young Hercules* $4\frac{1}{2}'' \times 3\frac{3}{4}''$	1773		
26. *Hercules and Omphale* $2'' \times 2\frac{1}{4}''$	1773		
27. *Cupid Shaving His Bow* $3'' \times 2\frac{1}{4}''$. 'From a picture of Correggio's in the Queen's house'. This subject made also in sizes down to $1\frac{1}{2}'' \times 1''$	1773	E25–18523 13 March 1774	The source painting, then attributed to Correggio, is now assigned to Parmigianino
28. *Sacrifice to Aesculapius* $4'' \times 3\frac{3}{8}''$	1773		
*29. *The Three Graces* $3'' \times 2\frac{1}{4}''$ and sizes down to $2'' \times 1\frac{1}{2}''$	1773	E25–18752 25 April 1777 (Jasper)	
†30. *Marriage of Cupid and Psyche* Flaxman $11\frac{1}{2}'' \times 16''$. 'Modelled from the celebrated gem in the duke of Marlborough's cabinet'. Also in sizes down to $1'' \times 2\frac{3}{4}''$, 'which last is a cast from the gem itself'	1773	LHP 13 January 1771; E25–18571 4 December 1774	A second source, a carved ivory, is mentioned in 1774. The finest model (Plate C20) is invariably assigned to John Flaxman, but no sound evidence has ever been quoted to substantiate the claim for Flaxman. The quality of the modelling, however, suggests his work (see notes to Plates 134–136)

31. *The Judgement of Paris* $2\frac{1}{2}'' \times 3''$	1773		See also 183
32. *Boys Playing With a Goat* $3\frac{3}{4}'' \times 4\frac{3}{4}''$ and sizes down to $2\frac{3}{4}'' \times 4''$	1773		Probably after François Duquesnoy (*Il Fiammingo*) (1594–1643)
33. *Cassandra* $7\frac{1}{4}'' \times 4\frac{1}{2}''$. 'A fine figure in high relief from a gem in the king of France's cabinet'	1773		This, and the next subject, have been attributed to John Bacon senior (Eliza Meteyard, *The Wedgwood Handbook*, London, 1875, p. 137, and others copying) but no evidence has been found to substantiate this.
34. *Diomedes Carrying Away the Palladium* $3'' \times 3''$	1773		
35. *Bacchanalian Boys* $3\frac{1}{2}'' \times 5''$	1777		Probably after Duquesnoy
36. *Bacchanalian Boys* $3\frac{1}{2}'' \times 5''$	1777		Probably after Duquesnoy
37. *A Bacchante and Children* $6'' \times 8''$	1773		
38. ⎫ *Fauns Representing Four* 39. ⎪ *Different Stages of Life* 40. ⎰ *From Youth to Old Age* 41. ⎭ $9'' \times 7''$	1773		
42. *Farnesian Hercules* $4'' \times 3''$	1773		
*43. *Omphale* $4'' \times 3''$	1773		
†44. *Apollo* $4'' \times 3''$	1773		
45. *Piping Faun* $4'' \times 3''$	1773		
*46. *Venus* $4'' \times 3''$	1773		
47. *Adonis* $4'' \times 3''$	1773		
48. *Ceres* $4'' \times 3''$	1773		
49. *Venus Belfesses (Callipygous)* $4'' \times 3''$	1773		See also 66
50. *Althaea, Mother of Meleager, Burning the Firebrand* $3\frac{1}{2}'' \times 2\frac{1}{2}''$	1773		
51–6. *Dancing Nymphs* Each $10'' \times 7\frac{3}{4}''$	1773	E25–18318 20 August 1770;	Nos. 51–65 (63 is omitted from the
†57–9. *Centaurs* Circular. Diameter $11\frac{1}{2}''$	1773	E25–18336 [?January] 1771;	Catalogues) are described as 'Figures
60. *Polyphemus* Circular. Diameter $11\frac{1}{2}''$	1773	E25–18478 July 1773;	from paintings in the ruins of Herculaneum;
†61. *Marsyas and Young Olympus* Circular. Diameter $11\frac{1}{2}''$	1773	E25–18481 20 July 1773;	the models brought over by the marquis of

Item		Year	Reference	Notes
62. *Papyrius and His Mother* Circular. Diameter $11\frac{1}{2}''$		1773	E26–18820 28 March 1778 (Jasper);	Lansdown'. In production by June 1769
†64. *A Bacchanalian Figure* Circular. Diameter $11\frac{1}{2}''$		1773	E25–18244 JW to Cox June 1769 (No. 61)	
†65. *Bacchanalian Figure* Circular. Diameter $11\frac{1}{2}''$		1773		
66. *Venus Belfesses (Callipygous)* $10\frac{1}{2}'' \times 7\frac{3}{4}''$		1773		
67. *Zeno* $10\frac{1}{2}'' \times 7\frac{3}{4}''$		1773		
68. *Cupid Reposing* $2\frac{1}{2}'' \times 3''$		1773		
†69. *Judgement of Hercules* $11'' \times 15''$. 'Modelled agreeably to lord Shaftesbury's idea of representing the subject'.		1773		
70. *Bacchanalian Triumph* 'long square tablet', $9'' \times 21''$		1773		This and the following subject were copied from two bas-reliefs by Clodion (Claude Michel, 1738–1814)
71. *Bacchanalian Sacrifice* 'long square tablet', $9'' \times 21''$		1773		
72. *Death of a Roman Warrior* 'long square tablet; from an ancient sarcophagus at Rome'. $11'' \times 20''$		1773	E25–18654 14 February 1776	
73. *A Lion* $3\frac{1}{2}'' \times 4\frac{1}{2}''$. 'From an antique'		1773		
74. *Perseus and Centaur* $3\frac{3}{4}'' \times 3''$		1773		
75. *Hercules and Theseus Supporting the World, or The Power of Union* $3\frac{1}{2}'' \times 2\frac{3}{4}''$		1773		
76. *Head of an Old Satyr* $6'' \times 4\frac{1}{2}''$. 'In a fine style, and highly finished'		1773		
†77. *Night* $7'' \times 5\frac{1}{2}''$		1773	E25–18276 16 December 1769;	77 and 79 are copied from an antique gem (Lionardo Agostini, *Gemmae et Sculpturae Antiquae*, 1685, Plate 116) and known also as *Venus and Cupid*, *Night shedding Poppies*, and *Ceres and Triptolemus* (1779 Catalogue). *Day* is attributed to John Bacon senior.
†78. *Day* $7'' \times 5\frac{1}{2}''$	Bacon	1773	E25–18278 28 December 1769;	
79. *Night* $20'' \times 14\frac{1}{2}''$		1773	E25–18641 6 January 1776 (White Jasper)	
80. *Day* $20'' \times 14\frac{1}{2}''$	Bacon	1773		
81. *Meleager and Atalanta Killing the Calydonian Boar* $6'' \times 7''$		1773		
82. *A Bull* $2\frac{1}{4}'' \times 3''$. 'Finely modelled from the antique'		1773		

83. *Jupiter and Semele* $3'' \times 2''$		1774		
*84. *Hunting* $5\frac{1}{2}'' \times 12''$		1774	E25–18523 13 March 1774	
*85. *Bringing Home the Game* $5\frac{1}{2}'' \times 12''$		1774	As 84	
86. *Music* $5\frac{1}{2}'' \times 12''$		1774	As 84	
87. *The Arts* $5\frac{1}{2}'' \times 12''$		1774	As 84	
88. *Fire* $13'' \times 10\frac{3}{4}''$. 'Emblematic representation'		1774	Invoice 1–114 from Hoskins & Grant 21 March 1774	This and the following three subjects are evidently the '4 Ovels of the Elements'
89. *Air* $13'' \times 10\frac{3}{4}''$		1774		supplied by Hoskins & Grant in March 1774
90. *Earth* $13'' \times 10\frac{3}{4}''$		1774		for £1 16s. 0d. the set
91. *Water* $13'' \times 10\frac{3}{4}''$		1774		
92.				This number is omitted from the Catalogues
93. *Lyre and Two Sphinxes* $10'' \times 22''$		1774	As 88	Supplied by Hoskins & Grant in March 1774 for 6/–
†94. *Large Head of Medusa* Circular. Diameter 5″. 'From an exquisite marble in the possession of Sir W. Hamilton'	Flaxman	1777	E25–18693 12 September 1776 E25–18719 25 November 1776	Usually attributed to Flaxman. Described also by Josiah as 'Gorgons head'
†95. *Medusa* Circular. Diameter 3″. Another model		1777		
96. *Medusa* $1\frac{1}{2}'' \times 2''$. Profile, 'with wings'		1777		
97. *Medusa* $1\frac{1}{2}'' \times 2''$. Another profile		1777		
*98. *Jupiter* Oval $8'' \times 6''$	(J. FLAXMAN)	1777	Invoice 1–204, March–April 1775, receipted by John Flaxman junior for his father	This subject, and the nineteen following, were supplied to Wedgwood by John Flaxman senior in 1775, the receipt being signed on his behalf by John Flaxman junior. All were 'Basso Releivo' [*sic*], and each (except the heads of Bacchus and Ariadne) was charged at 10/6d, the prices indicating that all were casts rather than original models in wax. Which, if any, of these models may be attributed to the younger Flaxman is problematic.

505

506

508

510

507

509

511

505. Bacchus and Panther. *Solid pale-blue and white jasper. Oval* $6\frac{15}{16}'' \times 9''$ *(17.6 × 22.8 cm). Mark:* WEDGWOOD. c.1785–90. Dwight & Lucille Beeson Collection, Birmingham Museum, Alabama

506. The Three Graces. *Black basaltes. Oval height 9'' (23.0 cm). Mark:* WEDGWOOD J. c.1880. Christie's, New York

507. Omphale. *Dark-blue jasper dip. Oval height* $3\frac{3}{8}''$ *(8.5 cm). Mark:* WEDGWOOD & BENTLEY. 1776–80. Dwight & Lucille Beeson Collection, Birmingham Museum, Alabama

508. Venus. *Blue jasper dip. Oval height* $3\frac{3}{8}''$ *(8.5 cm). Mark:* WEDGWOOD c.1785. Dwight & Lucille Beeson Collection, Birmingham Museum, Alabama

509. Hunting. *Solid pale-blue and white jasper. Diameter 5'' (12.5 cm). Mark:* WEDGWOOD J. c.1875.

510. Bringing Home the Game. *Description as 509.*

511. Jupiter. *Solid pale-blue and white jasper. Oval height* $7\frac{7}{16}''$ *(20.0 cm). Mark:* Wedgwood & Bentley. 1776–80. All Dwight & Lucille Beeson Collection, Birmingham Museum, Alabama

*99. *Juno* Oval 8″ × 6″			As 98	
†100. *Apollo* Oval 8″ × 6″			As 98	
101. *A Muse* Oval 8″ × 6″ (probably the subject invoiced as 'Euterpe')			As 98	
102. *Contemplative Muse* Oval 8″ × 6″ (probably the subject invoiced as 'Sappho')			As 98	
103. *Hercules Strangling the Lion* Oval 8″ × 6″			As 98	
*104. *Hercules Binding Cerberus* Oval 8″ × 6″			As 98	
105. *Meleager* Oval 8″ × 6″ (probably the subject invoiced as 'Hercules and the Boar')		1777	As 98	
106. *Justice* 7″ × 5½″		1777	As 98	
*107. *Minerva* 7″ × 5½″		1777	As 98	
108. *Hope* 7″ × 5½″		1777	As 98	
109. *Melpomene* 8″ × 6″		1777	As 98	For discussion of Flaxman's *Muses* see pp. 141–3
110. *Comedy (Thalia)* 8″ × 6″		1777	As 98	
111. *Dancing Nymph* 8″ × 6″		1777	As 98	
112. *Head of Bacchus* 8″ × 6″		1777	As 98	
113. *Head of Ariadne* 8″ × 6″		1777	As 98	
114. *Spring* (Head) 10″ × 8″		1777	Ms. 1–204 25 March 1775– 19 June 1775	The first of four 'Bass Releivos of the Seasons' invoiced by Flaxman at 2 guineas the set
†115. *Summer* (Head) 10″ × 8″		1777	As 114	
116. *Autumn* (Head) 10″ × 8″		1777	As 114	
117. *Winter* (Head) 10″ × 8″		1777	As 114	
†118. *Birth of Bacchus* 5¾″ × 7½″. 'From the antique'	W. HACKWOOD	1777	E25–18641 6 January 1776	Priced at 36/– (E25–18660 10 March 1776)
119. *Isis* (Head) 3″ × 2½″		1777		
120. *Ariadne* (Head) 2¾″ × 1¾″		1777		This and the next are smaller versions of 113 and 112
121. *Bacchus* (Head) 2¾″ × 1¾″		1777		
*122. *Pan* (Head) 3″ × 2⅜″		1777		See Plates 515–6

*123. *Syrinx* (Head) $3'' \times 2\frac{3}{8}''$		1777		
124. *Perseus and Andromeda* $6'' \times 5''$		1777		
125. *Indian Bacchus* 'companion to No. 76'		1777		
126–130. *Five Bacchanalian Figures* $6'' \times 4''$. 'From an antique vase'	Flaxman	1777	E25–18617 August 1775. 1–56 21 January 1769, invoice from Mrs Landré	Probably figures from the 'Borghese' vase, and modelled or cast from a copy in the collection of George Grenville (later second Earl Temple and first Marquis of Buckingham) at Stowe
131. *Lion and Two Boys* or *The Force of Love* $5\frac{1}{2}'' \times 7\frac{1}{4}''$		1777		
132. *Lion and Three Boys* or *The Force of Love* $3\frac{3}{4}'' \times 5''$		1777		
133. *A Mask* Circular. Diameter $2\frac{1}{2}''$		1777		
134. *A Mask* Circular. Diameter $2\frac{1}{2}''$		1777		
135. *Cupid and Hymen* $3\frac{1}{4}'' \times 5''$		1777		
136. *Cupid Inflaming the Mind* $3\frac{1}{4}'' \times 5''$		1777		
137. *A Philosopher Reading on the* *Immortality of the Soul* $3\frac{1}{4}'' \times 2\frac{1}{4}''$		1777		
138. *Dead Jesus, With the Virgin* *and Boys* $2\frac{1}{2}'' \times 4\frac{1}{2}''$		1777		
139. *Pan Reposing With Young* *Satyrs* $6'' \times 8''$		1777		
140. *Fauns Sacrificing* $8\frac{1}{2}'' \times 15''$		1777		
*141. *Aesculapius* $4'' \times 3\frac{1}{4}''$		1777		
*142. *Hygeia* $4'' \times 3\frac{1}{4}''$		1777		
143. *A Vestal* $4'' \times 5''$		1777		
†144. *Artemisia* $4'' \times 5''$		1777		
145. *Cupid on a Lion* or *The Power of Love* $4\frac{1}{8}'' \times 3\frac{1}{4}''$		1777		
146. *Indian Bacchus* $4'' \times 5''$		1777		
147. *Roman Matron* $4'' \times 3\frac{1}{4}''$		1777		
148. *Sophonisba* $4'' \times 3\frac{1}{4}''$		1777		

149. *Hercules* $4'' \times 3\frac{1}{4}''$		1777		
150. *A Piping Faun* $4'' \times 3\frac{1}{4}''$	Flaxman	1777	E25–18617 August 1775	One of the figures from the 'Borghese' vase. See 126–30
151. *Abundantia* $4'' \times 3\frac{1}{4}''$		1777		
152. *Medea Rejuvenating Jason's Father* $4'' \times 3\frac{1}{4}''$		1777		
153. *Bacchanalian Triumph* $7\frac{1}{2}'' \times 9\frac{3}{4}''$	Flaxman	1777	E25–18617 August 1775	Figures from the 'Borghese' vase as a tablet
154. *An Antique Male Figure, Holding a Seal Upon His Lips, With a Greyhound* Height $9''$		1777	E25–18681 July 1776 (list); E25–18675	This, and the following thirty-three subjects, were moulded by William Bedson from Sir Robert Newdigate's collection of antique marbles and plaster casts at Arbury Hall, Warwickshire, in June 1776. The quoted comments below are from Josiah's list of July 1776
155. *Hebe and the Eagle* $7'' \times 4\frac{1}{2}''$		1777	19 June 1776; E25–18676 20 June 1776	
156. *Venus Belfesses* (Callipygous)* Height $7''$		1777		
†157. *Hercules Farnese* Height $7\frac{1}{4}''$		1777		Arbury list No. 4
†158. *Sacrificing Figure* Height $7''$		1777		Arbury list No. 5 (?). 'A male figure wearing only a cloak over the shoulder'
159. *Vestal* Height $4''$		1777		Arbury list No. 6
160. *Juno* $4\frac{1}{4}'' \times 4\frac{1}{2}''$		1777		Arbury list No. 7
161. *Euterpe* $4\frac{1}{4}'' \times 4\frac{1}{2}''$		1777		Arbury list No. 8
*162. *Female Figure and Urn* Height $4\frac{1}{2}''$		1777		'A Female Cloathed – leaning with her head to an Urn, & imbracing it with both her hands. The Vase ornamented with a Garland, & stands upon a Pillar. . . . A Modern Figure'
†163. *Fame &c.* $4\frac{1}{4}'' \times 4\frac{1}{2}''$		1777		'A Winged Figure (Fame or Victory) Writing upon an Oval Tablet, or Shield, which is supported by a pillar upon which is an Anchor, & with her foot upon a Turband'

* Either from delicacy or from ignorance of the meaning, Josiah often wrote this as 'Bellface' (see, for example, E25–18681 July 1776). Subjects numbered 156–60 were omitted from the 1787 Catalogue.

512. Juno. *Solid pale-blue and white jasper.
Oval height* $7\frac{7}{16}''$ *(20.0 cm). Mark:*
Wedgwood & Bentley. *1776–80.*

513. Hercules Binding Cerberus. *Solid
pale-blue and white jasper. Oval height* $7\frac{3}{8}''$
(18.6 cm). Mark: WEDGWOOD & BENTLEY.
1776–80.

514. Minerva. *Solid blue and white jasper.
Oval height* $6\frac{1}{2}''$ *(16.5 cm). Mark:*
WEDGWOOD & BENTLEY. *1776–80.*
All Dwight & Lucille Beeson Collection,
Birmingham Museum, Alabama

515. Pan. *Pale-blue and white jasper with
darker-blue dip. Oval height* $3''$ *(7.6 cm).*

Unmarked. Wedgwood, 1778–80. Holburne of
Menstrie Museum, Bath

516. Pan and Syrinx. *Grey-blue jasper
with pale-blue jasper dip. Oval* $4\frac{3}{8}'' \times 5\frac{3}{8}''$
(11 × 13.6 cm). Mark: WEDGWOOD &
BENTLEY. *The two heads were catalogued
singly (nos. 122 and 123) but both were probably
copied from Volume I, Plate 49 of B. de
Montfaucon's* L'Antiquité expliquée et
représentée en figures, *1719.* Dr & Mrs
Alvin M. Kanter Collection

517. Cupid Inflaming the Mind. *Solid
grey-blue jasper with darker-blue jasper dip.
Oval height* $5\frac{1}{8}''$ *(13 cm). Mark:*
WEDGWOOD & BENTLEY. *1778–80.*

518. Aesculapius. *Solid pale-blue and white
jasper. Oval height* $3\frac{5}{16}''$ *(8.3 cm). Mark:*
Wedgwood & Bentley. *1776–80.*

519. Hygeia. *Solid grey-blue and white
jasper. Oval height* $3\frac{5}{16}''$ *(8.3 cm). Unmarked.
Wedgwood, 1776–80.* All Dwight & Lucille
Beeson Collection, Birmingham Museum
of Art, Alabama

520. Female Figure and Urn. *Blue jasper
dip. Oval height* $4\frac{1}{2}''$ *(11.4 cm). Mark:*
WEDGWOOD. *c.1785. Sometimes incorrectly
catalogued as 'Andromache' (Cf. Plate 1,231).*
Wedgwood Museum

*164. *A Conquered Province* $11'' \times 7''$, and sizes down to $2\frac{3}{4}'' \times 2\frac{1}{8}''$	1777	1–49 Invoice from P. Stephan	This subject appears on the Arbury Hall list, but it was also modelled in wax by Pierre Stephan in 1774. The Newdigate model is described as 'High relief', $8'' \times 7''$
165. *Flora* (Head) $9'' \times 8''$	1777		Arbury list No. 12
166. *Sleeping Venus* $4'' \times 11''$. 'Clothed'	1777		Arbury list No. 13
167. *A Priestess* Height $6\frac{3}{4}''$	1777		'Female Figure, Cloathed' Arbury list No. 14
168. *Venus and Cupid* $5'' \times 4''$	1777		Arbury list No. 15
169. *Diomede Carrying off the Palladium* $3\frac{1}{2}'' \times 2\frac{7}{8}''$	1777		Arbury list No. 16
170. *Triumph of Ariadne* $10\frac{1}{2}'' \times 14\frac{1}{4}''$. 'With choral figures'	1777		'Ariadne drawn by two panthers, with Pan &c'. Arbury list No. 17
171. *A Sacrifice to Peace* $3\frac{3}{4}'' \times 2\frac{3}{4}''$	1777		Arbury list No. 18 [?] Much reduced
172. *Group of Four Female Figures* $9'' \times 10''$	1777		Arbury list No. 19
173. *A Sacrifice* $10'' \times 14''$	1777		Arbury list No. 20
174. *A Bacchanalian Piece* $8'' \times 10\frac{1}{2}''$	1777		Arbury list No. 21
175. 176. 177. 178. *Four Bas-Reliefs by Giovanni da Bologna* Each $3'' \times 4\frac{1}{2}''$	1777		'4 Bassreliefs from the Cabinet presented by John of Bolognio to . . .[?] one of which is the presenting of the Cabinet – The rest are Modern Figures & modern stories'. Arbury list Nos. 22–5
179. 180. *Two Bas-reliefs by Giovanni da Bologna* Each $2\frac{1}{8}'' \times 5''$	1777		'From the same Cabinet – Modern Figures'. Arbury list Nos. 26–7
181. *Winged Cupid Upon a Swan* $2\frac{3}{4}'' \times 2\frac{1}{2}''$. 'From a gem'	1777		'Winged Cupid riding upon a Swan'. Arbury list No. 28
182. *Winged Cupid Flying Away with a Swan* $2\frac{3}{4}'' \times 2\frac{1}{2}''$. 'From a gem'	1777		'Winged Cupid Flying away with a Swan, or rather a *Goose*'. Arbury No. 29
183. *Judgment of Paris* $5\frac{1}{2}'' \times 6''$	1777		This, and the four following subjects, are evidently the previously unidentified Arbury list Nos. 30–4, listed by Josiah as '5 Pieces of
184. *Vulcan With Mars and Venus in the Net* $5\frac{1}{2}'' \times 6''$	1777		

185. *Rape of Helen* $5\frac{1}{2}'' \times 6''$		1777		John of Bologni's – Classic stories in the
186. *Death of Adonis* $5\frac{1}{2}'' \times 6''$		1777		Stile of our Feast of the Gods &c. but not so good for our purposes'.
187. *Bathing Nymphs* $5\frac{1}{2}'' \times 6''$		1777		Arbury list No. 34
188. *Goat and Boys* $3\frac{3}{4}'' \times 5''$		1777		
189. *Triumph of Silenus* $4\frac{1}{2}'' \times 7\frac{1}{2}''$. 'From a gem'		1777		
190. *Triumph of Bacchanalian Boys* $1\frac{1}{2}'' \times 2''$		1777		
191. ⎫ *Processions of Little Boys* &c. 192. ⎭ Each $2'' \times 6''$		1777		
193. *Four Boys at Play* $3\frac{3}{4}'' \times 5''$		1777		
194. *Three Boys at Play* $3\frac{3}{4}'' \times 5''$		1777		
†195. *Panther and Bacchanalian Boys* $7\frac{1}{2}'' \times 10''$		1777		Sometimes misdescribed as *Romulus and Remus*
*†196. *Sacrifice to Hymen* to match No. 30, different sizes	Flaxman	1777		
*197. *Andromache* Circular. Diameter $8\frac{1}{2}''$	J. Bacon Senior	1779	E25–18762 5 June 1777	
198. *A Conquered Province* Circular. Diameter $8\frac{1}{2}''$	J. Bacon Senior	1779	as 197	
†199. *An Offering to Flora* $7\frac{1}{2}'' \times 17''$ and $8\frac{1}{4}'' \times 19''$		1779	E25–18847 n.d. [1778]	As *Sacrifice to Flora*, this was bought by Sir Lawrence Dundas, and was the largest then made in jasper
†200. *Sacrifice to Bacchus* $8\frac{1}{4}'' \times 19''$ and $9\frac{1}{2}'' \times 22''$		1779		
†201. *Triumph of Bacchus* $6\frac{1}{2}'' \times 14''$ and $7\frac{1}{2}'' \times 10''$	W. Hackwood	1779	E25–18641 6 January 1776; E25–18655 21 February 1776	See 118
†202. *Apotheosis of Homer* $7\frac{1}{2}'' \times 14''$ and smaller sizes	J. Flaxman	1779		See pp. 135–6 and references quoted
†203. *The Nine Muses* $8'' \times 25''$; with festoons or garlands $10'' \times 25''$	Flaxman	1779		See pp. 141–3 and references quoted
†204. *The Muses With Apollo* $6'' \times 18''$. In two pieces, for friezes to chimney-pieces with No. 202 for the tablet	Flaxman	1779		As 203
†205. *Dancing Hours* $6'' \times 18''$ or $5\frac{1}{4}'' \times 14\frac{3}{4}''$; with festoons or garlands $10'' \times 25''$	Flaxman	1779		See pp. 137–8 and references quoted
†206. *Birth of Bacchus* $11'' \times 23''$. From Michelangelo's seal	W. Hackwood	1779	39–28408 Commonplace Book p.118 (1779)	The original gem (carnelian) in the cabinet of the King of France reputedly belonged to Michelangelo

*207. *Triumph of Love* $6\frac{1}{4}'' \times 11''$		1779	
†208. *Sacrifice to Love* $9\frac{1}{2}'' \times 21''$ or $10\frac{1}{2}'' \times 25''$		1779	
209. *Triumph of Venus* $8'' \times 17''$ or $9'' \times 20''$		1779	
210. *Hero and Leander* $17'' \times 8''$ or $20'' \times 9''$		1779	
211. *Priam Begging the Body of Hector from Achilles* $14'' \times 11\frac{1}{2}''$ or $17\frac{1}{2}'' \times 13''$		1779	
212. *Triumph of Bacchus and Ariadne* $9\frac{1}{2}'' \times 23''$ or $10\frac{3}{4}'' \times 26''$		1779	
213. *Boys and Goat, Bacchanalians* $7'' \times 11\frac{1}{2}''$ or $9'' \times 12\frac{3}{4}''$		1779	
214–223. *The Nine Muses and Apollo* in separate pieces $8'' \times 5\frac{1}{2}''$ or $3\frac{1}{2}'' \times 2\frac{1}{2}''$	Flaxman	1779	See pp. 141–3 and references quoted. Dimensions reversed in Wedgwood Catalogues
224. *Young Hercules* $4'' \times 6\frac{1}{4}''$		1779	
†225. *Ganymede and the Eagle* $5'' \times 6\frac{1}{4}''$		1779 E25–18790 3 November 1777; E25–18822 4 April 1778	
226. *Meleager and Atalanta Killing the Calydonian Boar* $8'' \times 11\frac{1}{4}''$ or $6\frac{1}{4}'' \times 15''$		1779	
227. *Tragedy, Comedy and Apollo* $6'' \times 9\frac{1}{2}''$	Flaxman	1779	Melpomene and Thalia from the set of the nine Muses
228. *A Horse* $4\frac{1}{2}'' \times 5\frac{3}{4}''$		1779 1–56 Invoice from Mrs Landré undated	Perhaps the model supplied by Mrs Landré
*229. *Bacchus With an Urn and Grapes* $3\frac{3}{4}'' \times 2\frac{1}{2}''$		1779	
230. *Boys at Play* $2\frac{3}{4}'' \times 1\frac{3}{4}''$		1779	
†231. †232. †233. †234. *The Four Seasons* in separate pieces $3\frac{3}{4}'' \times 4''$ or $1\frac{1}{2}'' \times 2''$		1779	Usually attributed to Flaxman in error for Nos. 114–17 (e.g. Bruce Tattersall, 'Flaxman and Wedgwood', in David Bindman (ed.), *John Flaxman RA*, London, 1979, No. 23). The Flaxman 'Seasons' are specifically described by Wedgwood as 'Heads'

521

522

523

524

525

526A

526B

526C

526D

521. A Conquered Province. *Plaster block mould. Height 12⅜″ (31.3 cm). Unmarked.* Wedgwood Museum

522. Andromache. *Plaster block mould. Height 12″ (30.4 cm). Unmarked.* Wedgwood Museum

523. Terpsichore. *Black-painted plaster. Oval height 8¼″ (21.0 cm). Unmarked. From the model by John*

Flaxman junior (see Plates 138 and 139). Wedgwood Museum

524. Triumph of Love. *Solid pale-blue and white jasper. 9″ × 7″ (22.7 × 17.8 cm). Mark:* WEDGWOOD & BENTLEY. 1777–80. *This representation of* Omnia vincit Amor, *showing Cupid subduing Pan, has been variously catalogued as 'Faun and Cupid', 'Autumn', etc.* Buten Museum

525. Bacchus with an Urn and Grapes. *Solid pale-blue and white jasper. Oval height 3″ (7.6 cm). Mark:* WEDGWOOD. *c.1785.* Wedgwood Museum

526. The Four Seasons. *Black-painted plaster. Ovals height 5¾″ (14.6 cm). Unmarked.* Wedgwood Museum

†235. *The Frightened Horse* $11\frac{1}{4}'' \times 17\frac{1}{2}''$. 'From Mr. Stubbs's celebrated picture, and modelled by himself'	G. Stubbs	1787	LHP 13 August 1780; LHP 21 August 1780	See pp. 143–4 and references quoted. Modelled in August 1780
†236. *The Fall of Phaeton* $12'' \times 21\frac{1}{2}''$	G. Stubbs	1787	LHP 28 October 1780; LHP 12 November 1780	See pp. 143–4 and references quoted. Modelled in October–November 1780
†237. *A Roman Procession* $9\frac{1}{2}'' \times 21''$		1787		
†238. *An Offering to Peace* $6\frac{1}{2}'' \times 11\frac{1}{2}''$. 'From a design of lady Templetoun's' or 'smaller size'	Lady Templetown (Hackwood)	1787	E26–1958 27 June 1783; W/M 1508 23 July 1785 Josiah to Fox	See pp. 156–7.
239.				
†240. *Friendship Consoling Affliction* $7'' \times 8\frac{3}{4}''$ and sizes down to $3'' \times 4''$	Lady Templetown (Hackwood)	1787	As for 238	
†241. *Group of Three Boys* $5\frac{1}{2}'' \times 4\frac{1}{2}''$. 'From designs of lady Diana Beauclerk's'	Lady Diana Beauclerk	1787	W/M 1508 23 July 1785 Josiah to Fox; 2–1360 21 September 1789 (Hackwood account)	See pp. 157–9. 'Repaired' by Hackwood, 1789
†242. *Group of Two Boys* $5\frac{1}{2}'' \times 4\frac{1}{2}''$ and sizes down to $3\frac{1}{2}'' \times 2\frac{3}{4}''$	Lady Diana Beauclerk	1787	As for 241	
†243. *Four Boys Single* $4\frac{1}{2}'' \times 3\frac{3}{4}''$ and sizes down to $3'' \times 2\frac{1}{4}''$	Lady Diana Beauclerk	1787	As for 241	
†244. *Bacchanalian Tablet* $26'' \times 5\frac{1}{2}''$. 'Of the six preceding articles, under arbours with panthers' skins in festoons &c'	Lady Diana Beauclerk	1787		As for 241. The grouping was varied, and the three groups 241–3 were arranged also in two tablets.
245. *Venus in Her Car Drawn By Swans, With Attendant Cupids* $4\frac{1}{4}'' \times 9''$. 'From Le Brun'		1787		From a design by Charles Le Brun (1629–90)
246. *Cupid Watering the Swans* $4\frac{1}{4}'' \times 9''$		1787		After Le Brun. Pair to 245
247. *Domestic Employment* $3\frac{1}{2}'' \times 4\frac{1}{4}''$ and sizes down to $1\frac{1}{2}'' \times 2''$. 'From a design of Miss Crew's'	Emma Crewe	1787		
†248. *Domestic Employment* $4\frac{1}{2}'' \times 5\frac{3}{4}''$ and sizes down to $2\frac{1}{2}'' \times 3''$. 'From lady Templetoun'	Lady Templetown (Hackwood)	1787		As for 238. This, and the five following numbers (eight subjects in total), are all assigned to Lady Templetown by Josiah in the 1787 Catalogue
249. *Family School, and Companion Piece* (untitled) $4\frac{1}{2}'' \times 5\frac{3}{4}''$ and sizes down to $2'' \times 3\frac{1}{4}''$	Lady Templetown (Hackwood)	1787		For 'Companion Pieces' to 249–50 see Appendix J:II

†250. *Study, and Companion Piece* (untitled) $3'' \times 3\frac{3}{4}''$ and sizes down to $1\frac{3}{4}'' \times 2\frac{1}{4}''$	Lady TEMPLETOWN (Hackwood)	1787		
*251. *Maria* *The Bourbonnais Shepherd* Pair. Each $3\frac{3}{4}'' \times 3''$ and sizes down to $2\frac{1}{4}'' \times 1\frac{3}{4}''$	Lady TEMPLETOWN (Hackwood)	1787		Subjects from Sterne's *Sentimental Journey* published in 1768. See p.156. Dimensions reversed in Wedgwood Catalogues
252. *Genii* $3'' \times 7''$ ('measured diagonally') and sizes down to $1\frac{3}{4}'' \times 3\frac{3}{4}''$	Lady TEMPLETOWN (Hackwood)	1787		
253. Companion piece to 252 (untitled) $1\frac{3}{4}'' \times 3\frac{3}{4}''$	Lady TEMPLETOWN (Hackwood)	1787		See Appendix J:II
†254. *Infant Academy* † *Music* Pair. 'Different sizes from' $5'' \times 6\frac{1}{4}''$ to $2\frac{1}{2}'' \times 3\frac{1}{4}''$	Hackwood W. HACKWOOD	1787	Invoice L2–1354 20 October 1785	The first 'from a picture by Sir Joshua Reynolds'. The second modelled in wax by Hackwood
†255. *Blindman's Buff*, 'a group of boys' $5\frac{1}{2}'' \times 13''$ and sizes down to $3'' \times 9''$	J. FLAXMAN	1787	2–1335 28 October 1782 Flaxman to Wedgwood; ?Invoice 2–1339 28 March 1784 (wax)	Designed with *Game of Marbles* and *Triumph of Cupid* (in two pieces) as groups 'to decorate the sides of teapots', but *Blindman's Buff* only is listed in the 1787 Catalogue
†256. *Commercial Treaty with France* $11'' \times 9''$	J. FLAXMAN	1787	2–30193 23 December 1786 Josiah to Flaxman	This and the following subject were modelled by Flaxman in 1786.
†257. *Commercial Treaty With France* $11'' \times 9''$	J. FLAXMAN	1787	Flaxman	See pp. 161–4 and references quoted
258. *Coriolanus. With His Wife and Mother Persuading Him to Return* (sic) *to Rome* $6'' \times 9\frac{3}{4}''$	J. FLAXMAN	1787	Invoice 2–1339 12 December 1784 (wax); E2–30191 20 October 1785	Both Flaxman and Josiah seem to have been unfamiliar with the history of Coriolanus, who was persuaded by Volumnia and Veturia to spare Rome, not to return to it
*259. *Sacrifice to Hymen* *Sacrifice to Concordia* Pair. Circular. Diameter $10''$		1787		
260. *Offering to Love* *Conjugal Fidelity* Pair. $4\frac{1}{2}'' \times 5\frac{3}{4}''$ or circular, diameter $4''$		1787		
261. *The River Thames* *Isis* Pair. Sizes from $2\frac{3}{4}'' \times 3\frac{1}{2}''$ to $2'' \times 3''$		1787		

262. *Jupiter, Eagle and Ganymede* $3\frac{1}{2}'' \times 2\frac{3}{4}''$		1787		
263. *Triumph of Cybele* $3\frac{1}{4}'' \times 6\frac{1}{2}''$		1787		
264. *Hymen* $5'' \times 3\frac{3}{4}''$		1787		
†265. *Apotheosis of Homer* $7\frac{1}{2}'' \times 15\frac{1}{2}''$	J. FLAXMAN	1787		See pp. 135–6 and references quoted
266. *Apotheosis of Virgil* $7\frac{1}{2}'' \times 15\frac{1}{2}''$. Pair to 265	Flaxman	1787		See p. 136
*267. *Cupid Sharpening His Arrows* Circular. Diameter 5″		1787		
*268. *Cupid Stringing His Bow* Circular. Diameter 5″. Pair to 267		1787		
*269. *The Graces Erecting the Statue of Cupid* $10\frac{3}{4}'' \times 9''$		1787		
†270. *The Young Seamstress* 'From a design of Miss Crew's' and Companion Piece (untitled) $4'' \times 2\frac{1}{2}''$ and sizes down to $2\frac{1}{4}'' \times 1\frac{1}{4}''$	EMMA CREWE	1787		See p. 157
†271. *Sportive Love* $4'' \times 3\frac{1}{4}''$ and sizes down to $2\frac{3}{4} \times 2\frac{1}{4}''$. 'From lady Templetoun'	Lady TEMPLETOWN (Hackwood)	1787		This and the two following subjects are assigned to Lady Templetown in the 1787 Catalogue
†272. *Charlotte at the Tomb of Werther* $5'' \times 4''$ and sizes down to $2\frac{3}{4}'' \times 2\frac{1}{4}''$	Lady TEMPLETOWN (Hackwood)	1787		
273. *Contemplation* and Companion Piece (untitled) $4'' \times 3\frac{1}{4}''$	Lady TEMPLETOWN (Hackwood)	1787		See Appendix J : II
274. *Diana Visiting Endymion* $8\frac{1}{2}'' \times 27\frac{1}{2}''$. 'From the celebrated bas-relief in the Capitol at Rome'		1787		
275. *Hercules in the Garden of the Hesperides* $5\frac{1}{2}'' \times 17''$. 'From a beautiful Etruscan vase in the collection of Sir William Hamilton, now in the British Museum'	J. FLAXMAN	1787	2–30191 20 October 1785. Flaxman to Wedgwood, price £23	See pp. 136–7 and references quoted

527A

527B

527A

527B

528

529

530

527A. Sacrifice to Hymen *and* Sacrifice to Concordia. *Black-painted plaster. Diameter 14″ (35.5 cm). Unmarked. c.1785* Wedgwood Museum

527B. Sacrifice to Concordia *and* Sacrifice to Hymen. *Black basaltes. Diameter 10¼″ (26.0 cm). Mark :* WEDGWOOD. *c.1787.* Christie's, New York

528. Cupid sharpening his Arrows. *Plaster. Diameter 5¾″ (14.6 cm). Unmarked.* Wedgwood Museum

529. Cupid stringing his Bow. *Plaster. Diameter 5¾″ (14.6 cm). Unmarked.* Wedgwood Museum

530. Endymion sleeping on the Rock Latmos. *Solid grey–blue and white jasper. 13⅜″ × 10″ 34.0 × 25.4 cm) Mark :* WEDGWOOD ENDYMION on the ROCK LATMOS BB 46 1919. *Modern replica by 'Bert' Bentley, 1919.* Mr & Mrs David Zeitlin Collection

II

Four subjects, unnamed in the 1787 Catalogue, are shown in the list of Class XII bas-reliefs in the Oven Book (also a Price Book) Ms. No. 54–30020:

Juvenile Feast 220
Rural Employment 221
Love Consoled by Friendship 222 (cf. No. 240)
Juvenile Conversation 223

These numbers evidently do not refer to those in the 1787 Catalogue (they were perhaps early mould numbers), but the subjects may be identified with the four untitled 'companion pieces' by Lady Templetown catalogued as numbers 249, 250, 253 and 273.

The following bas-relief subjects were modelled in Italy between 1788 and 1790. Not all of them are known to have been reproduced in the form of jasper or basaltes tablets or medallions, and none is listed in Wedgwood's Catalogues. The reference numbers, and the greater part of the information concerning these subjects, have been taken from the manuscript 'Account of the Letters from and to Mr Angelo Dalmazzoni at Rome', 1788–90 (W/M 1526). The sizes listed have been noted from surviving examples in jasper. See also pp. 141–5.

4. *Priam Kneeling Before Achilles Begging the Body of His Son Hector.* Modelled in wax by Camillo Pacetti, 1788. $6'' \times 15\frac{1}{2}''$ (also larger size, length $22\frac{1}{2}''$)
11. *Marcus Aurelius Making His Son Commodus Caesar.* Modelled by Camillo Pacetti, 1789
12. *Apotheosis of Faustina, Wife of Marcus Aurelius.* Modelled by Camillo Pacetti, 1789. Finished by Hackwood (L2–1356 14 May 1789)
25. *The Fable of Prometheus.* Modelled by Camillo Pacetti, 1788. From the description, and the price paid for the model, it appears that this was a very large composition which is not known to have been reproduced as a whole. Certain figures and groups may have been reproduced separately
†37. *Triform Goddess (Diana, Luna, Hecate).* Modelled by Camillo Pacetti, 1788. $9\frac{1}{4}'' \times 7\frac{1}{2}''$
†41. *Aesculapius and Hygeia.* Modelled by Camillo Pacetti, 1788. $8\frac{1}{4}'' \times 6\frac{7}{8}''$ also $9\frac{1}{2}'' \times 8\frac{1}{4}''$
42. *The Simulacrum of Hygeia, to Whom a Woman is Making an Oblation.* Modelled by Camillo Pacetti, 1788
43. *A Faun, With Three Spartan Bacchantes.* Modelled by Camillo Pacetti, 1788
*†53. *Endymion Sleeping on the Rock Latmos.* Modelled by Camillo Pacetti, 1788. $10'' \times 8''$, and $9\frac{1}{4}'' \times 7\frac{1}{2}''$
17. *The Whole Life of Achilles*, in five pieces. Modelled by Camillo Pacetti, 1788, comprising:
   †1. The birth and dipping of Achilles
   †2. Thetis delivering Achilles to Centaur, and Achilles on the back of Centaur hunting the lion. $6\frac{1}{2}'' \times 18\frac{1}{2}''$
    3. Achilles in Scyros among the daughters of Lycomedes. $6'' \times 17\frac{1}{2}''$
    4. Achilles and Hector in combat before the walls of Troy
   †5. Achilles dragging Hector around the walls of Troy. $6\frac{1}{4}'' \times 18\frac{1}{4}''$
   All five subjects were copied or adapted by Pacetti from the Luna marble disc or puteal given to the Capitoline Museum, Rome, by Pope Benedict XIV. A sixth scene from the life of Achilles, also by Pacetti (see No. 4) was taken from a different source, the so-called sarcophagus of Alexander Severus and Julia Mammaea in the Capitoline Museum.
†–. *Achilles in Scyros Among the Daughters of Lycomedes* (erroneously described as *Sacrifice of Iphigenia*). A second version of this subject (see above No. 17.3), attributed to Camillo Pacetti, and adapted from the same source as No. 4 to which it may have been intended as a companion piece. $6'' \times 15''$
†26. *The Nine Muses.* Modelled in wax by Giuseppe Angelini (1742–1811) and copied from the Sarcophagus of the Muses in the Capitoline Museum (see p. 141)
†26. *Reclining Figures* (sometimes described as *Banquet* or *Roman Banquet*). Modelled in wax by Giuseppe Angelini, 1789, from 'the top of the urn of the Muses. 3 Nymphs & 3 Silenuses'
35. *The Fable of Meleager.* Modelled by Giuseppe Angelini, 1789. This is sometimes confused with No. 72, *Death of a Roman Warrior*, but is a much larger composition using, in part, the same source.
38. *Apollo and the Muse Erato* ('before a simulacrum which is not characterised'). Modelled by Angelini, 1789
44. *Apotheosis of a Young Prince* (a composition in three parts: 'on the right a young prince . . . and by him, Diana . . . in the middle he is seen already deified between Jupiter & Juno with Venus & Pallas. . . . On the other side is the act of his apotheosis; the same is raised by Mercury'). Modelled by Angelini, 1789
57. *Several Geniuses Representing the Pleasures of the Elysian Fields.* Modelled by Angelini, 1789
58. *Two Fauns, Two Bacchantes & A Silenus.* Modelled by Angelini, 1789

†55. *Pluto Carrying Off Proserpine* (also described as *The Rape of Persephone* and *The Procession of Persephone into the Underworld*). Modelled by Angelini, 1789. 9″ × 26¼″ (possibly 'finished' by De Vaere. See below)

Angelini was responsible also for models numbered 22, 30, 48, 49, 60 and 62, but none of these subjects is titled or described in the correspondence from Rome.

The following subjects were the work of John De Vaere while he was in Rome in 1789–90 (see E26–19008 11 February 1790 Josiah to John Flaxman):

† *The Discovery of Achilles* (a third version of *Achilles in Scyros*. See No. 17.3 and second unnumbered model attributed to Pacetti listed above). Modelled by John De Vaere, 1789–90, probably working from an engraving of a sarcophagus in Winckelmann's *Monumenti Antichi Inediti*, 1767 (Vol. I, fig. 87). 9″ × 17″. (See also E2–30197 20 January 1790, Flaxman to Wedgwood)
* *Orestes and Pylades*. Modelled by De Vaere, *c.*1790. 7¾″ × 22¼″
* *Judgement of Paris*. Attributed to De Vaere, *c.*1790. 7″ × 18½″
  Rape of Proserpine. Finished by De Vaere 'in a most beautiful manner'. (See L1–213 28 March 1789 Flaxman to Wedgwood)

The following subjects have been recorded in jasper, but neither modeller nor the date of modelling have been identified with certainty:

* *The Nereids*. Variously attributed to Henry Webber and Camillo Pacetti. Probably modelled in Rome *c.*1790. 6″ × 21½″
  Nymphs Decorating a Statue of Priapus. Attributed to Henry Webber, *c.*1790. Oval 8⅞ × 7″
  Vitruvian Scroll. Previously attributed to Richard Westmacott, but supporting evidence for this has not been found. The scroll usually identified with this description (see Eliza Meteyard, *Memorials of Wedgwood*, London, 1874, Plate XXIII, and Frederick Rathbone, *Old Wedgwood*, London, 1898, Plate VI) could not easily be mistaken for Vitruvian
* Education of Bacchus. Probably copied in Rome *c.*1790, but unrecorded. The source is a sarcophagus in the Capitoline Museum, but, in some versions of the Wedgwood tablet, only part of the composition has been used for the tablet, which thus appears incomplete. 6¾″ × 11¼″
  Apollo Instructing the Youthful Bacchus (known also as *Apollo and the Three Graces*). Probably modelled in the Rome atelier, *c.*1790, but unrecorded. 6½″ × 15″
  Procession of Deities. Copied, probably in Rome *c.*1790, from the *Puteal of the Twelve Gods* now in the Capitoline Museum (formerly Albani collection). This composition appears to have been used more often on vases than on tablets
* *Three Warriors and a Horse*⎞ (These subjects have been shown by Carol Macht, *op. cit.*, pp. 28–31, to have been *Two Warriors and a Horse*⎠ adapted from the sides of the sarcophagus from which Pacetti copied *Achilles in Scyros* ('*Sacrifice of Iphigenia*', see above) and *Priam Kneeling Before Achilles Begging the Body of His Son Hector* (see No. 4 above), and it is a reasonable assumption that these, too, are Pacetti's work, *c.*1790. Both circular. Diameter 6⅝″
† *Volumnia, Wife of Coriolanus*. Probably modelled *c.*1790. The source of this subject is an engraving published in d'Hancarville, *op. cit.*, Vol. II, Plate 26. It is often erroneously catalogued as *Penelope and Her Maidens*. Carol Macht, *Classical Wedgwood Designs*, New York, 1957, p. 118, describes it as 'Volumnia, Mother [*sic*] of Coriolanus'. 6″ × 9⅛″

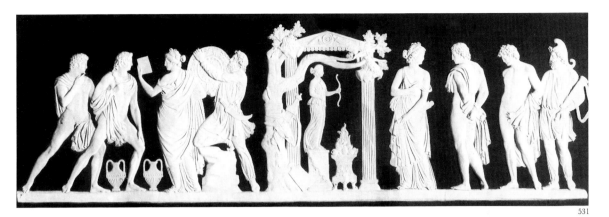

531

532

533

531. Orestes and Pylades. *Black jasper dip. 9½″ × 22½″ (19.0 × 57.3 cm). Mark:* WEDGWOOD. C.*1795.* Dwight & Lucille Beeson Collection, Birmingham Museum, Alabama

532. Judgement of Paris. *Solid black and white jasper. 7″ × 18½″ (17.8 × 47.0 cm). Mark:* WEDGWOOD. C.*1790.* (Photograph: Wedgwood)

533. The Nereids. *Solid pale-blue and white jasper. 6⅜″ × 21½″ (16.2 × 54.7 cm). Mark:* WEDGWOOD. C.*1870.* Mr & Mrs David Zeitlin Collection

534

534. Education of Bacchus. *Solid blue and white jasper. 7″ × 22⅞″ (17.7 × 57.0 cm). Mark:* WEDGWOOD *c.1920.* Dwight & Lucille Beeson Collection, Birmingham Museum, Alabama

534A. Education of Bacchus. *Solid blue and white jasper. 6¾″ × 11¼″ (15.8 × 29.8 cm). Mark:* Wedgwood. *c.1785.* Photograph: Wedgwood (reproduced from Eliza Meteyard's *Wedgwood and His Works,* 1873, Plate III)

534A

535. Apollo instructing the Youthful Bacchus. *Green jasper dip. 6½″ × 15¾″ (16.5 × 40.0 cm). Mark:* WEDGWOOD. *c.1880.* Christie's, New York

536. Three Warriors and a Horse. *Solid grey–blue jasper. Diameter 6¼″ (16.0 cm). Mark:* WEDGWOOD. *c.1785.* British Museum

537. Boy leaning on his Quiver with Doves etc. *Solid blue and white jasper. Oval height 6¼″ (15.8 cm). Mark:* WEDGWOOD. *c.1788–95. Uncatalogued. This medallion is evidently the subject described in the 'Extract of Memorandums by Mr Webber' (MS. W/M 1769 8 May 1782) but may not have been produced before 1788.* Dwight & Lucille Beeson Collection, Birmingham Museum, Alabama

536

537

535

APPENDIX K

Busts

CLASS XI, SECTION I

The information in this Appendix is based on the lists of subjects, with sizes, published in the Wedgwood & Bentley and Wedgwood Catalogues between 1773 and 1787. Sources quoted are generally those who supplied casts or moulds, and, unless otherwise stated, these were all of plaster. Many of these, certainly the majority though no full list is possible, were 'repaired' by William Hackwood. The sizes published in the Catalogues are not precise, and should be accepted as useful guides. Specimens of subjects whose sizes do not nearly conform to those listed should, however, be carefully examined in the knowledge that they are likely to be of later manufacture or busts fitted with replacement socles.

All the busts listed were produced in black basaltes and in white jasper with white jasper or black basaltes bases, and those marked § were produced in blue and white jasper (see pp. 183–5 and Appendix L 42).

It is noteworthy that both James Hoskins and his partner Benjamin Grant, who supplied most of the casts for Wedgwood & Bentley busts, are recorded as working for John Cheere in 1751, the first as foreman, the second as an apprentice (*London Evening Post*, 10–12 December 1751).

	First Catalogue	Source	Reference	Remarks
From 4 to 4½ inches high				
83. *Homer* §	1779			
84. *Bacchus* §	1779	Hoskins & Grant(?)	L1–116 28 June 1779 (?)	This and the next may be reduced versions of 'Large busts' of these subjects invoiced in 1779.
85. *Ariadne* §	1779	As 84		
86. *Voltaire*	1777			Not Flaxman's. See below
87. *Montesquieu*	1777			
88. *Rousseau*	1777			Not Flaxman's. See below
89. *Pindar* §	1779			
90. *Aristophanes* §	1779			

The following subjects are recorded in letters or invoices, or are known from surviving examples, but do not appear in any of the Catalogues between 1773 and 1787.

Voltaire Busts of Voltaire and Rousseau were invoiced by John Flaxman junior in March 1781
Rousseau (E2–1330 26 May 1781) at 8/– each, a price that indicates casts of small busts, and it is tempting to suppose (see M. H. Grant, *The Makers of Black Basaltes*, London, 1910, p. 170) that these are the busts listed as 85 and 87. It is, however, unlikely that even Flaxman, who was not especially prompt with his invoices, should have waited as long as four years before requesting payment. It is not impossible that the work was overlooked and added to a much later invoice, but in that case it would be usual to mention this on the invoice.

Figures 1769[*]–95

*Jasper from c.1779

The descriptions of figures listed in this Appendix are reprinted, with the original dimensions, from the Wedgwood Catalogue of 1787.

All but the last six subjects were originally produced in black basaltes, sometimes bronzed, but jasper examples of many – notably the 'Fiammingo' boys, the sphinxes, griffins and tritons – are known, and trials of terracotta figures were certainly carried out. The production of black basaltes figures, reproduced from the original moulds, continued into the twentieth century.

	First Catalogue	References	
11. *Five Boys*, 'from Fiammingo', length 5″	1773	E25–18303 26 May 1770; ? Invoice 1–56 21 January 1769 from Mrs Landré	The 'Sleeping Boys' after Duquesnoy, almost identical to the five *Enfants du Roi* produced by Sèvres from the same source c.1755. Not to be confused with the 'Infant reclining figures' after Della Robbia produced c.1785
12. *Grecian Sphinxes*, pair, length 6″	1773	E25–18289 10 February 1770	
13. *Grecian Sphinxes*, pair, length 12″	1773	E25–18289 10 February 1770	
14. *Grecian Sphinxes*, pair, length 5″ (different models)	1773	As 12	
15. *Egyptian Sphinxes*, 'with the lotus, to hold candles', length 6″	1773	As 12	
19. *Tritons*, pair, 'from Michael Angelo', height 11″	1773	E25–18269 19 November 1769	
28. *Venus Rising from the Sea*, 'upon a pedestal richly ornamented with figures representing the seasons'. Height 6½″	1779		
36. *Cupid*, 'on a pedestal'	1787		This, and the following six subjects, were apparently introduced as jasper figures and are evidently those described in the 1787 Catalogue as 'A small assortment of figures . . . now made in the jasper of two colours, the effect of which is new and pleasing'. See pp. 185–7 and Appendix K 83–5 and 89–90
37. *Hebe*, 'on a pedestal'	1787		
38. *'Small Statues'*, on pedestals	1787		
39. *Mars*, on a pedestal	1787		
40. *Venus*, on a pedestal	1787		
41. *Jupiter*, on a pedestal	1787		
42. *Small Busts*, 'with emblematic terms'	1787		

Notes and References

PART ONE
The Wedgwoods, Master Potters

1. The term 'Art Pottery' may be used as a synonym for 'Studio Pottery' – that is, ceramics (generally earthenware or stoneware) produced individually, without precise repetition of shape and design. The term came to be widely used after the Philadelphia Centennial Exhibition of 1876, particularly for American pottery (e.g. Rookwood).

2. Basil Williams, *The Whig Supremacy 1714–1760*, Oxford, 1962, p. 114; P. Mantoux, *The Industrial Revolution in the Eighteenth Century*, London, 1906 (paperback edn, London, 1964), p. 387.

3. The memorial tablet erected by Josiah Wedgwood's sons in the parish church of Stoke-on-Trent in 1802 records Josiah's date of birth as 'August 1730'. Wedgwood's nephew and later partner, Tom Byerley, gave his uncle's date of birth as 12 July 1730, the date officially recorded for his baptism. It was common for weak or sickly babies to be baptised without delay.

4. Josiah Wedgwood's Indenture to his brother, Thomas Wedgwood, 11 November 1744. Quoted by Eliza Meteyard, *The Life of Josiah Wedgwood*, 2 volumes, London, 1865–6, Vol. I, pp. 222–3, no. 1.

5. This illness has been firmly established by earlier biographers as occurring in 1741–2, when Josiah was eleven or twelve. This is plainly an error, since the resulting damage to his knee would have invalidated his later Indenture, under the terms of which his brother was bound to teach him the 'Art of Throwing'. See Robin Reilly, *Josiah Wedgwood*, 1992, pp. 4–5.

6. Wedgwood Ms.29–19121. Josiah Wedgwood's *Experiment Book* was transcribed, after 1781, by Wedgwood's secretary and assistant, Alexander Chisholm, as a fair copy of the original. The introduction was probably added at the same time, but a partial draft of it in Josiah's hand exists in an earlier, undated, record.

7. E25–18073 17 June 1765, Wedgwood to his brother John.

8. In 1848, Joseph Mayer, a prosperous silversmith and Wedgwood collector, discovered a large quantity of manuscript material being sold by a Birmingham scrap merchant for use as wrapping paper. The enormous pile of paper, which Mayer immediately acquired, was found to contain almost the entire series of Wedgwood's letters to Bentley, besides a great number of Wedgwood invoices, memoranda and business records.

9. W/M 1826 'Warrington Novr 15 1767' (Bentley's handwriting). Endorsed 'Basis of the Agreement between W&B Novr 15 1767' in another hand.

10. Wedgwood Ms. 96–17760 30 April 1768.

11. E25–18199 n.d. [about 17 June 1768]; E25–18204 6 July 1768

12. E25–18392 23 August 1772.

13. E25–18232 [12 or 16] February 1769; E25–18240 1 May 1769; E25–18314 2 August 1770.

14. E25–18240 1 May 1769.

15. E25–18256 16 September 1769.

16. E25–18196 24 March 1768.

17. Wedgwood Ms.2–30188 5 February 1784, John Flaxman Jnr to Josiah Wedgwood; and 2–30189 (draft) 20 February 1784, Josiah Wedgwood to John Flaxman Jnr. The interior of Etruria Hall was destroyed early in this century and it has not proved possible, from the slender evidence that has survived, to reconstruct Flaxman's design.

18. E25–18521 [7 March] 1774.

PART TWO
Jasper, 1774–95

1. LHP 13 January 1771.

2. E25–18432 31 December 1772.

3. This is demonstrated by reference to Josiah's letters of 31 December 1772 (E25–18432) and 1 January 1775 (E25–18578) quoted in the text.

4. See John Tindall, 'Josiah Wedgwood: Chemist', in *Josiah Wedgwood: 'The Arts and Sciences United'*, Barlaston, 1978, pp. 21–3; and John Chaldecott, 'Josiah Wedgwood: Scientist', in *ibid.*, pp. 16–20.

5. William Burton, *Josiah Wedgwood and His Pottery*, London, 1922, p. 186; Sir Arthur H. Church, *Josiah Wedgwood, Master Potter*, London, 1894, p. 34.

6. E25–18650 3 February 1776.

7. E25–18651 6 February 1776.

8. E26–18991 23 January 1790, Josiah to M./V. Brandoin; 1787 Catalogue.

9. E25–18433 2 January 1773.

10. E25–18162 10 August 1767; E25–18166 8 September 1767; E25–18159 n.d. [about 18 July 1767]; E25–18170 24 October 1767; Wedgwood Ms. 39–28408 Commonplace Book pp. 134–41, 281–6.

11. Wedgwood Ms. 96–17693 David Rhodes's expenses for 10–12 May 1775.

12. E25–18636 30 December 1775.

13. E25–18651 6 February 1776.

14. E25–18645 21 January 1776.

15. E25–18443 6 February 1773.

16. E25–18521 7 March 1774.

17. E25–18548 21 July 1774.

18. E25–18555 30 August 1774.

19. *Ibid.*

20. E25–18556 3 September 1774; E25–18557 5 September 1774.

21. E25–18562 6 November 1774; E25–18567 21 November 1774.

22. E25–18573 12 December 1774; E25–18575 18 December 1774.

23. E25–18573 12 December 1774; E25–18575 18 December 1774; E25–18576 26 December 1774.

24. E25–18573 12 December 1774.

25. E25–18578 1 January 1775.

26. E25–18576 26 December 1774; E25–18578 1 January 1775; E25–18583 14 January 1775; E25–18632 10 December 1775. It is possible that this last letter is wrongly dated and should be redated 1774.

27. E25–18557 5 September 1774.

28. E25–18582 8 January 1775.

29. Quoted by Robin Reilly and George Savage, *Wedgwood: The Portrait Medallions*, London, 1973, p. 363.

30. E25–18576 26 December 1774.

31. E25–18579 1 January 1775.

32. E25–18581 5 January 1775.

33. E25–18584 15 January 1775.

34. *Ibid.*

35. *Ibid.*

36. E25–18578 1 January 1775.

37. E25–18584 15 January 1775.

38. E25–18613 1 August 1775.

39. E25–18612 23 July 1775; E25–18614 6 August 1775.

40. E25–18640 4 January 1776; E25–18641 6 January 1776; E25–18642 14 January 1776; E25–18643 18 January 1776.

41. E25–18660 10 March 1776.

42. E25–18650 3 February 1776; E25–18654 14 February 1776; E25–18655 21 February 1776; E25–18656 21 February 1776; E25–18659 3 March 1776.

43. E25–18679 2 July 1776.

44. E25–18734 10 July 1777.

45. E26–18835 11 May 1778.

46. Memorandum 3–514 14 May 1776; E25–18671 21 May 1776: 'The cracking of the Bas reliefs cannot be got over at present – I believe those you receive crack'd go upon the way to you.'

47. E25–18673 6 June 1776.

48. E25–18671 Postmark 29 May 1776; E25–18672 29 May 1776; E25–18687 8 August 1776; E25–18717 16 November 1776.

49. E25–18658 28 February 1776; Commonplace Book 28–410 p. 109 13 January 1783; E25–18656 21 February 1776; E25–18673 6 June 1776; E25–18661 15 March 1776.

50. See also E25–18698 24 September 1776 for '1211, or the waxen body' distinguished from jasper.

51. E25–18659 3 March 1776; E25–18701 30 September 1776; E25–18680 5 July 1776; E25–18683 10 July 1776.

52. E25–18746 13 April 1777.

53. E25–18796 24 November 1777; LHP 24 December 1786, Wedgwood to R.L. Edgeworth; E25–18740 19 March 1777.

54. E25–18749 21 April 1777; E25–18707 'Memorandum of an Agreement made the 25th of October 1776 . . .'; E25–18573 12 December 1774.

55. E26–18919 23 August 1779.

56. E25–18734 25 January 1777; E25–18753 28 April 1777; E25–18771 17 July 1777; E25–18790 3 November 1777.

57. E25–18792 10 November 1777; E25–18803 17 December 1777.

58. E26–18853 6 October 1778.

59. W/M 1455 'Memorandum Nov' 23 1777 Jasper Composition'. Later dated copy in the hand of Alexander Chisholm.

60. E25–18802 15 December 1777.

61. *Ibid.*

62. Tassie's signature, or name with inscription and date, appearing on the truncation of a number of jasper portraits provides evidence of Wedgwood's use of Tassie's models; evidence of Tassie's use of Wedgwood's models is in the letters from James Tassie to Alexander Wilson 4 January 1779 – 28 December 1797 (Glasgow City Archives TD68/1).

63. E25–18667 7 May 1776; E25–18679 2 July 1776; E25–18707 25 October 1776.

64. Glasgow City Archives TD 68/1 24 August 1782, James Tassie to Alexander Wilson: 'PS perhaps you may be surprised at the number of pastes in the Empress's Cabinet, the reason is there is an Intaglio of each and an impression of each in the reased [raised] White Enamel the Cabinet consists of 200 Drawers and the whole number of subjects are 6076 the exterior part of the Cabinet adorned with near 100 heads & figures. I purchased a large Collection of figures from Mr Wedgwoods for the purpose.' See also letter of 9 July 1785.

65. E25–18654 14 February 1776.

66. E25–18575 18 December 1774.

67. E25–18859 4 November 1778.

68. E25–18680 5 July 1776.

69. E25–18682 Postmark 9 July 1776.

70. E25–18775 1 and 2 August 1777.

71. *Ibid.*

72. E25–18756 15 May 1777; E25–18760 23 May 1777. As early as February 1773 Josiah had told Bentley: 'If you want to match anything the Rule must be for the size of any Subject, an Eighth in an inch larger in the mould than when fired' (E25–18444).

73. The set of monarchs is mentioned in Josiah's letter (LHP) of 28 November 1771. The rest have been identified by comparison with medals. So, too, were the following portrait medallions in the 'Illustrious Moderns' series: Lord Chesterfield, Abraham Demoivre, Cardinal Fleury, Martin Folkes, Sir Andrew Fountaine, Louis XV, Francesco di Maffei, Duke of Marlborough, Duke of Montagu. See Reilly and Savage, *op. cit.*, and *The Dictionary of Wedgwood*, Woodbridge, 1980, p. 118.

74. E25–18615 9 August 1775.

75. E25–18734 25 January 1777.

76. 123 of them are listed in the 1773 Catalogue.

77. E25–18714 28 October 1776 Draft of letter Wedgwood to Paul Elers; E25–18719 23 November 1776; E25–18734 25 January 1777; E25–18772 19 July 1777; E25–18780 29 August 1777; E25–18826 11 April 1778.

78. The unmarked black dip trial portrait of Honora Sneyd Edgeworth (d.1780) in the Victoria & Albert Museum may sensibly be dated 1780–1. The portrait was modelled in 1780 at the request of Richard Lovell Edgeworth, and this example is inscribed verso 'Ground & head 2 of Last 1559/1 of 3614/Black wash'. See LHP 10 May 1780 and also Reilly and Savage, *Portrait Medallions*, p. 126.

79. E26–18878 25 February 1779; E26–18880 1 March 1779; 96–17696 4 March 1779, Wedgwood to W. Brock; E26–18882 8 March 1779; Oven Book 13 March 1779; E26–18884 14 March 1779; E26–18891 26 May 1779.

80. E25–18258 20 September 1769.

81. E25–18304 28 May 1770.

82. E25–18318 20 August 1770; LHP 7 September 1771.

83. LHP 30 November 1771; E25–18520 2 March 1774; E25–18558 11 September 1774; E25–18641 6 January 1776; E25–18679 2 July 1776.

84. E25–18680 5 July 1776.

85. E25–18738 10 March 1777.

86. E25–18805 22 December 1777.

87. See Reilly and Savage, *Portrait Medallions*, pp. 95–8, and 163–8, 327–8, 333–5; also p. 49.

88. E26–18862 Endorsed 'Rec'd Novr 21 1778'.

89. See Reilly and Savage, *Portrait Medallions*, p. 334; Oven Book for 13 and 20 April 1782.

90. Cockerell's description of him. David Watkin, *C.R Cockerell*, London, 1974, p. 100.

91. Sir Joshua Reynolds, *Discourses on Art*, ed. Robert R. Wark, New Haven and London, 1975, Discourse Three, Delivered to the Students of the Royal Academy on the Distribution of Prizes, December 1770.

92. LHP 7 September 1771.

93. E25–18579 1 January 1775 (Second part); E25–18583 14 January 1775; E25–18584 15 January 1775.

94. E25–18608 8 July 1775; E25–18611 20 July 1775.

95. Wedgwood Ms. 1–204 March and April 1775, Bill from J. Flaxman to Wedgwood & Bentley.

96. An example is in the British Museum (Cabinet 598–9). See Reilly and Savage, *Portrait Medallions*, p. 216.

97. E25–18617 8 August 1775.

98. E25–18682 Postmark 9 July 1776.

99. See Reilly and Savage, *Portrait Medallions*, pp. 361, 365–73. These wax portraits were lost for many years and discovered, in a very broken condition, by Robin Reilly in 1970. They were carefully restored, using the Wedgwood jasper copies as models, in the Conservation Department of the Victoria & Albert Museum. This work afforded unusual insights into Flaxman's methods and the strength of his wax composition.

100. The list of Hackwood's models is certainly far from complete, but his recorded portraits number twenty-two (against Flaxman's thirty-six), with a further eight confidently attributed to him.

101. Wedgwood Mss. 1–20 and 1–21 November 1798, Receipts from De Vaere to Wedgwood.

102. See W/M 1769 'Extract of Memorandums by Mr Webber to be presented to Mr Wedgwood', which records the date of Webber's agreement to go to Etruria as 8 May 1782 and of his arrival there as 2 July 1782. See also Wedgwood to Sir W. Hamilton 24 June 1786 (E26–18976).

103. For evidence of some of these transactions see the James Tassie–Alexander Wilson correspondence, Glasgow City Archives TD 68/1.

104. E25–18558 11 September 1774.

105. Wedgwood Ms. 2–939 30 April 1787.

106. E.g. marble bust of Frederick Augustus, Duke of York in the collection of HM The Queen at Windsor Castle; the plaster of Sir William Herschel in the National Portrait Gallery, London; identical versions of a marble bust of R.B. Sheridan at Windsor Castle, the Victoria & Albert Museum and the Museum of Art, Carnegie Institute, Pittsburg. See Terence Hodgkinson, 'John Lochée, Portrait Sculptor' in *Victoria & Albert Museum Yearbook*, London, 1969, pp. 152–60.

107. LHP 24 March [1788], Josiah Wedgwood II to Wedgwood.

108. *Universal Magazine*, 1791, p. 238.

109. But see Hodgkinson, *op. cit.*

110. A wax portrait closely resembling the Wedgwood medallion of Princess Charlotte Augusta is in the collection of HM The Queen at Windsor Castle. This has been attributed to Charles Peart, but on grounds of style might be assigned to Lochée.

111. Exhibited at the National Portrait Gallery, London, 3 October 1973 to 5 January 1974. See Catalogue by Robin Reilly, *Wedgwood Portrait Medallions: An Introduction*, London, 1973, No. 23a. The bust is signed and dated 1779.

112. Earl of Ilchester (ed.), *The Notebooks of George Vertue*, Walpole Society XX, 7 volumes, London, 1930–5, Vol. II, p. 47.

113. Hugh Tait, 'Wedgwood, Flaxman and Silvanus Bevan', in Wedgwood Society *Proceedings*, No. 3, 1959, p. 127.

114. E26–18860 8 November 1778.

115. E26–18929 9 October 1779.

116. Tait, *op. cit.*, p. 130 and Plate 16 D (Caption).

117. See note 95.

118. See note 72. See also Commonplace Book 39–28410 p. 63 where the diminution of dry bodies in firing is noted as from 10.82 to 11.00 inches in clay down to 10 inches fired.

119. L. Richard Smith, *Captain James Cook: The Wedgwood Portrait Medallions*, Sydney, 1979, p. 15.

120. E25–18614 6 August 1775.

121. Huntington Library MO 50256 26 April 1789, Mrs Montagu to Leonard Smelt.

122. E25–18394 30 August 1772.

123. E25–18404 14 September 1772: 'Can you enamel grounds upon our bisket intirely unglazed and unpolish'd for Mr Adam?'

124. E25–18849 1 September 1778.

125. E26–18855 16 October 1778.

126. E26–18898 19 June 1779. Although Josiah does not mention any architects' names in this letter, Eliza Meteyard accuses Chambers of 'talking down' the jasper tablets (*The Life of Josiah Wedgwood*, 2 volumes, London, 1865–6, Vol. II, p. 378). Alison Kelly, *Decorative Wedgwood*, London, 1965, p. 76, questions this accusation, but Josiah's letter of 1 July (E26–18903) quoted below makes it clear that it was indeed Chambers who persuaded the Queen not to buy Wedgwood & Bentley's tablets.

127. E26–18903 1 July 1779.

128. E26–18911 19 July 1779.

129. E26–18860 8 November 1778.

130. E26–18863 22 November 1778.

131. Kelly, *op. cit.*, pp. 76–7.

132. *Ibid.* p. 12.

133. Eliza Meteyard, *The Wedgwood Handbook*, London, 1875, pp. 153–8. It is not clear what is meant by Meteyard when she refers to 'Reduced price after the death of Bentley'. There is no evidence of any general reduction in prices of ornamental ware during that thir-teen-month period. It is possible that prices of certain models, stocks of which were inflated or considered overpriced, were temporarily reduced, but no record of such a reduction has been found. Nor are Meteyard's 'Warehouse prices' easily related to invoices, particu-larly since no details of sizes of the tablets and plaques concerned appear in Christie's catalogue. The sizes of those listed in suites of tablets, friezes and blocks for chimneypieces may be deduced with some accuracy, but those described as 'for pictures' cannot be identified or priced in detail. Meteyard's 'Warehouse prices' must therefore be regarded with suspicion.

134. Meteyard, *Life*, Vol. II, p. 378; David Buten, *18th-Century Wedgwood*, New York, 1980, p. 146; and especially Neil McKendrick, John Brewer and J.H. Plumb, *The Birth of a Consumer Society: The Commercialization of Eighteenth-century England*, London, 1982, p. 116.

135. Certain lots (e.g. 1,142) are listed as sold to 'Wyatt' or 'Holland' but the identification of these buy-ers with the architects of the same names is supposition.

136. Quoted by Kelly, *op. cit.*, p. 95.

137. See Kelly, *op. cit.*, pp. 100–3 and Plates 44–6.

138. E26–18951 30 July 1779.

139. This is first mentioned in an undated letter (E25–18847), probably written about 8 August 1778, as 'the new tablet of Homer &c'. The first reference to Flaxman as the modeller of this design is in a letter from Sir William Hamilton to Wedgwood in July 1786 (John Rylands Library, Manchester, English Mss. 1110).

140. P.H. d'Hancarville, *Collection of Etruscan, Greek and Roman Antiquities from the Cabinet of the Hon. William Hamilton*, Naples, 1767, Vol. III, p. 31.

141. T. Bentley to Sir W. Hamilton, 26 February 1779 (Collection Mrs R.D. Chellis).

142. Wedgwood Ms. 32–5365 22 June 1779, Sir W. Hamilton to Wedgwood.

143. E25–18845 19 August 1778.

144. This is most certainly the model of which Flaxman wrote to Wedgwood on 13 December 1785 (Wedgwood Ms. 2–1337): 'I hope, however, on com-paring this model with that of Homer and Hesiod, you will find it very superior.'

145. Wedgwood Ms. 2–30191 20 October 1785, J. Flaxman to Wedgwood.

146. D'Hancarville, *op. cit.*, Vol. II, Plate 127.

147. Wedgwood Ms. 2–1337 13 December 1785, J. Flaxman to Wedgwood.

148. Wedgwood Ms. 2–1339 August 1787 Invoice, J. Flaxman to Wedgwood.

149. E25–18847 n.d. [April?] 1778.

150. P.S. Bartoli, *Admiranda Romanorum Anti-quitatum*, 1693, Plate 63. This plate was re-engraved for inclusion in Bernard de Montfaucon's *L'Antiquité expliquée*, 5 volumes and supplement 5 volumes, Paris, 1719, Vol. III, Plate CLXXIII.

151. According to Bellori's life of Nicolas Poussin

(*La Vite de' pittori, sculptori ed architetti moderni*, 1728, p. 428), copies of the *Danseuses Borghese* and other antique reliefs were taken in Rome in 1641 and cast in bronze, to the order of Louis XIII, for the Louvre. The bronze tablet in the Wallace Collection, London, may be one of these. See Sir Claude Phillips, 'A Bronze Relief in the Wallace Collection', in *Burlington Magazine*, Vol. IV, 1904, pp. 111–24.

152. E25–18788 [27 October] 1788.

153. Wedgwood Ms. 1–204 March 1775, Invoice, J. Flaxman senior to Wedgwood.

154. Bruce Tattersall, 'Flaxman and Wedgwood', in David Bindman (ed.), *John Flaxman R.A.*, London, 1979, p. 52.

155. E25–18788 [27 October] 1777.

156. E25–18789 29 October 1777.

157. Carol Macht, *Classical Wedgwood Designs*, New York, 1957, p. 87, follows Meteyard, *Life*, Vol. II, p. 367, and Harry Barnard, *Chats on Wedgwood Ware*, London, 1924, p. 201, in stating that the countermand came too late to prevent Flaxman from completing the set. Tattersall, *op. cit.*, p. 52, states that the remaining Muses were made up from stock, including the variants on figures from the *Dancing Hours* group.

158. W/M 1526 'Account of Letters from and to Mr Angelo Dalmazzoni at Rome' 1788–90, No. 26. This set has previously been attributed to Camillo Pacetti (Meteyard, *Life*, Vol. II, p. 590).

159. Montfaucon, *op. cit.*, Vol. I, Plate XXX.

160. The suggestion (Tattersall, *op. cit.*, p. 52) that Urania is a version of Erato in reverse does not bear serious examination.

161. *Ibid.*

162. A painting of this subject from a private collection, and an etching from the British Museum were shown in the 'Stubbs & Wedgwood' Exhibition at the Tate Gallery 19 June–18 August 1974 (Catalogue Nos. 20–1).

163. LHP 13 August 1780.

164. LHP 1 August 1780.

165. A blue and white jasper example impressed 'WEDGWOOD & BENTLEY' was in the Oster Collection, but was sold privately before the auction sale of the collection at Sotheby's, London, in November 1971 and May 1972.

166. The Wedgwood design was evidently taken from an engraving based on a painting in enamel colours on copper ('Stubbs & Wedgwood' Catalogue No. 16). This was Lot 89 on the second day of the sale of Stubbs's studio in 1807 and fetched 310 guineas, the highest price in the sale. The watercolour portrait of George Stubbs by Ozias Humphry RA (National Portrait Gallery, London) shows the artist holding this enamel, which is plainly signed and dated 1778.

167. LHP 28 October 1780.

168. LHP 12 November 1780.

169. E25–18641 6 January 1776.

170. E25–18655 21 February 1776.

171. Macht, *op. cit.*, pp. 45–6.

172. Montfaucon, *op. cit.*, Vol. III, Pt 2, Plate CXXXIV.

173. E25–18678 2 July 1776.

174. E25–18681 [?] July 1776.

175. E25–18679 2 July 1776.

176. E26–18976 16 June 1787, Wedgwood to Sir W. Hamilton (draft); Wedgwood Ms. 2–30197 20 January 1790, Wedgwood to Sir W. Hamilton.

177. Wedgwood Ms. 2–1342 24 December 1788, J. Flaxman to Wedgwood. The wax, which is noted as never used by Wedgwood, was sold as Lot 82 in the sale of 'The collection of the late Miss Flaxman and Miss Denman' at Christie's, 26 April 1876. Wedgwood Ms. 1–210 15 March 1788, J. Flaxman to Wedgwood.

178. E.g. Wedgwood Mss. 1–210 15 March 1788; 1–213 28 March 1788; 2–30197 20 January 1790. J. Flaxman to Wedgwood.

179. Wedgwood Ms. 2–1342 24 December 1788, J. Flaxman to Wedgwood.

180. Wedgwood Mss. 2–1342 24 December 1788; 1–213 28 March 1788; 1–210 15 March 1788; 2–30197 20 January 1790. J. Flaxman to Wedgwood.

181. Wedgwood Ms. 1–148, 'Memorandum of an agreement made on the 16th day of July in the year of our Lord, 1787, between Josiah Wedgwood of Etruria in Staffordshire Esquire of the one part and Henry Webber of Etruria aforesaid Modeller and Designer of the other part'.

182. W/M 1526 'Account of the Letters from and to Mr Angelo Dalmazzoni at Rome' 1788–90.

183. *Ibid.*

184. *Ibid.* Josiah originally said that he preferred the work of Giuseppe Angelini, and gave instructions that Pacetti was to work only on small figures from Homer (24 November 1789), but in his letter of 2 March and 18 April 1790 he corrected this, giving new orders that Mangiarotti was not to be employed any longer, and admitting that he had confused Pacetti's work with Angelini's.

185. *Ibid.*

186. *Ibid.*

187. This is illustrated in H. Stuart Jones, *A Catalogue of the Ancient Sculptures preserved in the Municipal Collections of Rome: The Sculptures of the Museo Capitolino*, Oxford, 1912, Plate 9.

188. The name has frequently been misspelt 'Templeton' (e.g. Meteyard, *Life*, throughout; Wolf Mankowitz, *Wedgwood*, London, 1953, throughout; and most recently Buten, *op. cit.*, throughout). Wedgwood misspelt it 'Templetoun' in the 1787 Catalogue.

189. E26–18958 27 June 1783, Wedgwood to Lady Templetown (draft).

190. W/M 1508 23 July 1785, Wedgwood to C.J. Fox.

191. W/M 1755 30 April 1785 Bill from Hackwood

for 'Modeling in wax twelve small subjects as accompanyments to Ly Templeton's [*sic*] Basso^5 £1.11.6'.

192. Not two only, as stated by Reilly and Savage (*Dictionary of Wedgwood*, p. 336). The fourteen appear in the 1787 Catalogue as Class II, Nos. 238–40, 248–53, 271–3; 239 is a smaller version of 238, and 249–51 and 273 are for pairs of subjects.

193. It is necessary to distinguish between the 1787 Catalogue as issued by Wedgwood, which includes a few notes of his own identifying the artists with certain subjects, and the Catalogue as reprinted by Meteyard (*Handbook*) to which she has added her own attributions, not all of which have stood the test of time and further research. Failure to make this distinction has led to the repetition of erroneous attributions and such remarkable statements as 'The 1787 Catalogue lists designs attributed by Meteyard to Lady Templetown' (Mrs L.S. Rakow, 'The Feminine Touch in Wedgwood', in Wedgwood International Seminar *Proceedings*, Vol. 12, 1967, p. 157).

194. These are listed in the 1787 Catalogue as Class II, Nos. 247 and 270.

195. Mrs Steuart Erskine, *Lady Diana Beauclerk, Her Life and Work*, London, 1903.

196. W/M 1508 23 July 1785, Wedgwood to C.J. Fox.

197. 1787 Catalogue Class II, Nos. 241–4.

198. See Eliza Meteyard, *Wedgwood and His Works*, London, 1873, Plate VII, 2 (Sibson Collection).

199. Wedgwood Ms. 2–30193 23 December 1786, Wedgwood to J. Flaxman.

200. R.J. Auckland, third Baron, Bishop of Bath and Wells (ed.), *The Journal and Correspondence of William, Lord Auckland*, 4 volumes, London, 1862, Vol. I, p. 427.

201. Wedgwood Ms. 3–1338 12 January 1787 (erroneously dated by Meteyard, *Life*, Vol. II, p. 486 to 16 January; and by Tattersall, *op. cit.*, p. 63 to 10 January) and 12 March, J. Flaxman to Wedgwood.

202. 1788 Catalogue Class II, Nos. 256–7.

203. Wedgwood Ms. 17–15748 3 and 4 November 1789 Invoice to London Warehouse. First quoted by J.K. des Fontaines, 'The Bastille Medallion', in Wedgwood Society *Proceedings*, No. 3, 1959, pp. 150–1. In this article, later corrected (Wedgwood Society *Proceedings*, No. 6, 1966, p. 107, 'The Bastille Medallion Second Thoughts'), it was stated that basaltes medallions of this subject were copied from bronze medals by Bertrand Andrieu (1761–1822). Such medallions do exist in basaltes, but, although they are impressed WEDGWOOD, there is some doubt whether they were produced at the Etruria factory. The jasper medallions depict scenes which only superficially resemble those on Andrieu's medals. For the latter see M. Jones, 'Medals of the French Revolution', in British Museum, *Keys to the Past*, London, 1977 and *Médailles de la Révolution Française, Trésor de Numismatique et Glyptique*, Paris, 1836.

204. The second, theoretically possible, alternative of 'painting' the face of the moulded white jasper medallion with blue slip was clearly not used. This is evident in the blue shading *through* the thinnest parts of the white relief (viz. the clouds). No earlier example of the technique used by Wedgwood or any of his competitors has come to light.

205. LHP 28 July 1789, Wedgwood II to Wedgwood.

206. W/M 1460 29 July 1789, Josiah Wedgwood II to Wedgwood.

207. E26–19090 11 September 1790 Invoice of goods sent to London for shipment to Frankfurt.

208. These three are in the Byron and Elaine Born Collection. See Buten, *op. cit.*, p. 153, Plate 149.

209. This portrait was for many years wrongly identified as Prince Charles Edward Stuart, an identification corrected in Reilly and Savage, *Portrait Medallions*, p. 214.

210. E25–18700 28 September 1776.

211. Auckland, *op. cit.*, Vol. I, p. 133.

212. E.g. Buten, *op. cit.*, Plate 178 and see Oven Book 53–30014, February 1783.

213. Evidence of this is to be found in Josiah's letter to Byerley (Wedgwood Ms. 96–17711 6 April 1787) referring to a new 'Teapot on high feet. . . . they are called Vase Tea pots'. All known examples of this shape (Plate C38) are in solid blue jasper.

214. E25–18548 21 July 1774. It is possible that this reference is to 'large as life' portrait medallions, but context and date make a reference to busts more likely.

215. A larger bust of Plato (height 15 inches) marked 'WEDGWOOD & BENTLEY' is in the Museum of Fine Arts, Boston. This is described by Buten, *op. cit.*, p. 157, Plate 156, as of white jasper. Having not examined this piece, the author is unable to confirm the description. The illustration shows a body which looks more like terracotta, or even possibly block mould plaster.

216. E25–18564 16 November 1774.

217. E26–18866 5 December 1778.

218. Under Class XI, section II, No. 42, *Statues Animals &c*, not, as one might expect, under section I, *Busts*.

219. Wedgwood Ms. 2–1339 11 July 1783–10 August 1787, Invoice for work done during the period by Flaxman. Of the total charge of £188.4.2, the sum of £116.11.9 had already been paid. Several of the Flaxman wax models have survived, though much damaged, in the collection at the Wedgwood Museum, Barlaston.

220. Wedgwood Ms. 2–30188, J. Flaxman to Wedgwood.

221. Oven Book December 1783: '8 doz and 3 Chest Mon blue and white'.

222. Wedgwood Ms. 2–1339 8 March 1785, J. Flaxman to Wedgwood.

223. Barnard, *op. cit.*, p. 236.

224. E25–18596 1 April 1775: 'We send you some Jasper Candlesticks, Inkstands, and other articles immediately wanted today'.

225. E26–18859 4 November 1778.

226. LHP 5 October 1780.

227. LHP 28 October 1780.

228. A pair of these is illustrated by Mankowitz, *op. cit.*, Plate 77, where the figures are erroneously described as Ceres and Cybele, and attributed, without evidence, to Flaxman.

229. E45–29110 Byerley's Memorandum Book, p. 48, 23 March 1786.

230. Gaye Blake Roberts, 'A Selection of Works by Flaxman's Contemporaries Working for Wedgwood' in Bindman, *op. cit.*, p. 66; see also *Arts and Sciences United*, No. 168.

231. W/M 1769 'Extract of Memorandums by Mr Webber . . .'.

232. E53–30014 Oven Book for 21 and 28 December 1782. I am grateful to Mrs Lynn Miller for drawing my attention to this evidence.

233. LHP 12 November 1780.

234. W/M 1503 1 October 1807, T. Byerley to Josiah Wedgwood II.

235. E25–18614 6 August 1775.

236. E25–18232 [12 or 16?] February 1769.

237. E53–30016 Oven Book for 18 and 25 February 1786. This reference was unearthed by Mrs Lynn Miller.

238. Quoted by Aileen Dawson, *Masterpieces of Wedgwood in the British Museum*, London, 1984, p. 111.

239. E26–18976 24 June 1786, Wedgwood to Sir W. Hamilton.

240. Montfaucon, *op. cit.*, Vol. III, Plate XXXIV.

241. See Francis Haskell and Nicholas Penny, *Taste and the Antique: The Lure of Classical Sculpture 1500–1900*, New Haven and London, 1982, pp. 269–71, No. 63.

242. Dawson, *op. cit.*, p. 109.

243. Wedgwood Ms. 2–30188 5 February 1784, J. Flaxman to Wedgwood.

244. Wedgwood Ms. 2–30189 20 February 1784, J. Flaxman to Wedgwood.

245. For the most reputable interpretations see D.E.L. Haynes, *The Portland Vase*, 2nd revised edn, London, 1975; Bernard Ashmole, 'A New Interpretation of the Portland Vase', in *Journal of Hellenic Studies*, Vol. LXXXVII, 1967, pp. 1–17; J.G.F. Hind, 'Greek and Roman Epic Scenes on the Portland Vase', in *Journal of Hellenic Studies*, Vol. XCIX, 1979, pp. 20–5.

246. Haynes, *op. cit.*, p. 26, and Dawson, *op. cit.*, p. 113, take the view that the relationship of the themes 'must have been a coincidence'; but, if the themes have been correctly identified, it seems at least possible that it was not. Even in Roman times, and certainly by the sixteenth-century, this vase would have been prized as a superb example of the glass-maker's and cameo-cutter's arts, and it is sensible to suppose that great trouble would have been taken to match any repair, as nearly as possible, in colour, style and theme.

247. For a discussion of this correspondence, see Nancy T. de Grummond, 'Rubens, Pieresc and the Portland Vase', in *Southern College Art Conference Review*, Vol. III, No. 1, 1974.

248. This is reproduced in Dawson, *op. cit.*, p. 114.

249. Horace Walpole to the Countess of Upper Ossory, 19 August 1785. Mrs Paget Toynbee (ed.), *Letters of Horace Walpole*, 16 volumes, London, 1905, Vol. XIII, p. 308.

250. Wedgwood Ms. 33–24859 Receipt dated 10 June 1786 signed by Josiah Wedgwood and witnessed by Tom Byerley.

251. Montfaucon, *op. cit.*, Vol. V, Plate XIX.

252. E26–18976 24 June 1786, Wedgwood to Sir W. Hamilton.

253. E25–18701 30 September 1776.

254. E26–18976 24 June 1786, Wedgwood to Sir W. Hamilton.

255. *Ibid.*

256. W/M 1460 12 April 1791, Josiah Wedgwood II to Wedgwood.

257. E26–18976 24 June 1786, Wedgwood to Sir W. Hamilton.

258. An excellent brief account of the various interpretations is given in Haynes, *op. cit.*, Appendix pp. 27–32. For the purposes of this book, the most relevant is Josiah Wegwood's own, which appears in a long letter (E26–19004 endorsed 'Oct 1789') to Erasmus Darwin (see also Josiah's *Account of the Barberini, now Portland Vase. With various explications of its bas-reliefs that have been given by different authors*, London [1788?]). Josiah thought that the frieze represented death and the entrance of the soul into Elysium. It is probable that he was familiar also with the interpretations of Bartoli, *Gli antichi sepolchri*, Rome, 1697, p. xii, Plates 84–6; Montfaucon, *op. cit.*, Vol. V, Plate 19; and perhaps also with P.H. d'Hancarville, *Recherches sur l'origine, l'esprit et les progrès des arts de la Grèce*, London, 1785, Vol. II, pp. 142–60, Plates 9–11.

259. E26–18976 24 June 1786, Wedgwood to Sir W. Hamilton.

260. *Ibid.*

261. Sir W. Hamilton to Wedgwood, July 1786. This letter, quoted at length by Wolf Mankowitz, *The Portland Vase and the Wedgwood Copies*, London, 1952, pp. 28–30, and then in the manuscript collection at Barlaston (prior to its removal to the archives at Keele University) has since disappeared.

262. E26–18976 24 June 1786, Wedgwood to Sir W. Hamilton.

263. This belief was finally confuted by P.J. Mariette, *Traité des pierres gravées*, Paris, 1750; for Peiresc's identification of the vase as made of glass, see de Grummond, *op. cit.*

264. Dawson, *op. cit.*, p. 119, states that 'Wax models

were made from which working moulds were taken.' Such a direct method would quickly have resulted in damage, through wear and tear, to the working moulds which, after the return of the Vase to its owner, could have been replaced only from the waxes, which, in turn, would soon have deteriorated beyond further use. For such an important work, Josiah would certainly have required the more permanent 'block' moulds to be made, from which working moulds could be repeated.

264. E26–18976 24 June 1786, Wedgwood to Sir W. Hamilton.

266. LHP 24 March 1788, Josiah Wedgwood II to Wedgwood.

267. Uncatalogued letter (copy in the hand of Chisholm) 25 April 1788, Wedgwood to Dr W. Heberden.

268. E26–18976 24 June 1786, Wedgwood to Sir W. Hamilton.

269. E26–18993 9 May 1790, Wedgwood to Josiah Wedgwood II.

270. W/M 1455 Memorandum 23 November 1777.

271. Josiah to Auckland 5 July 1789. Eden Mss. printed in *Athenaeum Journal*, No. 1694, 17 April 1860.

272. This is claimed by both the Dwight and Lucille Beeson Collection, Birmingham Museum of Art, Alabama, and the Fitzwilliam Museum, Cambridge.

273. E. Darwin to Wedgwood, October 1789. Darwin Mss. quoted by Meteyard, *Life*, II, p. 581.

274. The engraving is illustrated in Dawson, *op. cit.*, p. 121, Figure 88; and see Sir Geoffrey Keynes, *Blake Studies*, 2nd edn, Oxford, 1971, pp. 59–65.

275. M. de Luc, the Queen's private secretary, wrote to Wedgwood on 5 June 1790 (E82–14607) apologising for not being able to accompany Her Majesty when she viewed the Vase, and asking if he might see it at a later date. Since the viewing at Sir Joseph Banks's house was held on the evening of Saturday 1 May, and it is unlikely this could have taken place prior to the vase being shown to the Queen, it is almost certain that it was displayed for her approval earlier that same day.

276. *The General Evening Post* was published between 1 and 4 May, and the *Gazetteer & New Daily Advertiser* on Wednesday 5 May. Both references were researched by Ann Eatwell of the Victoria & Albert Museum, and quoted in Dawson, *op. cit.*, p. 122.

277. This document, quoted in Mankowitz, *The Portland Vase*, p. 35, is dated 15 June 1790. Originally in the Wedgwood manuscript collection at Barlaston, it cannot now be found.

278. W/M 1460 20 July 1791, Josiah Wedgwood II to Wedgwood.

279. E30–22498 23 July 1791, Sir W. Hamilton to Wedgwood.

280. E25–18314 2 August 1770.

281. E26–18993 9 June 1790, Wedgwood to Josiah Wedgwood II.

282. W/M 1529 4 July 1790, Josiah Wedgwood II to Wedgwood.

283. W/M 1529 5 July 1790, Josiah Wedgwood II to Wedgwood.

284. Johanna A. Naber, *Correspondentie van de Stadhonderlijke familie*, The Hague, 1933, Vol. III, p. 59.

285. *Ibid.* Not less, according to the Princess, than fifty. Josiah II gave a list of them in his letter (W/M 1529) of 13 July 1790.

286. W/M 1529 5 July 1790, Josiah Wedgwood II to Wedgwood.

287. W/M 1529 13 July 1790, Josiah Wedgwood II to Wedgwood.

288. E33–24860 Byerley's Notebook. List of subscribers.

289. W/M 1529 5 July 1790, Josiah Wedgwood II to Wedgwood. The younger Josiah writes of his intention to set out for Amsterdam next day, and 'perhaps we shall see Mr Hope's great house on the way'.

290. W/M 1529 Postmark 14 September 1790, Wedgwood to Josiah Wedgwood II.

291. W/M 1460 Josiah Wedgwood II to Wedgwood.

292. W/M 1460 22 April 1791, Josiah Wedgwood II to Wedgwood.

293. Mankowitz, *The Portland Vase*, p. 41.

294. *Ibid.*, quoted p. 39.

295. *Ibid.*, quoted p. 47.

296. This accurate observation, which contradicts the information given in *ibid.*, p. 42, was made by Aileen Dawson *op. cit.*, p. 124, from a comparison of first-edition examples in the British Museum.

297. See particularly Mrs Dwight M. Beeson, 'Wedgwood's Copies of the Portland Vase', and Dr and Mrs L.S. Rakow, 'New Facts on the Portland Vase and the Wedgwood Portlands', in Wedgwood International Seminar *Proceedings*, No. 16, 1971, pp. 255–65, 218.

298. An article in the *General Advertiser* for 26 April 1786 describes the vase as being broken 'at least into three pieces and its original bottom was most certainly destroyed'. This is confirmed by the plaster copy made by Tassie from Pichler's mould in 1781–2, now in the British Museum. According to the *Gentleman's Magazine*, Vol. XVI, July–December 1786, p. 744, the vase was again 'repaired after its fracture by the Duchess of Gordon' (the notorious 'Jenny of Montreith'). Since it was in Wedgwood's hands by 10 June 1786, and remained with him long after the date of this article, this second 'fracture' most probably occurred between the death of the Duchess of Portland on 17 July 1785 and 24 April 1786.

299. *The Times*, 7 and 12 February 1845; *Gentleman's Magazine*, New Series, Vol. XXIII, p. 300.

300. A similarly idiotic loophole was exposed after the theft of Goya's portrait of the Duke of Wellington from the National Gallery in August 1961. On that occasion, the thief was charged only with damage to the

frame from which the portrait had been removed. The portrait was returned in May 1965.

301. E26–19001 28 June 1789, Wedgwood to E. Darwin.

PART THREE
Jasper 1795–1968

1. 142–29026 December 1790, Josiah Wedgwood II to Tom Byerley.

2. 'O.W. Order Book 1801–1812', uncatalogued.

3. *Ibid.*, 7 November 1801, 16 May 1802.

4. *Ibid.*, 14 May 1801 – 2 January 1802. The Oven Book entry for 16 and 23 January 1801 appears to be the first record of the beehive shape in jasper.

5. 'O.W. Order Book 1801–1812', uncatalogued, 13 April 1804.

6. 21 February 1801, Tom Byerley to Mowbray. Quoted by Meteyard, *op. cit.*, p. 182.

7. 'O.W. Order Book 1801–1812', 24 September 1801, 9 May 1803.

8. *Ibid.*, 20 May 1801 – 18 January 1810 *passim*.

9. *Ibid.*, 11 May 1807.

10. *Ibid.*, 11 October 1805.

11. *Ibid.*, 18 June 1811.

12. *Ibid.*, e.g. the 'Deep solid Blue Jasper' incense vase for 'Lord V P—', 11 May 1807 and 'Solid dark blue vases 148 Canopus' of 17 February 1808. For dip examples see 22 August 1810 and 8 September 1810.

13. Josiah Clement Wedgwood and Joshua G. E. Wedgwood, *Wedgwood Pedigrees*, Kendal, 1925, p. 26, fn. 1.

14. 60–32818 Pottery Memos, 1821–, n.d., *c.*1822–3.

15. Some credence is added to the theory by the presence of the memorandum in the somewhat miscellaneous Mosley collection of manuscripts and not, as might be expected, in the Etruria collection.

16. 'FW & GW Memoranda 1854–80', uncatalogued.

17. W/M 1602 1829–45; 19–17062 5 July 1829 – 17389 July 1843.

18. 60–32840 Abner Wedgwood's notebook, 'Blendings 1807–35'.

19. 60–32820 Pottery Memos, 1836–.

20. *Ibid.*, *c.*1839.

21. W/M 1621A series.

22. 60–32817 Pottery Memos, 1816– (1817).

23. W/M 1637 18 September 1844, 23 October 1844.

24. 60–32825 Pottery Memos, March 1845; W/M 1651 London orders November 1847.

25. William Evans, *The Art and History of the Potting Business*, Shelton, 1846, p. 52.

26. 'FW & GW Memoranda 1854–80', uncatalogued. Jasper, 15 February 1856.

27. '1843' Price Book, uncatalogued. List of jasper vases and prices, April 1860.

28. '1843' Price Book, uncatalogued: 'Sept 10/61' date pencilled in.

29. 60–32831 Pottery Memos, 1865–. This entry is undated but attributed to 1866.

30. *Ibid.*, *c.*1867–8.

31. *Ibid.*, *c.*1866–7.

32. 60–32828 Pottery Memos, 30 April 1866. The inclusion of a recipe for 1840 does not, of course, indicate that the jasper body was in production at that date in any form but as a dip and for bas-relief ornaments.

33. W/M 1415 23 February 1866, Frank Wedgwood to Godfrey Wedgwood.

34. 60–32833 7 June 1869.

35. *Ibid.*, 11 June 1869; 12 October 1869.

36. *Ibid.*, July 1869.

37. 'O.W. Price Book', uncatalogued, 7 June 1867 and October 1869.

38. 60–32833 Pottery Memos, 23 November 1869.

39. 'O.W. Price Book', uncatalogued, 26 February 1872.

40. *Ibid.*, October 1869.

41. 60–32834 Pottery Memos, 1871–2.

42. *Ibid.*

43. *Ibid.*, n.d., end of 1871.

44. *Ibid.*, 28 October 1872.

45. *Ibid.*, 25 February 1872.

46. *Ibid.*, 24 February 1872.

47. *Ibid.*, 24 November 1874, 2 February 1875, 12 August 1879, October 1879.

48. *Ibid.*, 21 December 1875.

49. *Ibid.*, 7 December 1875.

50. W/M 1612 1871–4.

51. Godfrey Wedgwood Private Letter Book 1872–81, 1 November 1876, 20 September 1876, Godfrey Wedgwood to Charles Toft.

52. *Ibid.*, 49–29463; Bert Bentley's Work Book, uncatalogued, *c.*1921.

53. 60–32835 Pottery Memos, 1 and 2 November 1880.

54. *Ibid.*, 5 October 1880. The bust was repaired and press-moulded by Isaac Cook, who made seven busts on 7 and 21 October 1881 ('O.W. Potters Book 1878–81' researched by Lynn Miller).

55. *Ibid.*, n.d. [November 1880], 1 December 1880.

56. E.g. Aileen Dawson, *Masterpieces of Wedgwood in the British Museum*, London, 1984, pp. 140–2.

57. Harry M. Buten, *Wedgwood Rarities*, Merion, Pennsylvania, 1968, p. 249.

58. W/M 1668 5 October 1882, Clement Wedgwood to George Darwin.

59. See Alison Kelly, *Decorative Wedgwood*, London, 1965, pp. 131–2.

60. Recipe Book *c.*1882, uncatalogued. I am grateful to Lynn Miller for bringing this to my attention.

61. 60–32836 Pottery Memos, 1882–4.

62. Godfrey Wedgwood Private Letter Book 1880, 2 June 1884, Clement Wedgwood to Halsey Ricardo (see also letters of 26 June, 22 September and 13 November 1884).

63. Since my own small part in this transaction has been mentioned in Tony Birks's *Lucie Rie* (London, 1987, pp. 48–9), it seems necessary to set down the course of events as I remember them. I had been introduced to Lucie Rie by a mutual friend some eighteen months before she was approached officially by Wedgwood and had visited her at her London studio in Albion Mews. I visited her again at about the time of the delivery of jasper clay to her studio, and some weeks later four prototype cups were delivered to the Wedgwood London showroom in Wigmore Street. Birks is correct in stating (from Lucie Rie's recollections) that 'The London director, Robin Riley [*sic*], was delighted with them'. I was doubtful that they could be made commercially, but this did not alter my opinion that the project should be pursued with a view to limited production, and this was, as I recall it, also the opinion of Maitland Wright. It did not, however, find favour with the production or design departments or, I think, with Josiah V, and their objections prevailed. I was under the impression also that Lucie Rie, whose visit to the Barlaston factory is not remembered by her with pleasure, expressed her opinion that the jasper body (the post-war composition created by Norman Wilson) was 'unsympathetic', and that she would have preferred a finer ceramic body to work with.

Birks's belief (*ibid.*, p. 49) that 'a Wedgwood launch of these designs could have set English industrial pottery at the end of the 1950s [*sic*] off in a new direction with far-reaching effect' seems to me to be greatly exaggerated. The co-operation of an artist and a manufacturer is not infrequently without any apparent influence on the industry as a whole (e.g. George Stubbs, Walter Sickert, Barbara Hepworth, Laurence Whistler), and, however regrettable it may be, the visible influence of the great British 'Studio' potters of modern times, such as Bernard Leach and Michael Cardew, on industrial pottery design has been slight. What was undoubtedly lost was the benefit to Wedgwood designers of working with a superb creative artist whose chosen medium is clay.

64. 18–16167 24 March 1810.

65. 60–32817 Pottery Memos 1817.

66. 60–32840 Abner Wedgwood's notebook.

67. 60–32818 Pottery Memos, 1821.

68. G.E. Stringer, 'Notes on Staffordshire Bas-Reliefs of the Eighteenth and Nineteenth Centuries', English Ceramic Circle *Transactions*, Vol. 4, Pt 1, 1857, pp. 2–6.

69. Oven Book for 24 December 1852.

70. W/M 1604 26 February 1818, 28 February 1818, [Postmark] 21 March 1818, 3 April 1818, 19 April 1818; 18–16443 22 June 1816; 18–18463 20 January 1817; 18–16396 May 1815; 18–16560 (date torn) end May 1818.

71. 18–16660 17 December 1820; 18–16706 8 July 1821; W/M 1602 21 July 1827, 8 August 1827; 18–16720 3 January 1823; 18–16724 18 January 1823; 18–16859 25 May 1824.

72. W/M 1621A 13 November 1828; 17–17062 8 July 1829; W/M 1602 31 October 1832; W/M 1637 19 April 1845.

73. 11–1837 20 April 1838; O.W. Potters Book 1841–6, 27 October 1843, 8 December 1843; 11–1837 9 November 1838, 26 June 1839; W/M 1602 28 June 1833.

74. T.H. Hayes notebook, uncatalogued, 1936–c.1950: 'Stone Bodies July 1941'.

75. 135–26936 28 May 1798, R.L. Edgeworth to Josiah Wedgwood II.

76. 7 October 1800, Bulstrode to Wedgwood's, quoted by Meteyard, *op. cit.*, p. 177.

77. 32–5363 14 August 1802, receipt from M. Chaptal.

78. Oven Book 9 September 1796 – 7 August 1802, entry for 13 and 20 January 1801.

79. 18–16832 November 1822, ordered for Mrs M. Rollason & Son, Birmingham.

80. O.W. Potters Book, uncatalogued, 15 January 1836.

81. O.W. Potters Book, 26 May, 26 June and 6 November 1839, 6 November 1840; W/M 1602 series 1839–42 *passim*.

82. W/M 1637 17 February 1845, 23 October 1844.

83. 60–32825 Pottery Memos, March–October 1845.

84. '1843' Price Book, uncatalogued, 18 May 1846.

85. W/M 1637 3 May 1845.

86. W/M 1651 London Orders 1847.

87. 60–32824 Pottery Memos, 1849.

88. '1843' Price Book, uncatalogued, April 1860.

89. O.W. Oven Book 1850–1, uncatalogued, 28 November 1850, 24 December 1850. I am indebted to Lynn Miller for these references.

90. Godfrey Wedgwood Private Letter Book, 18 May 1877.

91. 60–32835 Pottery Memos, November 1878.

92. *Ibid.*, November 1878.

93. 60–32833 5 April 1870, 24 August 1875.

94. Harry Barnard's 'Record', 1931.

95. The so-called 1839 edition was first described by Wolf Mankowitz, *The Portland Vase and the Wedgwood Copies*, London, 1952, p. 82 and Plates XV and XIX. No evidence is offered for this date or description and none has been discovered to sustain them.

96. See n. 84.

97. Robin Reilly and George Savage, *The Dictionary of Wedgwood*, Woodbridge, Suffolk, 1980, p. 276.

98. W/M 1637 3 May 1845; 60–32833 20 September 1870; '1843' Price Book, uncatalogued, prices of vases April 1860.

Glossary

Acanthus. Leaf motif based on the plant known also as 'bear's breech'. Common in classical art, it has been used by Wedgwood for painted decoration and relief ornament, and, in profile, for acanthus-scroll designs.

Anthemion. Stylised form of honeysuckle, common in neoclassical decoration and much used by Wedgwood for painted decoration and relief ornament.

Bas-relief. Embossed, carved or cast ornament in low relief. 'Bas-relief ware' is the name given to modern Wedgwood stoneware dipped in jasper, but, by definition, almost all jasper is ornamented in bas-relief.

Biscuit. Pottery or porcelain which has been fired but not glazed.

Block Mould. See *Mould*.

Body. The name given to the composite materials of which potter's clay is made.

Cameo. Ornament in relief (as distinguished from intaglio), and specifically that which is in one colour on a ground of another. The term was originally applied to antique Greek or Roman gems carved in low relief, and was later extended to objects carved from natural laminated material.

Casting (slip-casting). The process of forming shapes by pouring slip into dry plaster moulds which absorb moisture from the slip. When a sufficient thickness of clay has adhered to the inside of the mould, the remaining slip is poured away and the mould set to dry, after which the form is removed from the mould.

Cheese-hard (leather-hard). The state of unfired pottery after the evaporation of part of the moisture content. In this condition, not unlike leather in firmness and pliability, it may be turned on a lathe or ornamented by engine-turning. Clay ornament (e.g. jasper) is cheese-hard when it is applied or undercut.

Compotier. Correctly a bowl or deep dish, often on a foot or stand, for serving *compote* (cooked whole fruit). In the potteries the term is traditionally used also to describe small shallow bowls in various shapes suitable for serving nuts, olives, etc.

Conceit. A ceramic object in the form of an iced cake made for the decoration of the dinner table when flour for real cakes was in short supply.

Crazing. A network of fine cracks in the glaze of pottery or porcelain, usually the result of an accidental dif-ference in the rates of shrinkage of glaze and body in cooling, but sometimes caused by later reheating. The Chinese used controlled crazing as decoration on some of the finest wares, but this technique was seldom employed in Europe. Josiah Wedgwood succeeded in almost eliminating crazing from Queen's ware, but it appeared again on Wedgwood Queen's ware and Pearl ware in the nineteenth century.

Dipping. The process of glazing by dipping ware in liquid glaze. 'Jasper dip' is the name given to jasper of one colour dipped or washed in jasper slip of another colour.

Dry bodies. The name given to Wedgwood unglazed stonewares, including jasper, black basaltes, cane, rosso antico and drab.

Dunting. Cracking caused by stresses developing during the processes of firing and cooling. These may result from faulty design as well as incorrect firing, and may occur a month or more after manufacture. In a letter dated 26 September 1876 to Colonel Crealock, Godfrey Wedgwood wrote of dunting: 'This is an accident which sometimes happens to large pieces of ware after they are finished.' Dunting is not, however, confined to large pieces of ware.

Engine-turning. See Appendix D.

Fettling. The removal of excess clay, such as unsightly seam marks left after casting. This is done with a sharp knife while the ware is in the cheese-hard state.

Fire-crack. Crack occurring during the firing of a ceramic object, generally resulting from faulty design or clay mixing. Fire-cracks (sometimes erroneously described as 'age cracks') are always wider at one end, and must be distinguished from cracks due to impact, which are of even width. (See also *Crazing* and *Dunting*.)

Firing. The process of transforming clay into pottery or porcelain by the application of heat in a special oven or kiln, or of using heat in the same manner to fix glaze or decoration.

Frit (fritt). Ingredients of a glaze composition melted and ground together before use in the making of the glaze. Frits have many uses, including the preparation of artificial porcelain and ceramic colour stains.

Glaze. Glassy preparation applied to the surface of

biscuit ware to render it impervious to liquids. Salt glaze is a hard, transparent glaze with a pitted, 'orange-peel' surface, produced by throwing rock salt into the Kiln from above at a maximum degree of heat. Smear glaze is a thin deposit of lead glaze produced by smearing the inside of the saggar with glaze material.

Green ware. Unfired ware, complete from the potting but not yet sufficiently dried for firing.

Hovel. A building containing pottery ovens.

Intaglio. Design created by carving or incising below a flat surface: the opposite of cameo.

Lapidary polishing. A lapidary is a carver of hard-stones, who makes use of the principle that a substance will always be cut by another which is harder. Wedgwood employed lapidary techniques for the polishing of seals and cameos, the interiors and rims of cups and the edges of medallions. Jasper and basaltes are of approximately the same hardness as agate and may be polished with emery cloth.

Leather-hard. See *Cheese-hard.*

Mould. A cast, usually of plaster composition, taken from an original model so that many reproductions may be made. The hollow case mould is taken from the original model; a block mould in relief is taken from the case mould; and from the block mould the potter's (hollow) working mould is made. Further working moulds may be produced from the block mould as required. By this method the original case moulds, often irreplaceable, are protected from wear and may be made to last almost indefinitely.

Ornamenting. The process of applying relief decoration to ware while still in the plastic state. For the ornamenting of Wedgwood's jasper, clay is pressed into 'pitcher' moulds already cast in intaglio with the subject required. The clay relief is lifted out and applied ('sprigged') to the ware after moistening the surface. The ornament is fixed by gentle pressure of the crafts-man's fingers and subsequent firing. See Appendix C.

Repairer. A skilled workman, sometimes a modeller, responsible for the dissection of figure models, the moulding and casting of the various parts, their reassembly, propping and firing.

Saggar. A fireclay container in which the wares are placed inside the oven to protect them from direct contact with the flames and from impurities in the atmosphere of the kiln.

Scum. Whitish marks, caused by the surface crystallisation of soluble salts in the clay, appearing on biscuit ware and also on fired dry bodies. Wedgwood experienced much difficulty with this problem on nineteenth-century red and orange bodies.

Shard (sherd). In Staffordshire pronounced 'shawd'. A fragment of pottery.

Shraft. An accumulation of shards. A 'shraft tip' is a dump of broken ware from one or more potteries, often used also for general pottery factory waste.

Slip. Clay mixed with water to form a creamy consistency.

Sprigging. See *Ornamenting.*

Stoneware. Opaque, vitrified body fired at a high temperature, impervious to water without glazing.

Throwing. The process of making ware on a potter's wheel. Thrown ware is, by definition, circular in section.

Turning. The process of shaping on a horizontal lathe, similar to that used in the turning of wood or metal.

Undercutting. The process of sharpening the detail or ornament after it is removed from the mould and while it is in the cheese-hard state.

Vitrification. The conversion of a composition by intense heat into a glass-like substance. It is the final stage of fusion of a ceramic body in firing before deformation. Certain compositions, such as bone china, retain their forms at high temperatures because of the strength of their structure.

Short Bibliography

The following short list contains only those works which are directly concerned with Wedgwood's jasper, or to which reference has been made in the text or notes. The most comprehensive Wedgwood bibliography published appears in Robin Reilly's *WEDGWOOD*, 2 vols, 1989.

1. MANUSCRIPT MATERIAL

The Wedgwood collection of manuscripts deposited at Keele University and held temporarily at the Wedgwood Museum Barlaston, has provided most of the primary source material for this book. The principal subdivisions of the collection are:

Etruria Collection (E prefix), which includes the greater part of the surviving letters from Josiah Wedgwood to Thomas Bentley; Liverpool Collection (L prefix); Leith Hill Place Collection (LHP prefix); and Mosley Collection (W/M prefix). The E and L prefixes have been discarded here for all but the Wedgwood-Bentley letters unless the box and manuscript reference numbers are insufficient for identification.

Detailed references to all manuscript material quoted are given in the Notes and References.

2. PUBLISHED BOOKS

Bindman, David, *John Flaxman R.A.*, London 1979.

Birks, Tony, *Lucie Rie*, London, 1987.

Bourgeois, Emile, *Le Biscuit de Sèvres: Receuil des modèles de la manufacture de Sèvres au XVIIIe siècle*, Paris, 1909.

Burton, William, *Josiah Wedgwood and His Pottery*, London, 1906.

Caylus, Anne-Claude-Philippe de Thubières, comte de, *Receuil d'Antiquités Egyptiennes, Etrusques, Grecques et Romaines*, 7 volumes, Paris, 1752–67.

Clifford, Anne, *Cut-Steel and Berlin Iron Jewellery*, Bath, 1971.

Constable, *John Flaxman*, London, 1927.

Dawson, Aileen, *Masterpieces of Wedgwood in the British Museum*, London, 1984.

Erskine, Mrs Steuart, *Lady Diana Beauclerk, Her Life and Work*, London, 1903.

Evans, William, *Art and History of the Potting Business*, Shelton, 1846.

Farrer, K.E. (Lady Farrer) (ed.), *Letters of Josiah Wedgwood*, 3 volumes, Volume II, Manchester, 1903–6.

Finer, Ann and Savage, George (eds), *The Selected Letters of Josiah Wedgwood*, London, 1965.

Goodison, Nicholas, *Ormolu: The Work of Matthew Boulton*, London, 1974.

Gray, J.M., *James and William Tassie*, Edinburgh, 1894.

Gunnis, Rupert, *Dictionary of British Sculptors, 1650–1851*, revised edn, London 1968.

Hamilton, Sir William, and d'Hancarville, P.H., *Antiquités Etrusques, Grecques et Romaines*, 4 volumes, Naples, 1766–7.

Harris, John, *Sir William Chambers*, London, 1970.

Haskell, Francis, and Penny, Nicholas, *Taste and the Antique: The Lure of Classical Sculpture 1500–1900*, New Haven and London, 1982.

Haynes, D.E.L., *The Portland Vase*, 2nd revised edn, London 1975.

Hillier, Bevis, *Master Potters of the Industrial Revolution: the Turners of Lane End*, London 1965.

Honour, Hugh, *Neo-Classicism*, London, 1968.
  Romanticism, London, 1978.

Irwin, David, *John Flaxman, 1755–1826*, London, 1977.

Kelly, Alison, *Decorative Wedgwood*, London, 1965.

Macht, Carol, *Classical Wedgwood Designs*, New York, 1957.

McKendrick, Neil, Brewer, John, and Plumb, J.H., *The Birth of a Consumer Society: The Commercialization of Eighteenth-century England*, London, 1982.

Mankowitz, Wolf, *The Portland Vase and the Wedgwood Copies*, London, 1952.
  Wedgwood, London, 1953.

Meteyard, Eliza, *Choice Examples of Wedgwood's Art*, London, 1879.   *Memorials of Wedgwood*, London, 1874.
  The Life of Josiah Wedgwood, 2 volumes, London, 1865–6.
  Wedgwood Handbook, London, 1875.

Montfaucon, Bernard de, *L'Antiquité expliquée*, 5 volumes and Supplement 5 volumes, Paris, 1719.

Rathbone, Frederick, *Old Wedgwood*, London, 1898.

Reilly, Robin, *Josiah Wedgwood*, London, 1991.
  The Collector's Wedgwood, New York, 1980.
  Wedgwood. The New Illustrated Dictionary, Woodbridge, 1994.
  Wedgwood, 2 vols, London, 1989.
  Wedgwood Jasper, London, 1972.

Reilly, Robin and Savage, George, *The Dictionary of Wedgwood*, Woodbridge, 1980.
  Wedgwood: The Portrait Medallions, London, 1973.

Tassie, James, *Catalogue of Impressions in Sulphur of Antique and Modern Gems*, London, 1775.

Waring, J.B., *Masterpieces of Industrial Art and Sculpture at the International Exhibition, 1862*, London, 1863.

Watkin, David, *Athenian Stuart: Pioneer of the Greek Revival*, London, 1982.

Wedgwood, Josiah, *Account of the Barberini, now Portland Vase . . .* , London, 1788 (?).

3. PUBLISHED CATALOGUES

A. Wedgwood's Catalogues of Ornamental Wares

A Catalogue of cameos, intaglios, medals, busts, small statues, and bas-reliefs; with a general account of vases and other ornaments, after the antique, made by Wedgwood & Bentley, 4th edn, London, 1777, 5th edn, 1779.

Catalogue of cameos, intaglios, medals, bas-reliefs, busts and small statues; with a general account of tablets, vases, escritoires, and other ornamental and useful articles . . . , 6th edn, Etruria, 1787.

Illustrated Catalogue of Ornamental Shapes, n.d. (1878–80).

Catalogue of Bodies, Glazes and Shapes, current for 1940–50, Hanley, 1940.

B. Select List of Catalogues of Collections and Exhibitions

Art Journal, Special Issue, *The Crystal Palace Exhibition, Illustrated Catalogue*, London, 1851.

Adams, Elizabeth Bryding, *The Dwight and Lucille Beeson Wedgwood Collection at the Birmingham Museum of Art, Birmingham, Alabama*, Alabama, 1992.

Arts Council of Great Britain, *The Age of Neo-Classicism*, London, 1972.

Barnard, Harry, *Exhibition of replicas of eighteenth-century sculptured miniatures: Wedgwood's portrait medallions of illustrious moderns made and finished by Bert Bentley*, London, n.d. (1922).

Chaffers, William, *Catalogue of an Exhibition of Old Wedgwood at Phillips' Galleries, London*, London, 1877.

Des Fontaines, J.K., with Chaldecott, John, and Tindall, John, *Josiah Wedgwood: 'The Arts and Sciences United'*, London, 1978.

Early Wedgwood Pottery, (Catalogue of the Eustace Calland Collection), London, 1951.

Gatty, T., *Catalogue of a loan exhibition of the works of Josiah Wedgwood, exhibited at the Liverpool Art Club*, Liverpool, 1879.

Gorely, Jean, and Wadsworth, Mary, *Old Wedgwood from the bequest of Grenville Lindall Winthrop*, Fogg Museum of Art, Harvard University, 1944.

Gunsaulus, Frank W., *Old Wedgwood 1760–95: a collection acquired by . . . W. Gunsaulus, loaned to the Museum of the Art Institute of Chicago*, Chicago, 1912.

Henry E. Huntington Library and Art Gallery, *Wedgwood & Bentley Pottery from the Kadison Collection*, San Marino, California, 1983.

Hobson, R.L., *Catalogue of English Pottery and Porcelain in the Department of British Mediaeval Antiquities and Ethnography, British Museum*, London, 1903.

Record of the Collection in the Lady Lever Art Gallery, Port Sunlight, 3 volumes, Vol. II: *Chinese Porcelain and Wedgwood Pottery*, London, 1928.

Northern Ceramic Society, *Stonewares & Stone Chinas of Northern England to 1851*, Stoke-on-Trent, 1982.

Nottingham Castle Museum, *Catalogue of the Wedgwood in the Felix Joseph Bequest*, Nottingham, 1930.

Mr Wedgwood, Nottingham, 1975.

Rackham, Bernard, *Catalogue of English Porcelain Earthenware Enamels and Glass collected by Charles Schreiber Esq. M.P. and Lady Charlotte Schreiber . . .* , 3 volumes, Volume II, London, 1924–30.

Rathbone, Frederick, *A Catalogue of the Wedgwood Museum*, Etruria, 1909.

A catalogue of a collection of plaques, medallions, vases &c in coloured jasper and basaltes: produced by Josiah Wedgwood, 1760–1795 . . . formed by Lord Tweedmouth, London, 1905.

Old Wedgwood and old Wedgwood Ware: Handbook to the collection formed by Richard and George Tangye (Birmingham Museum & Art Gallery), London, 1885.

Reilly, Robin, *Wedgwood Portrait Medallions: An Introduction* (National Portrait Gallery exhibition), London, 1973.

Sanderson, Arthur, *Catalogue of a collection of plaques, medallions, vases, figures etc., in coloured jasper and basalte, produced by Josiah Wedgwood F.R.S., at Etruria, in the county of Stafford: 1760–1795, the property of Arthur Sanderson*, London, 1901.

Scheidemantel, Vivian J., *Josiah Wedgwood's Heads of Illustrious Moderns* (loan exhibition at the Chicago Art Institute), Chicago, 1958.

Tattersall, Bruce, *Wedgwood Portraits and the American Revolution*, National Portrait Gallery, Washington, 1976.

Wedgwood In London: 225th Anniversary Exhibition 1759–1984, Barlaston, 1984.

Index

Numbers in *italic* indicate black and white illustrations, numbers in **bold** indicate colour plates.